The Complete Guide to
Birds
of Britain & Europe

BTO

British Trust for Ornithology

The Complete Guide to

BIRDS
of BRITAIN
& EUROPE

CONSULTANT EDITOR
PAUL STERRY

Published by AA Publishing (a trading name of Automobile Association Developments Limited, whose registered office is Fanum House, Basing View, Basingstoke, Hampshire RG21 4EA; registered number 1878835).

Packaged for Automobile Association Developments Limited by D & N Publishing, Lambourn Woodlands, Hungerford, Berkshire.

First published in the UK in 2009

Find out more about AA Publishing at www.theAA.com/travel

A03689

ISBN: 978-0-7495-5862-8
Special sales ISBN: 978-0-7495-6135-2

A CIP catalogue record for this book is available from the British Library.

The British Trust for Ornithology (BTO) is a pivotal organisation in the conservation of birds in Britain, and further afield. Their research brings clarity to many of the complexities of British birdlife, aspects of migration and factors affecting their survival. Assisted by a small army of willing volunteers, the BTO carries out survey work and ringing studies that continue to reveal vital information about bird populations and so alert people to potential crises looming on the horizon. Every responsible birdwatcher should be a member, even if they do not participate directly in the fieldwork undertaken by the BTO.

Contributing authors: Dr Paul Sterry (consultant editor), Andrew Cleave MBE, Dr Andy Clements, Peter Goodfellow and Dr Mike Toms
Designer: Shane O'Dwyer
Production at AA Publishing: Stephanie Allen
Maps created by Gulmohur Press Pvt Ltd, New Delhi, India

The Publishers would like to thank Paul Sterry, Shane O'Dwyer, David and Namrita Price-Goodfellow (D & N Publishing), Mike Toms and the staff of the BTO, particularly Chas Holt (for checking the maps) and John Marchant (for checking the text), for all their hard work on this book and dedication to the project. A special thanks to Paul Sterry, without whom none of this would have happened.

Photograph previous page: male Stonechat.
Photograph below: adult winter Ross's Gull.
Photographs opposite page: juvenile Sabine's Gull (above) and adult summer female Grey Phalarope (below).

CONTENTS

HOW TO USE THIS BOOK

The *Complete Guide to Birds of Britain and Europe* serves a number of functions for the reader. It contains detailed and accurate descriptions for every bird species found on a regular basis in Europe, as well as a wealth of facts about their structure, habits and natural history. In addition, stunning photography and artwork make the book a visual celebration of the region's wonderful birdlife.

Maps of the region show the distribution for every regularly encountered species. Different colours depict differing seasonal status:

■ = PRESENT IN THE DEPICTED AREA YEAR-ROUND

■ = PRESENT IN SPRING AND SUMMER

■ = PRESENT IN WINTER

MAPS

This provides accurate and contemporary information about European birds – up-to-date facts, figures and details about food, nesting and lifespan; much of the information is condensed from the British Trust for Ornithology's online database BTO BirdFacts

BIRD FACTS

LONG-TAILED TIT

Aegithalos caudatus

Tiny-bodied, long-tailed bird, not related to true tits.

THE LONG-TAILED TIT is mainly sedentary, but at times of high populations many irrupt from their breeding grounds. Long-tailed Tits are territorial in the breeding season, after which they are gregarious, forming small flocks of around ten birds. These flocks defend a winter territory against others, and consist of parents, their offspring and helpers related to the male. A flock keeps together with the help of a constant 'conversation' of 'tsirrrup' calls, as its members restlessly hunt for food. The flock roosts communally, in a thick bush, huddled together on one horizontal perch.

IDENTIFICATION

Sexes similar. Adult birds from most of Europe have head and underparts whitish, washed with dusky pink on nape, and from belly to undertail coverts; black bands extend from bill, above the eyes to the mantle. Upperparts, wings and tail dull black, with pink scapulars and rump, and white tips and edges to graduated tail feathers. Pink tones wear off. Adult of subspecies from northern and eastern Europe has pure white head and noticeably white-edged tertials and secondaries; birds of southern subspecies have grey backs, darker faces, and little or no pink. Eyering reddish in all birds. Juvenile shorter and darker than adult, with dusky mask and drab upperparts.

Adult of Scandinavian race.

Adult of Western European race.

BIRD FACTS

VOICE Call low, repeated 'tsupp'; alarm trilled 'tsirrrrup'; song rapid repetition of calls

LENGTH 14cm

WINGSPAN 16–19cm

WEIGHT 7–9g

HABITAT Deciduous woodland; for nesting, thick scrub like gorse, bramble or briar

NEST Usually in a thorny bush; domed nest of moss, lichen and feathers

EGGS 8–12; white, unmarked or with minute reddish speckles

FOOD Insects, especially eggs and larvae of butterflies and moths

GREAT TIT

Parus major

adult male

THE GREAT TIT has the widest distribution in the world of all the tits. Birds from western and southern Europe are mostly sedentary but northern and central European birds, at times of high population, irrupt into other parts of Europe. Great Tits forage for food low down more than other tits. Those resident in beech woods may spend as much as 45 per cent of their time on the ground in late autumn searching for beech-mast. By contrast, in an oak wood they may spend 60 per cent of the time on low branches in search of insects. In winter they regularly come to bird tables.

Song is vary varied, often leading to misidentification.

Juveniles look very washed out and have yellow cheeks rather than white.

BIRD FACTS

VOICE Call loud 'tink, tink, tink'; song far-carrying 'teacher, teacher, teacher'

LENGTH 14cm

WINGSPAN 22.5–25.5cm

WEIGHT 16–20g

HABITAT Almost anywhere with trees, except coniferous forest; even in cities

NEST In hole in wall or tree, or nest boxes; moss base, cup lined with hair, wool and feathers

EGGS 5–12; white, speckled reddish-brown, larger than Blue Tit's markings

FOOD Great variety of adult and larval insects; spiders; seeds and fruits in winter

IDENTIFICATION

The largest common tit, with quite a long tail. Adult is basically yellow-green above and yellow below. Wings have black flight feathers, blue-grey coverts and black tertials, tipped white. Shows white wingbar and white outertail feathers. Distinctive head pattern comprises glossy blue-black cap with triangular white cheek patch. Black on chin and throat extends into bold, black stripe down centre of underparts, forming a wide black patch between legs on male, and much narrower one on female. Bill strong and black. Legs blue-grey. Juvenile similar to adult but has sooty crown, browner back, cheeks washed yellow and underparts duller yellow.

Large size and striking combination of colours make Great Tit unmistakable.

adult male

Superb colour photographs illustrate as wide a range of plumages, poses and behaviours as space permits, for every species found in Europe. Some of the images were taken especially for the book

PHOTOGRAPHS

Detailed descriptions are given allowing for easy recognition and separation from superficially similar or closely related species. Every recognisably distinct plumage is covered and, where appropriate, these include male, female, juvenile, summer and winter

Written by a team of experts, in part accessing information collected, collated and interpreted by the BTO, the main text provides the reader with a wealth of information about European birds. Subjects covered include feeding habits, behaviour, current population status and conservation concerns

IDENTIFICATION

Adult is the only European tit with bright-blue crown, bordered with white. Has dark lines from bill through eye, around back of head and around otherwise white cheeks. Upperparts yellowish-green, underparts sulphur-yellow, with small blackish central streak. Wings dark blue with white wingbar. Tail dark grey-blue. Bill short, black. Legs dusky blue. Female very similar to male but colours less bright. Juvenile washed yellow and lacks blue in plumage but similar to adult in other respects.

BLUE TIT
Cyanistes caeruleus

THE BLUE TIT is abundant in most habitats with trees, although it avoids conifers, and outside the breeding season even wanders to reedbeds and clifftops. It tends to feed high up in broad-leaved trees, foraging on twigs, buds and leaves, but will visit bird tables in winter. Blue Tits are inquisitive and agile birds: they tap reed stems to locate hidden prey and open only those stems that contain larvae. They are occasionally known to hang by one foot and grab food with the other and routinely hold hard seeds underfoot and hammer them with their bill; they can also solve bird-table puzzles in order to reach food.

Fledglings have same patterning as adults but yellower face.

BIRD FACTS

VOICE Call 'tsee-tsee'; alarm 'chirr.r.r'; song tremolo 'tsee-tsee-tsee-tsuhuhuhu'

LENGTH 11.5cm

WINGSPAN 17.5–20cm

WEIGHT 10–12g

HABITAT Anywhere with trees, even inner-city parks and gardens

NEST Hole in tree or wall, nest box; pad of moss, cup lined with hair and fine grass

EGGS 6–16; white with fine, reddish spots

FOOD Chiefly adult and larval insects and spiders; fruits and seeds in winter

DID YOU KNOW?

Blue Tits are extremely acrobatic, and unlike Great Tits are light enough to forage at the tips of even the thinnest twigs.

Male glides slowly towards a possible nest site to attract females to it; at other times flight action is fluttery.

DID YOU KNOW?

In Britain Blue Tits sometimes rip open tops of newly delivered milk bottles to drink the cream. They are also known to exploit the nectar in willow catkins and cherry flowers, a rich food source little used by other European birds.

To complement the main text and identification section, extended captions are intended to provide additional information that will aid recognition and identification, or details that will help with the determination of gender or plumage

The Complete Guide to Birds of Britain and Europe's lavish illustrations have been created by some of Britain and Ireland's finest artists. Some of the illustrations portray interesting behaviour while others focus on accurate detail for identification purposes

TITS **257**

Unusual and unexpected facts about European birds are presented in DID YOU KNOW? boxes that are distributed throughout the book; some relate to the species in question's plumage, others to behaviour or distribution

BIRDS WITHOUT BORDERS: THE EUROPEAN OVERVIEW

Within the context of Europe, Siskin migration is extremely complex, with the many regional populations migrating in entirely different directions and distances from others. We know this for certain thanks to ringing records.

BIRDS DO NOT respect political boundaries and for the sake of conservation the factors affecting European birds need to be seen not as single country issues, but in the context of the whole region; sometimes even further afield in the case of long distance migrants. Because of this, any conservation overview of European birds, and strategies to help them, must also cross political borders in order to be effective. Scientific research and sound analysis of data underpin environmental legislative decisions made in Europe. The British Trust for Ornithology (BTO) provides accurate information needed for correct decisions to be made in Britain and in the wider context of Europe. And their involvement with the European Bird Census Council (a loose grouping of partners in Europe) is essential.

SEASONAL VISITORS

Many familiar species are migratory, spending only part of the year within a particular country. As such, any efforts to protect species within an individual country also need to consider where they may be at other times of the year. The Reed Warblers that are summer visitors to Britain spend the winter in sub-Saharan Africa and break their autumn migration with stops in south-west France or Iberia. Similarly, many of the Robins breeding in Norway winter in the Low Countries, with some breaking their journey in Britain. What happens to 'British' Reed Warblers and 'Norwegian' Robins is therefore dependent upon what also happens to them in other countries. It is for this reason that researchers operating within the different European countries often collaborate with one another, either exchanging information from their individual schemes or combining their efforts on joint initiatives. The European Bird Census Council provides a forum for organisations such as the BTO to work in partnership.

ABOVE: Strong easterly winds forced this migrant REED WARBLER off track and it ended up on a seacliff in western England.

CHARTING MIGRATION

Central to European efforts to chart the movements and migration patterns of birds has been The Union of European Ringing Schemes (known as EURING). Established in 1963, EURING has enabled a high level of cooperation between the individual ringing schemes operating in 39 countries across Europe. Although the way these schemes operate may vary, they all collect information in the same way by using a series of standard data fields and recording codes. This allows data from different countries to be combined; some 4.8 million records of ringed birds are now stored in the EURING Data Bank, managed on behalf of EURING by the British Trust for Ornithology. These records are used by researchers to answer questions about migration at the European scale, highlighting key migration routes and distinct sub-populations that exist within species. Much of this information has been published in country-based atlases but some of it has also been combined as an online and interactive mapping tool, allowing those interested to follow the migration routes of European birds. Visit http://www.euring.org to access the migration mapping tool.

This MEDITERRANEAN GULL was ringed in France but spent the winter months on the coast of Hampshire in England. Had it not been ringed and colour ringed nobody would ever have known that it was not a local bird.

COUNTING FOR CONSERVATION

The efforts of bird ringers contribute to a wider pool of knowledge about Europe's bird populations. While ringing can tell us about where birds go, how long they live and, to a lesser extent, how productive they are, other approaches are needed to complete our understanding of bird populations. As with the approach adopted for studying bird movements, much of the work is organised within individual countries by national organisations, some of which utilise the enthusiasm of volunteer birdwatchers to collect the information required. Britain has perhaps the longest history of amateur naturalists contributing to our understanding of bird populations and through the British Trust for Ornithology (BTO) it has very much led the way in collecting impartial data that can be used to underpin conservation actions. Established in 1933, the BTO is a mix of professional (paid) ornithologists working in partnership with interested amateur (volunteer) birdwatchers. The concept behind this approach was that the Trust would act as the nucleus, stimulating and co-ordinating research into populations of wild birds and their changing fortunes, a pattern now being repeated in other European countries.

INSET: *Colour ringing allows observers to be certain that this migrating WHITE STORK is a bird that nests in the summer months in southern Sweden and spends the winter in Africa.*

RIGHT: *Changing weather patterns, linked to global climate change, also affect birds, in some cases allowing previously southerly species, such as the LITTLE EGRET, to spread northwards.*

UPS AND DOWNS AND SAFEGUARDING THE FUTURE

The changing fortunes of Europe's various bird populations, monitored through national and international schemes, are often linked to human activities: habitat use (such as the effects of urbanisation or afforestation), agricultural policy, hunting pressure and global climate change are examples. Many characteristic farmland species, such as Tree Sparrow and Corn Bunting, have declined across much of Europe because of agricultural intensification. Such changes are likely to continue and it is important that the processes involved are understood clearly. Annual monitoring programmes and periodic surveys allow this knowledge to be acquired and it is Europe's army of volunteer birdwatchers that will be key to delivering this much-needed information.

A CO-ORDINATED APPROACH

THE EURING SWALLOW PROJECT is a good example of co-ordinated efforts at work across Europe. Involving many hundreds of trained and licensed bird ringers, and operating in 25 different countries across Europe, Africa and Asia, the project set out to examine the migration behaviour of the familiar Swallow. A key feature of Swallow migration is the autumn roosts at which many thousands of Swallows gather prior to departure. Such roosts often form in reedbeds where, over water, the risk of predation is reduced. During this roosting phase the Swallows build up the fat reserves needed to undertake their long migratory journey. Because Swallows feed on the wing it had been assumed that they did not need to lay down fat reserves for migration. However, the Swallow Project has highlighted that Swallows do in fact lay down fat reserves and that the amount of fat deposited is related to how far the bird has to migrate. Those Swallows using migration routes that only require 'short hops' over unfavourable terrain lay down less fat than birds faced with a much longer journey across sea or desert.

ABOVE: *This migrant SWALLOW was grounded by heavy rain and strong winds on its return migration in spring. Such are the perils of long distance migration and birds are at the mercy of what the elements throw at them.*

LEFT: *BTO rings, like those used elsewhere in Europe, are made from lightweight, durable metal and marked with a unique number and contact address.*

IN CELEBRATION OF BIRDS

OVER THE PAST 150 million years or so, since they first took to the air, birds have evolved from their scaly, flying reptilian ancestors into some of the most beautiful and graceful creatures in the animal world. Their beaks and feet have become adapted to a remarkable variety of lifestyles and their feathers, which give them form and allow them to fly, are quite simply amazing.

EUROPEAN STORM-PETREL

GRIFFON VULTURE

SWIFT

BLACK-WINGED STILT

BLACKBIRD

ADULT WOODPIGEON

WOODPIGEON PRIMARY FEATHER

WOODPIGEON TAIL FEATHER

WOODPIGEON CONTOUR FEATHER

WHAT ARE BIRDS?

Birds are arguably the most familiar of all animal groups, their relative uniformity in structure making them instantly recognisable. While birds show tremendous variation in colour, plumage and bill shape and size, the shared feature of having a body covered in feathers underlines their common ancestry. Another characteristic that binds together most, though not quite all, bird species is the ability to undertake powered flight. But one final feature shared by all birds is that they reproduce by laying eggs.

FEATHERS AND PLUMAGE

The plumage of a bird has a number of different functions. As well as giving the bird its external appearance, it can be an indication of gender and social status, or provide camouflage from potential predators. Feathers are made from keratin, the same substance that forms our nails and hair. It is an amazing material: light, durable and waterproof. Feathers are good insulators, trapping a layer of air between the body feathers and the skin beneath them. Once the feather has finished growing it comprises entirely dead material and further changes require the growth of a new feather through moult. In some birds the process of losing and growing new feathers is staggered to a degree. But many birds have entirely different summer and winter plumages, achieved by moult: the Ptarmigan, with its extreme seasonal plumages, is a good example. Plumage differences between the sexes are typically most evident in the breeding season.

FEATHER TYPES

Each bird has a number of different feather types, serving different functions within the overall plumage. These include the flight feathers, which are stiff and elongated, held together along the line of the feather shaft by a series of barbules that effectively 'zip' the feather together. There are also contour feathers that cover the body, comprising a 'zipped' outer section and an unzipped fluffy inner section; the outer section provides protection, the looser inner section insulates the bird. Other feather types have more specialised functions.

FLIGHT

Various tracts of feathers are adapted for flight, particularly those along the rear edge of the wing and on the tail. These feathers are elongated (when compared to other body feathers), strengthened and shaped so that, collectively, they can provide the thrust, lift and manoeuvrability needed in the air. The most energetically costly component of flight is take-off. Once airborne, the process of flying becomes more efficient and many birds can cover a considerable distance with relatively little expenditure of energy. Some species further enhance their energetic effectiveness by soaring on thermals.

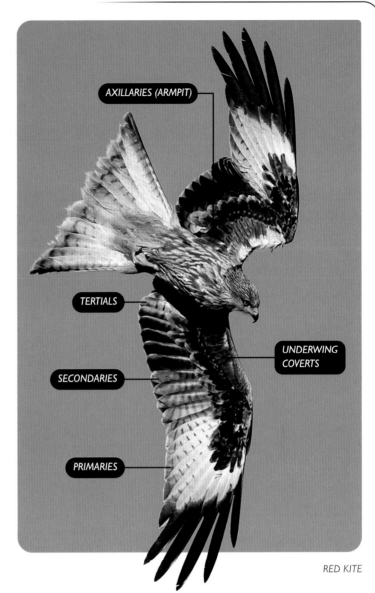

RED KITE

Capable of sustained gliding with barely a ripple of its flight feathers, the BLACK VULTURE is surprisingly manoeuvrable when it wants to descend to the ground quickly after food.

BIRD TOPOGRAPHY – NAMING THE PARTS

One of the best ways in which to improve your bird identification skills is to become familiar with the different parts of a bird. Each of the various feather tracts has its own name and knowing these will help you to understand the descriptions given in field guides and also to take notes that another birdwatcher will be able to understand.

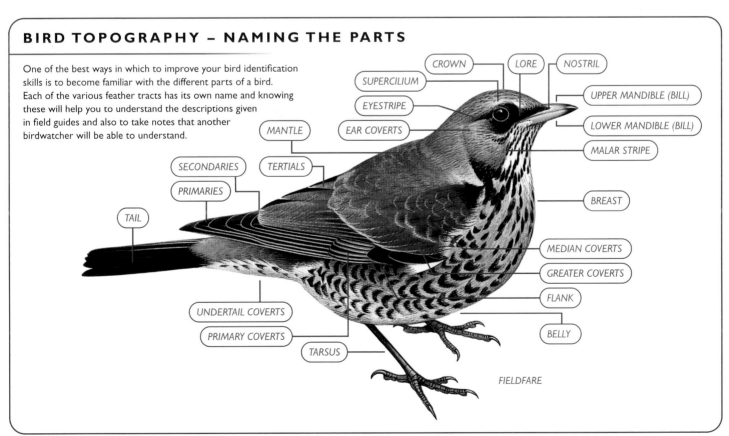

FIELDFARE

NESTS AND EGGS

LIKE THEIR REPTILIAN ancestors, birds lay eggs inside which their young develop. A hard, chalky outer casing protects the egg and the developing chick gains its nutrition from the egg's yolk. With the exception of seabirds such as the Guillemot (which lays, and incubates, its egg directly on a rock ledge), birds lay their eggs in a nest. These range in structure and placement from a simple scrape in the ground (as with many plovers) to fantastically intricate, woven and suspended structures like that of the Penduline Tit. But the vast majority of birds construct a variation on a cup-shaped nest, woven from, and lined with, a range of plant material. Such nests are typically sited in the cover of dense bushes to avoid detection by predators.

CHAFFINCH nest

ABOVE: *MALLARD ducklings are able to swim and feed for themselves from the moment they hatch, although typically under the wary supervision of their parents.*

WHAT ARE EGGS?

RAZORBILL 70mm

An egg consists of a yolk, which provides nutrition for the developing chick, the albumen (or egg-white), which protects the embryo, and a tough shell that protects the egg itself from damage. Birds' eggs come in all shapes, sizes and colours. Their shells have to be very strong, but weak enough for the chick to break out from inside. Many eggs are well-camouflaged – their colours and patterns cleverly blending into the background. Usually the size of the eggs is related to the size of the bird. The Mute Swan lays a particularly large egg (12cm long) while at the other extreme the Goldcrest lays an extremely tiny one (12mm long).

Like all songbirds and many other groups, SONG THRUSH chicks are entirely dependent upon their parents for food until the time they fledge.

YOUNG BIRDS

The young of birds that lay their eggs in a scrape or on bare ground usually leave the nest at once; they are known as nidifugous and are covered in well-camouflaged down as soon as they hatch. Those that are produced in well-protected nests are known as nidicolous – they remain within the security of the nest until they can fly. Nidicolous chicks are naked and blind when they hatch, and extremely vulnerable.

GREAT TIT 18mm

SONG THRUSH 27mm

SPARROWHAWK 40mm

LONG-TAILED TIT 14mm

LAPWING 50mm

OYSTERCATCHER 57mm

INCUBATION

It is essential that eggs are kept warm once they have been laid. The parent birds do this by sitting on the eggs – this is known as incubation. For the eggs to develop properly, a high, even temperature is essential. Most birds develop a brood patch, an area on the breast that loses its feathers and develops a rich supply of blood vessels.

A WOODPIGEON incubating its eggs in its rudimentary, twiggy nest.

Like many other warbler species, this GRASSHOPPER WARBLER feeds on invertebrates, primarily insects; this one has spotted a caddisfly.

LIFESTYLES AND ADAPTATIONS

ACROSS EUROPE THERE are birds in every conceivable habitat, from the highest mountain to the open oceans, and everywhere in between. And one species or another has evolved to exploit almost every available source of food. The range of bill and leg structures amongst European birds is astonishing, but once you know what to look for each is perfectly adapted for the food the bird eats and the habitat in which it lives. But birds' behaviour also plays a crucial role in ensuring the best possible chances of feeding, reproduction and survival.

AVOCETS are specialist feeders: they sweep their long, upcurved bills through the shallows.

DIET

Although there are a few generalist feeders, happy to snatch an opportunistic meal or exploit any food source, most birds are specialist feeders with rather specific diets. On occasions, the diet of a species may change with the seasons (some finches and buntings consume insects in summer, but feed almost exclusively on seeds in winter when invertebrates are scarce). But most birds have bills and bodies adapted to a fairly precise habitat and food source. Some birds are purely vegetarian, feeding perhaps on seeds or fruits, while many more specialise in catching invertebrates; the relative absence of insects in winter means that many species that feed on them migrate south. Other species are predators and specialist diets include fish as well as other bird species.

BILLS

A bird's bill (or beak) is an extension of its jaw. It has two parts – the upper and lower mandibles – both covered in a horny protective layer of skin. Like a human's, the lower jaw can move while the upper mandible is fixed to the skull. Nostrils are found on the upper mandible.

The main purpose of the bill is to aid feeding. Many sizes and shapes allow different birds to feed in different places and on a wide range of food. In addition to their usefulness in feeding, bills are used for preening, nest-building, and even as weapons of defence or attack. Some have special shapes or colours that are used in display.

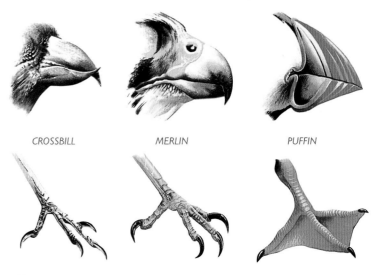
CROSSBILL   MERLIN   PUFFIN

FEET

Birds use their feet like humans do – for walking and balance. But they are far more versatile than ours and take on some of the equivalent functions of our hands. Birds use their feet to cling, climb, perch, dig, swim and even kill other animals. But basically there are three main types of feet. These are perching feet, those adapted for walking and wading, and those adapted for swimming. Like its bill, the precise appearance of any bird species' foot is adapted to suit its way of life and the habitat in which it lives. No bird has more than four toes, and some have fewer. Usually they have three toes pointing forward and one back.

SPARROWHAWKS have evolved to catch smaller birds in flight; this bird is chasing Chaffinches.

BEHAVIOUR

For many, the song of the NIGHTINGALE is the finest of all European birds. Rich, liquid and melodious, it often continues throughout the night.

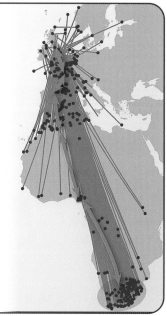

BIRDS ARE HIGHLY evolved animals with a sophisticated array of behaviour patterns that allow them to increase their chances of survival. Some of these allow them to rub along with members of the same species while others improve their chances of feeding successfully or finding a mate.

SOCIAL BEHAVIOUR

Getting along with neighbours of the same species is an important part of many birds' lives. Complex behaviour patterns allow, for example, colonially nesting birds to nest in relative peace within bill-stabbing distance of one another. It allows pair bonds to be developed and maintained in species that pair for life. And it enables the complex processes of courtship, mating, nesting and the rearing of offspring to take place.

ABOVE: Birds establish and maintain pair bonds using an array of behaviours between two individuals. To our eyes, behaviour such as this seemingly intimate moment between these ROOKS, can look sometimes like a display of affection.

RIGHT: During the breeding season, SNOW BUNTINGS are usually found in isolated pairs. But in winter (seen here) they form sizeable flocks that favour coastal grassland.

VOCALISATION

A few bird species are almost silent but most are vocal to varying degrees and under different circumstances. The apogee of bird vocalisation is song and it is amongst passerines that the finest examples are found. Typically it is males that sing and do so to advertise ownership of a breeding territory, and to attract and retain mates.

Most bird species have a repertoire of calls that serve a variety of behavioural functions. Amongst other things, these serve as alarm warnings to others (for example, at the discovery of a predator) and allow contact with other members of the species, for example when feeding or migrating.

FLOCKS

Outside the breeding season, many wader species, most ducks and geese, and several passerine species gather in huge flocks that feed and roost together. The principle of safety in numbers operates and with so many eyes on the lookout for danger, potential predators are usually spotted.

MIGRATION

Although some bird species are essentially sedentary, most take advantage of their ability to fly to move around the environment, often in search of food. Some simply disperse outside the breeding season in a seemingly random fashion. But others migrate; this predictable and typically annual flight takes them from one distinct area used for breeding to another used for wintering. The distances between the two can be continents apart. Migration is a response to the fact that most avian food resources, notably insects, are strongly seasonal in abundance. Most European summer migrants are insectivorous and breed during the long daylight hours that our northern summers provide. Insect abundance declines with the approach of winter and the insect eaters are forced to retreat south to latitudes where insects remain readily available. Other migrants move within Europe and are typically moving south and west to avoid colder weather further north and east.

Thanks to the efforts of British Trust for Ornithology ringers, we have a good understanding of SWALLOW migration. British Swallows migrate south through western Europe, cross the Sahara and winter in South Africa.

COASTS AND SEAS

THE MARINE ENVIRONMENT is full of life and it is little wonder that a wide range of birds has evolved to exploit the food resources on offer. The coast – where land meets sea – is strongly influenced by tides and is arguably the richest habitat in biological terms. It is certainly the most accessible to birds; waders and many wildfowl species depend on its mudflats and saltmarshes for invertebrates while the shallow seas provide fish for terns, grebes and divers. Cliffs and islands offer nesting sites for many true seabirds – auks and petrels for example – that otherwise shun the sight of land, while the open sea provides food aplenty for those seabirds specially adapted to cope with its rigours.

ABOVE: The oozing mud of estuaries and mudflats is rich in invertebrate life and European coasts are internationally important wintering grounds for significant numbers of waders. This KNOT flock represents just a tiny fraction of the population present on the Wash, on the English coast, from September to March. Half of the entire breeding population from Greenland and northeast Canada winter there – more than 185,000 individuals.

LEFT: This immature SABINE'S GULL may well have hatched from an egg laid on Spitzbergen. After fledging it will spend its entire life at sea – typically out of sight of land – until it returns to its breeding grounds next summer.

FAR LEFT: European STORM-PETRELS are truly remarkable seabirds that spend their entire lives at sea, apart from when they are nesting. How these tiny birds – just 14cm long – can cope with the rigours of the open ocean is a wonder. And even more amazingly, they locate their food, in part, by smell!

RIGHT: Following in the wake of a fishing trawler, this flock of LESSER and GREAT BLACK-BACKED GULLS have been joined by a lone GANNET and some EUROPEAN STORM-PETRELS. The gulls, and even the Gannet, benefit from the by-catch of the fishing industry – unwanted fish species caught and killed in the nets, and simply discarded overboard. By contrast, most of their seabird cousins are severely and adversely affected by the industrial scale of modern fishery – the nets simply out-compete them for the fish they depend upon to survive. This is reflected by the lack of breeding success seen in many populations of northwest European seabirds.

FRESH WATER

FRESH WATER IS essential for all forms of life away from the marine world
and it is hardly surprising then that freshwater habitats harbour great riches.
Influenced and defined by factors such as water chemistry and the flow rate
(or lack of it), each is a challenge in its own way for its wildlife inhabitants;
this includes the birds that exploit its invertebrates, fish and plants. Rivers
and streams have flowing water while in lakes and ponds the water is standing.
Fens and bogs are defined by the presence of permanently waterlogged, variably
inundated ground, the former having alkaline waters, the latter acid.

BELOW: DIPPERS are associated with fast-flowing rivers and streams, and are seldom seen anywhere else. Superbly adapted to a watery life, this individual is foraging for stonefly nymphs and caddisfly larvae in the shallows. But it will unhesitatingly submerge completely when it wants to feed in deeper water.

ABOVE: The smallest of its kind in Europe, the LITTLE GREBE is an unobtrusive resident on many slow-flowing streams, and a visitor to coastal wetlands in winter. Despite the downy 'powderpuff' appearance of its feathers, they are seemingly impervious to water as the droplets on this bird's back demonstrate.

ABOVE: Many wetland birds breed communally and this is particularly true of herons and egrets. This SQUACCO HERON was nesting in a mixed colony that included Little Egrets, Glossy Ibises and Night Herons.

Although some of Europe's great wetlands have suffered as a result of drainage and pollution at the hands of Man, many gems still survive. Arguably the finest is the Danube Delta, a huge, meandering network whose waters empty into the Black Sea. Romania holds the lion's share of the Delta's wetlands and also some 4,000 pairs of WHITE PELICANS – the vast majority of the European breeding population.

WOODLAND

THROUGHOUT EUROPE, WOODLANDS and forests provide excellent habitats for birds. Their obvious three-dimensional structure provides a wide variety of niches for feeding and nesting birds and are home to a great diversity of resident species; and the invertebrate communities they support underpin a significant proportion of Europe's summer migrant visitor species. European woodlands are themselves extremely diverse. They include the evergreen broadleaved forests of the Mediterranean and evergreen conifers (also a feature of the Mediterranean) that come into their own and dominate northern latitudes and many mountain ranges. And the deciduous forests that spread across temperate Europe have their own magic and are truly wonderful.

ABOVE: Black-and-white woodpeckers of various species are very much a feature of European woodlands. The GREAT SPOTTED WOODPECKER is by far the most widespread and it favours a range of deciduous wooded habitats.

RIGHT: Being essentially nocturnal, most owl species are easily overlooked. But a range of species occurs in European woodlands and, as important predators, they have a significant role to play in the ecology of the woodland they inhabit. This GREAT GREY OWL – more diurnal than most – is an enigmatic denizen of northern European forests.

RIGHT: Insects and other invertebrate life abound in most European woods in spring and summer. This bounty is what enables most of our summer migrant visitors, such as this WOOD WARBLER, to successfully raise their broods.

BELOW: In parts of its range where oaks predominate, the JAY plays a vital role in ensuring that new generations of trees are produced. In autumn, Jays bury countless numbers of acorns, as a cache of food for the winter. Many of these get overlooked subsequently by the hungry birds and of those that germinate a few go on to become mature oaks.

RIGHT: Favouring mixed conifer and broad-leaved woodland, the FIRECREST is one of the smallest European woodland birds. It specialises in catching tiny invertebrates and aphids feature heavily in its diet.

HEATHLAND, GRASSLAND AND FARMLAND

ACROSS MUCH OF Europe, Man has exerted his influence on the landscape for millennia. Lowland areas have been particularly affected, to the extent that the overall appearance of significant areas of countryside, and their botanical composition, is largely determined by human activities past and present. Heathlands, dominated by members of the heather family, flourish on acid soils after ancient tree clearance and subsequent periodic burns. Grassland areas are, in the main, the result of woodland clearance in times past and maintained as such by grazing or cutting; their botanical composition is determined largely by soil chemistry. Farmland embraces grassland in the bigger picture of course but, at its extreme, intensive arable farming attempts to exclude all but one plant species – the crop – from the land. The implications for wildlife biodiversity are profound.

ABOVE: HOBBIES are summer visitors to Europe that specialise in catching dragonflies (particularly shortly after their arrival here in spring) and flying birds later in the season. Hobbies favour open country for feeding and can be seen over heathland and farmland.

TOP LEFT: The GREAT BUSTARD is a bird of wide open farmland and grassland, restricted now to the Iberian Peninsula and eastern Europe. Despite its size, it is wary, and justifiably so since it has been heavily persecuted over the years. Today, its survival depends on the whims of farming and the enforcement of legal protection.

LEFT: In areas of western Europe subject to intensive agriculture, many areas of farmland offer precious little food for birds. But further east where agriculture continues at a slower pace things are noticeably different. For example, in Romania in 2001, when this photograph was taken, it was still possible to find feeding flocks of ROSE-COLOURED STARLINGS numbering tens of thousands; in this instance the birds were feeding on emerging craneflies and were doing the farmers a service. With Romania's accession to the European Union in 2007 it is hard to imagine that its agricultural system will not become more 'efficient'. So will these flocks become a thing of the past?

SCRUB

BIRDWATCHERS USUALLY RECOGNISE the significance of scrub, and its importance for songbirds including many warblers. But because it is essentially a colonising, transitional habitat – in many areas, a step on the way to becoming woodland – it is hard to define in ecological terms and often neglected (or worse, reviled) by conservationists. The term 'scrub' means different things to different people. Typically though it comprises woody, tangled shrubs and spreading climbers, of whatever species happen to be present in a given area. In a formal manner, these same shrubby species are often planted by Man to create hedgerows; the dense cover that results mimics woodland edge and is a rich habitat for birds. In the Mediterranean, a spectrum of scrub habitats often predominates, their appearances the result of historic tree clearance, underlying soil type and the degree of grazing (especially by goats) to which they are subjected; at one extreme is *maquis*, a habitat that comprises dense shrubs and small trees; at the other is *garrigue*, stony and sparsely vegetated (often with spiny plants) and usually with more bare ground than vegetation.

ABOVE: *Members of the warbler genus Sylvia are among the highlights for birders visiting the Mediterranean in spring.* RÜPPELL'S WARBLER *is a speciality of Greece and Turkey and singing males often perch in the open; this contrasts with the species' otherwise skulking habits.*

BELOW: CRETZSCHMAR'S BUNTING *is a characteristic bird of scrub habitats on the Mediterranean coasts of Greece and Turkey, and its rich plumage colours are a good match for the stony, sparsely vegetated habitats it favours. Bush-crickets, which are abundant in spring, feature heavily in its diet and that of its chicks.*

ABOVE: *A slightly awkward encounter between two of the Mediterranean's commonest and most colourful inhabitants:* HOOPOE (LEFT) *and* BEE-EATER (RIGHT). *Both feed primarily on invertebrates but find their food in different ways: the former probes the ground with its long bill, the latter catches flying prey on the wing.*

INSET: LINNETS *feed primarily on seeds and forage in suitable areas – weedy fields and arable fields – throughout the year. But in spring, patches of scrub are vital for nesting.*

UPLANDS AND TUNDRA

UPLAND HABITATS – mountains and moorlands – are challenging environments at the best of times. Sometimes they can be positively inhospitable and, even in summer, are often subjected to periods of freezing temperatures, driving rain or even snow. But despite this a hardy band of specialist birds make them their home. A few are truly resident; some are altitudinal migrants, escaping the worst of the winter weather by heading downhill; others migrate long distances, often to different habitats, for the winter. The winter months are also bleak on the frozen, treeless tundra that dominates Arctic regions and only a scattering of birds can tolerate these extremes. Come the spring, however, and insect and plant life flourishes, and vast numbers of migrant waders and wildlife make the tundra their home for the breeding season.

ABOVE: Barren, stony mountain plateaux are home to the DOTTEREL, during the summer months at least. Abandoning this rather forbidding terrain in autumn, they fly south, most spending the winter in North Africa.

LEFT: Surveying the surrounding tundra from its nest, this incubating PURPLE SANDPIPER laid its four eggs in a shallow scrape in the stony ground. With such hostile surroundings and chilly ground below, the parent bird's uninterrupted incubation is absolutely essential if the eggs are to hatch.

MEADOW PIPITS (BELOW LEFT) can be abundant on upland moors during the breeding season. It is their role in life to form a significant part of the diet of predatory MERLINS (BELOW), with which they share these habitats. The fate of the two are inextricably linked: in years when there are poor numbers and breeding success of Meadow Pipits, Merlins raise fewer offspring.

THE URBAN ENVIRONMENT

WITH AN EVER-GROWING human population, it is hardly surprisingly that the urban environment is significant in ecological terms: in Britain, for example, 10% of the available land area is devoted to private, domestic gardens. While the urban environment excludes large numbers of birds that would have been present had not towns, roads and the like removed their favoured habitats, many species live quite happily alongside Man. Some positively benefit – House Sparrows do extremely well in many towns and the majority of Swifts nest in buildings. Part of the attraction for birds is that features in the urban landscape mimic those in the wild. The sides of buildings resemble cliff faces, mature gardens often have a rich scrub layer akin to woodland edge, and parks can sometimes make good feeding grounds for open grassland birds.

BELOW: People living in towns and cities often do positive things to encourage birds in their gardens. The provision of food is one way, but these BLUE TITS are doing well in a nestbox provided by a thoughtful house owner.

BOTTOM: It is rare to find a SWIFT nesting anywhere other than in the roof space of a house, church or other tall building. Other than easy access to the outside, Swifts ask very little else of their chosen homes: the nest – such as it is – is typically sited on bare loft boards.

CONSERVATION

WE ALL KNOW the problems that beset our planet: global warming and greenhouse gas emission; insidious pollution of the terrestrial environment; agricultural intensification; housing development; pollution of the sea and the rape of its resources. This list goes on. As members of society, and consumers within it, we all contribute in one way or another to these problems. But potentially we are also the solution. All of us can make decisions that affect the environment for better or for worse: what we eat and where we source our food; how we travel; how we dispose of our rubbish. All these issues really can make a contribution at the personal level and, who knows, other people may well learn from positive examples.

Simply being a member or supporter of conservation and birdwatching organisations across Europe is also a really positive thing to do; if nothing else it adds weight of numbers to the voices that speak out on matters affecting the environment and the laws that govern the way we live. Give as much money as possible to conservation bodies for the purchase of land, thereby removing areas from threats such as development and intensive farming. But perhaps the most significant thing you can do is to become a member of, and information contributor to, the British Trust for Ornithology (BTO) if you live in Britain, or one of its sister organisations elsewhere in Europe. Striving to understand what is happening to our birdlife through rigorous and detached science, organisations such as the BTO have real power to influence important environment decisions made by governments – and ultimately, that's a good thing for all wildlife, not just birds. Nobody can ignore or dispute rigorous science and watertight analysis. You have obviously dug into your pocket to buy this book. So dig a little deeper and become a paid-up citizen scientist!

It's not all doom and gloom. At the start of the 20th century the BUZZARD had been exterminated from much of Britain, persecuted by gamekeepers and landowners. Poisoning by organocholorine pesticides was another blow, as it was for many other species. But with these pesticides banned and gamekeepers adopting a more enlightened attitude, its fortunes changed. From the 1980s onwards, and without the direct aid of conservationists, Buzzards spread back into many of their former haunts. Numbers are soaring. In a short space of time it has become widespread and is now possibly Britain's commonest bird of prey.

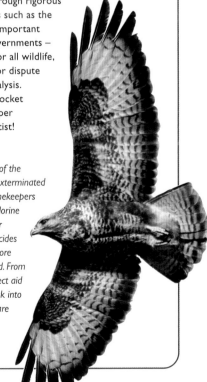

MUTE SWAN
Cygnus olor

NORTHWEST EUROPE IS the focus for the region's Mute Swans, the species being particularly widespread in Britain and Ireland. In spring, aggressive males engage in spectacular 'busking' displays with arched wings, their competitive spirits sometimes leading to serious fights. Watch the adult swans for any length of time and you will see them feeding. They sometimes graze in shallow water and upend in deeper water, using their long necks to uproot water plants. Unfortunately, they are prone to ingest fishermen's lost lead weights, which although banned in Britain are still used in parts of Europe, and which cause serious poisoning; abandoned fishing lines and hooks can also be a threat.

Male swans are aggressive in the breeding season, chasing off intruders by flying, and then swimming quickly towards them; this is called 'busking'.

Adult has all-white plumage although neck sometimes stained buffish. Bill is orange-red with large black knob at base. Juvenile buffish-brown with grubby-pink bill; acquires adult feathering during first year. When swimming, adult and juvenile hold neck in a more graceful 'S' shape than other swans. Sometimes flies in 'V' formation or diagonal lines.

juvenile

BIRD FACTS

VOICE Hoarse trumpeting, snorting and hissing calls; non-vocal wing noise in flight

LENGTH 145–160cm

WINGSPAN 210–235cm

WEIGHT 8–13kg

HABITAT Lakes, slow-flowing rivers, wet meadows and sheltered coasts

NEST Mound of vegetation beside water

EGGS 5–8; greenish, chalky

FOOD Mainly water plants; some small invertebrates

male

female

juvenile

In flight, wingbeats are deep and powerful; the wings make a unique creaking sound that serves the same purpose as other species' contact calls.

The Mute Swan's long neck allows it to exploit deeper water than geese or dabbling ducks.

ABOVE: *male*

male

female

Family group: adults with cygnets.

Much larger than superficially similar Bewick's Swan and with proportionately longer neck. Adult has all-white plumage, black legs and black bill with yellow patch at base; area of yellow larger than on Bewick's; wedge-shaped and extends beyond nostrils. Juvenile is pinkish-buff with black-tipped, pinkish bill, grading to white at base. Similar to juvenile Bewick's: best identified by larger size and association with adult birds.

The adult Whooper Swan is essentially pure white.

WHOOPER SWAN
Cygnus cygnus

THE SIGHT AND sound of an overwintering flock of Whooper Swans is a memorable one. Flying in 'V' formation flocks through flurries of snowflakes, or swimming through rising mists on a part-frozen loch, they appear far more at ease with wintry conditions than most human observers. As with Bewick's Swans, with which they seldom mix, family units remain together within the looser associations of winter flocks.

Family group in flight.

juvenile

Smallest swan in Europe. Adult has all white plumage. Legs black and bill black with irregularly shaped yellow patch at base; yellow does not extend beyond nostrils. Juvenile is buffish-grey and has black-tipped pink bill, fading to white at base; distinguished from juvenile Whooper Swan by its smaller size, and bill size and shape, but more importantly by association with adult birds.

adult   *adult*

BEWICK'S SWAN
Cygnus columbianus

FROM OCTOBER TO March Bewick's Swans can be found at traditional sites, which are coastal or lowland wetlands, from Denmark to Britain and Ireland. If especially cold weather spreads west during the winter, birds are sometimes forced to move ahead of it in order to continue feeding. On some traditional sites, individual birds can be recognised by their unique bill patterns. Watch a flock of Bewick's Swans for a while and you will notice that small family parties, comprising two adults and two or three youngsters, tend to stick together; this bond lasts throughout the winter, the parties having migrated from their high Arctic breeding grounds together as well.

Bewick's Swans are invariably seen in flocks; young birds are greyer and have pink and black bills.

Bewick's Swans that visit Europe in the winter breed in the northeast Arctic.

juvenile

GREYLAG GOOSE

Anser anser

Adults in flight.

THE PRECISE NATURAL distribution of Greylag Geese in Europe is now difficult to determine, since introductions and feral populations have confused the situation. Although some feral populations of Greylag Geese can be approachable, most are generally wary of man – justifiably so, as they are often persecuted and shot. If danger threatens, all the heads in a feeding flock will go up and, if the alarm continues, the birds may take to the air, running along the ground to take off. They fly on powerful wingbeats and the flock will sometimes engage in surprisingly aerobatic dives and plunges. Generally speaking, wintering flocks will not be found far from water, to which they retreat without hesitation should the need arise.

BIRD FACTS

VOICE Clattering clamour in flight, less bugling than other grey geese

LENGTH 75–90cm

WINGSPAN 150–180cm

WEIGHT 3–4kg

HABITAT Arable land, marshes, lakes

NEST Sheltered depression on ground, among vegetation

EGGS 4–6; creamy white

FOOD Grass, spilt crops, growing cereals

The Greylag Goose is the typical grey goose seen in much of Europe, especially during the summer months; this bird is an adult.

IDENTIFICATION

adult

Large, stoutly built goose with mainly grey-brown plumage. Most adult birds seen in western Europe have orange bills; eastern birds have pinkish bills. Legs pink in all adult birds. Shows pale margins to feathers on back. Lower belly and undertail white. Some birds have a few dark feathers on belly. In flight, shows grey on forewing, lower back and tail.

Family groups of Greylag Geese, comprising both adult birds and accompanying chicks (goslings), are a familiar sight on many European lowland lakes in spring and summer.

Smaller than superficially similar Bean Goose and with proportionately shorter neck and smaller bill. Bill dark with variable patch of pink, usually in the form of a band, near tip. Head and neck usually dark brown, breast and flanks paler brown and back greyish. Legs pink, although much duller in juvenile. In flight, wings look pale grey except for darker flight feathers; back and tail also paler than on Bean Goose.

adult

adult

The characteristic pink legs of this species are much duller in the juvenile; the variable pink patch on the bill makes this goose very similar in appearance to the Bean Goose in poor light.

adult

PINK-FOOTED GOOSE
Anser brachyrhynchus

THE PINK-FOOTED GOOSE is essentially an Arctic breeding species, with the entire world population migrating to northwest Europe in September and October. During the day, the birds usually feed on coastal fields, including a wide variety of plant material in their diet. As dusk approaches, they take to the air in vast flocks, streaming overhead in noisy skeins towards the safety of their saltmarsh roost on the shores. The species is still persecuted by hunters in some areas, as well as having to endure the rigours of the brief Arctic summer when breeding; in some bad seasons, few or sometimes no young are reared by entire breeding groups.

BIRD FACTS

VOICE Musical disyllabic or trisyllabic honking; also high-pitched, sharp 'wink-wink'
LENGTH 60–75cm
WINGSPAN 135–170cm
WEIGHT 1.8–3kg
HABITAT Breeds on uplands or tundra; in winter, on fields, roosting on estuaries or lakes
NEST Mound of vegetation on hummock or ledge; sometimes colonial
EGGS 3–5; white
FOOD Plant material; in winter, mainly stubble or grass

adult

Can generally be identified by chocolate-brown appearance, particularly on head and neck, and proportionately long neck. Bill dark with variable orange markings: in race *rossicus* orange limited to near bill tip, but in race *fabalis* orange much more extensive. Legs of both races orange. In flight, upperwings look all dark. Lower back is brown, separated from white-edged brown tail by white band at base.

adult fabalis

adult fabalis

BEAN GOOSE
Anser fabalis

IN EUROPE, THERE are two races of Bean Goose: *rossicus*, which nests at more northerly latitudes on open tundra, and *fabalis*, which favours taiga or boreal forest at slightly lower latitudes. Both races are migratory, moving south and west in autumn. Some winter in lowland areas, others around arable land and wetlands. They favour traditional sites, some of which have varying degrees of protection from hunting. When danger threatens, birds are quick to take to the air and are more able to rise in a near-vertical manner than many other goose species.

The Bean Goose is a particularly nervous bird in winter and favours large, open fields, where the flock can keep wary eyes open for danger; although similar in colouring to other geese, this species has very distinctive orange legs, a characteristic common to both races.

BIRD FACTS

VOICE Calls include a nasal cackle
LENGTH 65–80cm
WINGSPAN 150–175cm
WEIGHT 2–4kg
HABITAT Breeds on tundra and in northern forests; in winter, on arable and stubble fields
NEST Mound of vegetation, lined with down
EGGS 4–6; buffish but stained
FOOD Grasses and cereal grains

adult fabalis

WHITE-FRONTED GOOSE

Anser albifrons

THE WHITE-FRONTED GOOSE occurs in two races: the Siberian race *albifrons* overwinters in east and southeast Europe and also occurs along the coast of northwest Europe and southern England; the Greenland race *flavirostris*, numbering some 30,000 birds, overwinters in Ireland, Scotland and Wales. Although difficult to approach closely in most parts of their European overwintering range, the species is afforded special protection in a few areas, where hides allow the quarrelsome antics of busy feeding flocks to be watched at close quarters. Startled geese take to the air in huge, noisy flocks, flying in 'V' formations or chevrons.

Large goose, which, as adult, has white forehead not extending above eye. Siberian race *albifrons* has pinkish bill, while Greenland race *flavirostris* has orange-yellow bill. Plumage generally grey-brown, with underparts paler, but with variable black bands and crescents on belly; undertail white. Juvenile similar to adult but lacks white forehead. In flight, looks comparatively long-winged and more agile than Greylag.

adult albifrons

juvenile

adult albifrons

BIRD FACTS

VOICE Flocks utter musical ringing, laughing and yodelling calls; hissing and yapping calls on ground and non-vocal 'creaking' wings on taking to air

LENGTH 65–78cm

WINGSPAN 130–165cm

WEIGHT 1.5–3kg

HABITAT Breeds on boggy tundra; overwinters on water meadows and near estuaries

NEST Vegetation-lined depression on hummock

EGGS 5–6; very pale buff

FOOD Grass, roots, other vegetation

White-fronted Geese are very wary of intruders and take to the air in huge, noisy flocks if alarmed.

LESSER WHITE-FRONTED GOOSE

Anser erythropus

ALTHOUGH SMALL FLOCKS of Lesser White-fronts can be found by travelling to southeast Europe in the winter, birdwatchers from northwest Europe also stand a reasonable chance of finding a stray bird among flocks of White-fronted Geese. Picking out a bird is tricky: size alone is little use (White-fronts are variable) so concentrate on the bird's head markings, notably the eyering and white blaze.

Superficially similar to White-fronted Goose, but more compact and appreciably smaller when seen side by side. Bill on adult relatively small and pinkish-orange. White forehead extends above eye, which has conspicuous yellow eyering; white forehead absent in juvenile and eyering dull. Plumage on all birds mostly grey-brown, darker than White-front, with dark markings on paler belly. Undertail white. In flight, has fast wingbeats and is hard to distinguish from White-front.

BIRD FACTS

VOICE High-pitched yelping calls

LENGTH 55–65cm

WINGSPAN 120–135cm

WEIGHT 1.5–2.5kg

HABITAT Breeds on tundra; overwinters on meadows and fields

NEST Vegetation-lined mound on tundra hummock

EGGS 4–6; off-white

FOOD Plant material

adult

adult

RED-BREASTED GOOSE

Branta ruficollis

THE RED-BREASTED GOOSE is a scarce and declining species. It often nests in accessible sites, vulnerable to attack by ground predators. But nests are often near nesting Peregrines, the geese presumably gaining protection from the falcon's vigorous defence of its own family. Declining Peregrine numbers may affect Red-breasteds but hunting and habitat loss are factors too.

adult

A small but beautifully marked goose. Adult has complicated pattern of red, white and black on head, neck and breast. Back, wings and belly mostly black but shows conspicuous white stripe on flanks. Rear end white except for tail; white is most striking in flight. Juvenile similar to, but duller than, adult.

adult

BIRD FACTS

VOICE High-pitched, disyllabic call

LENGTH 53–56cm

WINGSPAN 115–135cm

WEIGHT 1–1.5kg

HABITAT Breeds on tundra; in winter, on steppe or sometimes arable land

NEST Mound of vegetation; usually built near bird of prey nest

EGGS 4–5; whitish

FOOD Plant material

The striking looking Red-breasted Goose is a rare but regular straggler to parts of western Europe; individual birds are invariably found among flocks of Brent, Barnacle or White-fronted Geese.

dark-bellied adult (bernicla)

light-bellied adult (hrota)

BRENT GOOSE

Branta bernicla

VISIT ALMOST ANY sizeable estuary on Europe's North Sea coast between October and February and you are likely to find large flocks of Brent Geese. Feeding out on the mudflats, they are unobtrusive, especially on dull days. Contact calls give their presence away, however, and they frequently take to the air when disturbed or in search of alternative feeding grounds. In late winter, when food supplies on the estuaries may be exhausted, flocks increasingly visit nearby arable land and grassland prior to the long migration back to their high Arctic breeding grounds.

BIRD FACTS

VOICE Deep, rolling bark

LENGTH 55–60cm

WINGSPAN 110–120cm

WEIGHT 1.5–2kg

HABITAT Breeds on tundra; in winter, on saltmarsh and coastal grassland

NEST Mound of vegetation on island or hummock in water

EGGS 3–5; off-white

FOOD Plant material, particularly eelgrass in winter

IDENTIFICATION

A small, dark goose. Adult has all-black head and neck except for white neck patch. Back and wings dark grey-brown except for black flight feathers. Rear end white, most noticeable in flight, but tail dark. Legs and feet black. Race *bernicla* has dark belly; race *hrota* has pale-grey belly. Juvenile has pale-edged feathers on back and lacks white neck; adult characteristics acquired during winter.

dark-bellied flock

adult dark-bellied

The white rear of the Brent Goose is best seen in flight; the white neck patch is more of a stripe, and far less prominent than that on the Canada Goose.

adult dark-bellied

adult dark-bellied

BARNACLE GOOSE

Branta leucopsis

IN EUROPE, THE attractive Barnacle Goose is seen as a winter visitor, arriving in October and departing in March. Studies have shown that distinct populations are represented within the breeding range, with little mixing or overlap between them. The sight of feeding flocks of these strikingly marked birds is memorable enough, but their flights at dawn and dusk are even more remarkable.

Barnacle Geese are the subjects of some controversy at their winter grounds on Islay, where they prefer the meadow grasses in fields 'improved' for sheep rearing.

BIRD FACTS

VOICE Short, sharp bark; repeated as yapping chorus by flocks

LENGTH 60–70cm

WINGSPAN 135–145cm

WEIGHT 1.5–2kg

HABITAT Breeds on tundra; overwinters on coastal grassland and saltmarshes

NEST Mound of vegetation on cliff ledge or island

EGGS 4–5; greyish-white

FOOD Plant material, including roots and seeds

The colours of these glossy black and white birds contrast even more in flight.

adult

IDENTIFICATION

A small, compact goose. Bill and eye black. Adults have white face and black neck. Back barred black and grey; underparts white. Legs and feet black. Juvenile has more blotched face and greyer chest. In flight, looks very black and white; flight feathers black, and shows conspicuous white rump when seen from above.

CANADA GOOSE

Branta canadensis

INTRODUCED TO EUROPE in the 17th century, Canada Geese seem to favour semi-urban or even man-made habitats and most birds are residents. Unlike their wild North American cousins, they are generally tolerant of human observers and flock behaviour can often be studied at close quarters. It soon becomes apparent that winter flocks in particular have an organised hierarchy. Within the flock, large family groups dominate smaller ones and show considerable aggression towards one another; not surprisingly, single birds come right at the bottom of the pecking order.

BIRD FACTS

VOICE Loud, resonant honking calls, usually two notes 'gor-rronk'; also a variety of other trumpeting notes

LENGTH 90–100cm

WINGSPAN 150–180cm

WEIGHT 4–5kg

HABITAT Ornamental lakes, flooded gravel pits and nearby meadows

NEST Pile of leaves and vegetation, usually near water

EGGS 5–6; cream or white

FOOD Roots, stems, leaves, etc of aquatic and waterside plants

adult Canada Goose

IDENTIFICATION

Europe's largest goose. Head and neck black, except for contrasting white patch on face. Plumage on back and underparts brown, except for white on undertail and black flight feathers; upperparts can look rather barred. Yellow-buff goslings follow parents. Juvenile birds duller than adults but soon indistinguishable.

Adults in flight.

Adult birds, accompanied by goslings, take to the water soon after the chicks hatch, as a means of avoiding ground predators.

Superficially similar to Ruddy Shelduck but with distinctive markings. Adult has pinkish bill and legs. Head and neck pale except for dark patch through eye and dark collar. Breast and underparts buffish-brown but with dark chestnut patch on belly. Back usually rufous-brown but sometimes greyish-brown. Juvenile is more uniformly buffish-brown, without clear markings on head or belly; legs and bill dull brown. In flight, adults show striking white forewing patches on both upper and underwing surfaces, green speculum and black flight feathers.

Adults fighting.

EGYPTIAN GOOSE
Alopochen aegyptiacus

IN EUROPE, THE Egyptian Goose has a long-established feral population in East Anglia and the Thames Valley, in England, and is abundant in the Netherlands and Belgium; individuals seen elsewhere are probably escapes from captivity. They are aggressive towards one another and this antagonism sometimes extends to other species, so Egyptian Geese do not usually mix with other wildfowl species. Birds often feed in more lush vegetation than do other wildfowl, and sometimes only their heads can be seen above the grass. They sometimes perch in trees.

BIRD FACTS

VOICE Distinctive loud braying calls
LENGTH 65–73cm
WINGSPAN 135–155cm
WEIGHT 1.5–2kg
HABITAT Seldom far from water, usually in fields and marshes
NEST Mound of vegetation under bush or in hole
EGGS 8–9; off-white
FOOD Mainly leaves and seeds of grass and cereal crops

FAR LEFT: Adults in flight.
CENTRE LEFT: adult
LEFT: adult

male

female

RUDDY SHELDUCK
Tadorna ferruginea

LIKE ITS COUSIN, the Shelduck, the Ruddy Shelduck is a hole-nesting species. Underground burrows are favoured, although birds are not averse to using holes in trees or unexpected locations such as derelict buildings. The young ducklings, which leave the burrow soon after hatching, can feed on their own almost immediately, but are guided and protected by both parents until able to fend for themselves. Family groups are seldom found far from water, to which they retreat if danger threatens.

BIRD FACTS

VOICE Noisy; flight call 'ang' or rolling 'aarl'
LENGTH 61–67cm
WINGSPAN 120–145cm
WEIGHT 1.1–1.5kg
HABITAT Variety of wetland habitats including river deltas
NEST In burrows or holes in trees
EGGS 8–9; white
FOOD Plant material and small invertebrates

An attractive and distinctive duck. Sexes similar. Adult has dark bill, eyes and legs. Head and upper neck buffish with clear demarcation from orange-brown body. In breeding season, only the male has black collar separating buff and orange plumage; sexes similar in other plumage respects. At rest, black wingtips can be seen. In flight, wings are strikingly black and white, the black being confined to the flight feathers. Juvenile similar to adult but duller.

Adults in flight, showing the striking black and white areas on the wing that are typical of the species; birds seen well outside the usual breeding range are most likely to be part of a developing feral population in Western Europe.

SHELDUCK

Tadorna tadorna

THROUGHOUT MUCH OF its European range, the Shelduck is essentially a coastal bird. It breeds along much of the north west European coast, from northern France to Norway, and is common around Britain and Ireland. Visiting the coast in spring, it always seems slightly odd to see a Shelduck emerge from an abandoned rabbit burrow: where rabbits are common, this is a favourite nesting site. Nesting birds will aggressively drive off others of their own species and will even attack young from different parents. After breeding has finished, Shelduck often congregate in favoured, traditional sites to moult all their flight feathers.

The bright colours of this striking species can be seen to great effect in flight.

ABOVE: *male*

ABOVE: *female;* BELOW: *male*

Although the Shelduck can be aggressive when nesting, the adult bird will show care and devotion to its own ducklings, and long lines of black and white youngsters can be seen following the female across shallow estuaries.

male

DID YOU KNOW?

An old Rabbit burrow is a good nesting site for the Shelduck.

A large and distinctively marked bird, the smaller female lacks the bill knob of the male.

female

juvenile

IDENTIFICATION

Adult has bright red bill and legs. Head and upper neck dark green; can look all dark in some lights. Rest of plumage comprises patches of white and black with conspicuous orange-chestnut breast band. Male has red knob at base of bill, while female shows pale feathering at bill base instead; sexes similar in other plumage respects. Juvenile is mottled and marbled brown and white; shows dull pink legs and bill. In flight, adult looks conspicuously black and white.

Male has yellow bill, green head showing sheen in good light, chestnut breast and otherwise mostly grey-brown plumage; shows black stern and white tail. Female has orange-yellow bill and rather uniform brown plumage. Eclipse male similar to female but more reddish on breast. In flight both sexes show white-bordered blue speculum.

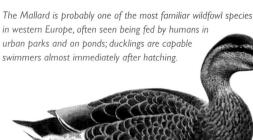

Male feeding.

MALLARD
Anas platyrhynchos

MALLARDS CAN BE found in almost any freshwater habitat and are occasionally seen around the coast as well. On urban lakes and at beauty spots where they are fed, Mallards seem to have lost most of their connections with the wild. They are often tame and respond to human visitors not by fleeing but by pestering them for scraps of bread. Under more natural conditions, Mallards can be seen feeding by dabbling in the shallows or up-ending to feed on the bottom mud. The small, fluffy ducklings swim almost from the moment they hatch.

BIRD FACTS

VOICE Female gives familiar quack; male a weak nasal note

LENGTH 50–65cm

WINGSPAN 80–100cm

WEIGHT 950–1,300g

HABITAT Almost anywhere with water

NEST Usually a depression on the ground

EGGS 9–13; bluish-green

FOOD Omnivorous; an opportunistic feeder

adult male

The Mallard is probably one of the most familiar wildfowl species in western Europe, often seen being fed by humans in urban parks and on ponds; ducklings are capable swimmers almost immediately after hatching.

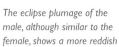

male

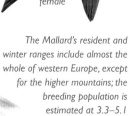

The eclipse plumage of the male, although similar to the female, shows a more reddish breast.

eclipse male

female

female

The Mallard's resident and winter ranges include almost the whole of western Europe, except for the higher mountains; the breeding population is estimated at 3.3–5.1 million pairs in northwest Europe, 350,000 in Britain alone.

male

female

male

Male and female Mallards are easily distinguished, but the bright orange legs are common to both sexes.

GADWALL

Anas strepera

As a breeding bird, the Gadwall occurs rather locally in western Europe, with perhaps a few tens of thousands of pairs breeding at latitudes from northern Britain south to southern Spain. A few hundred pairs breed in Iceland, but the species becomes much more common across its central Asian breeding range, and Gadwall are also common breeding birds in northwest North America. Recent estimates put the European breeding population at 20–30,000 pairs, rising to maybe 100,000 individuals in winter; roughly 20% of these occur in northwest Europe.

BIRD FACTS

VOICE Male utters nasal 'mair'; female gives quiet quack

LENGTH 45–55cm

WINGSPAN 85–95cm

WEIGHT 600–900g

HABITAT Breeds on wetlands with open water; in winter, on lakes and marshes

NEST On ground beside water

EGGS 8–12; pale pink

FOOD Seeds, plants and insects

adult female

adult male

Adult male has dark grey bill and head, and buffish-grey neck and back with black stern.

adult female

adult male

IDENTIFICATION

At first glance, a rather drab duck. Close views of male in good light reveal grey plumage comprising intricate vermiculation. Female recalls female Mallard with yellow bill and brown plumage. Juvenile resembles dull adult female. Both sexes are easily identified when swimming if flash of white speculum is revealed. This latter feature very obvious in flight, when white underwing also noticeable.

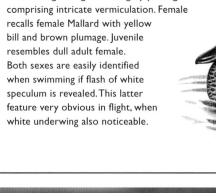

ABOVE: *male;* BELOW: *female*

DID YOU KNOW?

Outside the breeding season, from August to April, Gadwall are invariably found in flocks and identification of the females is far easier when male and female ducks are seen within the same flock than when females are alone; the species often associates freely with Coots.

An attractive dabbling duck. Male can look drab in dull light. In good light, reveals orange head with yellow forecrown. Breast pinkish, and back and flanks covered with soft, grey vermiculation. Underparts white and stern black. In water, appears to have black and white rear end. Female has mainly brown plumage with white belly and dark feathering around eye. In flight male shows conspicuous white patch on upper surface of innerwing.

WIGEON

Anas penelope

DURING THE BREEDING season, Wigeon are retiring and favour inaccessible wetlands; consequently, the species is difficult to see well at this time of year. From late August until April, however, flocks of Wigeon move south to spend the winter on coastal marshes and estuary saltmarshes, where they are much more visible. At low tide, the birds waddle across the oozing mud in a rather ungainly manner, feeding on eelgrass and algae. As the tide advances, they up-end in the shallows to feed.

BIRD FACTS

VOICE Male utters whistling 'whee-OO'; female gives grating purr

LENGTH 45–51cm

WINGSPAN 75–85cm

WEIGHT 600–900g

HABITAT Breeds on northern lakes and wetlands; in winter, on saltmarshes and coastal grassland

NEST On ground in cover

EGGS 6–12; pale buff

FOOD Plant material, mainly eelgrass and algae

Males in particular are well marked in flight.

male

female

female

female

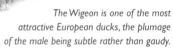

male

The Wigeon is one of the most attractive European ducks, the plumage of the male being subtle rather than gaudy.

male

BIRD FACTS

VOICE Distinctive, high-pitched, chirping 'krick'

LENGTH 34–38cm

WINGSPAN 58–65cm

WEIGHT 240–360g

HABITAT Shallow fresh water when nesting; in winter, on flood meadows or saltmarshes

NEST On ground, in cover

EGGS 8–11; off-white

FOOD Seeds, invertebrates

TEAL

Anas crecca

DESPITE BEING WIDELY hunted in much of its range, the Teal is still one of Europe's commonest ducks. Except in areas where they are protected from hunting pressures, Teal are wary of man and quick to take to the air, rising almost vertically from the water when alarmed. They fly off rapidly with whirring wingbeats and swerving flight patterns, flocks sometimes having a wader-like jizz. When undisturbed, the birds feed in very shallow water, thrusting their bills ahead of them into the soft mud as they walk.

The region's smallest duck. Male has attractive orange-brown head with large green patch from eye to nape, bordered with creamy yellow stripe. Back and flanks show grey vermiculation and underparts white. Black-bordered, creamy-yellow patches on sides of stern. Female and juvenile have grey-brown plumage; best identified by size and association with male. In flight, all birds show green speculum and white underwing.

Male in flight.

male

female

male

female

male

The Teal breeds throughout much of northern Europe; in North America it is replaced by a separate species – Green-winged Teal – formerly considered to be a subspecies of Teal.

male

DID YOU KNOW?

The Teal's winter range extends south of its breeding range and includes most of western and southern Europe; some populations in northwestern Europe are year-round residents.

An unusual duck, the most distinctive feature of both sexes being the broad, flattened bill. Male has green head with sheen in good light. Bright orange belly provides striking contrast with otherwise white breast and flanks. Back and stern dark and bill black. Female has mottled brown plumage. Bill dark but with lower edges orange. In flight, both sexes show blue forewing separated by white band from green speculum.

SHOVELER
Anas clypeata

SHOVELERS ARE DIFFICULT birds to observe during the breeding season, although pairs are sometimes seen performing aerobatic display flights above suitable territories. They are easier to watch at wetland reserves in winter, when small groups often gather to feed in the shallows. Continually on the move, feeding Shovelers walk slowly forward, using their bills to sieve food from the mud. Given the small size of the animals and plant debris on which they feed, it is not surprising that an almost constant intake of food is required.

BIRD FACTS

VOICE Quiet 'tuc' uttered by male; female quacks
LENGTH 44–52cm
WINGSPAN 70–85cm
WEIGHT 400–850g
HABITAT Shallow water
NEST Depression in ground
EGGS 9–11; buff
FOOD Mostly small invertebrates but some plant matter

DID YOU KNOW?

The characteristic shovel-like bill is ideal for sieving food.

ABOVE: *female*

Shovelers are often seen in pairs, even outside the breeding season; both share the same bill shape but the female (LEFT) is noticeably duller than the more colourful male (BELOW).

female

male

male

PINTAIL

Anas acuta

IN WESTERN EUROPE, the Pintail is a local and rather scarce breeder. In winter it is a different story, with some 60,000 birds present in northwest Europe, mostly in coastal districts, and 250,000 in the Mediterranean region. Even when seen from a distance, a male Pintail is easily identified by its gleaming white neck and breast, and long tail. Often seen in pairs or small groups in winter, Pintails are comparatively shy and unobtrusive wild birds, seldom accustomed to the close presence of humans. Although they often feed on coastal wetlands, they are also seen on mudflats in winter.

Male is an elegant duck with chocolate-brown head and white on underparts and on front of neck, forming narrow stripe up side of face. Flanks are grey and black with elongated feathers. Stern is buff and black, with long, upcurved tail. Female has dark-grey bill and largely brown plumage with long-bodied appearance. Juvenile resembles dull adult female.

BIRD FACTS

VOICE Male utters quiet whistle; female gives short quacks

LENGTH 51–66cm

WINGSPAN 80–95cm

WEIGHT 750–1,000g

HABITAT Open areas with shallow water

NEST Hollow on ground, usually in the open

EGGS 7–9; yellowish

FOOD Variety of plant and animal material

DID YOU KNOW?

In winter, coastal Pintails feed on a tiny mollusc called the Laver Spire Shell, found on mudflats.

Upended male, feeding in shallows.

male

female

male

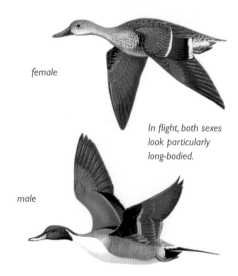

female

In flight, both sexes look particularly long-bodied.

male

Male is distinctive with broad, white crescent-shaped stripe over eye leading back to nape. Cap dark but head and neck otherwise reddish-brown. Breast brown, flanks grey and shows long, trailing black, blue-grey and white feathers on back. Female similar to female teal and best distinguished by association with male. In flight, blue forewing and green speculum of both sexes can be seen.

female

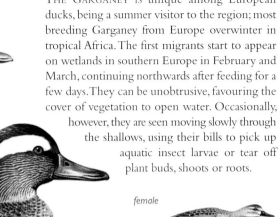

male

GARGANEY
Anas querquedula

THE GARGANEY IS unique among European ducks, being a summer visitor to the region; most breeding Garganey from Europe overwinter in tropical Africa. The first migrants start to appear on wetlands in southern Europe in February and March, continuing northwards after feeding for a few days. They can be unobtrusive, favouring the cover of vegetation to open water. Occasionally, however, they are seen moving slowly through the shallows, using their bills to pick up aquatic insect larvae or tear off plant buds, shoots or roots.

female

male

When alarmed, Garganey rise steeply from the water; their flight is direct and fast, without the swerves and twists that characterise Teal flight.

BIRD FACTS

VOICE Male utters characteristic mechanical-sounding rattle; female gives quiet quack

LENGTH 37–41cm

WINGSPAN 60–65cm

WEIGHT 320–500g

HABITAT Shallow wetlands and flooded meadows

NEST On ground, in thick tussock

EGGS 8–9; light brown

FOOD Aquatic insects and plants

ABOVE: male

LEFT: Female; confusingly similar to female Teal but greyer overall with pale spot at base of bill often noticeable and obviously different wing markings when seen in flight.

DID YOU KNOW?

The arrival of small parties of Garganey on marshes in the region is a sure sign that spring is on the way.

RUDDY DUCK

Oxyura jamaicensis

BIRD FACTS

VOICE Mostly silent

LENGTH 35–43cm

WINGSPAN 53–62cm

WEIGHT 400–700g

HABITAT Well-vegetated ponds, lakes and reservoirs

NEST Well hidden near water

EGGS 6–10; whitish

FOOD Mainly aquatic insect larvae; also seeds

IN POOR LIGHT and at a distance, a feeding Ruddy Duck might be mistaken for a Little Grebe: it also tends to dive frequently and bob up to the surface a few seconds later. But in good light Ruddy Ducks of both sexes are distinctive. In the spring, males display by rattling their bills and chest-beating, the result being a froth of bubbles surrounding their chests at water level. In the breeding season, they are rather retiring; they are easier to see in winter, when small flocks sometimes gather in open areas of water.

The male Ruddy Duck (above) can be distinguished by its bright-blue bill.

IDENTIFICATION

A so-called 'stifftail' duck, which often lives up to its name by raising its relatively long tail in the air. Male has mainly orange-brown plumage but with black cap, white face and bright-blue bill; stern white. Female has mainly grey-brown plumage but similar, distinctive outline. Often shows pale cheeks broken by dark line from base of bill. Seldom seen in flight.

male

female

female

female

This species appeared in Europe in the 1950s: birds escaped from Slimbridge Wildfowl and Wetland Trust reserve, England; they have increased ever since.

WHITE-HEADED DUCK

Oxyura leucocephala

BIRD FACTS

VOICE Mostly silent

LENGTH 43–48cm

WINGSPAN 62–70cm

WEIGHT 550–900g

HABITAT Shallow, well-vegetated lakes and pools; both freshwater and brackish

NEST Woven platform of reeds

EGGS 5–10; whitish

FOOD Plant material and small aquatic animals

THE WHITE-HEADED DUCK is one of Europe's rarest waterbirds, having its last strongholds in Turkey and the south of Spain; even here, not many more than a few hundred pairs are thought to breed. The White-headed Duck possesses one of the strangest bills of any duck and often swims with its bristly tail cocked in the air. The bird is, however, an excellent swimmer and diver, covering surprisingly long distances underwater and staying submerged for half a minute or more in its quest for water plants.

male

female

IDENTIFICATION

A 'stifftail' duck, superficially similar to, but larger than, Ruddy Duck. Male is distinctive with white head, black cap and eye and disproportionately large blue bill with strangely swollen base. Body plumage mainly brown. Female has brown body plumage and bill similar in shape to male's but dark grey in colour. Head shows dark brown cap down to level of eye and white face with dark line running from base of bill.

Despite subdued colouring, an attractive duck. Sexes similar. Plumage ground colour is grey-brown but covered with pale buff spots; these are particularly large and striking on breast, belly and back. Bill dark and shows dark smudge through eye. In flight has rather uniform brown wings.

Although Marbled Ducks are migratory in parts of their range, their movements in Europe are unpredictable and perhaps have more to do with changes in water level in favoured habitats than with seasons alone.

MARBLED DUCK

Marmaronetta angustirostris

WITH A DECREASING range and population, the Marbled Duck is now a rare bird in Europe, found mainly in southern Spain, where fewer than 200 pairs breed each year. Marbled Ducks are difficult birds to see, since they favour the cover of dense emergent vegetation and are also rather shy and re-tiring. Perhaps the best chances of getting a glimpse of the species can be had by visiting the Coto Doñana or Ebro Delta in Spain. Al-though Marbled Ducks will take to the wing, they seldom fly far and soon drop back into cover. They occasionally venture across open water but spend lengthy periods on shady waterside perches.

BIRD FACTS

VOICE Mostly silent
LENGTH 40–42cm
WINGSPAN 63–67cm
WEIGHT 400–550g
HABITAT Shallow, well-vegetated pools and lakes; freshwater and saline
NEST Shallow depression in dense cover
EGGS 7–14; off-white
FOOD Plant material and some invertebrates

Marbled Ducks typically feed unobtrusively in shallows, often in partial cover.

Male is extremely distinctive with long mane of dark feathers on cap and nape, broad, pale stripe above eye and radiating orange feathers on neck and breast. Underparts and back dark but flanks orange and shows sail-like feathers at rear end; undertail white. Female mainly grey-brown with white belly and larger white spots on neck and breast. Shows conspicuous white 'spectacle' around eye, and white throat and base to bill.

male

female

BELOW: male; BELOW RIGHT: female

MANDARIN

Aix galericulata

THE STRANGE-LOOKING Mandarin has its true range in eastern Asia, as its oriental name implies. In Europe, it is a popular bird in captivity and many sightings are in fact escapes. Although disregarded by many serious birdwatchers, the Mandarin has established several feral breeding populations in Britain – mainly in southern and central England, but also in southern Scotland. Despite its gaudy appearance, the Mandarin can be difficult to locate since pairs or small groups tend to feed among marginal vegetation and under over-hanging trees.

BIRD FACTS

VOICE Mostly silent
LENGTH 41–49cm
WINGSPAN 68–75cm
WEIGHT 450–600g
HABITAT Wooded rivers and lakes
NEST Hole in tree
EGGS 9–12; white
FOOD Plant material and some invertebrates

TUFTED DUCK

Aythya fuligula

FROM SEPTEMBER TO MARCH, over 1.2 million Tufted Ducks move to or through northwest Europe, mostly from their main breeding range in northern Europe, boosting the numbers of resident birds. Watch a winter flock of Tufted Ducks for any length of time and you will soon discover how difficult it is to estimate numbers. Each bird dives frequently and often for considerable lengths of time, also covering a considerable distance while swimming underwater. In many parts of their range, it has benefited from the increase in man-made water bodies such as reservoirs and flooded gravel pits.

Male is very distinctive, looking black and white at a distance. In good light, dark feathering has sheen. Bill is grey with white band towards end, and has black tip. Iris yellow and head bears crest feathers, which can be raised. Female has mostly brown plumage, slightly paler on belly and flanks. Bill pattern similar to that of male and iris yellow. Head bears short tuft of feathers, giving it a rather square outline. Some females have white patch at base of bill; this never as extensive as on female Scaup. Eclipse male similar to female. In flight, both sexes show white wingbar.

BIRD FACTS

VOICE Various harsh, growling notes

LENGTH 40–47cm

WINGSPAN 68–73cm

WEIGHT 600–1,000g

HABITAT Open water, including rivers

NEST On ground near water but well hidden

EGGS 8–11; greenish-grey

FOOD Mainly molluscs and aquatic insects but some plant material

The Tufted Duck's winter range extends to southern Europe wherever suitable habitats can be found.

TOP: *female;* ABOVE: *male*

Female could be confused with female Greater Scaup but note the peaked crown and different bill pattern; usually seen in association with male.

DID YOU KNOW?

The increase in suitable habitats for the Tufted Duck explains its success; winter is spent in large flocks on open water.

male

female

male

Male is superficially similar to male Tufted Duck. Can look black, grey and white at a distance, but rounded head has green gloss in good light. Bill grey with black nail at tip and yellow iris. Neck, breast and stern black, belly and flanks white and back soft grey with fine vermiculations. Female has mainly brown plumage but with yellow iris and conspicuous white patches at base of bill and on forehead and cheek. In flight, both sexes show white wingbars.

GREATER SCAUP
Aythya marila

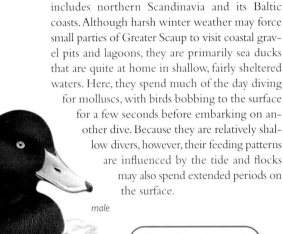

female

male

THE GREATER SCAUP's breeding range in Europe includes northern Scandinavia and its Baltic coasts. Although harsh winter weather may force small parties of Greater Scaup to visit coastal gravel pits and lagoons, they are primarily sea ducks that are quite at home in shallow, fairly sheltered waters. Here, they spend much of the day diving for molluscs, with birds bobbing to the surface for a few seconds before embarking on another dive. Because they are relatively shallow divers, however, their feeding patterns are influenced by the tide and flocks may also spend extended periods on the surface.

BELOW: *male;* BOTTOM: *female*

BIRD FACTS

VOICE Harsh, grating 'karr-karr' while flying

LENGTH 42–51cm

WINGSPAN 72–83cm

WEIGHT 900–1,200g

HABITAT Breeds on coastal tundra; in winter in shallow, coastal waters

NEST Close to tundra pools

EGGS 8–11; pale grey

FOOD Mainly molluscs

DID YOU KNOW?

In winter, Greater Scaup are local in the eastern Mediterranean, coastal northwest Europe and the Black Sea as well as on ice-free lakes in central Europe.

POCHARD

Aythya ferina

BIRD FACTS

VOICE Harsh,
growling notes

LENGTH 42–49cm

WINGSPAN 72–82cm

WEIGHT 800–1,200g

HABITAT Well-vegetated
pools in summer but
open water in winter

NEST On ground
near water

EGGS 8–10; greenish

FOOD Water
plants, seeds and
invertebrates

OUTSIDE THE BREEDING season, Pochards are in-variably seen in flocks, some of which can be quite sizeable. Birds of this species mix freely with Tuft-ed Ducks and spend much of their time diving for food. A large proportion of their diet comprises plant material such as seeds and shoots, which are most readily found in shallow waters; this explains the Pochard's fondness for the margins of well-vegetated lakes and flooded gravel pits. As a rule, Pochards tend not to become accustomed to peo-ple, although birds that are fed on urban lakes may prove to be exceptions.

Male is attractive and distinctive. Bill relatively long and black with broad, grey band across middle. Rounded head is reddish-orange and neck and breast are black. Underparts and back grey with intricate vermiculations. Stern black. Female has mottled brown and grey-brown plumage, mostly grey on back. Bill pattern and head shape as male. Usually shows pale 'spectacle' around eye. In flight, wings of both sexes appear rather uniform; belly of female looks pale.

From September to March perhaps as many as 250,000 Pochards are found in northwest Europe, some 80,000 of which occur in Britain alone.

female

male

female

male

The wings of both sexes look similar in flight; the male's contrasting dark head and neck and pale belly are distinctive, while the female's belly is much paler than the rest of the underparts.

ABOVE: *Male, showing the distinct and diagnostic bill pattern and head shape.* LEFT: *Female, showing the characteristic white 'spectacle' around the eye.*

Male is attractive and distinctive. Bill bright red. Head orange-brown and neck and body feathers mostly black except for grey-brown back and white flanks. Female has pink-tipped dark bill. Cap and nape dark brown but cheeks and throat conspicuously pale. Plumage otherwise brown. Eclipse male resembles female but retains red bill. In flight, both sexes show pale underwing and broad, white stripes on upperwing.

RED-CRESTED POCHARD

Netta rufina

IRRESPECTIVE OF THEIR origins, Red-crested Pochards are exciting birds to find anywhere in Europe. It often comes as a surprise to bird-watchers new to the species that this is a diving duck, an activity which it performs with great ease. Red-crested Pochards also feed in the shallows, however, and frequently up-end to feed in the manner of a Pintail or Mallard. In most parts of its natural range, the species is seen in pairs or small flocks, and is wary of man. An isolated, extralimital bird that is tolerant of people is likely to be an escape or part of a feral population.

BIRD FACTS

VOICE Mostly silent
LENGTH 53–57cm
WINGSPAN 85–88cm
WEIGHT 900–1,200g
HABITAT Fresh water with extensive cover; in winter, on lakes and flooded gravel pits
NEST In dense cover or waterside vegetation
EGGS 8–10; pale green
FOOD Mostly plant material

male

female

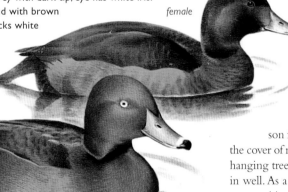

female

male

The pale underwing and broad white stripes on the upperwing are pronounced in flight.

male

As a European breeding bird, the Red-crested Pochard has a very local and patchy distribution, centred mainly on eastern and southeastern Europe and the Iberian peninsula.

Male has rather uniform chocolate-brown plumage with dark back and very conspicuous white stern. Bill grey with dark tip; eye has white iris. Female similar to male but duller and with brown iris. Juvenile similar to female but lacks white stern. In flight, looks slimmer than Tufted Duck and shows striking white wingbar; underwings pale.

FERRUGINOUS DUCK

Aythya nyroca

BOTH DURING THE breeding season and in winter, Ferruginous Ducks usually prove more difficult to find than most other diving ducks. The main reason for this elusiveness is their liking for the cover of marginal vegetation, particularly overhanging trees and shrubs, with which they blend in well. As a consequence, they are often found on surprisingly small bodies of water, much smaller than those favoured by their relatives.

female

male

BELOW LEFT: female; BELOW: male

BIRD FACTS

VOICE Female utters high-pitched, repeated 'karri'
LENGTH 38–42cm
WINGSPAN 63–67cm
WEIGHT 500–650g
HABITAT Shallow, well-vegetated lakes and pools
NEST On ground near water
EGGS 8–10; pale buff
FOOD Mainly plant material but some invertebrates

As with many other extralimital records of wildfowl, there is a possibility of 'escaped' birds being recorded.

EIDER

Somateria mollissima

EIDERS ARE ENGAGING birds to watch during the breeding season. Early on, the males perform crooning and cooing calls, throwing their heads and necks back in the process. Having mated, the females move ashore to nest on undisturbed beaches and grassland; their plumage affords them amazing camouflage while sitting on the eggs. When the young hatch, they are immediately led by the mother to the sea, where they often join with ducklings from other broods to form large 'crèches'. These are overseen by numerous 'aunties', who pay very close attention to their charges. Eiders feed on bottom-dwelling marine creatures and dive to reach them.

BIRD FACTS

VOICE Male utters humorous 'ah-whooo' during breeding season; otherwise silent

LENGTH 50–71cm

WINGSPAN 80–105cm

WEIGHT 1.5–2.5kg

HABITAT Coastal waters, usually close to shore

NEST On ground, often exposed; lined with down

EGGS 4–6; greenish-grey

FOOD Mainly molluscs, especially mussels

DID YOU KNOW?

Despite its dumpy appearance, the Eider walks well on land, albeit with a swaggering waddle.

male

IDENTIFICATION

A distinctive coastal duck with dumpy body and wedge-shaped bill following line of forehead. Mature male is unmistakable, with black and white markings on body; also shows lime-green markings on head and pink flush to breast. Full plumage not acquired until fourth year. Female has mottled brown plumage, looking rather barred on flanks. In flight, both sexes look heavy and ponderous with slightly drooping neck. Flies low over the water in lines.

female

females

female

male

female

Moulting and immature males have variably dark and white plumage.

Mature adult male has red bill expanded at base into basal knob. Head proportionately large with square outline; marked with pale blue-grey and green, the areas of colour outlined in black. Rest of body plumage black and white. Female similar to female Eider with mottled and barred brown plumage; pale on cheeks and around eye.

male

KING EIDER
Somateria spectabilis

KING EIDERS BREED in the high Arctic, but over-winter further south; they are found at this time around the coasts of northern Norway, and a few turn up every winter among Eider flocks off the Scottish coast. At the end of the breeding season, King Eiders gather in often sizeable flocks, first to move to moulting grounds and then to migrate to their overwintering quarters. These flocks remain together throughout the winter, when the birds feed in sheltered, coastal waters. Although King Eiders will feed in the shallows, they are capable of dives of 15m or more, mainly in search of bivalve molluscs on the seabed. They mix freely with Eiders.

BIRD FACTS

VOICE Male utters cooing calls during courtship; otherwise mostly silent
LENGTH 48–63cm
WINGSPAN 85–100cm
WEIGHT 1.4–1.8kg
HABITAT Breeds on Arctic tundra; in winter, on northern coasts
NEST Open ground, usually beside water
EGGS 4–5; olive
FOOD Mainly molluscs and crustaceans

BELOW: Female similar to female Eider but smaller with proportionately shorter bill.

RIGHT: Mature male has two sickle-shaped 'sails' on back.

HARLEQUIN DUCK
Histrionicus histrionicus

IN EUROPE, JUST 3–5,000 pairs of Harlequin Ducks are found in Iceland, and they do not move far in winter. In summer, they favour white-water areas where rivers crash and tumble over boulders and rocks. Here they plunge fearlessly into the torrent in search of insect larvae and other invertebrates. In the winter, the coastal waters they favour can be no less challenging, although they seldom venture far from land; Harlequins will also spend long periods resting on rocks above high tide mark.

BIRD FACTS

VOICE Occasionally utters high-pitched squeals but otherwise mostly silent
LENGTH 38–45cm
WINGSPAN 63–69cm
WEIGHT 500–700g
HABITAT In summer, on fast-flowing rivers; in winter, around coasts
NEST On ground, near water
EGGS 5–7; off-white
FOOD Mainly aquatic insect larvae in summer; in winter, mainly molluscs

male

Male is attractive and distinctive. Plumage mainly a mixture of blue and deep red with bold white stripes and spots on head and body. Female has more subdued, dark-brown plumage with white patch between base of bill and eye, and white spot behind eye. Eclipse male similar to female. All birds fly low over the water with fast, whirring wingbeats.

female

COMMON SCOTER

Melanitta nigra

IN THE WINTER months, the Common Scoter becomes widespread in European coastal waters, with more than 600,000 birds occurring in the region. In areas where they are common in the winter, Common Scoters form large flocks. They dive well, often in search of molluscs such as mussels and cockles; they also swim buoyantly, sometimes with their tails cocked up. They favour inshore waters and tend to avoid rough areas. During the breeding season, Common Scoters are distinctly wary of man and become very secretive.

A classic sea duck that can look all dark at a distance. Male has black plumage with black and yellow bill. Female has dark-brown plumage but much paler cheeks that show up well even at a distance or in flight. Invariably seen in flocks outside breeding season. Migrating flocks seen flying low over water, sometimes in lines but also in more tightly bunched packs with trailing stragglers.

male

female

Female; outside the breeding season, invariably associates with males.

male

winter flock

BIRD FACTS

VOICE Mostly silent but male utters quiet whistles in breeding season

LENGTH 44–54cm

WINGSPAN 80–90cm

WEIGHT 700–1,300g

HABITAT Breeds on upland moors and tundra; in winter, around coasts

NEST On ground, near water

EGGS 6–8; cream to buff

FOOD Mainly aquatic insect larvae in breeding season; in winter, dives for molluscs

RIGHT: male;
FAR RIGHT: female

VELVET SCOTER

Melanitta fusca

SEEN IN GOOD light, Velvet Scoters are stunning birds. Although they sometimes form small, one-species flocks of 20 or 30 birds, they are also seen during the winter in the company of Common Scoters. Seen side by side, Velvet Scoters are appreciably larger, and are closer in size and bulk to Eiders. They swim lower in the water and their greater size means they have more difficulty in taking to the air than their relatives; in flight, they look rather thick-set. Individual birds sometimes turn up inland during the winter months on reservoirs and flooded gravel pits, and they can be surprisingly tame.

Male has all-black plumage but is readily identified, even when among Common Scoters, by conspicuous white eye and white patch below eye. Bill black and yellow. Female has brown plumage with white patches between eye and base of bill and behind eye. In flight, both sexes show extremely conspicuous white wing patches; these are occasionally visible on swimming birds.

female

male

male

Like Common Scoters, flying birds look bulky; however, the white wing patch is immediately distinctive.

BIRD FACTS

VOICE Male utters whistling call in breeding season and female has grating call; silent at other times

LENGTH 51–58cm

WINGSPAN 90–100cm

WEIGHT 1.2–1.8kg

HABITAT Breeds on coastal moors and tundra; in winter, in coastal waters

NEST On ground, near water

EGGS 7–9; buff

FOOD Mainly molluscs and crustaceans

BELOW: Female, which lacks male's white eye patch and has little yellow on bill; BELOW RIGHT: male

Similar to Goldeneye but distinguished, even in silhouette, by steep, rounded forehead and relatively short, broad bill. Male has dark head with purple gloss and white crescent shape in front of yellow eye. Underparts mainly white and upperparts and stern dark; back shows small patches of white. Female has dark-brown head with yellow eye. Body plumage mainly grey-brown and underparts paler. In flight, both sexes show less white on inner wing than Goldeneye does.

female

Note characteristic head shape and relatively small bill of both sexes.

BARROW'S GOLDENEYE
Bucephala islandica

THE VAST MAJORITY of the world's Barrow's Goldeneye are found in the Pacific northwest of North America; in Europe, the species is represented by the 500–600 or so pairs that breed in Iceland and nowhere else. These are mostly resident and only move towards the coast when forced to do so by freezing conditions. The males court the females in May with much bobbing of heads, splashing and diving. Individual birds sometimes turn up in northwest Europe, but many of these may be escapes.

BIRD FACTS

VOICE Grunting calls accompany courting male's display; otherwise silent
LENGTH 42–52cm
WINGSPAN 67–85cm
WEIGHT 900–1,300g
HABITAT Breeds on Arctic lakes and rivers; in winter, on more coastal Arctic lakes and rivers and sometimes actually in coastal waters
NEST In rock crevice or tree-hole
EGGS 8–11; bluish
FOOD Aquatic insects, crustaceans and molluscs

male

Superb diving duck with peaked-cap profile to head, readily seen even in silhouette. Male has dark head with greenish sheen, white circular patch at base of bill and yellow eye. Body plumage mostly white except for dark back and stern. Female has reddish-brown head and dark grey bill with pink patch near tip. Body plumage grey-brown except for paler underparts and white neck.

Male; in flight both sexes show white patches on inner upperwing.

GOLDENEYE
Bucephala clangula

IN NORTHWEST EUROPE the Goldeneye is best known as a winter visitor, with more than 200,000 birds visiting the region between October and March. Within their usual overwintering range, Goldeneye are usually seen in flocks. They spend much of the time diving; when swimming buoyantly at the surface, the birds look hunch-necked with rounded heads. However, the sight of birds perched in trees or flying into or out of their tree-hole nest sites can be surprising. In many areas, Goldeneye readily take to the provision of nest boxes.

BIRD FACTS

VOICE Creaking display call but otherwise silent
LENGTH 42–50cm
WINGSPAN 65–80cm
WEIGHT 800–1,000g
HABITAT Breeds beside northern, wooded lakes; in winter on lakes and reservoirs, occasionally on coasts
NEST In tree-hole
EGGS 8–11; bluish-green
FOOD Aquatic molluscs, crustaceans and insect larvae

TOP: *male;* ABOVE: *female*

female

male

RED-BREASTED MERGANSER

Mergus serrator

FROM APRIL TO July Red-breasted Mergansers are found on suitable water bodies throughout Scandinavia and locally in northern Britain, Ireland and Iceland. Thereafter they move to coasts of northwest Europe. In winter, a lone distant bird could be mistaken for a grebe, with its slender neck and ragged head outline. At close range, the bill shape and colour are distinctive. It is hard to see the bill's serrated edges, which grip slippery fish prey, and after which this species and its near relatives are called 'sawbills'. The Red-breasted Merganser's fish-eating diet result in it being persecuted in some parts of its breeding range by people with commercial fishing interests.

BIRD FACTS

VOICE Mostly silent

LENGTH 52–58cm

WINGSPAN 70–85cm

WEIGHT 900–1,200g

HABITAT Breeds on clear, northern lakes and rivers; in winter, mainly in coastal waters

NEST On ground, well hidden

EGGS 8–10; buff to olive

FOOD Mainly fish

RIGHT: female
CENTRE RIGHT: male
FAR RIGHT: male

Slim-bodied duck with long, narrow sawbill. Male has red bill, legs and eyes. Underparts grey and finely marked, and back black and white. Female body plumage mainly grey-brown, although underparts paler. In flight, both sexes show white on innerwing; less extensive on female and divided by black bar.

Male (FAR LEFT) has dark-green head with untidy tufts, white neck and reddish-brown breast; female (LEFT) has red bill and reddish head.

GOOSANDER

Mergus merganser

IN EUROPE GOOSANDERS nest mainly in the north, although isolated populations also breed in Britain and the Alps; their winter range is rather wider. Goosanders swim buoyantly and winter groups often cruise in unison with great ease and at surprising speed across the water. They dive well and frequently, sometimes returning to the surface to consume their prey if the fish is particularly large. In late winter and early spring, when they have returned to their breeding grounds, male goosanders perform solitary or group displays, their antics including head-stretching and bobbing and water-rushing, where the male shoots rapidly across the surface of the water.

BIRD FACTS

VOICE Ringing calls uttered by displaying male; otherwise silent

LENGTH 58–66cm

WINGSPAN 82–96cm

WEIGHT 1.1–1.7kg

HABITAT Breeds beside northern lakes and rivers; in winter, favours lakes, reservoirs, flooded gravel pits and sheltered coasts

NEST In tree-hole or sometimes rock crevice; will take to nest boxes

EGGS 8–11; whitish

FOOD Fish

A large, attractive sawbill duck. At a distance, male can look black and white. At closer range and in good light, head has greenish gloss and white on body plumage suffused with pink. Bill red; lower back and tail grey. Female similar to female Red-breasted Merganser but has more elegant, reddish-brown head. Throat and neck white; body plumage mainly grey-brown with underparts paler.

BELOW: male
BOTTOM: female

female

male

In flight, female (centre) shows undivided white speculum and male shows entire white innerwing.

male

SMEW

Mergellus albellus

OUTSIDE THE BREEDING season, small parties of Smew are generally found on coastal lagoons or reservoirs, although they also occur on large, ice-free lakes from central Europe south to the Balkans. They are hardy birds and it usually takes severe conditions in mainland Europe to force them to move. During the breeding season, Smew are more difficult to observe, partly because of their favoured tree-hole nest sites. Old abandoned holes excavated by Black Woodpeckers are often chosen, and the species will also take to nest boxes.

male

DID YOU KNOW?

Most birds seen in western Europe in winter are 'redheads', comprising both young birds and almost identical females; they often consort with Goldeneyes.

BIRD FACTS

VOICE Mainly silent

LENGTH 38–44cm

WINGSPAN 55–70cm

WEIGHT 600–900g

HABITAT In breeding season, favours wooded lakes; in winter, on lakes, reservoirs and sheltered coasts and estuaries

NEST In tree-holes; nest boxes

EGGS 7–9; pale buff

FOOD Mainly small fish; some insect larvae

IDENTIFICATION

Small sawbill duck with narrow, serrated-edged bill. Male is distinctive and attractive with mainly white plumage but with black lines on body, around eye and on back; at close range, fine grey markings visible on flank. Female has grey-brown plumage, reddish-brown cap and white cheeks and chin. Immature drake resembles female. In flight, both sexes show white bars on wings.

female

IDENTIFICATION

An attractive sea duck with a distinctive outline. Plumage a mixture of black, white and brown but varies throughout year. Male has dark bill with pink band and long central tail feathers, often cocked upwards. In summer, head, neck and breast dark except for white patch around eye. Shows brown back and white underparts. In winter, male has much more white in plumage, face having buff flush and dark cheeks. Female lacks male's long tail and has grey bill. In summer, upperparts mostly brown and underparts white.
In winter, body brown but head white with variable dark markings.

LONG-TAILED DUCK

Clangula hyemalis

LONG-TAILED DUCKS ARE usually seen in flocks outside the breeding season, favouring the roughest of waters and easily riding breakers in windswept bays. They dive with ease and for long periods, members of a flock sometimes diving and surfacing together. Flocks are restless and regularly fly off a few hundred metres or further afield in search of better feeding. Long-tailed Ducks are vulnerable to oil pollution.

DID YOU KNOW?

Outside the breeding season Long-tailed Ducks range widely around coasts in northwestern Europe; winter populations in the southern Baltic are among the most important for this species.

BIRD FACTS

VOICE Very vocal, males having musical calls

LENGTH 40–47cm + male tail length

WINGSPAN 73–79cm

WEIGHT 600–800g

HABITAT Breeds on tundra; overwinters on sea coasts

NEST On ground, close to water

EGGS 6–9; greenish-buff

FOOD Mainly molluscs and crustaceans

female

female

male

female

male

Displaying male.

GREAT NORTHERN DIVER

Gavia immer

THE GREAT NORTHERN DIVER breeds mainly in North America, where it is known as the Common Loon. In Europe, its breeding range is limited to Iceland. During the breeding season its eerie wails seem to capture the spirit of the lonely north and the large, still lakes on which it breeds. In contrast, winter often finds this species on some of the roughest waters in Europe. Perfectly at home in a gale, the birds dive almost continuously in search of flatfish and crabs. On calm days the Great Northern, like other divers, can sometimes be observed rolling over on its side in order to preen all its feathers.

Size and markings make breeding-plumage bird distinctive; sexes are similar. Bill, head and neck black except for bands of narrow, white stripes on side of neck and under chin. Eyes red. Underparts white. Upperparts black except for tiny white spots and white chequerboard pattern on back; also black and white stripes on side of breast. Bill is large and grey with black tip, and neck often shows dark band on sides. Winter adult has dark upperparts and pale underparts. Juvenile similar but with grubbier underparts and pale fringes to upperpart feathers. In flight all birds show large wingspan and trailing feet.

first winter

BIRD FACTS

VOICE Only heard during breeding season: loud, eerie wailing calls

LENGTH 69–91cm

WINGSPAN 135cm

WEIGHT 3.5–4.5kg

HABITAT Breeds on large lakes; overwinters in sandy bays and around rocky coasts

NEST Depression in waterside vegetation

EGGS 1 or 2; greenish-brown with dark spots

FOOD Mainly fish but some crustaceans

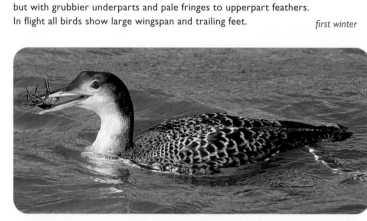

winter adult

RIGHT: *In summer, adult has spangled appearance and black head.*
INSET: *Summer plumage bird taking flight.*

BELOW: *Great Northern Diver nesting beside a lake on Iceland's Snaefellsnes Peninsula.*

RED-THROATED DIVER

Gavia stellata

THE RED-THROATED DIVER is widespread across northern Europe, although it occurs at comparatively low densities. In much of its European habitat, breeding is limited to small lakes and pools within flying distance of the sea, where it feeds. Shy and easily disturbed at the nest, it is protected by law in many countries. Red-throated Divers are superbly adapted to life on water and only venture onto land during the breeding season. In winter, they generally favour inshore waters but can still be difficult to spot, partly because they swim low in the water, and partly because they dive regularly for extended periods.

ABOVE: *winter adult*

DID YOU KNOW?

Except in very good light the red throat patch appears dark, almost black; it is the last part of summer plumage lost in autumn.

summer adult

BIRD FACTS

VOICE Only heard during breeding season: goose-like calls; deep, rhythmic quacking in flight; song rapidly repeated 'kwuk-uk-uk'

LENGTH 53–69cm

WINGSPAN 110cm

WEIGHT 1.2–1.6kg

HABITAT Breeds on northern coastal pools; overwinters around coasts

NEST A shallow depression in waterside vegetation

EGGS 1 or 2; dark, speckled brown

FOOD Mostly fish but occasionally crabs or shrimps

IDENTIFICATION

Sexes similar. Dagger-like bill and red eyes. In breeding season both sexes have red throat, black and white striping on nape and otherwise grey head and neck. Dark-brown back and white underparts. In winter, upperparts grey-brown with white speckling on back and white underparts. Juvenile similar to winter adult but with grubbier appearance to underparts. Swims low in water with superficially Shag-like appearance but head and bill have characteristic upward tilt. Looks goose-like in flight with neck outstretched; in winter, looks very pale in flight.

summer adult

Summer adult in flight.

juvenile

In territorial disputes rival males glide across surface of water calling loudly, in 'snake', 'penguin race' and 'plesiosaur' ceremonies.

BLACK-THROATED DIVER

Gavia arctica

INVARIABLY SEEN ON water, the Black-throated Diver swims buoyantly and dives smoothly, unlike the superficially similar Shag, which has a leaping dive. It breeds from May to August and favours large lakes, where it can both nest and feed. After nesting, Black-throated Divers move mainly to the coast and in winter disperse to in-shore waters of western Europe and the eastern Mediterranean. Following gales or severe winter weather, individual birds sometimes turn up on inland reservoirs elsewhere in Europe.

Sexes similar: grey head and neck with black throat and black and white stripes on side of neck and under chin. Sides of breast have black and white stripes that grade into black on back and upperparts; distinctive white chequerboard pattern on back. In winter, bill grey with black tip; plumage dark on upperparts and pale on underparts. Throat and cheeks often look conspicuously white; white patch on flanks at waterline. Juvenile similar to winter adult, but with neat scaly pattern on upperparts.

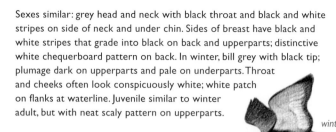

winter adult

winter immature

BIRD FACTS

VOICE Only heard during breeding season: raven-like croaks and wailing calls

LENGTH 58–73cm

WINGSPAN 120cm

WEIGHT 2–3kg

HABITAT Breeds on large lakes; overwinters around coasts

NEST Depression in waterside vegetation, often on an island

EGGS 1 or 2; olive-brown with black spots

FOOD Almost exclusively fish

summer adult

WHITE-BILLED DIVER

Gavia adamsii

THE WHITE-BILLED DIVER is a breeding bird of the high Arctic. In Europe it is mainly seen as a winter visitor; reasonable numbers regularly spend the winter off the coast of Norway and smaller numbers penetrate the northern North Sea. Unlike the Great Northern Diver, which prefers large lakes for nesting, the White-billed Diver is found beside a variety of water bodies, some quite small, in the breeding season. In the winter months it prefers waters further offshore than its near relative does. This predilection presumably explains why this is such a difficult bird to observe.

Superficially similar to Great Northern Diver except for bill, which is large, dagger-like and pale yellow. Head and bill characteristically held with upward tilt. In breeding plumage, head and neck are black except for bands of narrow, white stripes on sides of neck and under chin. Upperparts mostly black except for white chequerboard effect on back and scattering of small white spots. Underparts white except for black and white stripes on side of breast. Juvenile similar to winter adult.

summer adult

BIRD FACTS

VOICE Wailing calls on breeding ground, similar to Great Northern; otherwise silent

LENGTH 75–91cm

WINGSPAN 150cm

WEIGHT 5–6kg

HABITAT Breeds on high Arctic coastal lakes; overwinters in coastal waters

NEST Mound of vegetation beside water

EGGS 1 or 2; olive with dark spots

FOOD Mainly fish but also some crustaceans

LEFT: In winter, upperparts mostly dark brown and underparts white; head and neck grubby brown with dark smudge on side of neck and behind eye; face whitish.

RED-NECKED GREBE

Podiceps grisegena

Most easily confused with Great Crested Grebe, but smaller and more compact. Sexes similar. During breeding season, adult very distinctive with black-tipped yellow bill, silver-grey face, black cap and brick-red neck. In winter loses red neck, although a hint may remain in autumn birds. Black cap extends down to level of eye. Silver-grey cheeks look conspicuous and black-tipped yellow bill still a good feature. Juveniles have stripy heads but soon resemble winter adults. In flight, shows white wedges on leading and trailing edges of innerwing; less extensive than in Great Crested Grebe.

FOR MOST BIRDWATCHERS in western Europe, the Red-necked Grebe is most familiar as a winter visitor that appears in September and October and often stays into March or April. Red-necked Grebes often breed in loose colonies, but despite this they can be hard to see at this time of year, partly because of their choice of well-vegetated lakes and partly because of their retiring nature when nesting. Outside the breeding season, when they occur on open water, they can be easier to see, although their extended dives and the distances travelled underwater mean that views are all too brief and relocation is a frustrating business.

ABOVE: *summer adult with chick;* BELOW: *Summer adult preening.*

winter adult

summer adult

BIRD FACTS

VOICE During breeding season utters cackling and ticking sounds, and loud wails; otherwise silent

LENGTH 40–50cm

WINGSPAN 80–85cm

WEIGHT 500–800g

HABITAT Breeds on shallow lakes with abundant water plants; overwinters mainly on coastal waters

NEST Floating mound of aquatic vegetation secured to surrounding water plants

EGGS 4–5; white but usually stained reddish

FOOD Small fish, aquatic insects, shrimps

LITTLE GREBE

Tachybaptus ruficollis

Small, dumpy bird with powder-puff appearance to body feathers. Feathers at rear end are often fluffed up. Yellow-green legs and lobed feet sometimes visible in clear water. Shows lime-green patch at base of bill, which is dark with pale tip. In winter, appears paler brown but darker on cap, nape and back. Tail end is whitish; pale patch at base of bill.

BELOW: *winter adult, with characteristic rather uniformly brown plumage except for darkish cap and pale 'powderpuff' of feathers at stern.*

Wing-stretching summer adult showing white underwings.

THROUGHOUT MOST OF its range the Little Grebe is resident, but birds from eastern Europe and southern Scandinavia are migratory. Within their resident range, Little Grebes often move in the autumn from small areas of water to larger lakes less likely to freeze over; prolonged cold spells in winter may force birds to move to the coast. Little Grebes are excellent swimmers underwater, propelling themselves along using the lobed toes on their long feet. The feet are set well back on the body, which helps their swimming but hinders their ability to walk on land.

BIRD FACTS

VOICE High-pitched, whinnying trill

LENGTH 25–29cm

WINGSPAN 40–44cm

WEIGHT 140–230g

HABITAT Shallow-edged lakes, ponds, slow-flowing rivers and canals

NEST Floating tangle of aquatic vegetation attached to water plants

EGGS 4–6; white but usually stained reddish

FOOD Small fish, water shrimps, aquatic insects

In summer, looks mainly dark brown except for bright chestnut on neck and face.

BIRD FACTS

VOICE Barking 'rah-rah-rah' and a clicking 'kek'; most vocal in spring

LENGTH 46–51cm

WINGSPAN 85–89cm

WEIGHT 800–1,400g

HABITAT Breeds on lakes, gravel pits and slow-flowing rivers; occasionally on the sea in winter

NEST Floating heap of water plants secured to surrounding vegetation

EGGS 3–4; white but generally stained reddish by vegetation from nest

FOOD Mainly fish but some aquatic insects and molluscs

GREAT CRESTED GREBE

Podiceps cristatus

GREAT CRESTED GREBES occur patchily across much of central and southern Europe, their precise distribution being determined by the presence or absence of suitable wetland habitats. In freezing conditions the birds are forced to abandon their chosen lakes and occur in small numbers around the coasts of western Europe. The sight and sound of Great Crested Grebes displaying in spring is one of the highlights of the birdwatcher's calendar. During these ceremonial displays they exhibit a wide range of curious antics. Head-shaking, penguin dances with bills full of water plants, and ritual preening are all part of the varied show, which is usually accompanied by noisy outbursts from the excited birds.

Elegant waterbird with slender neck. Sexes similar. At a distance can look black and white. In breeding season has pink bill, white face, black cap and large, showy, orange-chestnut and brown ear tufts. Nape and back brown but underparts white. In winter, loses ear tufts and has mainly brownish upperparts and white underparts; black cap appears above level of eye and contrasts with white face. Bill pink. Juvenile in early autumn is stripy but resembles winter adult by late autumn. In flight, shows white wedges on leading and trailing edges of innerwing in all plumages.

The fluffy, striped young often take rides on the backs of their parents.

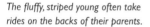

ABOVE: Ear tufts are lost in winter; bird always appears paler than Red-necked Grebe.

ABOVE: summer adult with chick.

TOP: summer adult; ABOVE: juvenile

RIGHT: Adult birds perform ritualised displays in spring, prior to nesting; these displays continue, sporadically, throughout the breeding season, reinforcing pair-bonds.

DID YOU KNOW?

During the head-shaking display (RIGHT) the crest is raised to make the bright colouring as obvious as possible.

A beautiful bird in breeding plumage, when neck, underparts and flanks are brick red and head black except for striking orange-yellow feathering from eye to ear tufts. Bill black with white tip, and eyes red. Back black, with small white tuft of feathers at rear end. In winter, appears mainly black and white and most easily confused with Black-necked Grebe. Cap is black, leading to narrow black line on nape, which widens on back of neck. Black back and white underparts. In flight, shows white patches on leading and trailing edges of innerwing; patch on leading edge is small.

SLAVONIAN GREBE

winter adult   *Podiceps auritus*

BIRD FACTS

VOICE Various screams and cries heard at nest

LENGTH 31–38cm

WINGSPAN 60–65cm

WEIGHT 350–450g

HABITAT Breeds on well-vegetated lakes and pools; overwinters on coastal waters

NEST Floating aquatic vegetation anchored to surrounding vegetation

EGGS 4–5; white but usually stained reddish

FOOD Fish

SLAVONIAN GREBES NEST in loose colonies on shallow, reedy lakes. A visit to a colony in May is well worthwhile, with plenty of bird activity to see. Displaying pairs engage in 'water rush' dances, swimming upright, each holding water plants in its bill, and racing across the water along parallel routes. In northwest Europe Slavonian Grebes are most familiar as coastal winter visitors to sheltered bays and estuaries. Because of their small size and frequent dives, however, they can be difficult to spot in rough winter seas.

ABOVE: winter adult
RIGHT: The spectacular orange-yellow eyestripe and tufts of breeding plumage birds are prominent in mating displays.

Superficially similar to Slavonian Grebe but with steep forecrown, upturned bill and upward-tilted head and bill. Sexes similar. Adult in summer plumage has black head, neck and back. Underparts brick red. Eyes red with orange-yellow feather tufts behind them. In winter has mostly dark upperparts and white underparts. Black cap looks more extensive than it does on Slavonian Grebe, while neck appears greyer and generally more grubby. In flight, shows white wedge on trailing edge of innerwing only.

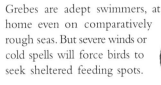

BLACK-NECKED GREBE

winter adult   *Podiceps nigricollis*

BIRD FACTS

VOICE Chittering trill

LENGTH 28–34cm

WINGSPAN 55–60cm

WEIGHT 250–400g

HABITAT Breeds on shallow, well-vegetated ponds; overwinters on coastal waters

NEST Floating or grounded mound of vegetation

EGGS 4–5; white but invariably stained brownish

FOOD Fish

THE BREEDING RANGE of the Black-necked Grebe shows little overlap with the Slavonian Grebe, but its distribution is patchy because of the specific habitat requirements of nesting birds. Larger lakes in western Europe sometimes hold breeding colonies, and the species nests sporadically in Britain. In winter, its range is similar to that of the Slavonian Grebe. Unlike other members of the family, the species often gathers in small flocks outside the breeding season. This alone is not enough to identify the species but the characteristic upward-tilted bill and head are distinctive even at a distance or in silhouette. Black-necked Grebes are adept swimmers, at home even on comparatively rough seas. But severe winds or cold spells will force birds to seek sheltered feeding spots.

ABOVE: Summer plumage has an attractive sheen to it; golden-yellow plumes on cheeks more straggly and unkempt-looking than those of Slavonian Grebe.
LEFT: winter adult

Summer adult, resplendent with its striking golden head plumes and beady red eye.

FULMAR

Fulmarus glacialis

Nests on sea cliffs, invariably in the company of other seabird species.

OVER THE LAST hundred years the Fulmar's range has expanded dramatically and today it occurs across much of the North Atlantic as far south as northern France. Throughout much of its range, the Fulmar nests on sea cliffs. Non-breeding birds often range far out to sea, especially during the winter months, but established nesting birds linger in the vicinity of the colony for much of the year. The Fulmar's stiff-winged flight pattern enables it to ride updraughts on cliffs as easily as it glides over the waves. Large groups tend to gather around trawlers and fish-processing ships. These long-lived birds usually pair for life and couples greet one another by bobbing and bowing their heads and cackling loudly.

IDENTIFICATION

Sexes similar. Superficially gull-like but distinguished by stiff-winged flight and large tube-nostrils. Adults have white head with dark smudge through eye. Bill comprises horny plates and has hooked tip and tube-nostrils. Wings relatively narrow and pointed; upperwing blue-grey and underwing white. Back and rump grey. Underparts white. Rarely seen northern birds may be all grey.

Adult, flying on stiffly held wings.

LEFT: *Nesting adult;*
BELOW: *Displaying adult calling to its mate.*

Rapid wingbeats alternate with low gliding over water.

Usually seen flying low over water. Sexes similar. At a distance, appears all black above and all white below. Body cigar-shaped and wings comparatively narrow and pointed. Tube-nostrils only visible at very close range. Upperparts almost black. Underparts white, including undertail feathering. Underwing white except for dark margin. Flies on stiffly held wings except in very calm conditions, when rapid wingbeats interspersed with long glides are used.

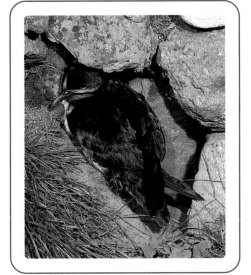

ABOVE: *Adult at entrance to nest burrow.*

Adult swimming.

MANX SHEARWATER

Puffinus puffinus

IN SUMMER IT is quite easy to see Manx Shearwaters from ferries and headlands in northwest Europe. Their burrowing nesting habits and the fact that they only return to the colony after dark, however, mean they are hard to see on land. During the day, the shearwaters are seen out to sea in long lines, banking from side to side and revealing alternately their dark upperwings and pale underwings. Wherever feeding is good, sizeable groups or 'rafts' gather to feed; the birds also mass in large numbers around their breeding islands at dusk.

Adults in flight.

DID YOU KNOW?

Manx Shearwaters are well-adapted seabirds, but are barely able to shuffle along on land.

Yelkouan Shearwater

BALEARIC SHEARWATER

Puffinus mauretanicus

YELKOUAN SHEARWATER

Puffinus yelkouan

FORMERLY CONSIDERED TO be races of Mediterranean Shearwater, the main range for both species is the Mediterranean where birders are only likely to see them at sea. They nest in burrows on remote islands and dangerous cliffs, and only return to land after dark. Yelkouan Shearwaters occur mainly in the eastern Mediterranean while Balearics favour the west; both can be seen from ferries and headlands and feeding birds often favour inshore waters, sometimes settling briefly where small fish are moving at the surface. After breeding has finished, some Balearics leave the Mediterranean and move to the Bay of Biscay; a few reach Britain.

Balearic Shearwater

IDENTIFICATION

Usually seen flying in long lines, low over water. Note short, cigar-shaped body and narrow, stiffly held wings. In flight, legs project slightly beyond tail. Yelkouan Shearwater has dark sooty brown upperparts and whitish underparts overall but with grubby undertail coverts. Balearic has warmer brown upperparts and buffish or dusky underparts, especially dark on undertail coverts.

CORY'S SHEARWATER

Calonectris diomedea

CORY'S SHEARWATER IS common throughout its breeding range and, like other shearwaters, it favours isolated rocky islands for nesting. Strong onshore breezes improve the likelihood of these seabirds coming close to land, and windy conditions also allow the observer to see their impressive aerobatic skills. With hardly a wingbeat, they ride the gusts and eddies, sometimes rising to considerable heights in the process. This immediately distinguishes them from other shearwaters, which seldom fly more than a few metres from the surface of the sea.

Cory's Shearwater

IDENTIFICATION

Large shearwater, similar to Great Shearwater but lacks that species' black cap and white nape band. Sexes similar. Bill large and yellow with black tip. Upperparts brownish except for darker wingtips and black tail; scaly effect caused by pale feather edges. At close range, faint pale base to tail sometimes visible. Underparts white except for leading and trailing edges to wings, which are dark, and brown face.

The species appears further north towards the end of the breeding season when sea temperatures rise; there are regular sightings off the French coast, and off Cornwall and southern Ireland.

GREAT SHEARWATER

Puffinus gravis

LIKE ITS COUSIN, the Sooty Shearwater, the Great Shearwater breeds in the southern hemisphere during the northern winter, and only passes through coastal waters of northwest Europe from July to September. A pelagic trip to the edge of the continental shelf at the right time of year offers the best chances of seeing good numbers of Great Shearwaters. The prospects of encountering this species closer to shore are slim, especially since the numbers visiting the region vary greatly from year to year. Onshore gales in late August or early September probably offer the best chances for observation from land.

Great Shearwater

IDENTIFICATION

Noticeably larger than Manx Shearwater. Invariably seen in flight on stiffly held wings. Sexes similar. Seen from above, dark cap is clearly separated from grey-brown mantle by white nape band. Upperwings and back dark, but pale feather edging to mantle and wing coverts visible in good light. White-tipped uppertail coverts produce white-rumped effect. Underparts white except for dark bands on underwing and dark belly and undertail feathering.

SOOTY SHEARWATER

Puffinus griseus

Sooty Shearwater

THE SOOTY SHEARWATER breeds on islands in the southern oceans, then embarks on a daunting clockwise journey around the North Atlantic, reaching Europe by late summer. Intrepid bird-watchers who venture out to the edge of the continental shelf between July and October will find that Sooty Shearwaters are not uncommon. Onshore winds down west-facing coasts of northwest Europe offer the likeliest opportunities of seeing them on land, although Sooty Shearwaters also pass through the North Sea in good numbers. You will probably need a telescope to see one clearly.

IDENTIFICATION

Invariably seen in flight; appears all dark except at close range or in very good light; however, identification is straightforward. Larger and longer-winged than Manx Shearwater. Body is cigar-shaped and bill long and thin compared with other shearwater species. Sexes similar. Body and upperwing are dark sooty brown. Underwings are mostly dark but show a pale, silvery stripe along their length, which can be conspicuous in good light.

EUROPEAN STORM-PETREL

Hydrobates pelagicus

EUROPEAN STORM-PETRELS (often referred to simply as storm-petrels) breed on remote, rocky islands and cliffs. The tiny birds are sometimes seen from ferry crossings, where they occasionally linger and follow in the wake of the boat. European Storm-petrels also congregate around fishing vessels to feed on the offal. This habit is exploited by pelagic birdwatching trips that use 'chum' (fish offal) to attract the birds.

Adult swimming.

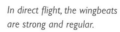

In direct flight, the wingbeats are strong and regular.

IDENTIFICATION

A tiny seabird, superficially recalling House Martin. Plumage usually appears all black except for conspicuous white rump. At close range, brownish edges to wing covert feathers may be revealed as pale bands, and white band on underwing sometimes visible. Legs black and trailing and bill black and slender, bearing delicate tube-nostrils.

DID YOU KNOW?

When the bird is feeding its flight can look fluttering; it also uses its feet to patter on the water.

Slightly larger than European Storm-petrel, with distinctly forked tail visible at close range. Wings relatively long and pointed. Plumage can appear all black. In good light, however, head, back and wing coverts look smoky grey; trailing edge of coverts shows pale feathering, producing a transverse wingbar. No pale bar on underwing. Rump conspicuously white; at close range, narrow grey bar revealed down centre. Varied flight pattern distinctive. Sometimes glides like shearwater then engages in darting, fluttering or hovering flight. Direct flight confident and powerful.

Does not patter its feet as often as European Storm-petrel, but legs may be dangled.

Erratic flight path recalls shearwater one minute and tern the next.

LEACH'S STORM-PETREL

Oceanodroma leucorhoa

WITHIN ITS EUROPEAN range, Leach's Storm-petrel occurs from May to October, the winter months being spent in the oceans of the southern hemisphere. For most European birdwatchers, the best opportunities for seeing this species come with the arrival of gales in September and October. If these happen to coincide with southerly autumn movements of Leach's Storm-petrels down the coasts of northwest Europe, the birds sometimes pass quite close to land. Sometimes large numbers of birds are driven by severe weather and a few appear inland.

BIRD FACTS

VOICE Agitated churrs and hiccups at nest; otherwise silent
LENGTH 19–22cm
WINGSPAN 45–48cm
WEIGHT 40–50g
HABITAT Breeds on remote islands; otherwise at sea
NEST In burrow
EGGS 1; white
FOOD Plankton, small fish

Adult swimming.

Summer adult, perched and drying wings.

Winter adult, perched and drying wings.

PYGMY CORMORANT

Phalacrocorax pygmeus

PYGMY CORMORANTS ARE colonial nesters and will often join colonies of other waterbirds. Here they are difficult to see, since they prefer to nest among the dense reeds for cover. Birdwatchers are more likely to see them swimming low in the water or perched on dead branches, either during the day, with wings outstretched, or at roost. Sometimes, however, Pygmy Cormorants can be seen soaring on rising thermals.

BIRD FACTS

VOICE Croaking calls at nest; otherwise silent
LENGTH 45–55cm
WINGSPAN 80–90cm
WEIGHT 600–750g
HABITAT Shallow, reed-fringed lowland lakes
NEST In trees or reedbeds
EGGS 3–4; pale green with chalky coat
FOOD Fish

Sexes similar. Compared with Cormorant, head and neck look proportionately short and tail looks proportionately long; these features are most noticeable in flight. Adult has mostly dark plumage except for chocolate-brown head. In breeding plumage, shows white flecks on head, breast and mantle. In winter, adult has whitish throat. Juvenile has brownish upperparts and paler underparts, belly and throat looking almost white.

Nesting adult.

CORMORANT

Phalacrocorax carbo

SEEN IN FLIGHT, the robust body and broad wings of the Cormorant give it a rather goose-like appearance. By contrast, on the water and at a distance Cormorants can resemble divers. They swim low in the water, with their heads tilted slightly upwards, and dive frequently and often for extended periods. Their adaptations to an aquatic life include modified feather barbs that allow air to escape and water to penetrate the plumage. Hence they can swim underwater efficiently, but their feathers soon get waterlogged. Birds often perch on posts with wings outstretched to dry.

Adult looks dark at a distance; at close range, has scaly appearance due to oily greenish-brown feathers on upperparts having dark margins. Both *carbo* (see illustration) and *sinensis* races have white thigh patches in breeding season. Extensive white feather tips, especially in *sinensis*, make head and nape look white as breeding starts. Much of white feathering lost outside summer months. Juvenile brown and scaly; looks palest on underparts.

BIRD FACTS

VOICE Guttural croaks at nest and roost; otherwise silent

LENGTH 80–100cm

WINGSPAN 130–160cm

WEIGHT 2.5–3.5kg

HABITAT Breeds colonially, mainly around coasts in western Europe but on inland lakes elsewhere; overwinters mainly around sheltered coasts but also on inland waters

NEST Pile of twigs, seaweed and flotsam in coastal nesters; in trees or reedbeds in some parts

EGGS 3–4; chalky white

FOOD Fish, especially flatfish and eels

Summer adult in flight.

Juvenile, with its wings outstretched.

Bill large and dark with hooked tip. Race carbo, from northwest Europe, has yellow base to bill and white throat.

Winter adult swimming.

Adult in breeding plumage; the white thigh patch is flashed in courtship display.

SHAG

Phalacrocorax aristotelis

UNLIKE ITS COUSIN, the Cormorant, the Shag is an entirely maritime bird, favouring deeper waters and rockier coasts than its relative. Shags are largely year-round residents, with adults faithful to the particular stretch of shore where they nest each year. In early spring adult birds engage in head- and neck-rubbing courtship displays, and are constantly adorning their large, untidy nests with some new piece of seaweed or flotsam, including items such as plastic bags and baler twine. The early start to nesting ensures that the young birds are in the nest when fish stocks are most productive.

Breeding plumage quite distinct from Cormorant's, and shape of feather line round gape is also different.

The chicks take 53 days to fledge and are tended and fed by their parents for several weeks after this.

BIRD FACTS

VOICE Grunts and clicks

LENGTH 65–80cm

WINGSPAN 90–105cm

WEIGHT 1.8–1.9kg

HABITAT Rocky coasts

NEST Heap of seaweed and vegetation on sheltered rocky ledge

EGGS 3; pale blue with chalky deposit

FOOD Fish, mainly sand eels and herrings

Non-breeding adult swimming.

IDENTIFICATION

Smaller than superficially similar Cormorant and seldom seen in similar habitats. Sexes similar. In poor light, adult looks all dark. At close range, breeding birds have oily-green plumage, bottle-green eyes, yellow gape and upturned crest. In winter, crest and sheen are lost or less obvious. Lores feathered on Shag, bare on Cormorant. Juvenile is pale brown with white chin; Atlantic birds have brown underparts but those from Mediterranean have white on belly. In flight, has proportionately shorter and more rounded wings than Cormorant and faster wingbeats.

juvenile

adult

In flight, body shape is distinctive, even from a distance.

adult with chick

BELOW: Gannet breeding colony

GANNET
Morus bassanus

THE GANNET IS Europe's largest breeding seabird. Gannets are a common sight off many west-facing headlands along the coast of northwest Europe. On most days they will simply stream by in long lines, but now and again birdwatchers may be lucky enough to see them feeding. If conditions are particularly good, and shoals of Mackerel or Herring are near the surface, gannets may gather in large numbers. They plunge-dive from a considerable height, folding their wings right back just before they enter the water.

IDENTIFICATION

Large size and black and white adult plumage distinctive. Adult looks all white except for yellow-buff head, black wingtips and dark legs. Feet webbed; at close range, pale blue visible along toes. Bill dagger-like and pale blue-grey. Juvenile is dark brown, speckled with pale spots; acquires white adult plumage over five years or so, the upperwing and back being the last to lose immature feathering. Flight pattern includes long glides on outstretched wings, deep, powerful wingbeats in direct flight and characteristic plunge-dive feeding method.

BIRD FACTS

VOICE 'Arr', 'urrah', heard at colonies and from breeding flocks; otherwise silent

LENGTH 87–100cm

WINGSPAN 165–180cm

WEIGHT 2.5–3.5kg

HABITAT Breeds colonially on islands and inaccessible cliffs; otherwise at sea

NEST Pile of vegetation, seaweed and flotsam

EGGS 1; pale blue and chalky, later whitish and stained

FOOD Fish

GREY HERON

Ardea cinerea

BIRD FACTS

VOICE Call a loud and harsh 'frank'; young birds at nest give pig-like squeals

LENGTH 90–98cm

WINGSPAN 175–195cm

WEIGHT 1.1–1.7kg

HABITAT Wetland; sometimes on coasts

NEST Colonial; tangled stick construction in tree

EGGS 4–5; pale blue

FOOD Fish, frogs and other aquatic animals

THE GREY HERON is by far the most widespread heron in Europe. And because it ofen feeds in open habitats, it is also the easiest to see. It often stands motionless for hours on end, both when resting and when feeding. Early naturalists, seeing herons engaged in the latter pursuit, ascribed fish-attracting properties to the birds' legs. Of course, this is not the case and patience is the only secret they employ for their wait-and-see fishing. Grey Herons will also stalk their prey on occasion, using a slow, deliberate pace followed by a lightning strike of the bill. After a successful fish catch, Grey Herons usually preen. If the head or neck feathers are coated with fish scales and mucus, they are rubbed against powdery feathers on the chest. The powder makes preening easier.

Grey Herons are capable of standing motionless for hours waiting for fish to approach.

IDENTIFICATION

Adult head, neck and underparts mostly whitish, except for black feathering on neck and on head; has black, trailing tuft of feathers on head. Bill large, dagger-like and yellow. Legs long and yellowish-green. In flight, Grey Herons look huge with long, broad and rounded wings. Wingbeats slow and leisurely, and head and neck held kinked and pulled in. Legs held outstretched with toes held together.

Large, dagger-like bill is perfectly adapted for fishing.

Adult, taking flight.

BELOW: In adult, back and upperwings grey except for flight feathers; black and white carpal feathers appear as 'black shoulder' on resting bird.

BELOW: Juvenile similar to adult but underparts more grubby and streaked; black and white head markings less distinct.

DID YOU KNOW?

The breeding season is protracted, with the first eggs being laid in mid-February and the last young fledging in early September. Displays throughout the breeding cycle maintain the bond between the breeding pair.

PURPLE HERON

Ardea purpurea

Most attractively marked heron. Slightly smaller than Grey Heron, with more slender head and neck. Adult plumage appears mostly purplish-grey. Head and neck orange to buff, with black stripe along length down each side. Long breast feathers appear streaked and underparts look dark on standing bird. Upperparts purplish-grey. Juvenile appears more uniformly buffish-brown. In flight, adult upperwings look purplish-brown with black flight feathers; underwings look grey, except for dark maroon band forming leading edge.

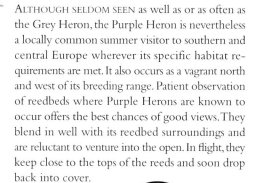

In flight, head is held in snake-like kink, and long, trailing legs show hind toes cocked upwards.

ALTHOUGH SELDOM SEEN as well as or as often as the Grey Heron, the Purple Heron is nevertheless a locally common summer visitor to southern and central Europe wherever its specific habitat requirements are met. It also occurs as a vagrant north and west of its breeding range. Patient observation of reedbeds where Purple Herons are known to occur offers the best chances of good views. They blend in well with its reedbed surroundings and are reluctant to venture into the open. In flight, they keep close to the tops of the reeds and soon drop back into cover.

adult bird with eel

Does not stand about in the open as much as Grey Heron, but is often flushed from the dense vegetation it favours.

BIRD FACTS

VOICE 'Kraank' call sometimes used, but mostly silent
LENGTH 78–90cm
WINGSPAN 120–150cm
WEIGHT 600–1,200g
HABITAT Extensive wetlands, especially in dense reedbeds
NEST Colonial; platform of reeds built in reedbeds
EGGS 4–5; pale bluish-green
FOOD Fish, frogs and other aquatic animals

Adult, with hunched neck typical of relaxed bird.

NIGHT HERON

Nycticorax nycticorax

Sexes similar. Adult face, neck and underparts pale grey; whitish on forecrown and around base of bill. Back black and wings grey, the contrast most noticeable in flight. In breeding plumage sports long, white head plumes. Legs yellowish except at start of breeding season, when pinkish. Immature has black-tipped yellow bill and dark-brown plumage adorned with large, pale spots. Underparts streaked.

Adult has black bill, black crown and large, red eyes.

THE NIGHT HERON is a summer visitor to Europe, present from April to September; because of its colonial nesting habits, detailed maps show its precise distribution in tight groups. Although a few birds overwinter in the Mediterranean region, the vast majority migrate to tropical Africa. The species occurs as a vagrant north and west of the breeding range. As the name suggests, the night heron is most active after dark. Outside the nesting period, hunched-up Night Herons can sometimes be seen in communal daytime roosts in trees, with long lines of flying birds leaving at dusk for their feeding grounds. They can sometimes be observed feeding in shallow water as the light fades.

BIRD FACTS

VOICE Raven-like 'kwaak' flight call
LENGTH 60–65cm
WINGSPAN 105–110cm
WEIGHT 550–700g
HABITAT Wetlands
NEST Colonially, usually in trees, twig platform
EGGS 3–5; pale blue
FOOD Fish, amphibians and insects

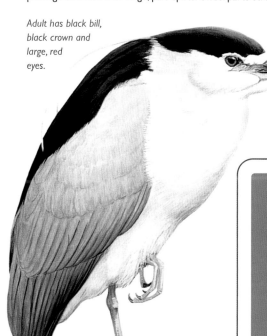

Adult perched.

Relatively slow wingbeats make flight action seem almost mechanical.

juvenile

BITTERN

Botaurus stellaris

BITTERNS ARE FAR more easily heard than seen: the male's loud, booming call can be heard up to 5km away on calm spring evenings in the vicinity of their reedbed habitat. Most birdwatchers have to satisfy themselves with brief views of birds flying low over the reeds and dropping into cover after a limited period in the air. During extreme winter weather, however, Bitterns do occasionally venture out into the open or are forced to move to wetland areas, where their camouflaged plumage is less effective. Damage done to wetlands has caused Bittern numbers to decline markedly, and their range to shrink.

Sexes similar. Large bird with mottled and marbled buffish-brown plumage. Darker streaks, barring and arrow-shaped markings afford excellent camouflage against reedbed. Neck long but often held in hunched posture. Cap and nape dark and shows dark moustachial stripe. Bill large, dagger-like and yellowish. Legs and feet yellowish-green with very long toes. When alarmed adopts motionless, upright posture with head and neck stretched skywards. In flight, often looks owl-like, with long and broad brown wings; trailing legs and forward-pointing head and bill clearly visible.

BIRD FACTS

VOICE During breeding season, male utters deep, resonant booming, 3–4 times in 5–6 seconds; otherwise silent

LENGTH 70–80cm

WINGSPAN 125–135cm

WEIGHT 900–1,500g

HABITAT Reedbeds; rarely in other wetland habitats – except during cold weather

NEST On ground among reeds

EGGS 5–6; olive-brown

FOOD Mainly fish, occasionally frogs

In flight, the brown plumage and rounded wings can make the Bittern resemble a giant Woodcock or owl.

Adult has a plump body, dagger-like bill and proportionately large toes, useful when walking through wetland vegetation.

DID YOU KNOW?

This species' skulking and secretive behaviour and excellently camouflaged plumage make it very difficult to observe: the best option for those seeking good views is to visit a reedbed reserve with hides, but even there patience and luck will be needed.

The Bittern's streaked and mottled plumage provides excellent cover among reedbeds.

Alert adult with head and neck held outstretched – sky-pointing – as a sign of anxiety.

Male has black-tipped yellow bill, greyish face, black cap and orange-buff, streaked underparts. Back and flight feathers black, contrasting with buffish-white wing coverts forming pale panel. Upperwing features most striking in flight. Female has much more subdued version of male's plumage, with reddish-buff face and underparts and streaked, brown back. Juvenile heavily streaked.

male

Pale upperwing panels can best be seen in flight.

Although unobtrusive and easily overlooked, Little Bitterns are common summer visitors to much of Europe.

male

LITTLE BITTERN
Ixobrychus minutus

THE LITTLE BITTERN is much easier to see than its larger cousin. Vigilant scanning of a suitable reedbed or wetland within the species' range will normally produce flight views, since Little Bitterns take to the wing regularly. Lucky observers may even see them clamber up reed stems to scrutinise the intruder before taking off in alarm. They then characteristically drop back down into the vegetation after a comparatively short flight. The Little Bittern occurs as a spring vagrant outside its normal breeding range and has even nested in Britain.

BIRD FACTS

VOICE Mostly silent but frog-like calls heard during breeding season; 'kerk' flight call

LENGTH 35–38cm

WINGSPAN 53–56cm

WEIGHT 140–150g

HABITAT Reedbeds and other well-vegetated wetlands

NEST Pile of vegetation among reeds

EGGS 5–6; white

FOOD Fish, frogs and aquatic insects

In the female, black elements of the male's plumage are dark brown.

Sexes similar. In breeding plumage crown and nape streaked, feathers on lower nape being long and plume-like. Underparts white. Bill greenish with black tip and eyes yellow. Legs greenish-orange. In flight, shows pure white wings and back. In non-breeding plumage, adult has dull-brown upperparts and streaked head and neck. Still strikingly white in flight. Bill yellowish with black tip. Juvenile similar to non-breeding adult.

In breeding plumage, standing bird looks mainly orange-buff with reddish tinge to back.

SQUACCO HERON
Ardeola ralloides

PRESENT IN THE region from April to September, most European Squacco Herons then migrate to tropical Africa. Vagrants appear north of the breeding range in Europe, most records referring to overshooting spring migrants. At first glance, a flying Squacco Heron could be mistaken for a breeding-plumage Cattle Egret. On closer inspection, the extensive buffish upperparts of the heron soon distinguish it, as do the species' habits. Unlike the more gregarious Cattle Egret, the Squacco Heron is generally a solitary bird, feeding by stealth in shallow wetland margins. When nesting, however, pairs often join large mixed colonies of other heron and egret species.

BIRD FACTS

VOICE Harsh croaks heard in breeding season; otherwise silent

LENGTH 45–47cm

WINGSPAN 80–90cm

WEIGHT 250–350g

HABITAT All sorts of wetlands

NEST Colonial; twig platforms built in trees

EGGS 4–6; greenish-blue

FOOD Fish, amphibians, aquatic insects

FAR LEFT: *Adult perched.*
CENTRE LEFT: *Adult in flight.*
LEFT: *Adult standing.*

SPOONBILL

adult

Platalea leucorodia

ALTHOUGH THE SPOONBILL's breeding range extends in a wide band across central Asia, and includes much of the Indian sub-continent, it is a distinctly local species in Europe at shallow lowland lakes and coastal lagoons. In the winter months, birds from southeast Europe tend to move to coastal wetlands around the shores of the eastern Mediterranean; those from the Netherlands move down the Atlantic coast of northwest Europe. Out of their normal range, Spoonbills are usually seen singly or in small parties, but around breeding colonies sizeable groups sometimes feed together.

BIRD FACTS

VOICE Mostly silent; occasional grunting sounds at nest

LENGTH 80–90cm

WINGSPAN 115–130cm

WEIGHT 1.4–1.9kg

HABITAT Shallow lakes, coastal lagoons

NEST Colonial; pile of twigs or reeds in reedbed or bush

EGGS 3–4; white with small, reddish spots

FOOD Small aquatic insects, fish, molluscs, crustaceans

IDENTIFICATION

Sexes similar. Resting birds often have bill tucked in and so can be mistaken for Little Egrets. Feeding birds distinctive, and identified by bill shape and feeding method, when bill is swept from side to side. Adult plumage all white, although can look rather grubby; shows buffish-yellow on breast in breeding season and long plumes on nape. Legs long and black, and bill long and flattened with spoon-shaped tip. In flight, carries head and neck outstretched and legs trailing. Immature has black wingtips.

ABOVE: *Outside the breeding season, Spoonbills are often seen flying in small flocks.*

Spoonbills fly with their heads and necks outstretched, and legs trailing.

DID YOU KNOW?

In Europe, Spoonbills are under threat from marsh draining and pesticides; they are also sensitive to disturbances at breeding time.

The Spoonbill's flat-tipped bill is ideally suited for filtering out small water animals from soft sediment or the water column.

Legs long and black, contrasting with yellow feet.

LITTLE EGRET
Egretta garzetta

WHEREVER LARGE, SHALLOW lakes or coastal wetlands are found in southern Europe, you will find Little Egrets in summer. The species' range has expanded northwards in recent decades and it is now common in southern Britain (and Ireland) and breeds there. A hunched-up roosting Little Egret may not inspire much admiration, but when striding purposefully through the shallows on its long legs, or poised motionless, waiting for a fish to pass by, it is a most elegant bird: it will stab at prey with unerring accuracy. On some occasions, the birds appear to shuffle their feet in front of them, apparently to disturb resting or hiding prey into tell-tale movement.

IDENTIFICATION

The most common pure-white, heron-like bird in Europe. Sexes alike. Slender and elegant appearance, with long neck. Bill long, dark and dagger-like. Bare skin at base of bill yellowish in breeding season but otherwise darker. Also sports long head plumes in breeding season. Appearance remains similar throughout year. In flight, shows broad, rounded wings and trails its long legs behind it.

Once prized and persecuted by the millinery trade for its long plumes, the species is now relatively common throughout its range.

BIRD FACTS

VOICE Harsh 'khaah' and other grating sounds heard at colony; otherwise mostly silent

LENGTH 55–65cm

WINGSPAN 88–95cm

WEIGHT 400–550g

HABITAT Shallow lakes and wetlands; also coastal lagoons and saltpans

NEST Colonial; twig platform in tree or among reeds

EGGS 3–5; greenish-blue

FOOD Fish, amphibians and other aquatic animals

ABOVE: *Adult in flight;* BELOW: *Adult catching stickleback prey.*

In flight, head and neck held in hunched-up posture.

CATTLE EGRET
Bubulcus ibis

VOICE During breeding season, utters barking 'aak' and other calls; otherwise silent

LENGTH 48–52cm

WINGSPAN 90–95cm

WEIGHT 300–350g

HABITAT Cultivated land and grassland, often alongside animals; also follows ploughs

NEST Colonial; platform of twigs or reeds or in tree

EGGS 4–5; whitish

FOOD Insects, invertebrates, small mammals, frogs, etc., disturbed by progress of herd animals

IN EUROPE THE Cattle Egret's main breeding range is southern and southwestern parts of the Iberian peninsula. But its range is expanding north and it bred in Britain for the first time in 2008. In contrast with the wait-and-see approach to feeding adopted by many herons and egrets, Cattle Egrets are far more active. This is especially true when flocks join herds of cattle or sheep. Ever alert, the birds keep pace with the animals in order to spot frogs and insects disturbed by their progress. Mornings and evenings see lines of birds flying between roosts and feeding grounds.

A stocky, white bird with a characteristic bulging throat. Sexes similar. Plumage pure white except during brief period of breeding season. Bill dagger-like and proportionately large; at height of breeding season pinkish-orange but otherwise yellow. Legs dull yellowish-green except, briefly, during breeding season, when pinkish-orange. In flight, wings broad and rounded, and legs trailing; neck held in typical hunched-up posture, giving large-headed appearance.

During the brief breeding season the feathers on the nape, mantle and breast have a warm, buffish tinge.

adults

Adult, at height of breeding season.

adult

GREAT WHITE EGRET
Ardea alba

VOICE Grating 'kraak' heard at colony and roost; otherwise silent

LENGTH 85–102cm

WINGSPAN 140–170cm

WEIGHT 1–1.5kg

HABITAT Extensive wetlands and large, reed-fringed lakes

NEST Colonial; pile of reeds or twigs in reedbeds or bushes

EGGS 3–5; pale blue

FOOD Fish, amphibians and other aquatic animals

GREAT WHITE EGRETS have a limited breeding range in the region but have recently spread to the Netherlands, north France, Spain and Latvia, and occur as vagrants as far north and west as Britain. Although they are colonial nesters, they tend to be solitary or are seen, at most, in small groups at other times. The leisurely way in which Great White Egrets wade through deep water differs from the more active approach often adopted by their smaller cousins. Birds also stand motionless for extended periods, stabbing or lunging with their bills at the crucial moment. As well as fish and frogs, Great White Egrets also eat mammals such as voles as well as water snakes.

Distinctly larger than Little Egret, with which it sometimes occurs, and with rather more statuesque proportions. Plumage pure white at all times; shows long, lacy plumes on lower back in breeding season. Bill black in breeding season but yellow at other times; patch of yellow skin at base of bill present at all times. Legs long; reddish on tibia in breeding season on adult but dark blackish at other times and in juvenile.

RIGHT: adult, in breeding season

BELOW: adult, non-breeding

In flight shows long, broad wings and long, trailing legs; head and neck held in hunched posture.

Similar in proportions and size to White Pelican but slightly larger. White plumage has blue-grey tinge; sports a back-curled mane in the form of curly feathers. Bill long and large and throat sac orange-yellow in breeding season but pink at other times. Legs grey in all plumages. In flight, adult seen from below has uniformly greyish-white wings, easily separating it from White Pelican. Seen from above, primary flight feathers are black, contrasting with otherwise pale plumage. Juvenile has more uniformly greyish-white underwing in flight than White Pelican. A consummate flier, able to soar and glide with ease.

DALMATIAN PELICAN

Pelecanus crispus

BIRD FACTS

VOICE Hissing and grunting calls heard at colony; otherwise silent

LENGTH 160–175cm

WINGSPAN 280–290cm

WEIGHT 10.5–11.5kg

HABITAT Shallow freshwater lakes

NEST Mound of twigs and vegetation

EGGS 2; white

FOOD Fish

DELIBERATE DESTRUCTION BY fishermen and wetland drainage have severely depleted the Dalmatian Pelican's numbers. They are often seen in the company of White Pelicans, both on migration through the region and at feeding or nesting sites. Like their relatives, Dalmatian Pelicans sometimes engage in group feeding, a dozen or more birds forming a semi-circle and driving fish into the shallows. More than 1kg is consumed each day by a single bird and fish up to 45cm can be swallowed.

adult, in breeding season

BELOW AND RIGHT: *adult, in spring*

BELOW: *adult, in spring*

Large, white waterbird. Often seen swimming in flocks when adult plumage looks all white, except for black wingtips. In good light, plumage can be seen to be tinged yellowish. Bill large and very long. Throat sac yellow to orange and shows bare patch of pink skin around eyes. Robust legs and webbed feet orange-yellow. From below, adult shows black flight feathers that contrast with otherwise white plumage. Juvenile has brownish plumage and yellow throat sac; shows brown flight feathers and brown leading edge to wing.

WHITE PELICAN

Pelecanus onocrotalus

BIRD FACTS

VOICE Grunts, growls and mooing calls heard at nest; otherwise silent

LENGTH 140–170cm

WINGSPAN 275–290cm

WEIGHT 10–11kg

HABITAT Shallow, lowland lakes and river deltas

NEST Mound of twigs and vegetation in reedbeds or on islands

EGGS 2; white

FOOD Fish

A TRIP TO northern Greece in spring offers the best opportunities for seeing this imposing species in Europe. With its long, broad wings, the White Pelican is every bit as proficient at soaring and thermalling as birds of prey. Birds are sometimes seen circling above their breeding grounds or in migrating flocks of several hundred individuals. They are also well adapted to an aquatic life, their webbed feet enabling them to propel themselves along quickly. White Pelicans are easily disturbed at their colonial nesting grounds.

The capacious throat sac is used to engulf whole shoals of fish if feeding conditions are good.

adults, in breeding season

The White Pelican is especially impressive in flight.

TOP: *Migrating flock;* ABOVE: *Feeding flock of adults.*

WHITE STORK

Ciconia ciconia

BIRD FACTS

VOICE Mostly silent; non-vocal bill-clapping at nest

LENGTH 100–115cm

WINGSPAN 155–165cm

WEIGHT 3–4kg

HABITAT Feeds in wetlands and fields adjacent to towns and villages

NEST Arrangement of twigs on rooftop; occasionally in tree

EGGS 3–5; white

FOOD Fish, frogs, small mammals, insects

ANYONE WHO HAS visited bird migration hotspots at the Bosphorus in Turkey or the Straits of Gibraltar in southern Spain will have lasting memories of migrating storks. Designed for soaring flight, the species favours narrow isthmuses, where thermals give enough lift to glide over the cooler seas. Flocks of more than 10,000 are not unknown and tens of thousands pass through each day when conditions are good. White Storks are easy birds to see during the breeding season. They favour small towns and villages, nesting on rooftops or churches and even taking to man-made platforms provided for them.

Unmistakable, given size and markings. Sexes similar. Standing, adult head, neck, back and underparts white; can look rather grubby. Wingtips black. Bill long, dagger-like and bright red. Legs long and red. In flight, soars impressively on long, outstretched wings, which look square-ended and have 'fingers' of primaries projecting. Body white except for black flight feathers when seen from above and below. Juvenile similar to adult but colour of bill and legs duller.

Adult feeding.

Adult in flight.

Bill-clapping display of nesting adults.

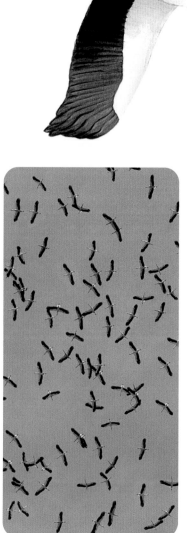

Migrating flock.

Sexes similar. From behind, plumage of adult looks all black; in good light, oily sheen also visible. From other views, white underparts can be seen. Legs long and red. In flight, has huge, broad wings, which look square-ended with 'fingers' of primaries showing; plumage all black except for white underparts extending to innerwing. Juvenile similar to adult but plumage browner and legs and bill dull greenish.

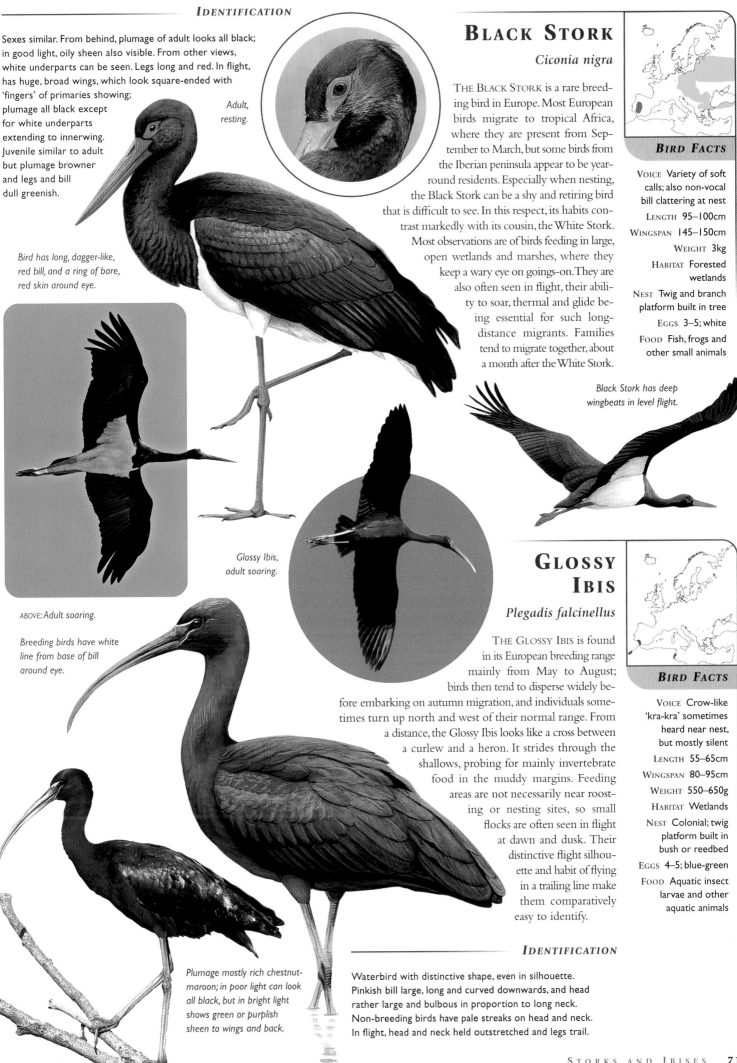

Adult, resting.

Bird has long, dagger-like, red bill, and a ring of bare, red skin around eye.

ABOVE: *Adult soaring.*

Breeding birds have white line from base of bill around eye.

Glossy Ibis, adult soaring.

Plumage mostly rich chestnut-maroon; in poor light can look all black, but in bright light shows green or purplish sheen to wings and back.

BLACK STORK
Ciconia nigra

THE BLACK STORK is a rare breeding bird in Europe. Most European birds migrate to tropical Africa, where they are present from September to March, but some birds from the Iberian peninsula appear to be year-round residents. Especially when nesting, the Black Stork can be a shy and retiring bird that is difficult to see. In this respect, its habits contrast markedly with its cousin, the White Stork. Most observations are of birds feeding in large, open wetlands and marshes, where they keep a wary eye on goings-on. They are also often seen in flight, their ability to soar, thermal and glide being essential for such long-distance migrants. Families tend to migrate together, about a month after the White Stork.

Black Stork has deep wingbeats in level flight.

BIRD FACTS

VOICE Variety of soft calls; also non-vocal bill clattering at nest
LENGTH 95–100cm
WINGSPAN 145–150cm
WEIGHT 3kg
HABITAT Forested wetlands
NEST Twig and branch platform built in tree
EGGS 3–5; white
FOOD Fish, frogs and other small animals

GLOSSY IBIS
Plegadis falcinellus

THE GLOSSY IBIS is found in its European breeding range mainly from May to August; birds then tend to disperse widely before embarking on autumn migration, and individuals sometimes turn up north and west of their normal range. From a distance, the Glossy Ibis looks like a cross between a curlew and a heron. It strides through the shallows, probing for mainly invertebrate food in the muddy margins. Feeding areas are not necessarily near roosting or nesting sites, so small flocks are often seen in flight at dawn and dusk. Their distinctive flight silhouette and habit of flying in a trailing line make them comparatively easy to identify.

BIRD FACTS

VOICE Crow-like 'kra-kra' sometimes heard near nest, but mostly silent
LENGTH 55–65cm
WINGSPAN 80–95cm
WEIGHT 550–650g
HABITAT Wetlands
NEST Colonial; twig platform built in bush or reedbed
EGGS 4–5; blue-green
FOOD Aquatic insect larvae and other aquatic animals

IDENTIFICATION

Waterbird with distinctive shape, even in silhouette. Pinkish bill large, long and curved downwards, and head rather large and bulbous in proportion to long neck. Non-breeding birds have pale streaks on head and neck. In flight, head and neck held outstretched and legs trail.

EGYPTIAN VULTURE

Neophron percnopterus

PRESENT IN THE region from April to September, Egyptian Vultures are associated with warm climates and are perhaps easiest to see in central and southern Spain. They favour eroded sandstone gorges or towering mountain slopes and, from mid-morning onwards, they soar to great heights on the rising thermals. By vulture standards, the Egyptian Vulture has a comparatively small, weak bill, which means that it is often obliged to feed on the scraps left over by other scavengers at a carcass; in some parts of its range it scavenges at rubbish dumps.

IDENTIFICATION

In flight, silhouette recalls a miniature Lammergeier with its wedge-shaped tail; wings proportionately broader and shorter than that species'. Sexes similar. Seen from below, adult has black flight feathers that contrast with otherwise rather grubby white plumage; at close range, black-tipped yellow bill, bald yellow face and yellow or pink legs visible. Juvenile similar shape to adult but all dark; full adult plumage acquired gradually over four years or so.

Adult in flight.

RIGHT: *juvenile*
FAR RIGHT: *adult*

LAMMERGEIER

Gypaetus barbatus

SOMETIMES REFERRED TO as the Bearded Vulture, the Lammergeier is Europe's scarcest and most local vulture species. It is found in the western Pyrenees, Turkey, the Caucasus, on Corsica and in northern Greece, with a total population of 50 to 100 pairs. Extremely fortunate observers may see one feeding. Although Lammergeiers will readily feed at a fresh carcass if the opportunity arises, they also have an amazing alternative means of getting a meal of bone marrow. Holding a large bone firmly in their feet, they take to the air and rise to a considerable height. When they are above a suitable flat rock the bone is dropped and shatters on impact. The Lammergeier then retrieves the pieces and swallows them whole.

IDENTIFICATION

A very distinctive bird of prey with very long and comparatively narrow wings and a long, wedge-shaped tail. Seen in good light, adults show orange-buff head and underparts; wings and tail black. At close range, black patch around orange eye can be seen along with black moustache-like feathers. Juvenile has similar flight silhouette to adult but is all dark.

RIGHT: *adult*

Adult soaring.

One of the most majestic of all birds in flight.

juvenile

Flight silhouette distinctive with long, broad and parallel-sided wings, which are square-ended but show splayed 'fingers' of primary feathers; soars with wings held flat. Head appears relatively small and tail is usually slightly fanned. Sexes similar. Plumage mostly dark brown but invariably appears all black because of distance at which most birds are seen. Seen at close range, has huge, black-tipped bill and bald head and neck with ruffled collar of feathers. Juvenile difficult to separate from adult in the field.

adult

BLACK VULTURE

Aegypius monachus

THE EURASIAN BLACK VULTURE is Europe's largest bird of prey and also one of its rarest. Although it was probably never numerous, persecution by farmers has reduced its numbers in the region to a few hundred pairs, the majority of these being found in central southern Spain. Given its size, it is not surprising that the Black Vulture takes precedence over other scavengers at a carcass. With its powerful bill and strong neck muscles, it can tear open the hide of even the largest animal, something which other, smaller vultures are not able to do; in this respect, Black Vultures do their cousins a favour by initiating the scavenging process.

Even at the great heights favoured by this species, its immense size is still apparent from a distance, especially when it is joined by smaller birds of prey such as Booted Eagles or is mobbed by Ravens; it dwarfs both these species.

adult

BIRD FACTS

VOICE Mostly silent
LENGTH 100–110cm
WINGSPAN 250–290cm
WEIGHT 7–11kg
HABITAT Seen at towering heights over all sorts of broken terrain, especially near mountains
NEST Twig platform built in tree
EGGS 1; white with reddish streaks
FOOD Carrion

Large, broad-winged vulture. Sexes similar. Adult has buffish-brown body plumage contrasting with dark flight feathers; contrast visible from above and below in flight and on perched birds. Head and neck bald and whitish but sometimes stained; has collar of ruffled feathers. In flight, looks small-headed and short-tailed. Wings long and broad, narrowing towards tips and showing pale barring against brown underwing coverts; soars with wings held in shallow 'V'. Juvenile generally similar to adult but underwing coverts rather pale with dark barring.

GRIFFON VULTURE

Gyps fulvus

ALTHOUGH REDUCED IN range and numbers, the Griffon Vulture is by far the commonest vulture of the region and, in most of its range, is a year-round resident. Given its size and usual indifference to man, it is also the easiest to see, especially when tens or even hundreds rise in spiralling fashion on a single thermal. Griffon Vultures are most numerous and widespread in the Iberian peninusla but they also occur in the eastern Mediterranean and a few birds still persist on Sicily. In contrast to their rather grizzly feeding habits, these are majestic birds in flight, able to soar for hours on end with hardly a wingbeat.

Prior to taking to the air, often sits facing the sun with its wings slightly spread.

adult

adult

adult

BIRD FACTS

VOICE Utters croaking calls near nest or roost; silent in flight
LENGTH 95–105cm
WINGSPAN 260–280cm
WEIGHT 7–10kg
HABITAT Warm, mountainous regions
NEST Pile of twigs on inaccessible cliff ledge
EGGS 1; whitish
FOOD Carrion

DID YOU KNOW?

Being dependent on rising thermals, Griffon Vultures are seldom seen in the air before ten in the morning.

GOLDEN EAGLE

Aquila chrysaetos

THE GOLDEN EAGLE is a widespread, although never common, raptor of mountainous regions. It often flies very high, covering a wide range every day, but when hunting it will usually fly low, dropping suddenly on its prey with talons outstretched. Most of its food is taken on the ground, but it will occasionally take a startled bird in flight. Adults are mostly sedentary, but juveniles will disperse to find unoccupied territories, during which time they are vulnerable to shooting. Elaborate aerial displays are performed in winter and early spring when pairs may perform downwards 'cartwheel' flights; some calls may be heard at this time from this otherwise silent species.

BIRD FACTS

VOICE Mostly silent, but some yelping calls, rarely heard

LENGTH 76–89cm

WINGSPAN 190–227cm

WEIGHT 3.5–6.5kg

HABITAT Mountainous regions, lowland forests and marshes; only where human habitation is absent

NEST On cliff ledges, rarely trees; large twiggy platform

EGGS 1–3; dull white, with red-brown blotches and flecks

FOOD Small mammals and birds; some carrion

DID YOU KNOW?

Both Golden Eagles and Buzzards soar on raised wings, so caution is needed when bird is viewed from a distance; the eagle is much larger, although a distant bird's size is not always apparent.

A large eagle with a long tail and long, broad wings held in a shallow 'V' when soaring and gliding. Looks dark from below but shows buff, grey and dark-brown markings above with paler head. Strong wingbeats are followed by one- to two-second glides in normal flight, but prey may be surprised by a steep dive, or low-level glide. Immatures have white wing patches and white tail with dark terminal band. Adult plumage attained after five to seven years.

adults

juvenile, first winter

immature, third winter

adult

adult

juvenile

The massive bill is impressive when seen close up; the crown and shaggy hind neck are washed golden-yellow.

In flight, has immense wingspan with broad, parallel-sided wings, which are square-ended with primaries resembling splayed 'fingers'. Tail relatively short and broad; white in adult birds but dark in juveniles. When seen perched, yellow legs and bill can be seen in adult; juvenile bill dark but yellow at the base. Adult head looks paler than body.

WHITE-TAILED EAGLE

Haliaeetus albicilla

A WHITE-TAILED EAGLE in flight is an unforgettable sight and few people can fail to be impressed by its sheer size. During the winter months, birds seldom rise to great heights, so the chances are good of getting superb views of them in low-level flight. Although White-tailed Eagles will take carrion and mammals at any time of the year, during the winter they often specialise in catching ducks and geese, hence their ties with wetland habitats. When hunting, they show surprising speed and agility for such a large bird.

BIRD FACTS

VOICE Yelping call
LENGTH 70–90cm
WINGSPAN 200–240cm
WEIGHT 4–6kg
HABITAT Associated with sea coasts and extensive wetlands
NEST Bulky mass of sticks in tree or on cliff
EGGS 2; white
FOOD Carrion, waterbirds, mammals, fish

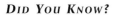

ABOVE: adult

RIGHT: Immature in flight.
BELOW: adult

DID YOU KNOW?

In many parts of their European range White-tailed Eagles are year-round residents, but birds from Russia migrate south and west in the autumn.

GREATER SPOTTED EAGLE

Aquila clanga

BIRD FACTS

VOICE Yapping call heard near nest

LENGTH 62–75cm

WINGSPAN 160–180cm

WEIGHT 1.6–2.2kg

HABITAT Forest and scattered woodland close to wetland areas

NEST Stick construction built in tree

EGGS 1–3; white, sometimes with reddish spotting

FOOD Mammals, reptiles and birds but also carrion

GREATER SPOTTED EAGLES are still fairly common in parts of their eastern European range. Vast tracts of undisturbed forest are not essential to them, and in fact small copses and scattered woodland will sometimes serve as a breeding site, provided that wetland areas lie close by. The bird's leisurely flight on downward-bowed wings can give the impression of a much larger bird. Although carrion can feature quite heavily in this species' diet, it also catches live prey in active, low-level flight. In favoured hunting areas, small numbers of eagles can sometimes be found perched on nearby posts and trees, waiting for a feeding opportunity to arise.

Appreciably larger than Lesser Spotted Eagle, but this is not always easy to see in distant, solitary birds. Best feature for separation in flight seen from below is greyish flight feathers, which appear paler than rest of feathering on wings and body (converse true in Lesser Spotted Eagle). Seen from above, adult plumage looks all dark; that of juvenile shows heavy white spotting on wing coverts and inner flight feathers with white 'shafts' on all primaries.

GREATER SPOTTED EAGLE

Juvenile heavily spotted.

GREATER SPOTTED EAGLE

adult

LESSER SPOTTED EAGLE

LESSER SPOTTED EAGLE

adult

LESSER SPOTTED EAGLE

Aquila pomarina

BIRD FACTS

VOICE High-pitched yapping call

LENGTH 57–65cm

WINGSPAN 135–160cm

WEIGHT 1.3–1.8kg

HABITAT In European breeding range, favours forests adjacent to wetlands

NEST Stick construction built in tree

EGGS 1–3; white, spotted with reddish-brown

FOOD Mainly small mammals, but also birds and reptiles

A REQUIREMENT FOR extensive and undisturbed forested areas for nesting and the juxtaposition of marshes and wet meadows for feeding inevitably limits possible breeding sites for Lesser Spotted Eagles; degradation or destruction of both these habitats may help explain its demise. Visit one of the eastern European countries, however, and your chances of seeing this species are good. Like other similarly sized raptors, Lesser Spotted Eagles soar effortlessly. They are often seen in low-level, rather laboured flight as well and will perch for extended periods on posts adjacent to feeding areas.

Juvenile shows white spotting on inner flight feathers.

adult

IDENTIFICATION

Comparatively small eagle but with proportionately long, parallel-sided wings, which appear rather square-ended in soaring flight with 'fingers' of primaries clearly visible. Seen from below, can look all dark; in good light, flight feathers always darker than brown body feathers in both adults and juveniles, a good feature for separating from similar Greater Spotted Eagle. Seen from above, adult shows tail and flight feathers darker than body feathers, narrow white band on base of tail and white 'shafts' on inner primaries. Juvenile similar to adult but has numerous white spots on inner flight feathers.

IMPERIAL EAGLE

Aquila heliaca

THE IMPERIAL EAGLE is a rare bird in Europe. It hunts in open, lightly wooded lowland areas where there are scattered tall trees for nesting. Much time is spent sitting on a low perch, sometimes even on the ground, but feeding forays are made at high altitude, often at great speed. The nest is a large, twiggy structure high in a tall tree, although very rarely it may be on a cliff ledge. This is normally a solitary bird, but very occasionally a few may be found at a good feeding spot. Its lack of fear of humans has led to it being heavily persecuted.

IDENTIFICATION

Adult is a very dark bird showing a creamy buff nape and greyish tail with a dark terminal band. Wings are long and narrow and held flat when soaring, but may be slightly raised with a flat tip when gliding. Tail appears long and narrow in adults, but juveniles show a more spread tail when soaring. Juvenile brownish-red, fading to paler buff-brown with streaked breast. Juveniles take four to five years to attain adult plumage.

BIRD FACTS

VOICE Deep raven-like 'gahk'

LENGTH 75–84cm

WINGSPAN 180–215cm

WEIGHT 2.5–4.5kg

HABITAT Mediterranean steppe, mixed lowland habitats with some tall trees

NEST High in large tree; twigs and branches, lined with green leaves

EGGS 2–3; dull white, sometimes with darker flecks

FOOD Small mammals and birds, waterfowl, some carrion

SPANISH IMPERIAL EAGLE

Aquila adalberti

THE REGIONS AROUND the Coto Doñana in the far south of Spain are one of the Spanish Imperial Eagle's strongholds, and here the birds spend much of the day sitting around in trees, where they are surprisingly easy to overlook. Spanish Imperial Eagles soar on rising thermals to great heights but can still follow movements on the ground and descend rapidly on an unsuspecting rabbit. The species was formerly considered to be a race of Imperial Eagle and not a separate species.

IDENTIFICATION

Seen in flight, wings look relatively long and parallel-sided; tail not normally fanned. Adult can look all dark but in good light shows dark brown plumage and white markings on scapulars and leading edge of innerwing; crown and nape are pale buff. Juvenile has pale-brown plumage except for dark flight feathers and tail; shows heavy white spotting on upper surface of flight feathers and, in good light, teardrop spots on wing coverts.

BIRD FACTS

VOICE Repeated, harsh barking call

LENGTH 75–85cm

WINGSPAN 180–215cm

WEIGHT 2.5–3.5kg

HABITAT Open woodland and fields

NEST Stick platform built in tree

EGGS 2–3; white with brownish markings

FOOD Mainly mammals but some carrion

Immense, relatively long-winged raptor with white scapular patches.

IMPERIAL EAGLE

SPANISH IMPERIAL EAGLE

IMPERIAL EAGLE adult

SPANISH IMPERIAL EAGLE immature

SHORT-TOED EAGLE

Circaetus gallicus

BIRD FACTS

VOICE Fluting calls by male, harsher notes from female

LENGTH 62–67cm

WINGSPAN 170–185cm

WEIGHT 1.2–2.2kg

HABITAT Dry, open habitats, with some maquis, garigue or scattered trees

NEST Top of low tree; deep cup of twigs, lined with green leaves

EGGS 1; white and smooth

FOOD Snakes, lizards

SHORT-TOED EAGLES favour open, warm habitats where there is an abundance of snakes. The usual method of hunting is to hover, or perhaps quarter low over the ground, dropping on to the prey with a rapid strike. Small prey items are carried into the air and moved around with the feet until killed, usually by ripping off the head, before being swallowed. Large snakes may be eaten on the ground or taken to a perch after being ripped up. Males are very vocal on the nesting site, which they defend vigorously, using the same nest many years in succession. Both sexes share in the incubation and care of the young.

A large, pale raptor, usually seen hovering or using updraughts, when underparts look very white. Wings broad and quite long in proportion to body size; tail narrow and square-ended. Darker head gives hooded appearance. Sexes have similar plumages but female is larger than male. May be confused with Osprey, but does not show dark carpal patches.

Adult, with snake prey.

adult

adult

DID YOU KNOW?

Short-toed Eagles overwinter in Africa; they often migrate in mixed flocks of other raptors across well-known migration routes such as Gibraltar and the Bosphorus.

The smallest European eagle, occurring in a pale and dark form. Dark form easily confused with Black Kite and juvenile Bonelli's Eagle; plumage varies from red-brown to blackish-brown, with buff tail darkening towards tip. For description of pale form see caption. Both dark and pale forms show a pale 'V' on upperparts formed by median upperwing coverts. Primary feathers in outstretched wings appear as typical eagle 'fingers'.

Pale form has pale underparts and wings except for dark flight feathers, dark-grey tail and greyish-buff head.

ABOVE: *pale form*

dark form

BOOTED EAGLE

Hieraaetus pennatus

THE BOOTED EAGLE is still relatively common in Spain, but is rarer elsewhere in southern and central Europe. This is one of the most vocal of the eagles, with several wader-like calls uttered near the nest site and during courtship. Booted Eagles sometimes hunt in pairs, swooping one after the other on prey, which may be pursued through the branches of trees or captured on the ground. A great variety of small birds, mammals, reptiles and insects are taken, with birds usually being beheaded and plucked before being eaten.

BIRD FACTS

VOICE Various whistling and cackling calls

LENGTH 45–50cm

WINGSPAN 100–130cm

WEIGHT 500–1,250g

HABITAT Wooded mountain slopes, open hilly country

NEST In tree, sometimes cliff face; large and twiggy with green leaves

EGGS 2; dull white, rarely marked

FOOD Small mammals, birds, reptiles and insects

The Booted Eagle can hang motionless at great height without hovering, and then dive straight down at breathtaking speed with legs extended forwards.

Adults are distinctive with very pale belly, dark terminal band to long tail, and contrasting dark underwings; lesser underwing coverts are whitish and flight feathers greyish at base giving distinctive pattern, but general effect is of dark wings. A variable pale patch shows on the upper back. Sexes similar. Wingbeats are quick and shallow, with wings held level and slightly forwards when soaring. When gliding, wings are gently arched and show straight rear edge. Juveniles are pale pinkish-brown below and darker on back.

Bonelli's Eagles often hunt in pairs along mountainsides and over rough ground, frequently using the same hunting areas every day; prey is usually captured on the ground and consists of medium-sized mammals such as rabbits and birds such as partridges; birds are also sometimes caught in flight.

adult

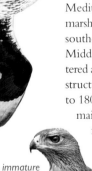

adult

immature

BONELLI'S EAGLE

Hieraaetus fasciatus

MOST BONELLI'S EAGLES remain near their breeding grounds all year, but outside the breeding season juveniles will migrate south towards the Mediterranean, where they will hunt over coastal marshes and plains. Bonelli's Eagles are found across southern Europe and North Africa as far as the Middle East, although they are very widely scattered and nowhere common. The nest is a very large structure, often used year after year, and may be up to 180cm high and 180cm in diameter, composed mainly of large branches up to 3cm thick, with fresh greenery added almost every day. Both sexes help with building or rebuilding the nest – a three or four month process.

BIRD FACTS

VOICE Shrill, piping calls

LENGTH 65–70cm

WINGSPAN 150–170cm

WEIGHT 1.5–2.5kg

HABITAT Mountainous and hilly country in Mediterranean region; sometimes marshes

NEST In tree or on cliff ledge; large, with many branches and some greenery

EGGS 2; white, with brown and lilac spots and lines

FOOD Small mammals and birds

BUZZARD

Buteo buteo

ALTHOUGH STILL COMMON in many parts of Europe, Buzzard numbers have decreased over the last century. In parts of the northwest of the range, however, there are signs that the species may be expanding its range again into formerly occupied areas. Where it is common, the Buzzard often attracts attention to itself with its mewing, cat-like call. Furthermore, unlike many other large birds of prey, Buzzards spend quite long periods perched on posts and dead branches in the open, often yielding good views to observers. They will also feed on the ground, searching mainly for earthworms and carrion.

VOICE Mewing 'peeioo'

LENGTH 50–55cm

WINGSPAN 115–130cm

WEIGHT 700–1,200g

HABITAT Hilly country, open farmland with adjacent woodland

NEST Stick nest built in tree or on crag

EGGS 2–3; white or bluish

FOOD Earthworms, rabbits, carrion

Soaring effortlessly overhead, several individuals may join a single thermal and stay aloft for hours on end.

adult

Adult, tearing prey apart.

Medium-sized bird of prey. Sexes similar. Colour extremely variable but almost always some shade of brown. Soars on broad, rounded wings held in a 'V' angle with barred tail fanned out. Upperparts usually dark brown, although flight feathers contrastingly dark in paler birds. Seen from below, wings and tail barred, the trailing edge of wings and terminal edge of tail noticeably dark. Some birds show dark collar and dark carpal patches. At close range, black-tipped yellow bill and yellow legs visible. Almost pure-white birds are occasionally seen.

RIGHT: From below, Buzzards can be highly variable, with colouring ranging from largely dark to largely white as this adult demonstrates.

Birds frequently perch in a hunched position on roadside telegraph poles.

RIGHT: Adult, with rabbit prey.

Superficially similar to Buzzard in silhouette but slightly larger and with proportionately longer wings and tail. Like that species, the Rough-legged soars on raised wings, but also regularly hovers. Seen from below, typically shows dark and white pattern: has dark belly patch, dark carpal patches on wings and tail with faint barring towards tip and broad, dark terminal band. Seen from above, conspicuous pale base to tail appears as white rump. Seen perched, dark belly often noticeable and head can look pale, especially in young birds.

*adult
male*

White tail with dark terminal band is diagnostic.

ROUGH-LEGGED BUZZARD
Buteo lagopus

BIRD FACTS

VOICE Similar mew to Buzzard but louder and lower
LENGTH 50–60cm
WINGSPAN 120–150cm
WEIGHT 700–1,200g
HABITAT Nests on tundra; in winter, on marshes, moors and downs
NEST Stick platform, on rocky ledge if available
EGGS 3–4; white, streaked with red
FOOD Mainly small mammals; in winter, may take birds and rabbits

THE ROUGH-LEGGED BUZZARD's low-level flight, conspicuous white-based tail and habit of hovering make it easy to identify even at a distance. Its diet comprises mainly small mammals and it is presumably a dearth of voles and mice in some winters that forces birds to spread more widely in Europe than in good rodent years. In the Arctic, lemmings are major prey items, these creatures having three- or four-year cycles of abundance. In good years large broods of Rough-legged Buzzards are reared while in bad years breeding success crashes.

Like Buzzard, soars on raised wings, but is larger, with proportionately longer wings and tail.

adult male

Sexes similar. Adult plumage extremely variable but perched birds generally show noticeably pale head and breast; latter separated from pale vent and undertail by broad, rufous band across belly. Seen from below in flight, shows reddish-brown underwing coverts and dark carpal patches; flight feathers white but with conspicuous and contrasting black tips to primaries and black trailing edge to secondaries. From above, reddish-brown mantle and upperwing coverts contrast with dark flight feathers; tail and head look very pale. Juvenile similar to adult but with faint barring on tail and less uniform coloration overall.

LONG-LEGGED BUZZARD
Buteo rufinus

THE LONG-LEGGED BUZZARD is essentially a bird of North Africa and western central Asia; in Europe it is perhaps most easily seen in Greece and European Turkey between April and August. Compared to the Common Buzzard, the Long-legged Buzzard looks large, pale and relatively long-winged. In good light, the rufous coloration is a useful identification feature as is the uniformly pale, unbarred tail. Long-legged Buzzards seem more inclined than other buzzard species to spend long periods of time perched on posts and rocks.

BIRD FACTS

VOICE Mewing call, similar to that of Buzzard
LENGTH 50–65cm
WINGSPAN 130–150cm
WEIGHT 800–1,100g
HABITAT Arid mountainous terrain and semi-desert
NEST Twiggy mound built on cliff ledge or crag
EGGS 3–4; pale greenish-white with darker blotching
FOOD Mainly small mammals and reptiles

adult

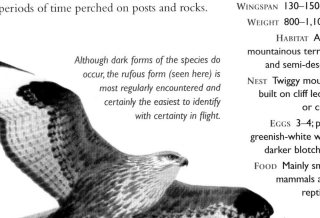

Although dark forms of the species do occur, the rufous form (seen here) is most regularly encountered and certainly the easiest to identify with certainty in flight.

adult

HONEY BUZZARD

Pernis apivorus

BIRD FACTS

VOICE Thin, mournful call, seldom heard

LENGTH 50–60cm

WINGSPAN 135–160cm

WEIGHT 500–1,000g

HABITAT Breeds in mature woodland

NEST In tree, often built on an existing nest

EGGS 2; whitish with red or chocolate markings

FOOD Mainly bee and wasp larvae but also other large insects and occasionally small mammals

WITHIN THEIR BREEDING range, Honey Buzzards are comparatively easy to see in flight, since they frequently soar over the forests and woods favoured as nesting sites with characteristically flat wings. When not in the air, however, they are secretive and seldom seen, even when feeding. In certain European locations (Falsterbo in Sweden and the Bosphorus in Turkey) huge numbers of Honey Buzzards can be seen at migration times. Passage migrants sometimes occur outside the usual breeding range. The species overwinters in sub-Saharan Africa.

Colour rather variable but usually dark brown above and pale underneath with dark barring. Seen from below in flight, wings are long and broad, tail is relatively long and head proportionately long and cuckoo-like. Shows pale throat but heavy barring from neck to base of tail; tail itself has several dark bars and conspicuous dark terminal band. On wings, flight feathers have dark tips and are barred, as are coverts. Dark patches on forewing are characteristic. At close range, pale head, yellow eyes (brown in juveniles) and yellow legs can be seen.

Migrating flock.

juvenile

ABOVE: *Adult male, drinking*; BELOW: *adult male*

TOP: *adult male*; ABOVE: *adult female*

The Osprey is a large, long-winged bird of prey, looking very pale below. Dark primaries and carpal patches give the underwing a distinctive pattern. Females and juveniles have a darker breast band on a buff background. The long tail has a broad, dark terminal band and three to four narrower dark bands.

OSPREY
Pandion haliaetus

AN OSPREY CIRCLING over a lake may resemble a large immature gull until it sights prey, when it will hover with deep, powerful wingbeats and dangling legs. It descends from its hunting flight in stages until ready to dive, which it does at high speed, sometimes disappearing below the surface before emerging with its catch. Both sexes share the care of the young, with the male doing most of the fishing while the female broods the chicks. Young birds will linger in the breeding area after the parents have migrated south, but will follow them after a month to the overwintering grounds in tropical Africa. The Osprey is found, either as a breeding or overwintering bird, all around the world and is one of the most widespread birds of prey; in Europe it is confined mainly to the north and Scandinavia.

BIRD FACTS

VOICE Shrill piping and yelping calls

LENGTH 55–69cm

WINGSPAN 145–160cm

WEIGHT 1.1–1.65kg

HABITAT Rivers, lakes, coastal areas

NEST Large; branches and twigs, moss lined; in tree

EGGS 2–3; white with red-brown spots and blotches

FOOD Fish

adult

The Osprey hits the water at high speed when fishing; if the fish is too large the Osprey will let it go, but birds have been known to drown as a result of claws catching in bones or scales.

adult

adult

DID YOU KNOW?

To help them grip fish Osprey have specially adapted talons that are long, of equal length and spiny below; large prey are turned to face forwards before the Osprey flies off, presumably to assist streamlined passage through the air.

The big stick nest is added to each year; it is usually built at the top of a pine tree.

HEN HARRIER

Circus cyaneus

ALTHOUGH CAPABLE OF rapid, direct flight, the flight pattern more usually associated with the Hen Harrier is a combination of leisurely wingbeats and long glides. In windy conditions, the birds seldom have to flap their wings, holding them instead in a pronounced 'V' shape. Because the Hen Harrier flies so low over the ground, it is easy to lose sight of when it is quartering over broken ground. Although highly territorial in the breeding season, during the winter months Hen Harriers will often roost communally, with up to a dozen birds flying into a chosen, sheltered spot at dusk.

VOICE Rapid, chattering 'ke-ke-ke' heard in nesting territory; otherwise silent

LENGTH 45–50cm

WINGSPAN 100–120cm

WEIGHT 300–550g

HABITAT Breeds on northern and upland moors and bogs; in winter, in lowland, open terrain, often coastal

NEST On ground, usually in heather, lined with rushes and grasses

EGGS 4–5; bluish-white, occasionally with reddish marks

FOOD Small mammals, birds and insects

Male has mainly pale-grey plumage, feathers on breast and belly being palest of all. Wingtips contrastingly black and shows conspicuous white rump in flight. At close range and when perched reveals yellow iris, black-tipped yellow bill and yellow legs. Female has brown plumage with owl-like facial disc and streaked underparts; shows conspicuous white rump in flight and strongly barred tail and underwing. Juvenile similar to female.

Adult male is mainly pale grey.

female

male

female

Adult female and juvenile are very similar.

MONTAGU'S HARRIER

Circus pygargus

THE MONTAGU'S HARRIER'S favoured hunting method is to fly low over the ground, its skilled use of breezes enabling it to fly at strikingly slow speeds. A tell-tale rustle will cause it to swerve in mid-flight and plunge, talons first, to the ground. Voles and mice are important food items but lizards, insects and small birds are also eaten, particularly in southern Europe. Seen near the nest, Montagu's Harriers circle and soar, pairs also performing dramatic food passes in mid-air. The species is a summer visitor to Europe and overwinters in Africa.

VOICE High-pitched 'yik-yik-yik' over breeding ground; otherwise silent

LENGTH 40–45cm

WINGSPAN 105–120cm

WEIGHT 300–400g

HABITAT Uses variety of habitats during breeding season including wetlands, arable fields, young plantations, heaths and moors

NEST On ground, lined with grasses

EGGS 4–5; pale bluish-white with faint rusty markings

FOOD Small mammals, birds, reptiles

IDENTIFICATION

Both sexes are superficially similar to Hen Harrier but wings look proportionately longer and more pointed. Male has mainly pale-grey plumage, palest on breast and belly. Seen from below, shows extensive black wingtips, two black wingbars and fainter, reddish wingbars on coverts; seen from above, has black wingtips, single black wingbar and white rump, less conspicuous than male Hen Harrier's. Female very similar to female Hen Harrier and best told by smaller white rump and wing shape. Juvenile similar to female but, seen from below, body and wing coverts reddish-orange.

Male has greyish plumage with black wingtips and black bars on underwing.

Female has white rump like female Hen Harrier, but is smaller; wings also look more pointed.

male

female

MARSH HARRIER

Circus aeruginosus

Graceful bird of prey with relatively long wings and long tail. Occasionally seen perched but more usually observed in flight low over ground, often with legs dangling. Seen from above, male has dark-brown back and wing coverts, which contrast with blue-grey flight feathers and tail. Wingtips black, and head and leading edge of innerwing pale grey-buff. Seen from below, underwing blue-grey except for black wingtips, body dark brown and tail grey. Female has mostly chocolate-brown plumage except for pale-buff forehead and cap, throat and leading edge to innerwing. Juvenile resembles female but pale markings less distinct.

WITH WINGS HELD in a pronounced 'V', Marsh Harriers quarter the reedbeds in a leisurely fashion, dropping down occasionally to catch a frog or small bird. They seldom fly more than a few metres above the height of the reeds when hunting. When courting and nesting, however, the male sometimes circles to a considerable height above his territory and will perform dramatic, stooping display flights. When the young have hatched, patient observers may even see spectacular food passes where the female takes to the air and turns upside down to receive prey from the male's talons.

BIRD FACTS

VOICE A plaintive, shrill 'kweeoo'

LENGTH 50–55cm

WINGSPAN 115–130cm

WEIGHT 500–800g

HABITAT Reedbeds and wetlands; sometimes over nearby farmland

NEST Bulky nest of reeds and twigs built among reeds

EGGS 4–5; bluish-white, often stained

FOOD Amphibians, birds and small mammals

RIGHT: Female's plumage is mostly brown.
LEFT: Male takes at least three years to acquire pale parts of plumage.

BELOW: Male (below) and female displaying.

BLACK-SHOULDERED KITE

Elanus caeruleus

IN SPAIN AND Portugal Black-shouldered Kites are mainly year-round residents that start nesting comparatively early in the year, sometimes in February. Although they favour open terrain, the presence of scattered trees and bushes is essential to the species. Nests are built among the branches but the trees also serve as vantage points for these keen-eyed raptors, which spend a large part of the day perched, scanning the ground below for the tell-tale movements of lizards and other prey. Nowadays, telegraph poles and overhead wires are also used as lookouts. Seen well in good light there can be no mistaking a Black-shouldered Kite. A distant flight view in poor light can be misleading, however, as the bird sometimes hovers like a Kestrel or glides and quarters like a Short-eared Owl.

Sexes similar. Upperparts mostly pale grey and underparts white. Head looks superficially owl-like and has staring red eyes with black 'eyebrows'. Has black-tipped yellow bill and yellow legs. In flight, which is buoyant and graceful, black wingtips and black on leading edge of innerwing look conspicuous. Often hovers or glides with wings in 'V' shape.

juvenile

Seen perched, looks somewhat large-headed and short-tailed; black patch on innerwing shows as a black 'shoulder'.

adult

BIRD FACTS

VOICE Mostly silent but utters thin scream in alarm
LENGTH 31–35cm
WINGSPAN 75–83cm
WEIGHT 230g
HABITAT Dry, open country with scattered trees
NEST Twig platform built in tree
EGGS 3–4; buff
FOOD Reptiles, small mammals and insects

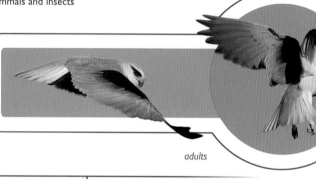

adults

BLACK KITE

Milvus migrans

adult

AS ITS SCIENTIFIC name suggests, the Black Kite is a migratory species and summer visitor to Europe, arriving in April or May and leaving again in August and September to overwinter in sub-Saharan Africa. Its range includes much of mainland Europe as far north as Germany; it is absent from Britain and Scandinavia as a breeding species but is seen as a rare passage migrant, mainly in spring. With eyes ever on the look-out for an easy meal, Black Kites glide in a leisurely manner over lakes, dipping to the surface to grasp a dead fish and making off with heavy wingbeats. In some parts of their range, Black Kites are associated with people, making a handsome living off discarded food and rubbish. In such circumstances, they often become bold and will visit markets and rubbish dumps with confidence.

BIRD FACTS

VOICE Gull-like whinnying call
LENGTH 55–60cm
WINGSPAN 145–165cm
WEIGHT 650–900g
HABITAT Wooded lakes and open country
NEST Twig platform in tree; sometimes in loose colonies
EGGS 2–3; white with red spotting
FOOD Scavenger, but will take small mammals, insects etc.

adult

Wings relatively long and broad and held flat when circling; tail is constantly twisted in flight to assist control.

IDENTIFICATION

In flight most easily confused with female Marsh Harrier. Sexes similar. Plumage mainly dark brown and can look all black in poor light. Head rather paler than body. Has black-tipped yellow bill and yellow legs. Tail forked, but not as deeply as Red Kite's.

adult

Sexes similar. Plumage mainly reddish-brown with paler head and deeply forked tail. Has black-tipped yellow bill and yellow legs. In flight, soars effortlessly, often with wings slightly kinked forwards. Seen from below, body and leading edge of innerwing are reddish. Wings are long and show translucent whitish patch near tips; tail is pale rufous.

adult

RED KITE
Milvus milvus

RED KITES HAVE a somewhat patchy distribution in Europe, being most common and widespread on the Iberian peninsula and across much of central France. Birds in the western part of the range are generally resident, while those in the north and east are summer visitors. Few birds of prey are more impressive in flight than the Red Kite. In good light the bird's colours are striking and, in flight, the observer can only marvel at its mastery of the air as it glides effortlessly overhead. Although Red Kites will hunt for earthworms and will snatch a small mammal if the opportunity arises, much of their diet, particularly during the winter months, consists of carrion. This puts them at risk from farmers who lace dead carcasses with poisons, not knowing what will come and eat them.

adult

BIRD FACTS

VOICE Shrill, quavering 'weoo-weoo-weoo'

LENGTH 60–65cm

WINGSPAN 155–185cm

WEIGHT 850–1,000g

HABITAT Typically associated with wooded valleys adjacent to areas of farmland or open country

NEST Stick and mud platform built in tree

EGGS 3–4; whitish but variably marked

FOOD Small mammals, birds, earthworms, carrion

FAR LEFT: *From below, rusty red body and underwing coverts contrast distinctively with pale head and white wing patches; wingtips are black.*

LEFT: *Seen from above, tail is orange-red, and brown innerwings contrast with dark flight feathers.*

LEVANT SPARROWHAWK

Accipiter brevipes

THE LEVANT SPARROWHAWK has a limited breeding range in Europe, but on migration passes through the Bosphorus in spring and autumn. Its over-wintering grounds are not known, but presumed to be in Africa. Levant Sparrowhawks favour warm lowland and coastal districts. Habitats chosen might include light woodland or olive groves, or farmland with only scattered trees. Levant Sparrowhawks do not use mid-air surprise attacks to catch prey, but circle at low level before dropping to catch prey on the ground.

Dashing raptor, superficially similar to Sparrowhawk. Adult male seen in flight appears very pale underneath except for pinkish flush to breast, black wingtips and dark barring on tail. At rest, head and back appear uniformly blue-grey; shows white throat, white vent and faint pinkish barring on breast and belly. Adult female similar to adult male but barring on underparts more prominent. When seen in flight from below, black wingtips contrast with pale wings. Juvenile recalls adult female but has teardrop-shaped dark spots and streaks on breast and belly; underwings show dark barring.

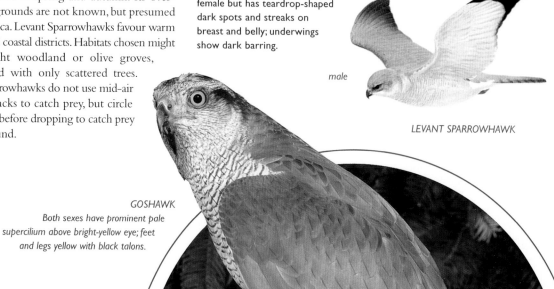

male

LEVANT SPARROWHAWK

BIRD FACTS

VOICE Harsh screaming call uttered near nest

LENGTH 33–36cm

WINGSPAN 65–75cm

WEIGHT 170–210g (male), 220–250g (female)

HABITAT Warm, dry woodland and farmland

NEST Twiggy structure on branch of tree

EGGS 3–5; pale green with faint darker markings

FOOD Mainly insects and lizards

GOSHAWK
Both sexes have prominent pale supercilium above bright-yellow eye; feet and legs yellow with black talons.

GOSHAWK

Accipiter gentilis

THE BEST TIME of year to look for Goshawks is in the early spring, in the early morning, when pairs display above their territories. Birds can be seen circling and stooping, often with their white undertail feathers fluffed out like a powder puff. At other times, Goshawks are generally shy and solitary, spending much of their time sitting un-obtrusively in cover. When prey is sighted, however, the Goshawk's flight is rapid and dashing, the bird often gliding at high speed through the trees or just above the tree canopy.

BIRD FACTS

VOICE Rapid, hoarse 'gek-gek-gek' heard at nest; otherwise silent

LENGTH 50–60cm

WINGSPAN 125–150cm

WEIGHT 600–900g (male); 1–1.4kg (female)

HABITAT Extensive forests, often of pine or beech

NEST Substantial stick platform, built in tree

EGGS 3–4; bluish-white

FOOD Birds, especially pigeons, squirrels, etc.

IDENTIFICATION

Large, dashing hawk, the female similar in size to Buzzard. Smaller male can be confused with female Sparrowhawk but note Goshawk's bulkier body, shorter tail relative to body size and longer wings, often held in an 'S' curve. Seen from below, both sexes look pale with grey barring on body, wings and tail; fluffy white feathers at base of tail often conspicuous. Both sexes have rather similar grey-brown upperparts. Juvenile has streaked underparts and less uniform upperparts.

female

male

DID YOU KNOW?

Goshawks are resident across most of their range, but birds in the far north and east move south and west in the autumn.

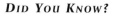

Male has blue-grey upperparts and whitish underparts bearing strong reddish-orange barring on body and underwing coverts. Undertail feathers white and tail barred. Female has grey-brown upperparts and whitish underparts with grey-brown barring. At close range, both sexes show yellow legs and black-tipped yellow bill; iris of male orange, that of female yellow. Juvenile similar to female but browner and streaked below.

SPARROWHAWK

Accipiter nisus

SPARROWHAWKS ARE OFTEN seen in low-level, dashing flight, but they will also occasionally soar, showing their short, rounded wings and long tail. The species has suffered greatly at the hands of man, both from the use of DDT and other agrochemicals and from sportsmen. Both these areas are now subject to tighter control, however, and numbers have recovered. Sparrowhawks are resident across most of their range although birds from the north of the region migrate south in the autumn.

BIRD FACTS

VOICE Harsh 'kek-kek-kek-kek'

LENGTH 30–40cm

WINGSPAN 55–75cm

WEIGHT 150–300g

HABITAT Mixed woodland, farmland with hedgerows; increasingly in urban areas

NEST Stick platform built in tree; may use foundation of another species' nest

EGGS 4–5; whitish

FOOD Small birds caught on the wing

Adult male is considerably smaller than female.

ABOVE: *juvenile*

adult male

LEFT: *male*

DID YOU KNOW?

Sparrowhawks catch prey either by surprise attack from a concealed perch or flight close to a woodland edge.

Adult female chasing Chaffinches.

HOBBY

Falco subbuteo

THE HOBBY IS expert at catching large insects like dragonflies on the wing. The prey is seized by the talons in a downwards stoop and eaten in flight, unless it is a small bird, which will be taken to a perch and plucked. Hobbies often hunt late into the evening, when bats may also be taken. Prey is usually captured high up, not low over the ground, and a high perch is normally chosen as an observation point before making the feeding flight. Nesting occurs late in the season so that the young can take advantage of the abundance of unskilled fledgling passerines. Hobbies overwinter in sub-equatorial Africa.

In flight, the wings look long and pointed, and the tail appears short, giving the impression of a large Swift. Adult's white cheeks and moustachial stripes show well in sitting birds, as do the red 'trousers' and vent. The streaked underside looks dark in flight. Males and females are almost identical, apart from the smaller size of the male, but juveniles are browner with pale feather-edging and a pale crown, and they lack the red colour.

BIRD FACTS

VOICE Sharp, scolding 'kew kew kew kew kew'

LENGTH 28–35cm

WINGSPAN 75–90cm

WEIGHT 130–340g

HABITAT Open habitats, marshes, heathlands

NEST In old Crow nest in high tree

EGGS 3; brownish-yellow with reddish spots yellowing with age

FOOD Insects caught on wing; a few small birds and bats

adult

The hobby flies on swift wingbeats, interspersed with short glides when hunting.

adult

adult

DID YOU KNOW?

Hobbies are widespread summer visitors to Europe, being most frequently seen in warm, open habitats such as heaths and extensive marshes.

Europe's smallest bird of prey, with a neat, light outline. Wings appear short and relatively broad but tail looks long and square-ended. Resembles small Peregrine. Male is greyish-blue above with reddish-buff underside. Female is noticeably larger than male, dark brown above and strongly patterned below. Juvenile resembles female but is darker with white patches on nape.

MERLIN

Falco columbarius

THE MERLIN'S SMALL size is compensated for by its strong, dashing flight and ability to startle small birds by coming upon them suddenly from its low hunting flight. It will sometimes soar or hang in the wind high overhead and can even hover briefly, but will normally keep low down. The Merlin's preferred ground nest site exposes it to danger from predators such as foxes (and in some parts of the region game-keepers), but new birds will nest year after year in nests where the previous occupants have been destroyed. In winter most Merlins move to estuaries, coastal marshes and open agricultur-al land where there are many small birds such as waders, pipits, finches and larks.

BIRD FACTS

VOICE Shrill
'kek kek kek'
LENGTH 25–30cm
WINGSPAN 60–65cm
WEIGHT 160–220g
HABITAT Moorland, upland bogs; winter on lowland heaths, coastal marshes
NEST On ground in heather and bracken; sometimes in old Crow nest in low tree
EGGS 3–5; light buff with dense brown-red blotches
FOOD Small birds

male

juvenile

male

DID YOU KNOW?

When not hunting, the Merlin will sit on a low perch where there is a sweeping view of the moorland, adopting a very upright posture.

The Merlin's hunting flight can be as low as 1m above the ground.

female

PEREGRINE FALCON

Falco peregrinus

FOLLOWING A CRASH in its numbers, Europe's Peregrine population is now recovering again, and birds can turn turn up in almost any habitat. Numbers are highest in northwest Europe, but Peregrines breed in much of the rest of Europe where suitable cliffs for nesting occur. Prey, in the form of a medium-sized bird like a Rock Dove, may be spotted from a lofty perch or from the air, and once identified it will be attacked by a high-speed stoop. Near the nest, aerial food passes may be witnessed: the male will present the female with prey as part of courtship or to feed to the young.

Large falcon with a compact body shape and broad-based, pointed wings. Shallow wingbeats with springy wingtips are characteristic, as is the dramatic high-speed stoop for prey from a great height. Adult is steely grey above with a paler grey rump. Has bold facial patterning with dark moustachial stripes. Juvenile is slightly slimmer and browner than adult, with pale feather edging on mantle and bold streaking below; facial markings less distinct than on adult and cere is grey-blue, not yellow.

BIRD FACTS

VOICE Shrill 'kek kek kek kek'

LENGTH 39–50cm

WINGSPAN 95–115cm

WEIGHT 600–1,300g

HABITAT Open, upland habitats; sea cliffs, coasts in winter

NEST On cliff ledge, sometimes high buildings; uses abandoned bird's nests

EGGS 3–4; creamy buff with many reddish-brown markings

FOOD Birds, mostly taken on the wing

DID YOU KNOW?

Small birds are often killed by the impact of the talons, but larger birds may be taken away to a perch to be killed and eaten.

The flight of a Peregrine across an estuary will cause panic among gulls and waders, which will take to the air with the result that one at least will end up as prey.

adult

Adult is steely grey above with a paler grey rump and pale underside with dark barring.

adult

adult

adult

Peregrines attack prey with a breathtaking stoop.

Frequently seen hovering with a characteristic long-tailed silhouette and downward-looking head. Male is colourful with spotted brick-red back, black primaries and grey tail and head. Female is more uniform with heavily spotted chestnut plumage, a barred tail and brownish streaked head. At a distance the sexes can appear similar. Juvenile resembles female but is more streaked on the underside.

male

KESTREL
Falco tinnunculus

THE KESTREL IS the commonest bird of prey over most of Europe. When in direct flight, the wingbeats are fast and shallow with a few glides, but the most distinctive behaviour is the ability to hover in a fixed position on rapidly beating wings or remain motionless on an updraught. When prey is spotted the Kestrel drops vertically. Prey is usually carried away to be eaten on a perch. Kestrels also hunt by sitting on wires and posts, and they will stalk earthworms on the ground as well. Kestrels have excellent eyesight and can continue hunting in very low light.

BIRD FACTS

VOICE Piercing 'kee-kee-kee', especially at nest site

LENGTH 33–39cm

WINGSPAN 65–75cm

WEIGHT 130–300g

HABITAT Cultivated country, heaths, moorland, roadsides and towns

NEST Old Crow nests, tree-holes, cliffs and building ledges; little nest material

EGGS 3–6; buff-white, almost covered with reddish-brown speckles

FOOD Mainly small mammals; some birds, reptiles, insects

Male is colourful and distinctive.

DID YOU KNOW?

Its hovering flight distinguishes the Kestrel immediately from that other common and widespread raptor, the Sparrowhawk.

Female (BELOW) has mainly chestnut plumage.

Perched Kestrels have a noticeably upright posture.

male

male

LESSER KESTREL

Falco naumanni

LESSER KESTRELS NEST colonially in old buildings and on rock faces and are often seen hunting together when there is an abundance of flying insects, their favourite prey. They often nest near human habitation and show little fear unless directly persecuted. Lesser Kestrels hover far less than Kestrels and have a lighter, more agile flight pattern. Food may be caught on the wing in the air or pounced on, but it is normally eaten in the air. Most Lesser Kestrels overwinter in Africa, but a few remain near the breeding sites all year, especially those in the southern part of the range.

BIRD FACTS

VOICE Rasping two- or three-note calls and trilling notes at colonies

LENGTH 29–32cm

WINGSPAN 58–72cm

WEIGHT 90–200g

HABITAT Mediterranean region; cultivated country, villages

NEST In hole in old building; colonial nester

EGGS 3–5; white with pale yellow-red spots

FOOD Insects

male (left) and female (right)

Small falcon with narrow wings and a longish slender tail. Male is strongly coloured with unspotted chestnut back, blue-grey innerwing and hood and pale-grey tail with dark terminal band. Female is slightly larger than male and has barred tail. Juvenile resembles female. In all birds claws are pale, not dark as in Kestrel.

Female has chestnut colouring and shows dark spotting on upperparts; primaries are dark.

Male has blue-grey head and unspotted chestnut back.

LANNER FALCON

Falco biarmicus

THIS LARGE FALCON is rare in Europe. Lanners often hunt in pairs, covering vast areas and ones where few other birds of prey occur. They sometimes skim low over the ground to startle a ground-dwelling bird or small mammal, but they will also pursue birds through the air. Lanners normally take over the nest of another bird, often evicting resident Crows or Ravens. They are mostly resident, making trips to their nesting sites outside the breeding season from time to time to check for intruders.

BIRD FACTS

VOICE Similar to, but quieter version of, Peregrine's call

LENGTH 43–52cm

WINGSPAN 95–115cm

WEIGHT 500–900g

HABITAT Mediterranean region; dry open country, mountains

NEST Rock ledge or tree; uses old nest of Crow or Raven

EGGS 3–4; dull white with yellow, red or brown blotches

FOOD Birds, some small mammals, reptiles, insects

IDENTIFICATION

Similar to Peregrine, but slightly slimmer with longer tail and uniformly broad wings with more rounded wingtips. Male has a rusty nape and dark blue-brown mantle with a pale, spotted underside. The larger female is similar but has a buff nape and more boldly spotted underside. In both sexes, the moustachial stripe is less pronounced than in the Peregrine. Juvenile is darker brown above than adult and more buff below with heavier brownish-black streaks. Flight feathers look pale on underwing.

Lanners lack the speed and agility of some falcons, but will still catch birds in flight.

adult

SAKER FALCON

Falco cherrug

THE SAKER FALCON may be seen circling high up with wings held straight and tail closed, or even hovering laboriously; in active flight, however, it has powerful wingbeats and may make its attack from a low-level flight path, dropping on to a small mammal at great speed. The Saker favours open habitats where hunting for birds is easy. It may spend long periods on a high perch watching for prey, but it will also range over 20km from its nesting site in search of food. This is a rare bird in Europe and is normally sedentary.

Plumage is overall much 'warmer' brown than similarly sized Lanner Falcon.

IDENTIFICATION

Sexes similar, although females are larger than males. Adult is greyish-brown above with pale-fringed feathers on the mantle. Head is noticeably pale with a lightly streaked crown. Underside is streaked, with the boldest markings on the flanks and 'trousers'. Most individuals show contrast on the underwing between pale flight feathers and darker coverts, although some very pale birds occur, where this is not obvious. Juvenile is generally darker than adult with bolder markings on the underside.

BIRD FACTS

VOICE Harsh 'kek kek kek'

LENGTH 48–57cm

WINGSPAN 110–125cm

WEIGHT 750–1,300g

HABITAT Open country, steppe

NEST On cliff or in tree

EGGS 3–5; buff, spotted with dark brown and black

FOOD Small mammals, birds, lizards, large insects

IDENTIFICATION

Some birds, mostly from high Arctic, are almost pure white, but dark lead-grey and brownish birds also occur in southern part of range. Southern birds have heavily barred plumage with pale patches and a pale forehead, darker eye patch and moustachial streak. The white underparts are heavily marked with spots and streaks, and the underwing shows almost translucent panels contrasting with darker coverts. Adult white high Arctic forms have almost no spots except on mantle, although dark tips to primaries can be seen; juveniles of this form are similar to adults but have black 'teardrop' marks on underparts.

White phase birds show hardly any spotting but do have dark wingtips.

GYR FALCON

Falco rusticolus

THE POWERFUL WINGBEATS of the Gyr Falcon enable it to fly quickly, low over the ground, and flush birds that it can then pursue with ease and catch in flight. It will, however, also drop on to small mammals on the ground. It often sits on a low rock lookout between irregular feeding forays. Gyr Falcons will also feed on carrion, which enables them to remain in the Arctic throughout the year, although birds from the most northerly regions will move south. Juveniles mostly disperse south to spend the winter along coasts and lowland plains.

Dark phase birds occur in the southern part of the range.

BIRD FACTS

VOICE A hoarse 'kee-a kee-a kee-a'

LENGTH 55–60cm

WINGSPAN 125–155cm

WEIGHT 1.1–1.75kg

HABITAT Arctic tundra, high mountains; high Arctic seabird colonies

NEST On cliff ledge in nest of Raven or Rough-legged Buzzard

EGGS 3–4; pale yellowish-white with variable red or dark red spots

FOOD Medium-sized birds, some small mammals

dark phase adult

RED-FOOTED FALCON

Falco vespertinus

RED-FOOTED FALCONS ARE frequently seen perching on a post or overhead wire, from which short forays are made to catch prey; occasionally, however, acrobatic flights are made, sometimes to high altitudes in search of high-flying insects. Breeding usually takes place late in the season when birds such as Rooks vacate their nests; nesting is often colonial and so birds are usually seen hunting together. Red-footed Falcons seem indifferent to human presence and may nest in close proximity to farms or villages. Red-footed Falcons are summer visitors to Europe and overwinter in southern Africa.

A small falcon resembling a short-tailed Kestrel at a distance. Male is distinctive with dark-grey plumage, pale, silvery primaries, deep rufous-red vent and thighs and red feet, eyering and cere; immature male similar to adult male but has paler underparts and pale face and throat. Adult female has orange or pale-yellow crown and underside, and barred, dark grey upperparts. Juveniles are streaked below and have darker, blotched upperparts and a barred tail, and like female have dark eye patches resembling a highwayman's mask.

BIRD FACTS

VOICE Highly vocal; 'kew kew kew' flight calls

LENGTH 28–31cm

WINGSPAN 65–75cm

WEIGHT 130–195g

HABITAT Open heaths, cultivated land, steppe, marshland

NEST Colonial; old Rook nests

EGGS 3–4; buff, heavily marked with spots and blotches

FOOD Insects, some small birds, frogs

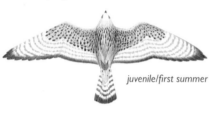
juvenile/first summer

immature male, first spring

immature male, late first summer

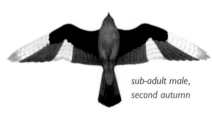
sub-adult male, second autumn

adult male

female

female

female

Adult female has bright orangey head and underside.

adult male

pale morph

ELEONORA'S FALCON
Falco eleonorae

ELEONORA'S FALCONS ARE at home on isolated, windy headlands in the Mediterranean, occurring from the Balearic Islands and Morocco eastwards to Cyprus. They appear late in the season when all other migrants have already arrived and commenced breeding. They delay nesting until late in the summer so that their young can capitalise on the offspring of migrant songbirds returning south to Africa. As well as taking small birds, Eleonora's Falcons will prey on large insects and occasionally bats, most prey being caught on the wing, and usually late in the day or very early in the morning. They will also hunt on clear, moonlit nights when large numbers of birds may be migrating. Eleonora's Falcons overwinter in East Africa and Madagascar.

BIRD FACTS

VOICE Hoarse, kestrel-like chatter; not often heard
LENGTH 36–42cm
WINGSPAN 90–105cm
WEIGHT 350–400g
HABITAT Sea cliffs and headlands, arid deserts
NEST On cliff ledge under overhang, in rock crevice or under dense bush; no nest material
EGGS 2–3; white or pale buff with brownish markings
FOOD Small birds, bats, insects

IDENTIFICATION

Appears rather slender and dainty but is actually larger than the Hobby. Tail longer than on other small falcons. Wings long and slender, giving an angular outline in flight. Pale and dark morphs occur, pale morph being three times more numerous. Dark morph looks almost black in flight; pale morph shows pale cheek, dark moustachial stripe and dark, streaked underside. Underwing shows contrasting dark coverts and paler primaries in both morphs. Juvenile similar to light morph adult but with buffish underparts and heavy streaks.

dark morph

Eleonora's Falcons' flight is light and acrobatic, perfect for intercepting swallows and martins, and they often give long displays over their nesting sites.

dark morph

pale morph

PHEASANT
Phasianus colchicus

ORIGINALLY INTRODUCED TO Europe from Asia, pheasants are now widespread and well established. Several strains are also regularly released for shooting, leading to a great variety of plumages being seen. Pheasants forage on the ground searching for plant food, but roost in trees at night. The males give a characteristic two-note crow, which can be heard up to 1.5km away, in order to establish their territory. They have a more frenzied call in response to danger and also when flying up to roost, when the whirring wingbeats may also be heard. Startled Pheasants can fly rapidly upwards from a standing start, but cannot sustain this for long.

Male has brightly coloured, iridescent plumage, with red wattles and glossy green head, some showing well-developed 'ear tufts'. White collar is present in some individuals. Tail very long and barred. Purplish-chestnut plumage shows scalloped pattern due to bold markings on each feather. Female has paler brownish-buff plumage with strong pattern on upperparts and flanks. Barred tail is shorter. Juvenile resembles female, but with duller, less strongly marked plumage.

purple form

female

female

LEFT: *Male, landing.*

male

LEFT: *female;* BELOW: *male*

GOLDEN PHEASANT

Chrysolophus pictus

SOLITARY GOLDEN PHEASANTS seen in Europe are invariably escapes. In a few areas in Britain, however, birds have been released in sufficient numbers to form seemingly stable feral populations. These are thought to be the only viable non-captive populations outside China. As in their native land, Golden Pheasants are extremely difficult to see in the mature conifer plantations or rhododendron thickets they favour in Britain. They are seldom flushed and usually retreat into cover by running long before an observer could hope to detect their presence.

IDENTIFICATION

Large, well-marked pheasant. Adult male has mainly orange-red body plumage except for yellow on crown and areas of blue and green on mantle and wings; shows conspicuous barring on nape. Tail broad and extremely long; brown with intricate pattern of fine, black lines. Adult female has roughly similar proportions to male. Body plumage mainly buffish-brown with dark barring. Juvenile similar to adult female but with shorter tail.

BIRD FACTS

VOICE Male utters crowing call during breeding season; otherwise both sexes rather silent

LENGTH Male 85–115cm; female 65–85cm

WINGSPAN 65–75cm

WEIGHT 550–700g

HABITAT Mountain woodland and scrub in natural range; birds introduced into Europe favour conifer plantations

NEST Shallow depression in ground

EGGS 5–10; white

FOOD Seeds, plant shoots and insects

LADY AMHERST'S PHEASANT

Chrysolophus amherstiae

IN ITS NATIVE China, Lady Amherst's Pheasant lives in woodlands and scrub at altitudes ranging from 2,000 to 4,600m and often feeds on bamboo shoots. It has been introduced into Britain at various times since 1900; today, it is on the verge of extinction in the wild. During the breeding season Lady Amherst's Pheasant is a secretive bird, running into cover to escape from danger, so despite its colourful appearance it is difficult to find. In winter, birds gather in larger groups but are still very secretive. They fly up into trees to roost at night, settling just before dark, usually without any calls or contact notes. Males may guard one or two females, which find a very secluded site for the nest on the ground.

BIRD FACTS

VOICE Hissing 'su-ik-ik-ik' calls at dusk roosts

LENGTH 60–120cm

WINGSPAN 70–85cm

WEIGHT 600–800g

HABITAT Mixed woodland with dense undergrowth

NEST Shallow scrape with some lining, under thick cover

EGGS 6–11; glossy buff or creamy white

FOOD Seeds, shoots, buds, roots, some insects

LADY AMHERST'S PHEASANT
The male's striking neck cape is fanned out in its courtship display, but the bird's secretive habits make this difficult to observe; the wing coverts have a bluish sheen in good light.

GOLDEN PHEASANT
male

GOLDEN PHEASANT
female

IDENTIFICATION

A very long-tailed pheasant with blue-grey legs and feet. Male is strikingly marked with dark glossy green and white, and has a colourful yellow rump with red at the base of the tail. Females are smaller with cinnamon-brown plumage and black barring on all feathers. Juvenile is similar to adult female but duller without rufous colouring on the crown.

RED GROUSE

Lagopus lagopus scoticus

RED GROUSE ARE restricted to northern Britain and Ireland and are most often seen when flushed from dense heather; the low, gliding flight alternating with bursts of rapid wingbeats, and the frantic call, are all most visitors will observe. In spring, males take up territories and stand on a raised hillock to call, but females are far more secretive. In very harsh weather Red Grouse will move to lower ground. Males guard territories in winter to ensure an adequate Food supply. Females need to feed well in the spring in order to breed successfully; they take some insect food, as do immature birds.

IDENTIFICATION

A plump gamebird that appears uniformly dark brown both on the ground and in flight; the wings are a dark grey-brown. Male is rich reddish-brown with red wattles and white-feathered legs. Female is pale buff-brown with pale feathered legs, but lacks the male's wattles over the eyes. Juvenile is buff-brown all over with pale feather margins.

male

WILLOW GROUSE

Lagopus lagopus lagopus

THE WILLOW GROUSE is the mainland Europe counterpart of Britain's Red Grouse. It is a wide-spread gamebird of open northern forests. Most birds are residents and do not migrate except for short distances within their ranges in search of winter food and territories. The strange laughing call of the male is sometimes uttered from within the cover of birch scrub and has a startling effect on passers-by; the calls of the female are quieter and shorter. For most of the time these are quiet birds that keep hidden.

IDENTIFICATION

A plump gamebird with liver-red to grey-brown plumage in summer and white plumage in winter. Male has red wattle over eye that is more prominent in spring, when white plumage is lost from the head first; by the end of summer male is more uniformly brown, but retains white primaries and black tail feathers, which are most obvious in flight. Female white in winter, but more tawny brown in summer than male and lacks his red wattle.

WILLOW GROUSE

winter male

summer male

summer female

RED GROUSE

male

female

male

female

Slightly smaller than Willow Grouse, which it resembles in winter, except that male has black lores in addition to red wattles. Both sexes appear all white in winter, except for black outertail feathers seen in flight. Plumage changes gradually through spring and summer, as snow melts, to more mottled grey-brown in male, and buff-brown in female. White primaries are retained in the wings, showing prominently in flight. Newly hatched young are downy and mottled buff-brown; juveniles similar to summer female but brown with darker feather edges.

PTARMIGAN

Lagopus muta

HARSH WINTER WEATHER is not as much of a problem to Ptarmigan as poor conditions in early summer, when the chicks are at their most vulnerable; these need a plentiful supply of insects. The variable plumage of the Ptarmigan helps it to blend in with the tundra as the snow recedes. Males may be seen displaying on prominent rocks with the better camouflaged females creeping around nearby. In winter, Ptarmigan form flocks, moving slowly over the snow in search of food, which they find by scratching with their feet, but as the breeding season approaches the males separate to find territories.

BIRD FACTS

VOICE Hoarse rattling 'karrrrr k k k k k'

LENGTH 34–36cm

WINGSPAN 54–60cm

WEIGHT 400–550g

HABITAT Open, stony tundra, high treeless mountain slopes

NEST Shallow scrape, sometimes sheltered by boulder; lining of moss and feathers

EGGS 5–8; rich glossy dark red with deep-brown spots, fading to yellowish-buff with black spots

FOOD Buds, shoots, berries, some insects

Nesting female.

summer male

winter male

summer male

summer female

winter male

DID YOU KNOW?

A Ptarmigan's wings are white all year – only the body plumage changes colour.

summer male

BLACK GROUSE
Tetrao tetrix

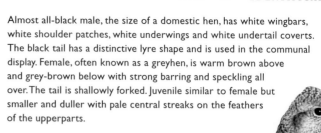

THE BLACK GROUSE prefers marginal forest areas with easy access to open areas such as bogs and moors, where it is usually seen feeding on the ground. Through the spring males may be seen displaying out in the open at dawn. When perched quietly high in a tree, however, Black Grouse can be very difficult to spot. Habitat loss and increased hunting have caused the numbers to drop in many regions. In much of their range, Black Grouse remain within their territories, but in the far north harsh weather may cause them to disperse to lower areas.

Almost all-black male, the size of a domestic hen, has white wingbars, white shoulder patches, white underwings and white undertail coverts. The black tail has a distinctive lyre shape and is used in the communal display. Female, often known as a greyhen, is warm brown above and grey-brown below with strong barring and speckling all over. The tail is shallowly forked. Juvenile similar to female but smaller and duller with pale central streaks on the feathers of the upperparts.

BIRD FACTS

VOICE Males make cooing calls and a sudden loud 'shoo-eesh'; females cackle

LENGTH 40–55cm

WINGSPAN 65–80cm

WEIGHT 800–1,250g

HABITAT Woodland close to bogs and heather moors

NEST Shallow grass-lined scrape on ground, under low bush

EGGS 6–11; glossy, pale buff or pale ochre with reddish-brown spots

FOOD Seeds, buds, berries, shoots; young eat insects

female

male

In flight, male's tail shape distinctive; female has slightly forked tail.

Adult male is unmistakable.

Adult female is greyer than female Red Grouse.

ABOVE: *female;* BELOW: *male*

Both sexes are very bulky with broad wings and tails, and strong, heavy bills. Male appears dark blackish-grey at a distance, but has glossy green chest and dark-brown wing coverts and upper mantle. Large, white patches on shoulders and whitish speckles on flanks and tail break up overall dark effect. Female has rufous-brown upperparts with chestnut patch on chest and paler-brown underside. Most of plumage is heavily barred with black above and black and white below. Juvenile resembles female but is smaller and duller; young males develop distinctive plumage in their first winter, but do not reach full size until the next year.

CAPERCAILLIE

Tetrao urogallus

THIS VERY LARGE grouse is the family member that is most tied to trees, and has an almost entirely vegetarian diet. It inhabits mature forests of pine, spruce, fir or larch and will also occur where there are birch and aspen; pine needles and other leaves form the major part of its diet. During courtship in the spring, males gather at display areas at dawn and emit very loud popping and clicking calls. At other times they are difficult to find, despite their large size, because of their tree-roosting habits. Large finger-sized droppings are clues to their presence. In rare cases the Capercaillie has hybridised with the Black Grouse.

BIRD FACTS

VOICE Very loud popping sounds, followed by 'drum roll'; various grunts and gulps

LENGTH 60–87cm

WINGSPAN 87–125cm

WEIGHT 3.5–5.5kg (male), 1.5–2.5kg (female)

HABITAT Coniferous forest with some bogs and shrubby areas

NEST Shallow depression on ground; sometimes old nest low in tree

EGGS 7–11; glossy yellowish-white with scattered brown streaks

FOOD Pine needles, shoots, some other leaves, berries

Displaying male.

female

Displaying male.

male

female

Capercaillies are sometimes flushed from their tree roosts, when the broad, rounded wings are noticeable.

adult male

adult female

DID YOU KNOW?

Birds can be found on the ground, often in the early mornings, taking grit to help their digestion.

HAZEL GROUSE

Bonasa bonasia

THE HAZEL GROUSE is a bird of dense lowland forests, found particularly where there are damp gullies and mossy hollows rich in bilberry, birch and alder, which provide fruits, seeds and buds for food. Hazel Grouse occur mainly in extensive, undisturbed lowland forests, but can be found at up to 2,000m. Becoming more scarce in France and Belgium and other parts of southern Europe, their main stronghold is now Scandinavia and northern Europe. Nests are concealed below vegetation and the Eggs are incubated by the female alone. After hatching, the young leave the nest within about 24 hours and are able to feed for themselves, although the mother stays close by and broods them at frequent intervals. After three weeks they can fly and reach buds and shoots in low branches. There is no migration in winter and so dispersal is very limited.

BIRD FACTS

VOICE High-pitched whistle, recalling Goldcrest

LENGTH 35–37cm

WINGSPAN 48–54cm

WEIGHT 370–450g

HABITAT Extensive mixed and coniferous forests

NEST On ground, under bush; grass-lined cup

EGGS 7–11; pale yellow-brown with darker red-brown speckles

FOOD Buds, shoots, fruits; some insects in summer

male

male

IDENTIFICATION

A compact gamebird with a grey rump and grey tail ending in a black and white band. Male has a black chin patch, red wattle over the eye, and a short crest. Head and neck are finely barred and underside heavily blotched. Female has a warmer brown coloration overall and is generally less boldly marked.

BLACK FRANCOLIN

Francolinus francolinus

THE BLACK FRANCOLIN is a very difficult bird to see, but its distinctive and far-carrying seven-note call, uttered from a low mound at dawn and dusk, advertises its presence. Normally it remains in thick, low cover and is difficult to flush, but in the breeding season various calls may be heard during the day and it can sometimes be glimpsed in gaps in the vegetation.

adult

BIRD FACTS

VOICE Harsh, shrill 'kek kek kek kek-ek-ek'

LENGTH 33–36cm

WINGSPAN 50–55cm

WEIGHT 400–500g

HABITAT Low-lying shrubby areas near water; dried-up river beds

NEST Shallow scrape, little lining

EGGS 8–12; glossy, pale yellowish-brown, sometimes white-spotted

FOOD Seeds, buds, roots, insects

IDENTIFICATION

In flight this partridge-sized bird shows dark outertail feathers and rich-brown, dark-barred wings. Male has a mostly black head and underside with white ear coverts and white flecks on the flanks. Wings are dark brown with black feather-centres, and tail is finely barred with black and white. There is a broad, chestnut collar. Female has a pale head, chestnut patch on neck, and overall brown plumage with black arrow-marks on all feathers. Juvenile resembles female but has dull plumage and faint markings.

ANDALUSIAN HEMIPODE

Turnix sylvatica

THE ANDALUSIAN HEMIPODE is a most elusive bird, possibly now extinct in Spain, keeping to the ground in thick cover unless flushed, when it will fly low for only a very short distance before dropping. Its smaller size, more striking markings, upright posture on landing and flight outline help distinguish it from the Quail. The normal roles of the sexes are reversed, with the male caring for the eggs and young; the more brightly coloured female initiates courtship.

Unusually, the female Hemipode is the more brightly coloured sex.

BIRD FACTS

VOICE At dawn female gives deep 'hoo hoo hoo' resembling distant cattle

LENGTH 15–16cm

WINGSPAN 25–30cm

WEIGHT 60–70g

HABITAT Dry, sandy areas with grass and scattered bushes

NEST Shallow scrape well hidden on ground in low vegetation

EGGS 4; glossy, pale buff or grey-white with black or red blotches

FOOD Seeds, insects

IDENTIFICATION

A small, secretive, Quail-like bird; adult has rusty red breast and boldly black-spotted flanks. The crown is brown and finely barred and has a creamy stripe, and the upperparts are brown with darker brown bars and cream streaks. The female is more strikingly marked than the male with overall browner colouring. Juveniles are very similar to males, but at close range show more spots on the chest and white spots on the upperparts.

When flushed, rounded shape, small head and pale underside are easy to see. Male is mostly yellowish-brown with dark brown barring on the upperside, a rufous chest and dark-streaked flanks. Head markings vary, but usually show some dark chestnut markings on the crown, through the eye, and on the cheeks and throat. Female resembles male but has less striking head markings; juvenile similar to female but has barred and spotted, not streaked, flanks.

Usually crouches but may stand higher to peer over vegetation.

DID YOU KNOW?

Quail are very widespread in Europe in the summer, especially in the warmer parts of southern Europe.

COMMON QUAIL

Coturnix coturnix

THE QUAIL GIVES its presence away by the male's persistent 'wet-my-lips' call, which is heard for hours on end, particularly around dusk, coming from the ground in dense vegetation such as a cornfield. Its reluctance to fly makes it very hard to see, and only if flushed will it take off with shallow wingbeats on a rapid flight to safety. Its more usual reaction to danger is to run, or simply squat. Quails spend the winter in sub-Saharan Africa, migrating south in small flocks; on their return from their feeding grounds, Quail sometimes overshoot their breeding grounds and end up in a variety of different habitats and more northerly locations than those in which they usually occur.

BIRD FACTS

VOICE Oboe-like 'wet-my-lips', repeated frequently
LENGTH 16–18cm
WINGSPAN 32–35cm
WEIGHT 85–120g
HABITAT Lowland grassland, agricultural land, pastures
NEST Shallow scrape in dense grassy area; some lining
EGGS 8–13; glossy whitish with brown blotches and spots
FOOD Seeds, insects

In flight, Quail shows relatively long, narrow wings.

Male has striking dark facial markings.

male

RED-LEGGED PARTRIDGE

Alectoris rufa

BIRD FACTS

VOICE Harsh repetitive 'kchoo kchoo-kchoo kchoo'

LENGTH 32–34cm

WINGSPAN 45–50cm

WEIGHT 400–550g

HABITAT Open country, farmland, lowland heaths

NEST Shallow scrape with grass lining; protected by low vegetation

EGGS 10–16; glossy, yellow or buff with reddish or grey blotches

FOOD Seeds, roots, leaves, few insects

THE RED-LEGGED PARTRIDGE prefers dry habitats, often where there is some bare ground, and avoids woodland and very wet areas. It nests on the ground and relies on finding plenty of insects when the young have first hatched. The Red-legged Partridge's call usually gives away its presence; it is heard when several birds are feeding in an area and need to keep in contact in dense vegetation.

A compact gamebird with overall greyish-brown colouring, but strongly marked flanks and head. Sexes are similar in appearance but males are larger. The head is grey and the rest of the upperparts and the chest are greyish-brown, but there is a more distinct grey band on the lower chest. The necklace meets over the bill and surrounds the white throat patch, and there is a bib of black streaks. The flanks are strongly barred with black and chestnut stripes on a white background. Juvenile lacks adult's head pattern and flank markings.

adult

adult

adult

adult

adult

CHUKAR

Alectoris chukar

BIRD FACTS

VOICE Short 'chuck' sounds; louder rhythmic call when flushed

LENGTH 32–34cm

WINGSPAN 47–52cm

WEIGHT 420–550g

HABITAT Dry, rocky mountain slopes, stony plains

NEST Shallow scrape, sheltered by rock; some lining

EGGS 8–15; glossy, cream or buff with red-brown spots

FOOD Seeds, mainly of grasses; some leaves and insects

THE CHUKAR CAN be difficult to locate when it crouches down, its greyish colouring enabling it to blend in with the background. During courtship, males show off their striped flanks to intimidate other males; they may also circle around on the ground tilting their heads and calling in order to establish dominance. Chukars rarely stray far from their home ranges, usually remaining in small groups; when flushed they fly strongly low over the ground, dropping quickly and continuing to run.

Adults have strongly patterned head and flanks, and red legs and bill.

adult

IDENTIFICATION

Compact, rounded gamebird. Sexes are very similar, showing grey heads and grey-brown upperparts, and a grey chest merging into a sandy underside. The white flanks are boldly barred with black and chestnut stripes and the black eyestripe extends down the neck to join on the chest, forming a dark necklace. Juvenile similar to adult but head and flank markings less distinct.

ROCK PARTRIDGE

Alectoris graeca

ROCK PARTRIDGES FLY only reluctantly, usually heading downhill and dropping to the ground quite quickly. They rarely stray far from their home ranges and usually live in small groups (covies). Although very similar to the Chukar, the Rock Partridge's preference for higher ground means the species are unlikely to be confused. Its calls are more varied than the Chukar's; the most frequent call is similar in pitch to the Nuthatch's.

BIRD FACTS

VOICE A four-note call and various shorter contact notes uttered by members of coveys

LENGTH 32–35cm

WINGSPAN 46–53cm

WEIGHT 500–800g

HABITAT Dry treeless mountain slopes, often south-facing

NEST Shallow scrape, sheltered by rock; some lining

EGGS 8–14; glossy, yellow-cream with reddish speckles

FOOD Leaves, buds, shoots, seeds; some insects when young

IDENTIFICATION

Very similar in appearance to the Chukar but chin and throat are pure white, not creamy buff, and the black necklace extends through the eyes and down to the base of the bill. Stripes on flanks are narrower and neater in appearance than on Chukar, and the chest and upperparts are greyer. The general impression at a distance is of very sharply defined set of markings. Juvenile similar to adult but, like on juvenile Chukar, head and flank markings are less distinct.

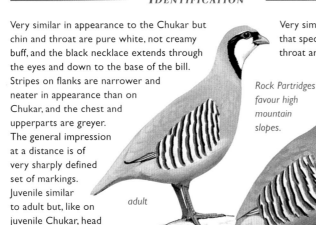

Rock Partridges favour high mountain slopes.

adult

BARBARY PARTRIDGE

Alectoris barbara

THE BARBARY PARTRIDGE is likely to have been introduced into its few sites in Europe, as the species is highly sedentary. This secretive bird remains concealed in low vegetation, usually running from danger to avoid breaking cover. If it does take to the air, the distinctive head pattern and horizontally held wings distinguish it from other partridges. The Barbary Partridge will often feed at dawn and dusk and hide during the day.

IDENTIFICATION

Very similar to Red-legged Partridge, but lacks that species' striking facial markings; the face and throat are grey and there is a collar of white spots on a dark-chestnut background, but no necklace. Most distinctive feature is the crown of dark chestnut with a light-grey supercilium. The upperparts are grey-brown with a pinkish tinge and the flanks are less boldly marked than in the Red-legged Partridge, with bars of black, buff and white.

adult

The Barbary Partridge will not fly unless approached very closely.

BIRD FACTS

VOICE Repetitive 'kchek kchek' and other harsh calls; also Curlew-like call in flight

LENGTH 32–34cm

WINGSPAN 46–49cm

WEIGHT 400–500g

HABITAT Dry, open habitats with low bushes at low altitudes and mountains up to 3,000m

NEST Shallow scrape, usually unlined

EGGS 10–14; slightly glossy, yellow-buff with fine reddish-brown markings

FOOD Leaves, shoots, seeds, some insects

IDENTIFICATION

This bird has a dumpy, rounded appearance, its head appearing particularly round with no neck. Underparts mostly grey. From a distance, upperparts look brown and plain, although on close inspection they are finely marked with darker brown and buff. Facial colouring is brick-red, contrasting with the grey underside. In flight, distinctive rusty outertail feathers are seen. Adult has dark chestnut horseshoe-shaped patch on underside, which is larger in male than female. Juvenile is browner than adult and lacks the horseshoe mark.

Female (FAR RIGHT) has less pronounced horseshoe mark on belly than male (RIGHT).

GREY PARTRIDGE

Perdix perdix

GREY PARTRIDGES AVOID very wet and very arid areas as these do not provide the nutritious plant foods they require. They use cultivated fields, tracks for dust-bathing and ditches for drinking. Like most partridges, the Grey Partridge is fairly sedentary, although birds will flock together in winter. In the far east and north of its range, deep snow will drive birds to move further in search of food. When alarmed they will run for cover, eventually taking flight in a flock and dropping quickly when out of danger.

BIRD FACTS

VOICE Harsh 'keirr-ik keirr-ik' at night, 'pitt pitt pik pirr pik' calls when alarmed and fleeing

LENGTH 29–31cm

WINGSPAN 45–48cm

WEIGHT 350–450g

HABITAT Lowland grassland, cultivated areas

NEST Shallow depression in low, thick vegetation; grassy lining

EGGS 10–20; glossy olive-brown

FOOD Seeds, buds, leaves, shoots; young eat some insects

male

CORNCRAKE

Crex crex

adult

THIS VERY SECRETIVE bird is hard to see but is easily located by the male's far-carrying call. Although it keeps to dense cover in meadows and hayfields, the male will sometimes perch on a stone wall to call or respond to the calls of another male. Corncrakes are summer visitors to Europe, where they attempt to nest in fields before the crops are harvested. Traditional methods allowed them to do this, but modern farming has made most areas unsuitable and this is now a very rare bird, restricted to a few localities where crops are harvested late in the season.

adult

Flies low, quickly drops into cover and then runs to safety.

adult

Adult males utter their 'crex crex' call incessantly through the night and early morning.

IDENTIFICATION

Similar in size to Water Rail but with shorter, yellowish-brown bill and noticeably long rusty wings when seen in flight. Upperparts of adult are grey-brown with dark centres to the feathers that form broken lines running the length of the body. Neck and supercilium are greyish, but underside is mostly brownish-buff turning to reddish-brown with white barring on the flanks. Sexes are identical apart from the lack of grey on the neck and face of the female. Juvenile resembles female but is paler, with light spots on the wing coverts. Legs are flesh coloured, darker in juveniles than adults, and the eyes are pale brown. Flight is weak and the legs dangle.

BIRD FACTS

VOICE Far-carrying, rasping 'crex crex' or 'crake crake'

LENGTH 27–30cm

WINGSPAN 46–53cm

WEIGHT 130–180g

HABITAT Hay meadows, driest areas of marshes

NEST On ground; shallow cup of leaves with slight canopy

EGGS 8–12; slightly glossy, greyish-green with reddish-brown spots and blotches

FOOD Invertebrates; some plant material

SPOTTED CRAKE

Porzana porzana

WHEN SEEN IN good light the Spotted Crake is not easily confused with any other small waterbird but its secretive habits make it difficult to locate; the 'whiplash' call, heard mostly at night, is the best guide to its presence. Outside the breeding season, Spotted Crakes are normally solitary. They keep to dense vegetation along the edges of rivers and lakes that have muddy margins, finding small food items at the surface of the mud or among plant roots; they are known to take a variety of small invertebrates and some plant material.

BIRD FACTS

VOICE Far-carrying 'dripping tap' call – 'hwitt hwitt'

LENGTH 22–24cm

WINGSPAN 37–42cm

WEIGHT 70–100g

HABITAT Sedges and rushes bordering lakes, ponds and rivers

NEST Cup-shaped on tussock in thick waterside vegetation

EGGS 10–12; glossy, olive-buff with reddish-brown and grey spots

FOOD Aquatic invertebrates, plant material

IDENTIFICATION

A small, compact waterbird, which at a distance appears all dark grey-brown or greenish-brown, but in good light looks spotted. The undertail is pale buff, the short pointed bill is red at the base with a yellowish-orange tip, and the legs and feet are bright olive-green. Females resemble males but have less grey on the face and underparts, with slightly more spotting. Juveniles resemble females but lack any grey tones and have less spotting and duller, olive-coloured legs.

Spotting on plumage only visible at very close range.

adult

juvenile

male

LITTLE CRAKE
Porzana parva

LITTLE CRAKES PREFER slightly deeper water than do other small crakes; they are more inclined to swim or even dive briefly and will also emerge into the open on the edges of reeds in the early mornings and at dusk. They will also sometimes climb up stems of bulrush and reedmace for short distances to reach food. Little Crakes are scarce in western Europe but in central and eastern Europe they are locally common around nutrient-rich lakes.

IDENTIFICATION

Male is olive-brown above with the feathers showing dark centres and buff margins; at close range the scapulars and mantle show some pale streaks. The face and underside are slate-blue or grey with pale streaking on the rear flanks and undertail coverts, which are not as striking as in the Water Rail. Female is pale buff beneath, rather than grey, and has a whitish face with faint barring under the tail. Juvenile is similar to female but is paler below; shows white supercilium and pale mottling on the chest and flanks; barring on the underside is darker than in female.

female

BIRD FACTS

VOICE Low accelerating croaking sounds, ending in a trill
LENGTH 18–20cm
WINGSPAN 34–39cm
WEIGHT 37–60g
HABITAT Reedbeds and swamps with still water and floating vegetation
NEST Shallow cup on raised tussock in thick waterside vegetation
EGGS 7–9; glossy, yellow-buff with brown spots and blotches
FOOD Aquatic invertebrates

IDENTIFICATION

A very small waterbird, the size of a House Sparrow, with colouring resembling a Water Rail. Adult upperparts are rufous brown with irregular whitish spots and streaks, and the feathers have dark centres. The face and chest are deep slate-blue and unmarked, but the rear flanks and underside as far as the tail are black with white barring. The legs are a dark flesh colour or dull olive, and the bill is green. The female is almost identical to the male but the throat and chest region are paler grey. Juveniles have the same upperpart colouring as adults, but are buff-coloured below and the bill is brownish. Has weak flight with dangling legs that is characteristic of smaller crakes.

BAILLON'S CRAKE
Porzana pusilla

THE BAILLON'S CRAKE's normal habit is to search for food among dense water plants and it rarely emerges into the open. It swims readily and can make shallow dives, so is often found in areas of deep water in large swamps and reedbeds. The frog-like call is produced mostly by the male, but females utter shorter, rasping notes near the nest. Its secretive habits make this a very difficult bird to observe. When alarmed it flicks its tail, showing the dark underside with white barring, and also flicks its head; the red eye can appear pale against the dark cheeks. Its relatively short wings help distinguish it from Little Crake.

BIRD FACTS

VOICE Rasping sounds resembling a finger scratching a comb
LENGTH 17–19cm
WINGSPAN 33–37cm
WEIGHT 30–50g
HABITAT Swampy areas with thick vegetation, streamsides, pond margins
NEST On ground in thick cover next to water; cup-shaped with canopy
EGGS 6–8; glossy, yellowish-buff with brownish streaks and spots
FOOD Aquatic invertebrates, some plant material

Adult male has slate-blue face and chest.

Plumage provides excellent camouflage in dense reedbeds.

WATER RAIL

Rallus aquaticus

THE WATER RAIL is more often heard than seen, being usually well concealed within dense reedbeds. At night in spring, males utter a rhythmic crake-like 'kipp kipp' call with many variations. Sometimes the rail will move out into the open to feed on muddy margins or to sun itself, when its slender, agile form can be seen. When moving through the reeds it may walk slowly, crouch, run, climb, or freeze at a hint of danger. Water Rails are widespread across Europe in suitable habitats, and most are sedentary, but Britain receives many visitors from the east during cold winters.

BIRD FACTS

VOICE Harsh squealing and grunting sounds; nocturnal 'kipp kipp' call

LENGTH 22–28cm

WINGSPAN 38–45cm

WEIGHT 100–140g

HABITAT Reedbeds, marshes, well-vegetated river and lake shores

NEST On ground in thick vegetation near water; cup shaped

EGGS 6–11; glossy, off-white with reddish-brown spots, mostly at blunt end

FOOD Aquatic invertebrates, insects, plant material

IDENTIFICATION

A secretive waterbird. Adult has mostly dark-brown colouring above and plain slate grey-blue below. The dark flanks are strongly barred and the tail is noticeably white beneath. The slender bill is red and slightly downcurved. The sexes are similar, but the female is a little smaller than the male with a slightly shorter bill. Juveniles are browner than adult on the underside and have a brown bill. In flight the long legs and toes trail conspicuously.

IDENTIFICATION

At a distance adult appears all black with a red shield on the face and yellow tip to the bill. A horizontal white line along the flanks and the black and white pattern under the constantly flicked tail make confusion with any other waterbird unlikely. Seen more closely in good light the plumage is black only on the head, while the rest of the upperparts are very dark brown and the underside is deep slate-grey. Before the autumn moult the worn plumage looks dusty and the white lateral line may disappear. Juveniles are brownish overall with paler flanks and chest, white chin and throat, and a buff rather than white lateral line. The undertail pattern resembles that of the adult.

RIGHT: Adults fighting.

MOORHEN

Gallinula chloropus

THE MOORHEN HAS adapted well to life in a variety of wetland habitats and is as likely to be seen out in the open grassland as on a deep lake or among dense reeds. Its fluttering take-off gives way to a relatively powerful flight, and it can also climb well and seek food on overhanging branches of waterside trees. During the breeding season Moorhens are rather secretive and solitary, nesting in concealed sites close to or even on the water. After breeding they may gather in larger groups in favourable feeding areas.

BIRD FACTS

VOICE Varied, loud calls, including harsh 'krreck' and rhythmic 'kipp kipp kipp'

LENGTH 32–35cm

WINGSPAN 50–55cm

WEIGHT 250–330g

HABITAT Wetlands, including urban park lakes, rivers, small ponds

NEST Near water, sometimes on floating platform; untidy cup of leaves, stems

EGGS 5–9; glossy, buff with brownish spots and blotches

FOOD Aquatic and terrestrial invertebrates, plant material

juvenile

adult

adult

CRESTED COOT
Fulica cristata

THE CRESTED COOT is a very rare bird in Europe. Where its restricted range overlaps with the Coot's, it can be difficult to pick out, even in the breeding season when its 'horns' are most prominent. When the species are seen together, the Crested Coot seems to have a slightly longer and stiffer neck than its common cousin, and a flatter head. A strange groaning or 'mooing' call is sometimes uttered from cover. This species is not as tolerant of human presence as the Coot and is also less inclined to emerge onto land to feed; it is also intolerant of colder conditions.

BIRD FACTS

VOICE Two-note 'clukuk' and a metallic 'croo-oo-k'

LENGTH 38–42cm

WINGSPAN 75–85cm

WEIGHT 800–900g

HABITAT Large water bodies with plenty of marginal vegetation

NEST Floating platform in shallow water, concealed by emergent vegetation

EGGS 5–7; slightly glossy, pale grey with dark-brown speckles

FOOD Mainly aquatic plants, especially roots and tubers, some invertebrates

IDENTIFICATION

Slightly larger than the Coot, but in other respects very similar. Sexes are identical. Adult has red knobs over the facial shield that can be seen at close range; at a distance they are not especially obvious and in winter they are smaller and duller than during the breeding season. In flight, wings lack the white edge to the secondaries seen in the Coot. Juvenile is drab brownish-black with a paler chin and throat, and a white centre to the belly. Adults and juveniles have slate-blue legs and feet.

Adult very similar to Coot but has slate-blue legs and feet.

The greenish feet have lobes on them to aid swimming; they are large and conspicuous on land and in flight.

COOT
Fulica atra

AN AGGRESSIVE WATERBIRD of larger bodies of water, the Coot defends a territory in spring against all comers. Coots prefer areas free of overhanging trees or steep banks and usually avoid fast rivers unless there is thick marginal vegetation. Outside the breeding season they will sometimes gather in large flocks and may be seen feeding confidently some distance away from the water's edge. They swim and dive quite well and fly freely, taking off by pattering across the water with rapidly flapping wings. This is the least retiring and secretive of the rail family, and is very confident on urban park lakes.

Coots are widespread across Europe where suitable water bodies exist, and are resident in the south and west.

BIRD FACTS

VOICE Loud repetitive 'kowk' and explosive shrill 'pitt'

LENGTH 36–38cm

WINGSPAN 70–80cm

WEIGHT 600–900g

HABITAT Larger ponds and lakes, canals, urban park lakes

NEST Platform of plant material over shallow water, hidden by tall plants

EGGS 6–10; slightly glossy, buff with dark speckling

FOOD Mainly aquatic plant material but some invertebrates also taken

IDENTIFICATION

A rounded, sooty-black waterbird, adult with gleaming white bill and facial shield and red eye. Sexes are identical, although the male is larger than the female. At close range, head and neck are seen to be the most intensely black, while flanks are greyer. In flight, wings have a pale rear margin. Juvenile is dull brown with pale face and throat, and a yellowish-grey bill.

PURPLE GALLINULE

Porphyrio porphyrio

THE PURPLE GALLINULE is a very scarce bird in Europe, found only in brackish marshes and areas of still water where there is ample plant material for it to feed on. It is adept at uprooting tubers and rhizomes of water plants, and can manipulate these in its feet to get at the central pith; it will also raid the nests of other waterbirds, taking eggs and chicks. Its slow walk is heron-like and it can swim or dive quite easily, sometimes emerging into open water, often at dawn or dusk. Most birds are resident and do not undertake long migrations.

BIRD FACTS

VOICE Variable, deeper versions of Moorhen calls, low 'chock chock'

LENGTH 45–50cm

WINGSPAN 90–100cm

WEIGHT 720–900g

HABITAT Marshes, reedbeds, tracts of bulrush, brackish swamps

NEST Large mass of leaves and stems over water in dense vegetation

EGGS 3–5; glossy, cream with maroon or grey spots and blotches

FOOD Aquatic plant roots and shoots, seeds, buds, invertebrates, frogs

IDENTIFICATION

Adult has violet-blue plumage with brighter blue face, and red legs, eyes and bill. Undertail is white. Sexes similar but male is larger. After breeding, the bill is duller and has dark patches. The bluest birds are those from the western Mediterranean; the Egyptian race has green tinges on the scapulars and back, and the Middle Eastern race has a green head and is paler blue. Juveniles are grey, with dull-red bill and legs and white throat.

adult

White undertail is exposed frequently when bird is nervous.

adult

GREATER FLAMINGO

Phoenicopterus ruber

FLAMINGOS ARE NOTORIOUSLY fickle in their breeding habits, attempting to nest only if feeding conditions are perfect and sometimes not even trying to breed in any given area for several years. Outside the breeding season, flocks of Greater Flamingos range widely around the Mediterranean, from Cyprus to northern Greece and from the Camargue to Andalucia. Individual birds seen out of their normal range are invariably escapes from captivity and are often the conspicuously red-kneed Caribbean race. Flocks of Greater Flamingos feed in close formation and interact with one another regularly; the groups are also very noisy.

IDENTIFICATION

Large and unmistakable bird, both standing and in flight. Adult plumage mainly pale pink but can look very washed out. Black-tipped pink bill is downcurved and banana-shaped. Neck very long and usually held in 'S' shape. Body compact and rounded. Juvenile is pale grey-brown with dark legs and black-tipped grey bill.

BIRD FACTS

VOICE Flocks utter 'kaa-haa' calls

LENGTH 125–145cm

WINGSPAN 140–165cm

WEIGHT 3–4kg

HABITAT Shallow brackish lagoons and saline lakes

NEST Colonial; mud platform

EGGS 1; white but usually stained

FOOD Mainly small, aquatic invertebrates

In flight, wings show black flight feathers and rosy-pink coverts; head and neck held outstretched and legs trailing.

Legs of adult (RIGHT) extremely long and pinkish-red; juvenile's are about two-thirds the length of the adult's.

The bill is used to filter out animals from the surface of the water: the head and neck are held downwards while the upside-down bill is swept from side to side.

Cranes search for food by walking slowly and probing with the large bill; plant material is the commonest food in winter but in the breeding season frogs, ground-nesting birds and invertebrates will also be eaten.

Adult Cranes are stately and imposing birds.

CRANE
Grus grus

CRANES ARE SOLITARY and nervous birds during the breeding season, but the rest of the year they congregate in large flocks. They nest in wetland areas, sometimes in boggy clearings in forested areas in the far north, using sites that afford them protection from predators. The Crane's elaborate dancing display is most commonly seen in spring, and involves wing-flapping, head-pointing and jumping. This sometimes precedes courtship, or may be performed by rival males. It is thought that Cranes pair for life. In the autumn Cranes migrate in small flocks and family groups in a tight 'V' formation to overwintering sites in Africa, India and southeast Asia; some use traditional European sites in France and Iberia. There are regular stop-over sites that are mostly protected from hunting.

IDENTIFICATION

A very large bird of upright posture, which moves in a steady and measured way on the ground. Sexes similar. Adult plumage is mostly grey but the head is much darker, appearing black at a distance, with a white band extending back from the red eye and a red crown. The chest and parts of the back have a pale-rufous tinge, and the tail and overhanging cloak of secondaries are darker. Juvenile is paler grey than adult with an unpatterned head and grey, rather than black, legs. In flight it shows long wings of even width with black flight feathers and a long extended neck and trailing legs.

BIRD FACTS

VOICE Loud bugling calls, plus 'kroo-krii kroo-krii' calls by pairs
LENGTH 110–130cm
WINGSPAN 200–230cm
WEIGHT 4.5–6kg
HABITAT Marshes, farmland, large boggy clearings in northern forests
NEST Large pile of vegetation with hollow top; on ground or in shallow water
EGGS 2; slightly glossy, variable colours from buff through olive to red-brown, spotted with red or dark brown
FOOD Invertebrates, small mammals, nestling birds, fruits, seeds

DID YOU KNOW?

On migration and in their winter quarters Cranes form large flocks and are easier to observe than in the breeding season.

DEMOISELLE CRANE
Anthropoides virgo

THE BEST CHANCE of seeing wild Demoiselle Cranes in Europe is to visit Cyprus during migration time: small numbers pass through from late March to mid-April, and larger numbers in late August and early September. Views in Europe are generally of distant flying birds, so certain separation from the Crane may be difficult. Size alone is not a good identifier but the Demoiselle Crane's neck is proportionately shorter. The greater extent of black on the neck is diagnostic, but often difficult to detect in flying birds. The Demoiselle Crane's call is higher pitched than its cousin's.

BIRD FACTS

VOICE Grating, honking flock calls uttered on ground and in flight
LENGTH 80–100cm
WINGSPAN 170–180cm
WEIGHT 2.4–2.8kg
HABITAT Steppe and upland grassland
NEST Shallow scrape on ground
EGGS 2; greyish-buff
FOOD Mainly plant material but some invertebrates

IDENTIFICATION

Superficially similar to Common Crane but smaller. Sexes similar. Adult has mainly pale blue-grey plumage, but is black from throat and neck to breast and has broad, black supercilium bordering grey crown. White nape plumes arise from behind eye. Iris red. Black flight feathers mostly hidden at rest but conspicuous in flight. Legs dark and bill yellowish. Juvenile has grubby brownish-grey plumage and lacks adult's head and neck patterns.

LITTLE BUSTARD
Tetrax tetrax

MALE LITTLE BUSTARDS display in the spring in the open; they give short rasping calls and make short jumps into the air. In flight they resemble gamebirds or possibly Mallards. The male's wings create a rhythmic whistling sound due to a short, narrow, fourth primary feather. Little Bustards are commonest in southwest Europe, where they are resident year round, but there are scattered breeding sites in France and Turkey. Their preferred habitat of open grassy plains leads them to use man-made sites such as airfields and military training grounds. Little Bustards are strong fliers; they take to the air if disturbed and are wary of people.

BIRD FACTS

VOICE Snorting 'knerr' or 'prritt' calls, various grunts and whistles

LENGTH 40–45cm

WINGSPAN 105–115cm

WEIGHT 600–950g

HABITAT Open grassy plains, large arable fields, grassy airfields

NEST Shallow scrape on ground in low vegetation

EGGS 3–4; glossy, olive-brown or green with darker streaks and spots

FOOD Plant material, invertebrates

female

male

Female (ABOVE) lacks black and white neck pattern.

In spring, displaying male Little Bustards (ABOVE) stand out in the open with their neck feathers splayed out.

IDENTIFICATION

A pheasant-sized bird with sturdy legs and a small head on a long thick neck. The overall body colour is speckled grey-brown with a white underside. Adult male has a strongly patterned black and white head and neck with a grey throat. Female lacks the male's black and white patterning, but has coarse speckling on the back. In flight, both sexes show white wings with black-tipped primaries and primary coverts, and a black and white tail rim. Juvenile is similar to female.

Male in full breeding plumage is very impressive; he performs an elaborate display in which he appears to turn inside out, exposing the white downy feathers.

GREAT BUSTARD
Otis tarda

Female is much smaller than male.

NORMALLY THE GREAT BUSTARD is a very shy bird and is difficult to observe; it keeps to open plains where it can spot danger easily and flee if necessary. The broad wings of the Great Bustard show a white panel in flight; this is much smaller in the female than the male, but both fly with strong, eagle-like wingbeats. Birds in the far east of Europe migrate south in the winter, but in the west of their range they disperse locally to more productive winter feeding areas. Great Bustards were once widespread across Europe, but have declined considerably.

BIRD FACTS

VOICE Mostly silent, but may give short, barking, alarm note

LENGTH 75–105cm

WINGSPAN 190–260cm

WEIGHT 12–16kg (male), 4–6kg (female)

HABITAT Open grasslands, lowland areas, wide river valleys and plains

NEST Shallow depression on ground in low vegetation

EGGS 2–3; glossy, variable pale colours with brown blotches

FOOD Plant material, invertebrates; few small birds and mammals in summer

IDENTIFICATION

Europe's heaviest bird. In the breeding season the displaying male has a bulging neck and a cocked-up tail that makes it appear even larger. Breeding males also have a strong chestnut chest band and white moustachial 'whiskers' extending back from base of bill. Outside the breeding season, male resembles female apart from his greater size. Female head and neck are grey with upperparts cinnamon-brown but strongly barred with black; the underside is white, giving the bird a three-coloured grey, brown and white appearance. Juvenile resembles adult female but has a buff neck.

male

STONE-CURLEW

Burhinus oedicnemus

A stocky wader with large, black and yellow eyes and stout, almost gull-like bill, which is black at tip. Sexes similar. Adult plumage is mostly sandy brown with darker streaks; underside is pale. At rest, wings show a white bar and dark lower edge; in flight, wings appear black with paler panels. Tail appears relatively long. When standing, the tarsus joint is prominent. Juvenile resembles adult but is less boldly marked.

STONE-CURLEWS ARE LARGELY nocturnal in their habits, giving their presence away by their eerie and far-carrying calls. During the day they rest quietly amongst low vegetation, remaining motionless even when approached closely. When flushed they fly off low over the ground with strong but shallow wingbeats, dropping into cover and running for a short distance before freezing again. Normally solitary, Stone-curlews gather together in small flocks after the breeding season and before embarking on migration; in some cases there are traditional gathering sites where they may congregate before heading south. Birds in southwest Europe are residents. Changes in agriculture and increased persecution have led to a great decline in numbers in many regions.

BIRD FACTS

VOICE Curlew-like flight call, and various high-pitched whistling and shrill wader-like calls at night

LENGTH 40–44cm

WINGSPAN 77–85cm

WEIGHT 440–500g

HABITAT Dry, open areas, semi-desert, arable land, heaths

NEST Shallow scrape in open position; lining of small stones, rabbit droppings

EGGS 1–3; slightly glossy, pale buff with brownish-purple streaks and spots

FOOD Soil invertebrates, small birds, mammals, frogs

Staring yellow and black eye gives Stone-curlew a stern appearance.

OYSTERCATCHER

Haematopus ostralegus

Adults have striking black and white plumage, a red eye, an orange-pink bill and red-pink legs. In winter, adults acquire a white chin stripe on the otherwise black neck. Newly fledged juveniles are exceptionally well camouflaged to resemble lichen-covered rocks. First-winter birds are paler than adults with a larger, white throat patch.

OYSTERCATCHERS ARE COMMON where there are shorelines that provide molluscs such as cockles and mussels to feed on; they open the shells with their powerful bills. They also take marine worms from mud, catching them by probing with their long bills. They roost communally so are normally found in areas that provide safe high-tide roosts as well as good feeding areas. In the breeding season the flocks disperse and they spread themselves out around the coast, along broad, stony rivers, and in a wide range of open, undisturbed habitats inland.

BIRD FACTS

VOICE Shrill piping calls, loud 'kubeek kubeek' alarm call

LENGTH 40–45cm

WINGSPAN 80–86cm

WEIGHT 450–700g

HABITAT Rocky shores, estuaries, large stony rivers, stony lake shores

NEST Shallow scrape in the open, lined with pebbles or shells; sometimes on promontory

EGGS 3; slightly glossy, buff-yellow with many dark spots, blotches, streaks

FOOD Molluscs, marine worms; earthworms for inland birds

Plumage is striking black and white with heavy orange bill; winter birds (LEFT) acquire white collar.

AVOCET

Recurvirostra avosetta

THE AVOCET USES its upcurved bill to sweep through liquid mud in search of tiny invertebrates; the side-to-side motion of the head is characteristic of this species. It prefers water about 10cm deep, a depth at which the long legs are hidden when wading. It can also swim if necessary, and frequently up-ends itself like a duck to reach deeper mud. In flight it often gives its clear, ringing call. Avocets are generally summer visitors to the coasts of northwest Europe but over 3,000 now remain in overwintering sites in southwest England.

Avocets are attentive parents, accompanying their chicks when they feed and seeing off potential predators.

adult and chick

BIRD FACTS

VOICE Varied calls, including a ringing 'pleet pleet'

LENGTH 42–46cm

WINGSPAN 77–80cm

WEIGHT 230–290g

HABITAT Estuaries, coastal lagoons, saltpans, shallow lakes

NEST Shallow scrape in the open, near water; some lining of shells, stones

EGGS 3–4; smooth, pale buff with brownish spots and blotches

FOOD Small invertebrates

adult

adult

IDENTIFICATION

A unique large, black and white wader with a strongly upcurved bill and long, blue-grey legs. The plumage is predominantly white with a black head and nape and black panels on the wings, which appear as oval panels in flight. From below, the Avocet looks all white in flight apart from black wingtips. Sexes identical and juveniles resemble adults except that the black element of the adult plumage is brownish instead.

adults

A very long-legged wader with entirely black and white plumage. The wings and mantle are black and the underparts are white, but the degree of black on the head is variable. In flight the white rump and long white wedge on the back show clearly, as do the trailing pink legs. The head may be all white or show varying amounts of black. The sexes are very similar except that breeding female usually shows pure white head and neck. Juvenile is paler on the mantle than adult, with sepia tinges to the darker feathers.

BLACK-WINGED STILT
Himantopus himantopus

THE BLACK-WINGED STILT has the longest legs, proportional to its size, of any bird, although in deep water it moves much like any other wader. Its long, slender bill is used to snatch at tiny insects in the air and on emergent vegetation, and it can also be used to probe into soft mud for tiny aquatic larvae; when probing for food in deep water the Stilt's head may be completely submerged. Black-winged Stilts prefer areas with high invertebrate populations and may nest in loose colonies. They are not tolerant of direct human disturbance, but seem to accept the presence of visitors who do not interfere with them.

BIRD FACTS

VOICE Varied short, nasal, bleating calls

LENGTH 35–40cm

WINGSPAN 67–83cm

WEIGHT 140–220g

HABITAT Coastal lagoons, shallow lakes, saltpans

NEST Shallow scrape near water, or raised platform over shallow water

EGGS 4; smooth, pale brown with black spots and blotches

FOOD Small aquatic invertebrates

adult male

Walks gracefully with delicate high steps.

adult female

female

All adults have a long black crest but the male's is longer than the female's.

LAPWING
Vanellus vanellus

THE LAPWING IS an agile bird in the air, performing displays over its territory at the start of the breeding season. The acrobatic swoops and dives are accompanied by the song of 'wee-willuch-coawhey-ee, willuch-coo-whey-ee'. It can take to the air with great ease and quickly turn to mob a predator. In winter, large flocks form near favoured feeding areas, and at the onset of snow or frost they will move south or west to find new areas. In the south and west, Lapwings are mostly year-round residents, but in the east and north they are summer visitors only.

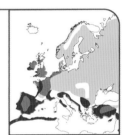

BIRD FACTS

VOICE Shrill 'peeoo-wit' and other more scratchy sounds

LENGTH 28–31cm

WINGSPAN 75–85cm

WEIGHT 190–300g

HABITAT Wet grasslands, marshes, open pastures

NEST In the open, slightly raised on tussock or mound; shallow scrape with lining of vegetation in wet areas

EGGS 4; smooth, olive, brown or pale with heavy streaks and spots

FOOD Soil invertebrates, especially beetles and earthworms

Adult has glossy green upperparts and all-white underparts apart from rich orange undertail coverts, seen when bird dips its head during feeding. Male when breeding has solid black chin and throat. At a distance, Lapwing appears all black and white, and in flight shows long, broad, black and white wings with white tips to three outer primaries. In winter, feathers have pale margins which give a scalloped appearance to the mantle; cheeks are buff rather than white. Juvenile resembles winter adult but has shorter crest and browner chest.

Adults vigorously defend nests against potential predators such as Magpies.

In flight, the black and white pattern on the underwing and distinctive rounded wingtips make identification straightforward.

GOLDEN PLOVER

Pluvialis apricaria

THE GOLDEN PLOVER is a bird of open moorlands and bogs where the vegetation is short enough to allow it to run easily. It feeds on the ground, pursuing small soil invertebrates, and takes flight only if disturbed. It will occasionally stand on a small tussock to survey its territory or use a grass clump to provide a little cover. Outside the breeding season Golden Plovers leave the high moorlands and move to lower levels to form flocks, sometimes mixed with Lapwings, on open arable lands, grass airfields and the upper reaches of estuaries. Only in the most severe weather will they move to the seashore.

Plump wader with short bill and rounded head and spangled golden-brown upperparts. In summer, male has black face and black underside separated from upperparts by broad white border. In flight it shows white underwings contrasting with black belly. Female similar to male but has less black on underside, sometimes restricted to belly; face is greyer than male's and white border to the black areas is less distinct. Northern birds (Iceland and Scandinavia) have far more black than southern birds (Britain). In winter sexes are similar, with no black on the underside and more uniform plumage overall. Juvenile very like winter adult but may show some faint barring on the underparts.

BIRD FACTS

VOICE A mournful, whistling 'pyuuh' or 'pyuu pu'

LENGTH 26–29cm

WINGSPAN 67–76cm

WEIGHT 150–220g

HABITAT Breeds on moorlands, bogs; overwinters on lowland pastures

NEST Shallow scrape on tussocky ground, sparse lining

EGGS 4; slightly glossy, greenish-olive or buff with darker streaks and blotches

FOOD Soil invertebrates, some berries and seeds

White underwings are characteristic of the species and a good feature to look for in flying birds.

Belly white in winter (LEFT) and black in summer (BELOW).

GREY PLOVER

Pluvialis squatarola

IN THE BREEDING season the Grey Plover is confined to the high Arctic, nesting on open ground beyond the tree line, but usually not on the coast or on islands. It has a circumpolar distribution. In autumn the whole population heads south. On their overwintering sites Grey Plovers may become territorial, defending good feeding areas, and there is evidence that they remain faithful to these sites over several years.

BIRD FACTS

VOICE Whistling
'pleeoo-wee'

LENGTH 27–30cm

WINGSPAN 71–83cm

WEIGHT 215–300g

HABITAT Breeds on
Arctic tundra;
overwinters on
muddy and sandy
seashores

NEST Shallow
scrape on dry
ground; lining
of small stones

EGGS 4; smooth, grey
or buff with darker
spots and blotches

FOOD Soil
invertebrates on
breeding grounds;
small molluscs,
crabs, worms,
etc. on shore

IDENTIFICATION

In summer, male is strikingly black below with pale head and white shoulders, and white-flecked upperparts. Female is duller than male and may show greyish cheeks and grey-brown upperparts. Winter adult (both sexes) lacks black belly and has more evenly marked dark grey, speckled upperparts.

LEFT: *In flight, underwing pattern shows distinctive black axillaries against a white background at all times.*

DID YOU KNOW?

Differs from Golden Plover in having much greyer speckled upperparts with no golden tinge.

ABOVE AND BELOW LEFT:
*Adult, breeding
plumage.*

BELOW: *Juvenile
resembles winter adult
(see above) but with
pale-buff wash to
plumage.*

DOTTEREL

Charadrius morinellus

REMOTE MOUNTAIN TOPS with sparse mosses and lichens are the preferred breeding habitat of the Dotterel. It is a very confiding bird on its breeding grounds, spending most of its time on the ground, running from danger rather than flying. Despite its bold markings, the stationary bird can be hard to spot. The traditional roles of the sexes are reversed in the breeding season, with the male taking most responsibility for the care of the eggs and young; it is the female who has the brightest colours and performs displays over a territory.

Distinctly patterned wader with no real affinity for water. In the breeding season, adult has broad, white supercilium and thin black and white chest band. Crown is very dark, framed by white eyestripes that meet on nape; face is whitish and rest of upperparts and neck are grey-brown. Belly is a rich chestnut with a darker centre and the undertail region is white. Female is generally brighter and more distinctive than male. In winter, colours fade to more uniform buff-brown with less markedly white supercilium. Juvenile resembles winter adult but has pale feather margins, which give a scalloped appearance.

female

juvenile

Male incubating.

BIRD FACTS

VOICE Soft 'pweet pweet' flight calls and trilling calls on ground

LENGTH 20–22cm

WINGSPAN 57–64cm

WEIGHT 86–130g

HABITAT Dry, open mountain plateaux; overwinters on arid grasslands

NEST Shallow scrape, often near large stone; moss or lichen lining

EGGS 3; smooth, buff with green tinge and darker red-brown blotches and streaks

FOOD Insects, small soil invertebrates

KENTISH PLOVER

Charadrius alexandrinus

MOST KENTISH PLOVERS are summer visitors to Europe, spending the winter on the west coast of Africa, although they can be found along the Mediterranean shore in winter. Like many small waders that nest on the shore, this species is subject in the breeding season to disturbance caused by human interference. It has adapted to changes in land use in some areas and has made use of salt-pans and gravel extraction areas, abandoning them as they become unsuitable. Where appropriate, safe nesting areas do occur the Kentish Plover can be almost colonial, with several nests being built within a short distance of each other.

Small, pale plover. Adult shows less black on head than Ringed Plover and breast band is incomplete. Breeding male has chestnut crown and black patch on forehead; female has brown replacing black and a grey-brown crown. In winter, male resembles female, with both becoming duller in appearance. Bill and legs are black, and both sexes appear longer-legged than the Ringed Plover. Juvenile plainer than adult, with greyer upperparts.

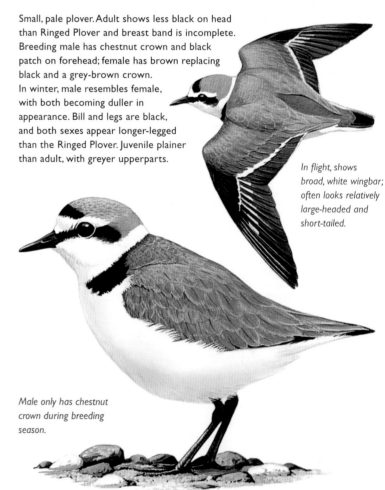

In flight, shows broad, white wingbar; often looks relatively large-headed and short-tailed.

Male only has chestnut crown during breeding season.

BIRD FACTS

VOICE Short 'kip' or 'peep' sounds

LENGTH 15–17cm

WINGSPAN 42–58cm

WEIGHT 40–54g

HABITAT Lagoons, estuaries, saltpans; mainly in Mediterranean

NEST Shallow scrape on ground, usually near water; lining of shells or pebbles

EGGS 3; not glossy, pale buff with black streaks and spots

FOOD Small worms, crustaceans, molluscs; insects when inland

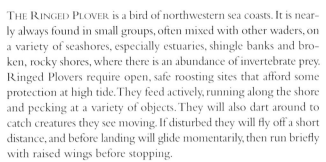
adult

RINGED PLOVER
Charadrius hiaticula

BIRD FACTS

VOICE A rising 'tooip' whistle, and a louder alarm 'te-lee-a te-lee-a'
LENGTH 18–20cm
WINGSPAN 48–57cm
WEIGHT 54–74g
HABITAT Seashores, estuaries, large lake shores, tundra
NEST Shallow scrape in open, near water; lining of small pebbles, shells
EGGS 3–4; slightly glossy or dull, pale buff with black spots and blotches
FOOD Invertebrates, mainly worms, molluscs, shrimps, larvae

THE RINGED PLOVER is a bird of northwestern sea coasts. It is nearly always found in small groups, often mixed with other waders, on a variety of seashores, especially estuaries, shingle banks and broken, rocky shores, where there is an abundance of invertebrate prey. Ringed Plovers require open, safe roosting sites that afford some protection at high tide. They feed actively, running along the shore and pecking at a variety of objects. They will also dart around to catch creatures they see moving. If disturbed they will fly off a short distance, and before landing will glide momentarily, then run briefly with raised wings before stopping.

Prominent white wingbar seen in flight.

adult and chick

IDENTIFICATION

Small, stocky wader with mostly plain colouring but striking facial markings. Upperparts of adult grey-brown and underparts pure white; in summer, legs and bill base are orange, but in winter bill may be all-dark. Head is strikingly marked with black cheeks and black line over the brow; there is a black chest ring. In winter, black fades and looks worn. Sexes are almost identical, although some females have less distinct black markings than males. Juvenile resembles adult, but has a scalloped appearance on upperparts due to pale feather edges, and partial brownish breast band. Striking white wingbars show well in flight in both adults and juveniles.

adult

LITTLE RINGED PLOVER
Charadrius dubius

BIRD FACTS

VOICE Falling 'kiu' flight call and plaintive 'krree-u krree-u'
LENGTH 14–15cm
WINGSPAN 42–48cm
WEIGHT 33–48g
HABITAT Dry, open habitats, gravel beds, lake shores, and similar man-made sites
NEST Shallow scrape on bare ground near water; some lining of stones
EGGS 4; not glossy, buff or stone-coloured with many brown spots and streaks
FOOD Insects, spiders, aquatic invertebrates

LITTLE RINGED PLOVERS are summer visitors to Europe, arriving on their mostly inland breeding grounds in early spring from their overwintering quarters in northern tropical Africa. They have adapted well to human activities such as gravel extraction, which expose the type of terrain they prefer to nest on. They are very secretive when nesting, but their far-carrying calls are good clues to their presence. If disturbed by a predator a nesting bird will perform an elaborate distraction display, dragging its wings or pretending to feed in order to lead attention away from the nest.

DID YOU KNOW?

Little Ringed Plovers are absent from the far north and avoid densely vegetated areas and very wet habitats.

IDENTIFICATION

Small, slender wader. Sexes similar. Adult has dull-brown upperparts and pure white underparts with a strongly patterned head. Bright-yellow eyering stands out well against the black cheeks. Bill is all black and legs are dull pinkish-brown. When seen in flight, the lack of any wingbar at any time is diagnostic for this species. Juvenile looks like faded version of adult with indistinct head and chest markings.

adult and chick

COLLARED PRATINCOLE

Glareola pratincola

BIRD FACTS

VOICE Tern-like calls and short rhythmic nasal calls

LENGTH 24–27cm

WINGSPAN 60–68cm

WEIGHT 68–95g

HABITAT Dry, open habitats with shallow pools, large saltmarshes

NEST Shallow scrape in bare, open areas

EGGS 3; smooth, not glossy, cream with dark spots, blotches and streaks

FOOD Invertebrates, especially insects caught in flight

THE COLLARED PRATINCOLE rarely wades in water to feed, preferring drier, open habitats, such as the uppermost reaches of saltmarshes and dry steppe areas in the Mediterranean region. Its normal method of feeding involves flying in a large flock in pursuit of airborne insects. It will enter shallow water to drink and preen, and often nests near water because there may be a more abundant supply of insects in the vicinity. Collared Pratincoles are summer visitors to the Mediterranean region; the greatest numbers occur in Spain, where many thousands nest.

No other European small wader (apart from Black-winged Pratincole) has combination of a very short bill, forked tail and long wings. At a distance, adult upperparts appear dark sandy or olive-brown with darker primaries and tail feathers. Underside is divided into pure white belly, light-olive chest and buff throat, clearly demarcated by thin black necklace stretching from eye to eye under chin. Gape of bill is bright red. Outside breeding season, adults have far less distinct necklace and more mottled throat and chest. Juvenile looks more speckled than adult because of pale margins to feathers; necklace is absent.

In flight, wings have chestnut lining and white trailing edge, and rump is white.

adult

Adult in breeding plumage.

Very gregarious, both in breeding season and on migration.

BLACK-WINGED PRATINCOLE

Glareola nordmanni

BIRD FACTS

VOICE Churring calls at nest; squeaky call uttered in flight

LENGTH 25cm

WINGSPAN 60–65cm

WEIGHT 90–100g

HABITAT Steppe grassland, usually close to water

NEST Shallow scrape

EGGS 4; olive green with darker spots

FOOD Insects; mainly caught in flight but sometimes on ground

IN WEST AND northwest Europe, Black-winged Pratincoles occur only as vagrants. The species is rarely seen on passage; a trickle of birds is noted in early autumn, however, in the eastern Mediterranean. Birds sometimes disperse in late summer prior to migrating, so a trip to eastern Austria or Hungary can provide sightings. Separation from the Collared Pratincole can be problematic. The black underwing is diagnostic, but the Collared Pratincole's reddish underwing often looks dark when seen against the light. Better pointers are the Black-winged Pratincole's uniformly coloured upperwing, and absence of white trailing edge to secondaries.

IDENTIFICATION

Superficially very similar to Collared Pratincole. Sexes similar. Summer adult at rest looks rather tern-like in silhouette. Plumage essentially dark sandy brown, palest on underparts. Has creamy-buff throat outlined and bordered by black and white lines. In flight, recalls tern or outsized hirundine. Shows forked tail and white rump. Upperwings uniformly dark sandy brown, lacking white trailing edge to innerwing and contrasting dark wingtip seen in Collared Pratincole. Underwing all-dark, lacking reddish-brown underwing coverts of Collared Pratincole. Winter adult (not seen in region) has pale feather margins on upperparts, giving scaly appearance, and less clearly defined throat markings. Juvenile recalls winter adult but looks even more scaly on back and on breast.

summer adult

As a breeding species, the Black-winged Pratincole is essentially a bird of steppe grassland, occurring on lowlands to the north of the Black Sea and at similar latitudes eastwards into central Asia; it occasionally breeds further west, sometimes among colonies of Collared Pratincoles.

Smallest European sandpiper, all ages of which have black legs and short black bill. In summer upperparts are mostly rusty red with dark feather centres; the centre of the crown looks darker. In winter mostly grey-buff above and white below. Larger feathers have dark central shafts, visible at close range. Juvenile resembles summer adult but is paler with a white 'V' on the reddish-brown upperparts and white underparts.

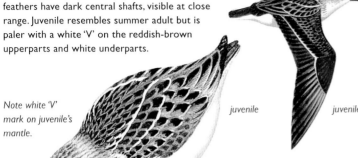

Looks small in flight; shows narrow white wingbar and dark line over white rump, and grey tail.

juvenile

juvenile

LITTLE STINT
Calidris minuta

THIS TINY WADER uses its short bill to pick insects from the surface of mud or plants. It is an active bird when feeding, running and darting in search of prey, which is detected by sight. In winter the Little Stint is usually found in small backwaters and quieter areas of saltmarshes, entering water less frequently than most larger waders. It often occurs in mixed flocks with other small waders, when its smaller size and more active feeding method help distinguish it. There are several similar species of small sandpiper, so accurate identification can be extremely difficult.

BIRD FACTS

VOICE A short 'tip' contact note and 'svee svee svee' display on breeding grounds

LENGTH 12–14cm

WINGSPAN 28–35cm

WEIGHT 20–40g

HABITAT Breeds on tundra; overwinters on muddy wetlands

NEST In the open, near water; shallow cup, lined with leaves

EGGS 4; glossy, pale green to buff, with dark chestnut streaks and blotches

FOOD Insects on tundra; tiny invertebrates on seashore

Note white 'V' mark on juvenile's mantle.

juvenile

summer adult

Very small sandpiper with short legs and rather long tail. Breeding birds look greyish-buff above with some feathers showing dark centres and chestnut fringes. In winter adults have grey-brown plumage above and white underparts; grey colouring extends further down on chest and is more clearly demarcated than in winter plumage Little Stint. For description of juvenile, *see* caption. Paler clay-coloured legs also separate this species from Little Stint at all times.

TEMMINCK'S STINT
Calidris temminckii

TEMMINCK'S STINTS PREFER slightly richer habitats than Little Stints during the breeding season, nesting in grassy areas with willow scrub, usually near rivers or pools. They seem to need sites with plenty of look-outs, in the form of rocks or tree stumps, as well as good feeding areas. They often nest near isolated buildings. They are likely to appear in small groups on migration and may use quite small pools as temporary stop-overs. If startled, Temminck's Stints will shoot rapidly upwards following a jerky flight path and move off for quite a distance before settling again.

BIRD FACTS

VOICE A ringing 'tirrr'

LENGTH 13–15cm

WINGSPAN 30–35cm

WEIGHT 22–36g

HABITAT Nests in tundra and mountainous Arctic regions; overwinters mostly on inland marshes

NEST Shallow cup on open ground with plant lining

EGGS 4; glossy green-grey fading to buff, with brown spots

FOOD Small insects, worms

Juveniles are warm buff above with pale edges to the larger feathers, giving a scaly appearance.

Adult in breeding plumage never as rusty red above as breeding plumage Little Stint; some adults show a few grey winter feathers on mantle.

DUNLIN

Calidris alpina

Winter birds of all ages (1st winter seen here) lack the black belly and have evenly marked dark grey, speckled upperparts.

HUGE FLOCKS OF Dunlin congregate on the shores of western Europe in autumn and winter. They are active feeders, seen in busy flocks pecking at small food items and probing to short depths in soft mud. Occasionally whole flocks take to the air and give an exciting display, changing colour from grey to white as they wheel and turn before settling again to start feeding. Within a flock there may be some variation in appearance, birds from the southernmost breeding populations in Britain and Iceland having a smaller and less distinct belly patch and a shorter bill.

BIRD FACTS

VOICE Harsh, rolling 'krreee' in flight; longer display over nest site

LENGTH 16–22cm

WINGSPAN 35–40cm

WEIGHT 36–57g

HABITAT Breeds on moorlands and tundra; overwinters on estuaries, sandy shores, lake shores

NEST Concealed in vegetation on ground; shallow scrape with some lining

EGGS 4; slightly glossy, pale brown or olive with darker blotches

FOOD Insects on tundra; small worms, shrimps, molluscs, etc. on shores

summer male adult

IDENTIFICATION

Small wader. Sexes similar. In summer has black belly and mostly white underside. Upperparts are chestnut and black, neck and chest are streaked and undertail region is white. For description of winter adult, *see* caption. Juvenile recalls moulting adult, but black breast patch is replaced by darker streaks especially on flanks; upperparts have paler appearance than adult due to buff fringes to feathers.

summer male adult

Bill varies greatly in length according to race, but is black and slightly downcurved in all plumages.

juvenile

Looks generally brown in flight, with distinct, narrow, white wingbar.

CURLEW SANDPIPER

Calidris ferruginea

FOR A BRIEF period in summer the male Curlew Sandpiper has rich red coloration, seen on spring passage birds in the central and eastern Mediterranean. Most birds seen in western Europe occur in autumn and are in juvenile plumage; they are usually seen in mixed flocks of small waders and can be picked out by their elegant long legs and curved bill, and white rump seen in flight. Curlew Sandpipers, like other small waders, are able to deposit body fat very quickly, which enables them to undertake long migrations without regular stopovers. This bird winters mainly in tropical Africa.

juvenile

Juveniles have buff-orange tint on upperparts and chest and pure white underside.

BIRD FACTS

VOICE A clear, ringing 'krillee' in flight

LENGTH 18–20cm

WINGSPAN 38–45cm

WEIGHT 45–90g

HABITAT Breeds in high Arctic; overwinters on seashores, lakes

NEST On dry ground, near water; shallow depression

EGGS 3–4; smooth, buff with many dark brown spots and blotches

FOOD Insects on tundra; worms, shrimps on shores

IDENTIFICATION

In summer has rich red underside and dark upperparts. Fresh plumage looks 'mealy' at first owing to pale feather edges, but becomes darker with wear. Winter adults are very pale grey above with light streaking on upper chest; underparts pure white. For description of juvenile, *see caption*. In all plumages, long black legs, long, black, curved bill and white rump distinguish this species from other small sandpipers.

summer adult

IDENTIFICATION

The darkest of all small sandpipers, but with a thin white wingbar showing in flight. Adults in breeding plumage have strongly marked upperparts with brown, chestnut and whitish colours on larger feathers, and dull yellow legs and bill-base. For description of winter adult, *see caption*. Juvenile recalls winter adult but has more distinctly patterned appearance than adult.

PURPLE SANDPIPER

Calidris maritima

THE PURPLE SANDPIPER overwinters further north than any other wader. It is usually found in small flocks on rocky headlands and islands where there is some wave action and sufficient tidal range to expose rocks to feed on. Purple Sandpipers' favourite food is small molluscs and invertebrates picked from rock crevices on the seashore, but they will also follow behind Turnstones and take food left behind after stones or algae have been flipped over. On their breeding sites they can be very tolerant of intrusion, and they are also fairly confiding at overwintering sites where human disturbance is kept to a minimum.

LEFT: In winter plumage, adult is dark grey above and paler grey below with dark streaks on breast.

BELOW: summer adult

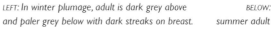

BIRD FACTS

VOICE A short, variable, 'kewitt' call and an agitated call on nest site

LENGTH 20–22cm

WINGSPAN 40–44cm

WEIGHT 59–80g

HABITAT Breeds on tundra and moors; overwinters on rocky shores

NEST Small cup on open ground with sparse lining

EGGS 4; slightly glossy, olive to buff with dark blotches and spots

FOOD Insects, spiders and some fruits on tundra; invertebrates on shore

BIRD FACTS

VOICE A loud 'plitt' flight call; short frog-like trill in display

LENGTH 20–21cm

WINGSPAN 36–42cm

WEIGHT 48–75g

HABITAT Breeds on high Arctic tundra; overwinters on sandy shores

NEST On bare ground; small shallow scrape

EGGS 4; slightly glossy, greenish-olive with darker spots

FOOD Insects on breeding grounds; shrimps, kelp flies on winter shores

SANDERLING

Calidris alba

THE SANDERLING HAS a distinctive method of feeding on sandy shores, running in and out of the surf, snatching morsels of food from the sand as a large wave retreats. The hind toe is missing in this species, perhaps as an aid to running along the shore. Only when a large rock or obstruction is reached will the Sanderling, usually found in small flocks in winter, take to the air. Sanderlings can be found on almost any stretch of sandy shore around the world during the northern winter, and there is evidence that some use the same overwintering sites several years in succession.

Small wader with relatively short, straight bill. In breeding plumage, has rusty-red upperparts with black markings on larger feathers giving a mottled appearance. Chest is rusty red, clearly demarcated from the pure white underside. For description of winter adult, see caption. Juvenile strongly marked above with black and white on upperparts, and with warm-buff tinge to mantle and neck areas. All ages and plumages have black legs and bill, with broad white wingbar seen in flight.

Winter adult in flight.

Summer bird has rusty-red upperparts and white underparts.

Winter adults look all white at a distance, but at close range are seen to have pale grey upperparts with white fringes to feathers.

BIRD FACTS

VOICE Short, slightly nasal 'kwett' in winter; fluting calls on breeding grounds

LENGTH 23–25cm

WINGSPAN 50–60cm

WEIGHT 120–190g

HABITAT Breeds on high Arctic tundra; overwinters on coasts

NEST Shallow scrape in the open, near water; sparse plant lining

EGGS 3–4; slightly glossy, green with brown markings

FOOD Insects and some plant material on tundra; worms, shrimps, etc. on seashore

KNOT

Calidris canutus

WHEN BREEDING ON the tundra, the Knot population is spread out over a vast area, each pair requiring a large territory, but in winter Knots gather in huge flocks, the bulk of those overwintering in Europe being found around the shores of Britain. When breeding, the Knot prefers to be near freshwater, but in winter it is almost exclusively coastal and remains very close to the water's edge. Very high tides force Knots to huddle in tightly packed flocks for roosting, but they are always the last birds to be pushed off the shore by the rising tide.

In summer, adult has orange-red underside, white undertail coverts and mostly buff upperparts, strongly patterned with chestnut and yellow patches; the largest feathers have black and white markings on them. Winter adult has grey upperparts and white underparts. Juvenile very similar to winter adult, but has warmer brown or pinkish-buff wash with no grey tints. Black and white terminal bands on feathers of upperparts produce scalloped appearance.

RIGHT: summer plumage

winter flock

juvenile

summer plumage adult

GREENSHANK
Tringa nebularia

THE GREENSHANK IS a scarce breeder in Scotland, but more widespread across Scandinavia, Russia and Siberia. It moves south for the winter and is a common passage migrant in autumn. The slightly upturned bill is ideal for catching prey in shallow water, and the Greenshank is adept at running after small fish such as sticklebacks, with its bill below the surface. When caught, the fish is lifted from the water before being swallowed. Greenshanks favour quiet backwaters and shallow creeks, normally avoiding open beaches and areas with strong wave action.

BIRD FACTS

VOICE Clear three-syllable 'chew chew chew' call

LENGTH 30–35cm

WINGSPAN 60–70cm

WEIGHT 130–240g

HABITAT Breeds on bogs and marshes; overwinters on coasts, lake shores, riversides

NEST On ground near rock or tussock; shallow scrape with sparse lining

EGGS 4: slightly glossy, buff, heavily marked with brownish spots and streaks

FOOD Invertebrates, fish fry, tadpoles

Pale wedge-shaped patch extending along the back is common to adults and juveniles.

IDENTIFICATION

Mostly grey wader with long green legs and slightly upturned bill; sexes similar. In summer, grey upperparts have darker markings, forming bands along wings; arrow-shaped markings on breast and flanks give streaked effect. For description of winter adult, see caption. In flight, tail looks pale and white and wedge-shaped rump patch extends up the back in both adults and juveniles.

FAR LEFT: Nesting adult in breeding plumage. LEFT: In winter, Greenshank are pale grey above with dark feather margins, bordered with white, and pure white undersides.

Juvenile plumage browner than adult's, with neater streaks on neck and breast.

REDSHANK

Tringa totanus

THE REDSHANK IS both a familiar sight and a familiar sound on coastal marshes and wet meadows across much of Europe. Its readiness to take to the air and give its ringing alarm call has earned it the country name of 'warden of the marshes'. When displaying near the nest site the Redshank gives a persistent 'tyoo tyoo tyoo' while rising and falling on rapidly beating wings. When landing, it raises its wings briefly, showing the pure white underside.

At all times adult has orange-red legs and reddish base to bill. Summer plumage grey-brown. Extent of dark markings on grey background varies considerably and birds from more northerly areas have darkest markings. In winter, darker markings fade and bird appears almost uniformly grey-brown above and very pale below. Juvenile has dull orange legs and base to bill. Shows dark streaks on underside and pale feather margins on mantle, giving slightly mealy appearance. End of tail is barred and outer edges of wings are dark.

BIRD FACTS

VOICE A far-carrying and persistent 'klu-klu-klu' alarm call and a two-syllable 'tu-hu'

LENGTH 27–29cm

WINGSPAN 55–65cm

WEIGHT 105–165g

HABITAT Wet meadows, coastal marshes in summer; estuaries and shores in winter

NEST Shallow depression on open ground, with lining

EGGS 4; slightly glossy, olive or pale green with dark brown spots and blotches

FOOD Insect larvae, earthworms, marine invertebrates

Breeding adult giving the alarm.

BELOW: Adult in winter plumage.

The white trailing edge of the wing and white rump are evident in flight on juvenile and adult birds alike.

BELOW: Adult in breeding plumage.

Elegant wader with long, red legs, which are darkest during the summer months. Sexes similar. For description of summer adult, see caption. Winter adult has essentially pale-grey upperparts and white underparts. Juvenile similar to winter adult but with grey barring on underparts.

SPOTTED REDSHANK
Tringa erythropus

THE SPOTTED REDSHANK breeds in the Arctic. On their breeding sites males help with incubation and the care of the young, remaining long after the females have left. Spotted Redshanks often feed in groups, making a distinctive stabbing movement with their long bill. They wade in quite deep water and swim at times, up-ending like ducks. They will also run after small prey items, reaching out and stabbing with their bills. If startled they will shoot upwards, giving a shrill, whistling call and showing the wedge-shaped rump.

BIRD FACTS

VOICE A shrill 'chu-witt' call, plus a repetitive buzzing 'krruu-ee' uttered in display

LENGTH 29–32cm

WINGSPAN 55–65cm

WEIGHT 130–200g

HABITAT Bogs and tundra in summer; coasts and estuaries in winter

NEST Shallow depression on open ground with sparse lining

EGGS 4; slightly glossy, olive to pale green with brown spots and blotches

FOOD Insects in soil and water on tundra; marine invertebrates on shore

full breeding plumage

In summer, Spotted Redshank has sooty black plumage relieved by pale margins to the feathers on the upperparts

BELOW: *partial breeding plumage*

winter adult

The absence of a white wingbar in flight immediately distinguishes the Spotted Redshank from its cousin.

BELOW: *Both sexes of this distinctive long-legged, long-billed wader have very pale plumage in winter.*

GREEN SANDPIPER

Tringa ochropus

THE GREEN SANDPIPER is a nervous and agitated bird, taking flight readily if disturbed, when it will give its clear, three-note call. Its usual habit, however, is to sit tight and not take flight until approached very closely. In winter it can be found in places where no other wader is likely to occur. Quite small ditches and enclosed water bodies such as watercress beds are favoured, and although this is usually a solitary bird, several may be found in close proximity to one another in suitable feeding areas.

BIRD FACTS

VOICE A shrill, three-note 'tuEEt-wit-wit' given in flight

LENGTH 21–24cm

WINGSPAN 50–60cm

WEIGHT 70–90g

HABITAT Boggy areas with open woodland near by; streams, lake margins, watercress beds

NEST Uses old nest of thrush or pigeon

EGGS 4; slightly glossy, cream with red-brown blotches and streaks

FOOD Invertebrates, fish fry

IDENTIFICATION

From a distance, looks almost black and white both when feeding and when in flight; dark wings contrast with white rump and belly. Upperparts of adult dark olive-green, fading to grey-green on head. In winter, white spots seen in summer birds are absent and underparts look gleaming white. Juvenile has buff-brown spots on dark upperparts; neck and chest streaked.

ABOVE: *adult*

adult

adult

Very black and white in flight; note the dark underwings.

Adult shows white eyering, dull white spots on back and bright white underside.

WOOD SANDPIPER

Tringa glareola

THE WOOD SANDPIPER is a common breeding wader of the far north of Europe and Scandinavia. From late summer onwards migrants turn up in Britain and western Europe on their way to Africa; these are mainly juveniles. Eastern birds head south for India and Australasia. Passage migrants turn up in a variety of habitats from coastal marshes to flooded meadows and riversides. They usually avoid exposed coasts, preferring shallow, brackish or freshwater areas where they can hunt for small aquatic invertebrates or beetles and insect larvae in adjacent grassy areas.

BIRD FACTS

VOICE Flight call is a whistling 'jiff jiff'; rolling display call uttered on breeding sites

LENGTH 19–21cm

WINGSPAN 50–55cm

WEIGHT 55–75g

HABITAT Open forests with boggy areas, marshes, riversides

NEST On ground in dense vegetation, sometimes in old nest in tree

EGGS 4; slightly glossy, pale green or buff with dark brown spots and blotches

FOOD Invertebrates, fish fry, tadpoles, a few seeds and algae

IDENTIFICATION

Compared with other small sandpipers, such as Common and Green, has longer legs and is slimmer. Adults in worn plumage look brownish-grey; sexes similar. Juvenile is browner than adult and has streaked neck, chest and flanks. In flight all ages show pale underwings (wings of Green Sandpiper are dark below), barred tail and white rump.

Barred tail and white rump are evident in flight and common to all ages.

ABOVE: *adult in spring*

breeding plumage

Sexes similar. Adult in summer has grey to grey-brown upperparts and pale underparts with dark streaks. Adult winter plumage light grey above and almost white below. Dark shoulder patch contrasts with pale grey mantle; at close range dark feather quills and pale margins give slightly scaly appearance. Olive-green legs yellower in spring. Juvenile pure white below with browner upperparts than adult.

Straight, thin bill characteristic of species.

breeding adults

MARSH SANDPIPER

Tringa stagnatilis

THE MARSH SANDPIPER is instantly recognisable by its delicate proportions, especially its long, slender bill and legs. If seen in flight the rapid take-off, agility in the air, wedge-shaped white rump and trailing legs are good identification features. It breeds well inland, preferring freshwater marshes where there is short vegetation for concealment. When feeding on land it adopts a crouching posture to pick up food items. Marsh Sandpipers are rare visitors to western Europe, turning up as migrants on their way from their breeding grounds in far eastern Europe and Russia.

Breeding adult

The Marsh Sandpiper's proportionately long legs give it an elegant appearance.

BIRD FACTS

VOICE A clear, whistling 'kiew', repeated frequently

LENGTH 22–25cm

WINGSPAN 50–55cm

WEIGHT 55–100g

HABITAT Lake margins and marshes in summer; lake shores and sheltered seashores in winter

NEST Shallow depression in short vegetation; some lining of grasses

EGGS 4: slightly glossy, cream or buff with dark reddish-brown spots and blotches

FOOD Insects, molluscs, crustaceans

Adult upperparts appear plain grey-buff at a distance, but darker feather centres and pale margins give delicately patterned appearance close up; this patterning is less obvious outside breeding season. Underside pure white with small white patch extending up in front of shoulder. Juvenile very similar to adult but with more scaly appearance owing to pale feather fringes. Legs always grey-green and bill dark brown with dull yellowish base.

adult

Flies on strongly bowed, stiffly held wings.

DID YOU KNOW?

When perching on a boulder, the Common Sandpiper bobs its rear end constantly.

Short-legged wader with elongated body, accentuated by its crouching posture.

COMMON SANDPIPER

Actitis hypoleucos

THE COMMON SANDPIPER is widespread in Europe, its breeding range embracing a huge range of climates and habitat types. In winter there is a migration southwards, although small numbers remain in northwest Europe throughout the winter. The Common Sandpiper is an active bird, constantly bobbing up and down even when perched. It walks or runs in search of food, and is adept at stabbing at insects with its bill. When flushed, it will fly away so low over the water that it appears to touch it with its wingtips; it characteristically utters its shrill call as it takes to the wing.

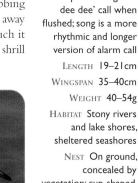

BIRD FACTS

VOICE A shrill and penetrating 'hee dee dee' call when flushed; song is a more rhythmic and longer version of alarm call

LENGTH 19–21cm

WINGSPAN 35–40cm

WEIGHT 40–54g

HABITAT Stony rivers and lake shores, sheltered seashores

NEST On ground, concealed by vegetation; cup-shaped, lined with plant material

EGGS 4; glossy, buff with red-brown spots and streaks

FOOD Insects and other invertebrates

adult

adult

TURNSTONE

Arenaria interpres

THE TURNSTONE IS a familiar seashore bird in winter. Its name is appropriate as it does indeed find food by turning over stones with its short, strong bill, but it feeds in a variety of other ways as well, foraging among seaweeds and probing into mud. Its short, powerful bill can also be used for breaking into crab and mollusc shells. Rotting kelp on beaches provides a good source of kelp fly larvae, which Turnstones relish and from which they very quickly gain weight; their body weight can increase significantly in a few days, enabling them to make long migrations with only short stop-overs.

For description of breeding-plumage male *see caption*. Breeding-plumage female is duller than male, with darker streaked head and less chestnut on upperparts. In winter, upperparts of both sexes uniform grey-brown and head and neck mottled grey. Juvenile resembles winter adult but dark feathers have buff edges, giving scaly appearance. In flight, wings show bold black, white and chestnut patterning at all ages.

winter adult

winter adult

In winter this stocky, short-billed wader can be found on a range of coasts, from exposed rocky shores to sheltered estuaries; its dull-orange legs are distinctive.

In breeding plumage male has black and white facial markings, chestnut upperparts with darker bands, pure white underside and orange legs.

BIRD FACTS

VOICE Short, nasal alarm calls uttered by feeding birds, and longer urgent-sounding call given in flight

LENGTH 21–24cm

WINGSPAN 49–55cm

WEIGHT 80–140g

HABITAT Breeds on coastal tundra; overwinters on seashores

NEST On a slight mound in the open, or in a crevice in rock; shallow scrape with sparse lining

EGGS 4; slightly glossy, buff or pale olive with heavy blotches and spots

FOOD Wide range of marine invertebrates, plus insects on tundra

---

WHIMBREL

Numenius phaeopus

More distinctive markings than Curlew, with two dark stripes on the crown.

THERE IS SOME overlap in the breeding ranges of the Curlew and Whimbrel, but the Whimbrel extends further north and is also more widespread. In winter Whimbrels can be found around the coasts of all the southern continents. They are often seen on estuaries in small groups and when a flock is startled they will all take off, uttering the characteristic seven-note call. Whimbrels seem to be more restless birds than Curlews, using estuaries only as stop-overs. They readily take flight and are only really settled when on the breeding grounds.

IDENTIFICATION

Smaller than Curlew but otherwise superficially similar. Crown has two dark stripes and pale supercilium. Sexes are similar and juvenile resembles adult apart from pale buff spots on crown and wing coverts.

In flight, looks much smaller than Curlew and has more rapid wingbeats.

BIRD FACTS

VOICE A seven-note trill in flight; a brief Curlew-like call in display

LENGTH 40–46cm

WINGSPAN 75–85cm

WEIGHT 430–575g

HABITAT Tundra, moors and bogs in summer; seashores in winter

NEST Shallow depression on open ground; sparse lining

EGGS 3–4; slightly glossy, olive-green with dark brown spots and blotches

FOOD Invertebrates, insects on tundra; marine worms, etc on shore

The pale V-shaped area on the Curlew's back is clear when seen in flight.

CURLEW
Numenius arquata

THE HAUNTING MELODIOUS call of the Curlew is a characteristic sound of upland bogs and moors in spring as males establish nesting territories. The 'cour-lee' call can be heard all year round; Curlews normally live in large flocks in winter and they are very vocal. The long, curved bill of the Curlew is used to good effect when feeding in soft mud, and the tip of the bill can also be used to extract soft-bodied creatures such as molluscs from their shells. Sometimes the Curlew can be seen with its head almost horizontal as it seeks insects on grass tussocks.

IDENTIFICATION

Large wader with long downcurved bill. Female larger than male and has longer bill, but both have similar plumage. In summer, fresh plumage has warmer yellowish tinge than in winter. Lower mandible is pink-flesh coloured in winter. Juvenile plumage very similar to adult; juvenile male has significantly shorter bill than juvenile female.

BIRD FACTS

VOICE A mournful 'cour-lee'; also a tuneful bubbling trill when displaying

LENGTH 50–60cm

WINGSPAN 80–100cm

WEIGHT 600–1,000g

HABITAT Upland moors and bogs in summer; coasts and marshes in winter

NEST On ground, sometimes on tussock; large depression with grassy lining

EGGS 4; glossy, green to olive with brownish spots, blotches and speckles

FOOD Insects, soil organisms; worms, molluscs, crustaceans on seashore

DID YOU KNOW?

The long, curved bill of the Curlew is a perfect adaptation to feeding in damp ground.

Adult feeding on crab.

adult

BLACK-TAILED GODWIT

Limosa limosa

Breeding plumage bird flexing its bill tips.

IN THE BREEDING season, freshwater marshes, especially if rather dry and grazed by cattle, are favoured Black-tailed Godwit breeding sites, with the birds nesting semi-colonially. Once the young have fledged they are taken away to wetter areas, such as lake shores and estuaries, where the feeding is more productive. Black-tailed Godwits' long legs enable them to wade in quite deep water and they feed by making deep probes into the mud. They walk slowly forwards with the bill held vertically down, making short stabs, and then suddenly probe deeply and emerge with the prey, which is swallowed immediately.

IDENTIFICATION

In breeding plumage head and neck are brick-red and upperparts and chest are mottled with black, chestnut and grey, the colours forming broken bars on upper chest. Underside is mostly grey-white. Amount of red coloration in breeding season is very variable, some adult females being almost grey in summer. Winter birds are pale grey above and grey-white below. Juvenile is warm buff below with brown and buff plumage above.

Long-legged, slim wader with long, straight bill.

ABOVE: moulting adult; BELOW: juvenile

BIRD FACTS

VOICE Excited, nasal, 'kee-wee-wee-wee' calls uttered near nest

LENGTH 36–44cm

WINGSPAN 70–80cm

WEIGHT 230–400g

HABITAT Breeds on damp meadows, boggy areas; overwinters on estuaries, marshes

NEST Shallow scrape in the open; lining of grass and leaves

EGGS 3–4; slightly glossy, greenish-olive or brown with dark brown spots

FOOD Invertebrates found by probing in soft mud

In flight all ages show half black and half white tail, white wingbar and trailing black edge to wing.

summer plumage

Flock showing white underwings and black on tail.

ABOVE: summer male; BELOW: winter

Bill is slightly shorter than Black-tailed Godwit's and has an upwards tilt.

BAR-TAILED GODWIT

Limosa lapponica

THE BREEDING SITES of the Bar-tailed Godwit are restricted to the treeless tundra, but there are many overwintering sites in western Europe and the Mediterranean region. Adults arrive on the breeding sites in late May and return south in July to August. Juveniles follow during August to October and may form mixed flocks with other larger waders on good feeding areas. Feeding methods are similar to the Black-tailed Godwit's, but the Bar-tailed is more energetic. It often walks forwards sweeping its head from side to side with its bill held vertically downwards, the lower mandible vibrating slightly to help locate prey.

IDENTIFICATION

Superficially similar to Black-tailed Godwit, but shorter legged and stockier; if seen in flight, lacks that species' distinctive wingbars and tail markings. In summer plumage male has a dark rusty-red underside and mottled chestnut and dark-brown upperparts; larger female has warm-buff underparts and slightly paler upperparts. For description of winter plumage, see caption. Juvenile browner above than winter adult, with patterning similar to Curlew.

Slightly smaller and paler than curlew, with which it sometimes associates.

In winter both sexes are buff-grey above with white undersides; grey feathers have dark central shafts, giving lightly streaked effect above.

winter adult

BIRD FACTS

VOICE Nasal 'ke-vu' with variations for alarm or flight calls

LENGTH 33–42cm

WINGSPAN 70–80cm

WEIGHT 240–380g

HABITAT Breeds on tundra; overwinters on muddy shores

NEST Shallow scrape on dry patch in marshy area; sparse lining

EGGS 3–4; slightly glossy, green-olive, with brown spots, blotches and speckles

FOOD Invertebrates: insects on tundra; worms, shrimps, etc. on shore

BELOW: juvenile

RUFF
Philomachus pugnax

IN THE BREEDING season male Ruffs gather in leks near their nesting sites and display their colourful plumage. They also perform elaborate dances with much leaping and bowing and occasional moments of freezing so that the plumage can be shown off to best effect. By June most of the male's colourful feathers will be moulted and they will look like larger versions of the females. During the autumn passage, juveniles predominate in Ruff flocks, their buff colouring distinguishing them among other, similar waders. On return passage in spring all birds tend to look greyer, but some males will already be showing signs of their display plumage.

male

Unusual wader with distinctive appearance in breeding season and great variation between the sexes and individuals. For description of breeding male, see caption. Smaller female is also variable in appearance, having mostly buff upperparts with varying degrees of darker mottling and streaking. In winter adult male loses 'ruff' and resembles female, both sexes losing warm buff wash to plumage.

male

Breeding male has elaborate neck and head feathers that may be any colour from black to white with numerous brown shades in between; the 'ruff' may be spotted, barred or plain.

Female and displaying males.

juvenile

BIRD FACTS

VOICE Mostly silent, may make quiet drawn-out squeak

LENGTH 26–32cm (m); 20–25cm (f)

WINGSPAN 54–56cm (m); 45–52cm (f)

WEIGHT 130–230g (m), 80–130g (f)

HABITAT Sedge-covered swamps, wet meadows, lake margins, muddy pastures

NEST Shallow scrape with grass lining; concealed by overhanging vegetation

EGGS 4; slightly glossy, green-olive, with dark brown streaks and spots

FOOD Invertebrates caught in shallow water, wet soil or from grasses

---

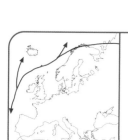

GREY PHALAROPE
Phalaropus fulicarius

AN ALTERNATIVE NAME for the Grey Phalarope is the 'whale bird', a name acquired through its habit of feeding on the backs of surfacing whales while overwintering at sea, and gathering in flocks in areas where whales are feeding because of the fish and plankton driven to the surface. Grey Phalaropes regularly turn up in small numbers in northwest Europe on autumn migration, usually after storms, and occasionally hundreds are driven inshore. They usually remain for a few days, feeding in the characteristic phalarope way of swimming with rapid turns, before continuing on their migration south.

Grey Phalaropes stay out at sea for the whole winter.

BIRD FACTS

VOICE A sharp 'pik' alarm call; rolling 'prruut' uttered by female in summer

LENGTH 20–22cm

WINGSPAN 37–44cm

WEIGHT 42–68g

HABITAT Breeds on high Arctic tundra; overwinters at sea in tropical regions

NEST On ground in low vegetation near water; shallow cup with plant lining

EGGS 4; slightly glossy, olive with blackish spots and blotches

FOOD Insects, molluscs, crustaceans and some plant material on tundra

IDENTIFICATION

Has broader, less pointed bill than Red-necked Phalarope. Breeding female has brick-red underparts, brown back and black and white facial markings. Breeding male similar to breeding female but colours less intense. Winter adults grey above and white below with black 'panda' mask through eye. Juvenile in autumn similar to winter adult but with irregular pattern of brown-fringed black feathers on otherwise grey upperparts.

ABOVE: *Role reversal occurs in the breeding season, with the female having the brighter plumage.*

winter adult

Bill very thin and pointed. For description of breeding female, *see* caption. Breeding male similar to female but colours subdued. Winter plumage adults of both sexes, rarely seen in Europe, have ashy-grey upperparts and white underparts and look black and white at a distance. Juvenile recalls male with washed-out summer plumage showing paler flanks and undersides, and brown wash on neck.

BELOW: Female has striking plumage in summer, with rusty-red neck and upper chest, slate-grey head and white throat.

RED-NECKED PHALAROPE

Phalaropus lobatus

THE RED-NECKED PHALAROPE is instantly recognised by its habit of swimming in search of food, and often spinning round and round to stir up aquatic insect larvae, which it picks from the water with lightning-quick pecks of its bill. In the breeding season it favours shallow freshwater pools from sea level to altitudes of 1,300m. At this time of year the usual male/female roles are reversed, with the female being the brightest in colour and initiating courtship. The male's more subdued appearance makes him most suitable for sitting on the eggs and he assumes all responsibility for the care of the young.

BIRD FACTS

VOICE Calls include short 'kitt' or 'kirrik' sounds

LENGTH 18–19cm

WINGSPAN 34–40cm

WEIGHT 30–48g

HABITAT Breeds on open tundra; overwinters at sea in tropical regions

NEST On ground in vegetation; shallow cup lined with leaves

EGGS 4; slightly glossy, olive with spotting and blotches at blunt end

FOOD Invertebrates caught on water while swimming; mostly insects in summer

LEFT: females
FAR LEFT: juvenile

DID YOU KNOW?

From the point of fledging, juvenile is as adept at swimming as an adult bird.

Larger and more rotund bird than Snipe, with attractive red-brown plumage, particularly noticeable when seen from behind in flight. Upperparts rufous-brown and marbled with black and white; underside paler and barred with dark grey-brown stripes. Long bill is dark flesh colour, becoming darker at tip. Sexes similar and juvenile very similar to adult.

WOODCOCK

Scolopax rusticola

THE SO-CALLED 'RODING' flight of the male Woodcock is usually all that is seen of this very secretive bird. On spring and summer evenings the male flies around the same area with rather jerky wingbeats, usually at treetop height. If flushed from the woodland floor, which is difficult to do because it sits tight until approached very closely, the Woodcock darts off through the trees on a zigzag path and drops quickly when at a safe distance. The female is particularly retiring and rarely leaves the nest during incubation. The young are very active soon after hatching and can fledge in three weeks.

Russet plumage and broad, pale bars on head and wings afford bird excellent camouflage when nesting on leafy woodland floor.

BIRD FACTS

VOICE A grunting 'oo-oorrt' call in flight, followed by a shrill squeak

LENGTH 33–35cm

WINGSPAN 55–65cm

WEIGHT 290–325g

HABITAT Damp woodlands

NEST On ground in woods, concealed by vegetation; shallow cup with lining of leaves

EGGS 4; slightly glossy, pale buff with brownish spots and blotches

FOOD Earthworms, soil invertebrates

When silhouetted against the sky, plump shape, broad wings, long bill held downwards and bat-like flight distinctive.

SNIPE

Gallinago gallinago

BIRD FACTS

VOICE A sneeze-like call when flushed; rhythmic, repetitive 'tick-a tick-a' on breeding grounds

LENGTH 25–27cm

WINGSPAN 40–50cm

WEIGHT 90–130g

HABITAT Bogs, wet meadows, upper reaches of saltmarshes

NEST Small cup hidden by vegetation in damp area

EGGS 4; slightly glossy, pale green to olive, with red or brown dark blotches

FOOD Invertebrates

IN ADDITION TO its distinctive long bill, the Snipe also has a characteristic feeding action, unlike that of other waders. It probes into soft mud with a very jerky action, vibrating the tip of the bill slightly. The tip is sensitive and food can be sucked up without the bill being withdrawn from the mud. The bird will fly off if disturbed, usually on an erratic flight path, before dropping to safety. In the breeding season males perform aerial displays, making a strange bleating sound with their tail feathers, which stick out as they dive through the air.

Sexes similar. Upperparts are brown with pale stripes; larger feathers have dark centres and pale margins, giving scaly appearance. Flanks are barred and underside is greyish-white. Juveniles almost identical to adults.

Very long-billed wader with distinctively patterned head and back.

LEFT: *adult*   ABOVE: *adult*

displaying adult

Short tail is barred and has buff margin.

adult

adult

Legs dull green and bill pale reddish-brown with darker tip in both adults and juveniles.

JACK SNIPE

Lymnocryptes minimus

BIRD FACTS

VOICE A brief sneezing sound when flushed, otherwise silent except for muffled, whistling display call near nest

LENGTH 17–19cm

WINGSPAN 36–40cm

WEIGHT 40–70g

HABITAT Breeds on tundra bogs; overwinters on lowland marshes

NEST Grass-lined cup on ground near water; hidden by vegetation

EGGS 4; smooth, olive to dark brown with many darker spots and blotches

FOOD Insects, worms, molluscs taken from soft mud and from surface

THE JACK SNIPE is far less sociable than the Snipe, normally occurring in low densities and usually only seen when flushed. It prefers to feed in areas where there is some covering vegetation and will freeze until approached to within about 1m before suddenly shooting upwards, turning slightly and dropping again. At the last moment it will open its wings to brake and then vanish into cover. The relatively short bill is a good guide to identification if the bird is seen in flight. Its flight is more direct than the Snipe's and looks rather weaker. On the ground the Jack Snipe moves rather awkwardly with plenty of tail bobbing and crouching. It is usually silent, but its display call has been likened to the sound of distant horses galloping.

Small, short-billed snipe with conspicuous pale-yellow stripes running along back. Overall impression is of greenish-brown patterned back and boldly marked head. Legs and feet are green. Sexes are similar and it is usually not possible to distinguish juveniles from adults.

Relatively short bill is yellowish with a darker tip.

When keeping still among grasses and sedges, pale back stripes give Jack Snipe excellent camouflage.

GREAT SNIPE

Gallinago media

THE GREAT SNIPE is normally only seen when flushed, as it tends to sit tight until approached to within a few metres. Boggy woodland clearings, willow scrub and mountain slopes are usually chosen as nesting areas; plenty of open wet patches and tussocks for display purposes are required. Males congregate in groups and display on tussocks, making strange chirping sounds and a more wooden bill clattering. Sometimes several males perform 'flutter jumps' as well. The females are much more secretive, nesting beneath thick cover and remaining silent.

BIRD FACTS

VOICE Mostly silent, but gives short 'itch' call, and has a chirping display call on territory

LENGTH 27–29cm

WINGSPAN 45–50cm

WEIGHT 185–225g

HABITAT Marshy areas in mountains and lowlands

NEST Concealed on ground in thick vegetation

EGGS 4; slightly glossy, buff with dark-brown spots and blotches

FOOD Earthworms and other soil invertebrates

Has darker belly than Snipe and distinctive white outertail feathers; plumage brightest during breeding season.

adult

IDENTIFICATION

Larger and plumper than Snipe, with slightly shorter bill, longer legs, stronger barring on the belly and more strongly patterned wing coverts. In flight, white outertail feathers and white wingbars are diagnostic; bird also appears larger than Snipe, with more rounded body shape and wings. Flight pattern is more laboured than Snipe's and usually straight, not zigzagged; the bird settles rather abruptly by dropping into cover. In winter plumage becomes duller because of wear of buff and cinnamon feather margins. Sexes similar and juveniles essentially indistinguishable from adults in the field, although white markings are less clear.

GREAT SNIPE displaying adult

BROAD-BILLED SANDPIPER

Limicola falcinellus

THE BROAD-BILLED SANDPIPER is a scarce wader with scattered breeding sites across northern Scandinavia and Siberia; it only turns up in western Europe as a scarce migrant. If mingled with Dunlin the bill tip and crown markings are the best features for identification. In summer the Broad-billed Sandpiper is found on boggy ground between 250 and 1,000m, choosing nesting sites that are almost floating; it prefers areas with plenty of *Sphagnum* moss, cotton grass and sedges. In winter the species seems to like wetter areas, where there is plenty of soft mud to probe.

IDENTIFICATION

Slightly smaller than Dunlin, with longer body profile and more sharply downturned bill tip. In breeding and juvenile plumage, head shows pale stripes similar to Snipe, and pale supercilium. Upperparts pale in early summer owing to broad, pale feather fringes; these are lost with wear and plumage gradually becomes richer brown. In winter looks similar to winter-plumage Dunlin but the pale crown stripes can still be seen in good light and the legs appear muddy grey-green. Juvenile recalls breeding-plumage adult but with pale margins on upperparts.

BIRD FACTS

VOICE Rasping 'chrreeeit' and mechanical-sounding 'swirr swirr swirr'

LENGTH 16–18cm

WINGSPAN 34–37cm

WEIGHT 29–49g

HABITAT Breeds on bogs in sub-Arctic

NEST Small cup in tussock on boggy ground

EGGS 4; smooth, pale buff with red-brown speckles

FOOD Invertebrates, some seeds and small fruits

BROAD-BILLED SANDPIPER Adult in breeding plumage.

BELOW: GREAT SNIPE adult

GREAT SKUA

Stercorarius skua

THE LARGEST OF all the skuas is an aggressive bird that allows no intruders, including humans, anywhere near its nest or young. The Great Skua readily attacks if provoked and shows no fear of any predator. Nesting colonies are normally near colonies of other seabirds, where there are easy meals to be had throughout the breeding season. Great Skuas follow other birds at sea and, although they can catch fish for themselves, they typically attack other birds, catching the fish they drop before it hits the water.

Bulky bird, adult reminiscent of juvenile gull but darker and far more heavily built. Juvenile similar to adult but usually darker; may show pale tips to larger feathers on upperparts. When standing on land, short legs and small feet obvious in all birds; when swimming, looks especially bulky and buoyant.

BIRD FACTS

VOICE Utters harsh 'tuk tuk' alarm calls and other fierce contact notes

LENGTH 53–66cm

WINGSPAN 125–140cm

WEIGHT 1.2–1.8kg

HABITAT Seabird cliffs and islands in summer; overwinters at sea

NEST Shallow scrape on ground; sparse lining of leaves and feathers

EGGS 2; smooth, chestnut-brown or paler with variable brown spots and blotches

FOOD Takes fish from other seabirds, plus eggs, chicks, fish from sea

juvenile

adult

DID YOU KNOW?

The Great Skua will harrass other seabirds into dropping their prey.

In flight, adult looks broad-winged and short-tailed, sometimes with two slightly projecting central feathers.

adult

The white flashes on the dark wings are seen well in flight and during aggressive displays on land when the wings are raised over the head.

BELOW: *Adults displaying.*

ARCTIC SKUA
Stercorarius parasiticus

Adult occurs in pale, intermediate and dark phases, pale being commonest in north and dark commonest in south of range. Dark phase birds have sooty brown plumage all over with darker cap and yellowish tone to sides of face. Pale phase birds are paler grey on mantle with grey-brown cap; flanks and ventral region light grey-brown and rest of underside, head and neck white. Pale phase birds show some straw yellow around the neck. Legs and bill are black in pale and dark phases, and both have all-dark wings with pale white flashes. Juvenile plumage very variable, pale phase birds having pale heads and light brown plumage with darker markings below, giving scaly appearance; dark birds are almost all dark with a slightly paler head.

THE ARCTIC SKUA is the commonest of the skuas on the coasts of northwest Europe and the Arctic ocean. Arctic Skuas are argumentative birds, screaming at each other and fighting over territories in breeding colonies. Defiant birds raise their wings high over their heads to show the white patches and attack any intruders, including humans. The skuas can perform exciting aerial displays to startle a smaller bird into dropping a fish. They will sometimes sit on a rock near a seabird colony and watch for a returning bird with a fish and then attack at the last moment by flying at high speed like a falcon.

BIRD FACTS

VOICE Utters a Kittiwake-like 'kee-aah', and short 'kukk' calls

LENGTH 46–67cm

WINGSPAN 97–115cm

WEIGHT 360–590g

HABITAT Breeds on coasts near other seabirds; overwinters at sea

NEST Shallow depression on open ground; sparse lining of leaves and feathers

EGGS 2; smooth, olive or brown, rarely blue, with brownish spots and blotches

FOOD Harries other birds to make them drop food

Almost falcon-like appearance in flight, with long, slender wings and long tail; has dashing, acrobatic flight when pursuing other birds.

Pale phase adult chasing Kittiwake.

dark phase

BELOW: *dark phase adult*
BOTTOM: *intermediate phase adult*

POMARINE SKUA

Stercorarius pomarinus

THE POMARINE SKUA'S principal summer food is lemmings, but it will also take eggs and chicks of other birds and eat carrion; it will even attack and kill smaller birds. It is very agile in the air, so is able to pursue seabirds returning to their young with food and scare them into dropping it. Pomarine Skuas can also catch fish for themselves if necessary. In summer they feed mostly on or near to land, but in winter they move far out to sea, following other birds and spending most of their time where there are upwelling currents, which provide rich feeding.

BIRD FACTS

VOICE Harsh, gull-like 'kowk' or 'geck' anger calls and higher mewing contact calls

LENGTH 65–78cm

WINGSPAN 113–125cm

WEIGHT 640–870g

HABITAT Breeds on high Arctic tundra, overwinters at sea

NEST Shallow depression on open ground

EGGS 2; slightly glossy, olive or brown with dark brown spots and blotches

FOOD On breeding grounds, lemmings, eggs, chicks of other birds and fish caught by harrying other seabirds; a food-pirate at other times of year

Juvenile pale brown with darker brown barring; white wing flashes are visible, but tail streamers are absent.

juvenile

IDENTIFICATION

Large, gull-like bird with heavy bill, large head and barrel-shaped body. Adult plumage very variable, with most birds occurring as pale phase and smaller number as dark phase. Pale phase birds are black-brown above and on upper chest and vent; belly white and nape pale yellow. Dark chest markings sometimes form complete band. Dark phase birds have sooty brown plumage all over; bronze wash to plumage seen only in good light.

Wings long and broad at base, and tail relatively long with twisted streamers in full adult plumage; both light and dark forms have white wing 'flashes' seen on both surfaces and showing very clearly in flight.

pale phase adult

adult

LONG-TAILED SKUA

Stercorarius longicaudus

THE BREEDING SUCCESS of the Long-tailed Skua is highly dependent on the populations of lemmings and other small rodents in the tundra and treeless regions of the Scandinavian mountains; in bad rodent years it may fail to breed altogether. The clutch size is also determined by the abundance of small mammals available to the females before breeding. Non-breeding birds live in loose flocks and hunt overland for food, usually away from the nesting areas. Of all the skuas, this is the species most likely to be seen well inland. This is a rare bird in northwest Europe, seen far less frequently on migration than the other species.

BIRD FACTS

VOICE Short 'kreck kreck' calls, and more drawn-out cackling calls for display

LENGTH 35–58cm

WINGSPAN 92–105cm

WEIGHT 250–380g

HABITAT Breeds on tundra; overwinters at sea

NEST Shallow depression on open ground with sparse lining

EGGS 2; slightly glossy, olive-green to buff with brownish spots and blotches

FOOD Rodents on tundra, plus fish, insects, carrion, berries; mainly fish-eater at sea

Smaller than other skuas, with narrow wings, long tail and slender body; like other skua species, however, powerful chest makes head appear relatively small.

IDENTIFICATION

In breeding plumage adult has greyish-brown mantle and flanks, which contrast with darker wingtips and feathers. Cap is black and sides of face and neck are pale yellow; breast is pale, darkening towards ventral region. Bill short but thick.

juvenile   *adult*

Juvenile's plumage variable, but most birds are very dark with paler feather margins, giving barred appearance; overall tone greyer than juvenile Arctic Skua.

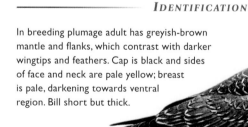

Adult has black wingtips and grey mantle; head and body otherwise pure white and bill plain yellow during summer months. In winter head and neck show grey-brown flecks and bill duller than in summer adult, some individuals showing dark tip. Immature shows extensive brown in wings in first winter and broad, black terminal tail band. In second winter wings almost completely pale grey. Immatures have black bills at first, these becoming dull flesh colour before turning yellower in second winter.

1st winter

winter adult

COMMON GULL

Larus canus

THE COMMON GULL is not in fact the commonest of the gulls of the region, being confined mainly to breeding colonies in northern Europe. In winter birds disperse to the seas and marshes relatively close to their breeding sites. The Common Gull can feed at sea like other large gulls but is also adept at feeding on land; it has learnt to exploit foods like cranefly larvae and earthworms, turned up when fields are ploughed. The Common Gull population seems to have increased in the 20th century, an indication of how this species has adapted to modern fishing and agricultural methods.

BIRD FACTS

VOICE Shrill 'keeow' and mewing 'gleeoo' calls

LENGTH 38–44cm

WINGSPAN 110–125cm

WEIGHT 300–480g

HABITAT Coasts, freshwater lakes, marshes

NEST Shallow cup of plant material on open ground, sometimes over water

EGGS 3; smooth, olive or pale blue-green with brown streaks and spots

FOOD Fish, marine invertebrates, insects, earthworms

Smaller and neater in profile than Herring Gull, and adult has dark eye.

BELOW: summer adult
BOTTOM: 1st winter

Wings show black primaries with white flecks in flight.

BLACK-HEADED GULL

Chroicocephalus ridibundus

THE BLACK-HEADED GULL is one of the commonest European gulls, breeding over a huge area of central Europe and Scandinavia. In winter, Black-headed Gulls turn up in most habitats from agricultural land, city parks and coastal marshes to the open sea, where they will follow fishing boats. The Black-headed Gull is an opportunist feeder, taking a wide range of foods; modern agriculture and waste disposal have provided it with good feeding in winter, so the population has increased. In winter many birds congregate in huge roosts, dispersing during the day to regular feeding areas.

In flight, all non-juvenile plumages show white leading edge to wing with black border to primaries on upperwing. Summer adult has dark chocolate brown head, colour extending to middle of head but not onto nape. Bill red with dark tip and legs dark red. Juvenile is buffish white; subsequently, immature birds acquire grey mantle with brown and black wing coverts and black terminal tail band; legs and base of bill in immature birds are dark flesh coloured.

BIRD FACTS

VOICE Utters harsh screaming calls; very vocal near nests and when in feeding flocks

LENGTH 38–44cm

WINGSPAN 94–105cm

WEIGHT 160–310g

HABITAT Sheltered seashores, lakes, marshes, urban parks, farmland

NEST Shallow scrape with lining of leaves and feathers; on bare ground or amongst marshy vegetation

EGGS 2–3; smooth, variable, green, greyish or brown with darker spots and blotches

FOOD Insects, earthworms, marine invertebrates, plant matter; some household waste and scraps

summer adult

1st winter

White leading edge to upperwing distinctive in all post-juvenile plumages.

Underside of wings dark grey with thinner white leading edge.

In winter, adult's head is white with two blackish smudges around and behind eye; legs and bill paler than in summer.

winter adult

juvenile

immature, 1st winter

immature, 1st summer

adult, winter

adult, summer

In flight, wings of adult appear pure white at the tips. In winter, summer adult's black head is lost and bird appears white apart from dark smudges around and behind eye. First-winter bird has black terminal band on tail, black primaries, mostly grey secondaries and brownish-grey wing coverts. Second-winter bird has mainly pale grey mantle but still shows black near tips to primaries and partial black head.

winter adult

MEDITERRANEAN GULL

Larus melanocephalus

MEDITERRANEAN GULLS PREFER flat areas such as saltmarshes for nesting, and are most wide-spread around the Mediterranean and Black Seas. Small numbers also breed in northwest Europe. Adults will fly great distances from the colony each day to feeding areas, and will form large flocks in places where there are hatches of insects such as flying ants. The Mediterranean Gull seems to be most at home on the coast, and usually avoids fly-ing far from the sight of land. In winter it frequently joins mixed feeding flocks of gull species in har-bours or near refuse tips, where there is scope for scavenging.

BIRD FACTS

VOICE Deep, nasal calls, mostly heard in spring; generally silent in winter

LENGTH 36–38cm

WINGSPAN 98–105cm

WEIGHT 250–350g

HABITAT Coasts and lagoons; lake shores mainly in Mediterranean area

NEST Shallow depression lined with grass and feathers

EGGS 3; smooth, cream or buff with dark brown spots and speckles

FOOD Insects, fish, marine invertebrates

In summer plumage, adult has black head with incomplete white eyering giving impression of eyelids.

DID YOU KNOW?

From a distance, adult can look all white but close-up view reveals very pale grey mantle.

2nd winter

summer adult

LITTLE GULL

Hydrocoloeus minutus

FROM A DISTANCE, a Little Gull in flight appears to flicker as the dark underwing contrasts with the pale mantle. Its energetic and vigorous flight, with frequent dips down to the water to pick up food, distinguishes it from other larger gulls. It can rise vertically for short distances and hover briefly before dipping down again. When at sea, small flocks will follow in the wake of ships or hover over areas of turbulent water. Little Gulls breed in colonies in marshy areas, nearly always over fresh water, but occasionally they nest on very sheltered stretches of coast where there is emergent vegetation; they may form mixed colonies with Black-headed Gulls. In winter they usually remain offshore and are seldom seen in large numbers.

juvenile

2nd autumn

IDENTIFICATION

Smallest gull of the region, with vigorous tern-like flight. Wings of adult are black on underside with trailing white edge. Mantle is pale blue-grey and rest of plumage is white but suffused with pale pink. In summer, head is all black; in winter, adult has paler head with dark-grey cap and black spot behind eye. In breeding season legs and bill are red; legs fade to flesh colour and bill becomes black in winter.

1st summer

summer adult

Immature birds in their first autumn and winter have characteristic black 'V' markings on upperwings.

1st winter

DID YOU KNOW?

The bulk of the Little Gull population is found in northeastern Europe and Russia; in winter many move as far as southwest Europe and southern Britain.

Elegant gull with proportionately slender wings and relatively large bill. In flight, mantle looks pale silvery grey with trailing white edge and contrasting black tips to primaries; inner primaries have a few white flecks. Bill mostly red with black and yellow tip. Legs black. Juvenile has mostly grey-brown plumage, darker mantle and black bill. In second winter, juvenile shows dark primaries, mostly grey mantle, and black terminal band to white tail. At this stage bill is red, with black and yellow tip.

Juvenile recalls juvenile Lesser Black-backed Gull.

1st winter

adult

Adult has very pale plumage.

AUDOUIN'S GULL
Larus audouinii

AUDOUIN'S GULL IS a rare breeding bird of the Mediterranean, nesting in colonies that are safe from human interference and usually no more than 50m above sea level. It is a very graceful bird in flight, spending much time wheeling and gliding in search of food; its excellent manoeuvrability enables it to catch fish easily and it stands out among the bulkier Yellow-legged Gulls. Audouin's Gulls can pick food from the surface of the sea without needing to slow down; only in strong winds will they alight on the water to catch prey. During severe storms they will also feed on land, taking insects and worms.

DID YOU KNOW?

This is a rare gull, but the world population has increased since the 1970s to over 18,000.

SLENDER-BILLED GULL
Larus genei

THE LONG, POINTED bill, which is not in fact especially slender, and the shallow forehead and long neck ensure that the Slender-billed Gull stands out easily from other gulls, such as Black-headed Gulls, with which it often mixes. It is good at catching fish and can make shallow dives or dip with its bill while in flight. It will also feed on the shore, picking invertebrates from the surface. Birds breeding away from the coast catch insects in flight, and some will visit outfalls to scavenge. In summer, when fish shoals are close to the surface, large excited feeding flocks will form, sometimes in association with other gulls.

non-breeding adult

summer adult

IDENTIFICATION

Adult similar to adult winter Black-headed Gull but completely lacking dark markings on head. Slightly larger than that species, however, with longer, broader wings and with slower wingbeats in normal flight. It often flies in 'V' formation like larger gulls. Adult has pale grey mantle with leading white edge to wings and black-tipped primaries; white underside is suffused with pink in summer. Long bill is orange with dark tip, and legs are paler orange than Black-headed Gull's. Juvenile has pale orange legs and bill, and wings have buff and dark brown coverts; shows tiny smudge of grey behind eye. If seen in mixed flocks with other gulls, appears to have proportionately long bill and small eye at all times.

In the breeding season the adult Slender-billed Gull shows a pink flush to its underparts.

KITTIWAKE
Rissa tridactyla

KITTIWAKES ARE FOUND in huge colonies around the sheer sea cliffs of Europe's northernmost coasts, where they are very noisy. At important mixed seabird colonies they are often the most numerous species. Breeding birds enjoy access to fresh water for washing, and sometimes take surrounding vegetation back to the nest. Kittiwakes are not truly migratory but they do disperse into the open Atlantic and North Sea during the winter. During autumn gales, flocks of Kittiwakes pass the shores in apparently effortless buoyant flight, even over the most stormy seas.

Slightly larger than Black-headed Gull but has more compact body and proportionately long wings. Summer adult (BELOW LEFT) has bright white head, neck, underparts, rump and tail. At all times of year bill pale yellow, and legs and feet brownish-black. Juvenile (BELOW RIGHT) has diagnostic blackish zigzag across grey and white upperwing.

BIRD FACTS

VOICE Utters the musical cawing of its name, 'kit-ee-wak'

LENGTH 38–40cm

WINGSPAN 95–120cm

WEIGHT 305–525g

HABITAT Breeds on sheer, high sea cliffs; open sea in winter

NEST Compacted cup of mud, grass and seaweed on cliff ledge

EGGS 1–3; smooth, pale buff, lightly spotted and blotched dark brown

FOOD Marine fish and invertebrates

Kittiwakes build their nests on tiny ledges on sheer cliffs.

adult

Apart from conspicuous 'W' on wings, immature bird also shows blackish hind collar, black mark on face and dark tip to very slightly forked tail; bill black.

Nesting colony on seacliff.

Smaller than Kittiwake, with narrower wings, more deeply forked tail and buoyant tern-like flight action. Summer adult has dusky-grey head with thin black lower border around neck; lower neck and underparts pure white. Mantle is grey, and tail and rump are white; upperwing shows smart and diagnostic triangular pattern of grey coverts, white inner primaries and secondaries, and black outer primaries. In winter, the adult bird loses its dark hood but retains the dusky streaking on the nape of its neck. Bill black with yellow tip at all times; legs and feet blackish-grey. Juvenile has similar upperwing pattern to adult but with grey elements of plumage replaced by warm brown; shows dark tip to tail.

adult

juvenile

juvenile

SABINE'S GULL

Larus sabini

DESPITE THE DISTANCE of its summer haunts from northwest European seas, Sabine's Gulls are seen regularly from these coasts, mostly in late autumn when storms move the birds from open seas to inshore shelter. This gull is small and dainty, almost tern-like in its erratic and buoyant flight, its forked tail adding to this similarity. Care is needed to distinguish this species from the juvenile Kittiwake, which has a superficially similar upperwing pattern with an additional black wingbar across the coverts.

BIRD FACTS

VOICE Various grating cries and whistling calls

LENGTH 27–32cm

WINGSPAN 90–100cm

WEIGHT 155–210g

HABITAT Arctic coastal lowlands; open seas in winter

NEST Shallow unlined depression

EGGS 2; smooth, olive, variably marked, dark brown mostly at broad end

FOOD Invertebrates, small fish, occasionally carrion

summer adult

DID YOU KNOW?

Sabine's Gulls undertake trans-equatorial movements to winter in seas off southern Africa.

HERRING GULL

Larus argentatus

HERRING GULLS ARE able to exploit a wide range of habitats and food sources. They can feed on the seashore and in the open sea, and can also scavenge in refuse tips and feed on agricultural land. They will take small migrating birds over the sea, and frequently prey on other smaller seabirds on nesting colonies. Herring Gulls nest colonially, and also feed and roost in large numbers outside the breeding season, but they also may be seen in small numbers on migration after the breeding season. It is suspected that Herring Gulls pair for life, and pairs are reported to have returned to the same nest site for as long as twenty years.

Adult plumage – silvery grey mantle with black wingtips flecked with white – is acquired in the fourth year. Large bill is yellow with orange spot near tip of lower mandible. Eye is yellow and legs are pink. Immatures are mottled brown in first winter with dark eye and bill, and dirty-pink legs. In second winter, have more grey in mantle, and iris becomes paler. Before attaining full adult plumage, black wingtips may look very pale, potentially causing confusion with Iceland or Glaucous Gulls.

summer adult

BIRD FACTS

VOICE Utters long 'aahhoo' calls and deep chuckling notes

LENGTH 55–67cm

WINGSPAN 130–158cm

WEIGHT 800–1,100g

HABITAT All types of coastline, large lakes, rivers

NEST Large cup of vegetation; on ground, sometimes on buildings

EGGS 2–3; smooth, olive to brown, with numerous dark-brown spots and streaks

FOOD Diet very varied; will eat almost anything organic that it can swallow

DID YOU KNOW?

Herring Gulls have very expressive calls and behaviour and can show aggression by defiant postures and loud calls.

winter adult

1st winter

2nd winter

YELLOW-LEGGED GULL

1st winter

Larus michahellis

THE YELLOW-LEGGED GULL is able to feed in a variety of ways and has adapted to modern fishing methods, frequently following fishing vessels and scavenging on waste; it is most likely to be seen near harbours or feeding at outfalls and refuse tips. It is now far more common than any other gull in the Mediterranean.

BIRD FACTS

VOICE Utters raucous 'aahhoo' calls and deep chuckling notes

LENGTH 55–67cm

WINGSPAN 130–158cm

WEIGHT 800–1,000g

HABITAT Mediterranean region, Black Sea

NEST Large, untidy cup of vegetation on ground

EGGS 2–3; olive to brown with darker spots and blotches

FOOD Wide range of fish and marine invertebrates, plus anything found by scavenging

IDENTIFICATION

Very similar to, and formerly considered a race of, Herring Gull; adult differs in having yellow legs and darker grey mantle when compared to western European Herring Gulls. In winter, adult lacks dark mottling on head and neck, characteristic of Herring Gulls. At all times, bill is richer yellow and has larger red spot near tip than Herring Gull. Three separate races of Yellow-legged Gull are recognised by experts; these are very similar, and are not considered here. Immature birds are brown as juveniles and in first winter; legs dark. Acquire adult's white head and body plumage, grey mantle and yellow legs through successive moults over subsequent two years.

adult

adult

adult

LESSER BLACK-BACKED GULL

Larus fuscus

THE LESSER BLACK-BACKED Gull is a migrant over much of its range, spending its winters at sea but generally staying close to the coast in summer. In recent years more birds have remained inland in winter, where they have learnt to exploit man-made resources such as refuse tips and agricultural land. They often gather in large roosts on reservoirs near cities. Many immature birds remain on the overwintering grounds, south of their breeding grounds, for one or two years, so birds in second- and third-year immature plumage are not often seen in northwest Europe in summer.

Occurs as three races in Europe, all of which have bright yellow legs. Adults of western race, *graellsii*, are slate-grey on mantle and can be confused with Yellow-legged Gull; wingtips show less white on black primaries than this species. Birds breeding around Baltic belong to race *fuscus*, and are black above, looking like slim Great Black-backed Gull but with only a single white spot on primaries. Scandinavian birds of race *intermedius* show characteristics of both of others. Juvenile has brown plumage, darker than juvenile Herring Gull, especially when seen in flight. Adult plumage acquired over subsequent two years. At successive moults, head and body become whiter, and brown on wings replaced by grey.

Black wingtips clearly darker than dark-grey wings and mantle.

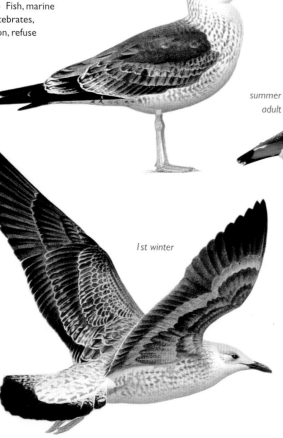

2nd winter

summer adult

1st winter

First-winter bird (ABOVE) has all-dark flight feathers; in second winter (TOP), acquires grey back and pale bill.

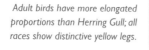

winter adult

Adult birds have more elongated proportions than Herring Gull; all races show distinctive yellow legs.

adult

GREAT BLACK-BACKED GULL

Larus marinus

THE GREAT BLACK-BACKED Gull can be solitary but in many areas prefers to breed in loose colonies. It often breeds in the company of other seabirds, which may then become its source of food. The species is not completely migratory, and some Great Black-backed Gulls move offshore in winter; over half the European population uses waters around Britain at this time. Flocks feed around fishing trawlers at sea and in harbours, where they often roost on buildings. Recently developed scavenging habits at rubbish dumps have probably resulted in an increase in the population.

IDENTIFICATION

Much larger and bulkier than Herring Gull, with large angular head, heavy bill and broad back. Sexes similar. Adult in summer has white head, neck, rump and tail. Back and upperwing slaty black with white tips to primaries forming row of white spots on closed wingtip. Underparts white. Bill yellow with red spot on lower mandible towards tip. Legs and feet pink. In winter, adult head and neck streaked with brownish-grey. Juvenile and immature plumages mottled dark brown and white, with whiter rump and blackish terminal band to tail; bill black.

DID YOU KNOW?

Great Black-backed Gulls scavenge at carrion but will also happily bring down adult seabirds returning to colonies with food, either to steal the morsels or kill the birds themselves; auks are particularly vulnerable to these attacks.

BIRD FACTS

VOICE Utters deep barking 'owk uk-uk-uk'; also various other wailing and squeaking calls

LENGTH 64–78cm

WINGSPAN 150–165cm

WEIGHT 1–2.2kg

HABITAT Breeds on coastal islands, stacks, beaches and saltmarshes, occasionally inland at freshwater lakes; continental-shelf waters in winter

NEST Heap of seaweed, vegetation and debris on ground, cliff or roof

EGGS 2–3; smooth, olive brown, blotched dark-brown and grey

FOOD Omnivorous and opportunistic; predator of smaller seabirds and scavenges widely

Unlike with Herring Gulls, black blotches on wings increase in second and third years.

ABOVE: *2nd winter*

Juveniles in flight are similar to young Herring Gulls, but head is paler and tail more clearly banded.

1st winter

1st winter

GLAUCOUS GULL

Larus hyperboreus

THE GLAUCOUS GULL prefers coastal breeding sites facing open seas, especially cliffs separated from the sea by a shelf of grassland. It shares its breeding sites with geese and auks, which helps its piratical feeding methods. When found together with the Iceland Gull this species requires care with identification: it is almost always larger, and its angular head and heavy bill give it a much fiercer expression than its smaller relative. The Glaucous Gull is not completely migratory; some individuals disperse only as far south as winter ice forces them to. Storms in early winter move birds further south and west, and at these times they can be found in considerable numbers on west European coasts.

Larger than Iceland Gull but usually smaller than Great Black-backed Gull. Looks pale and white-winged at all times. Summer adult has pale grey back and upperwing, otherwise plumage completely white, including wingtips. In winter, head and neck streaked brown. Pale eye, yellow bill with red spot, and pink legs and feet at all times. Immature plumages white with uniform pale mottled brown gradually lost by moulting until all-white by third year; bill pink with black tip.

Winter adult has streaked head and neck.

winter adult

BIRD FACTS

VOICE Short, high-pitched yapping and wailing calls

LENGTH 62–68cm

WINGSPAN 150–165cm

WEIGHT 1.2–2.1kg

HABITAT Breeds on small islands on Arctic and sub-Arctic coasts; overwinters on bays and harbours

NEST Large pile of seaweed and debris

EGGS 2–3; smooth, buff, blotched and spotted dark brown

FOOD Omnivorous; predator and scavenger, and food-pirate of other seabirds

DID YOU KNOW?

In winter, the best places to look for Glaucous Gulls are harbours where fishing boats dock and process their catches.

RIGHT: 2nd summer
BELOW: 1st winter

ABOVE AND RIGHT: adult

ICELAND GULL

Larus glaucoides

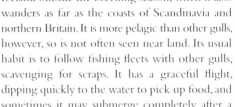

Smaller than Herring Gull, with more rounded head and smaller bill. Absence of black on wingtips at all times is good identification feature but may lead to confusion with Glaucous Gull; Iceland Gull is smaller and more graceful in flight. At rest, wingtips project further beyond end of tail. Juvenile and first-winter bird very similar to juvenile Glaucous Gull, with essentially white plumage mottled pale brown, but bill is brown-grey, not pale pink. Second-winter bird has pale, marbled grey upperparts and pale, streaked head and underparts. Pale grey bill has dark sub-terminal band.

THE ICELAND GULL breeds off the coast of Green-land and northeast Canada, but may be seen in Iceland outside the breeding season, when it also wanders as far as the coasts of Scandinavia and northern Britain. It is more pelagic than other gulls, however, so is not often seen near land. Its usual habit is to follow fishing fleets with other gulls, scavenging for scraps. It has a graceful flight, dipping quickly to the water to pick up food, and sometimes it may submerge completely after a plunge. Sometimes it follows boats into harbour in a mixed flock with other gulls.

BIRD FACTS

VOICE Utters shrill version of Herring Gull's 'aahhoo' call

LENGTH 52–60cm

WINGSPAN 130–145cm

WEIGHT 730–870g

HABITAT Breeds on Arctic islands; overwinters at sea

NEST Does not breed in region

EGGS Does not breed in region

FOOD Mainly fish; will also take carrion, plankton, eggs and chicks of other birds

Very pale appearance and rounded head profile immediately separate Iceland Gull from all large gulls other than Glaucous Gulls.

BELOW: winter adult

TOP LEFT: winter adult; BOTTOM LEFT: 2nd winter; BELOW: 2nd winter

BLACK TERN

Chlidonias niger

VOICE Squeaky harsh 'kik-keek' call; growling 'krrr' when on nest

LENGTH 22–24cm

WINGSPAN 64–68cm

WEIGHT 60–85g

HABITAT Continental, fresh or brackish waters, rich in floating and emergent vegetation

NEST Low heap of waterweed or shallow scrape lined with waterweed

EGGS 2–4; oval, glossy, cream, spotted and blotched dark brown

FOOD Insects and aquatic invertebrates; some small fish and amphibians

THE BLACK TERN is a breeding bird of eastern Europe with many scattered colonies to the west, especially round the swampy meadows and pools of the Netherlands. Birds return in May to breeding waters, where they are loosely colonial. Foraging adults fly buoyantly over water, dipping to the surface to take invertebrate prey. Black Terns are migratory, overwintering in tropical West Africa. During migration periods large numbers can some-times be seen in northwest Europe. The spring movement is most impressive: in favourable conditions, many thousands pass through reservoirs and lakes, and along coasts, often on the same day.

Smaller than all sea terns, with shorter, less forked tail. Summer adult dark slate-grey, with head almost black and upperwing ash-grey. Rump and uppertail grey. Underwing very pale grey, vent and undertail coverts white. In winter, grey upperparts and white underparts reminiscent of sea terns, but upperparts darker and with black smudge at shoulder. Moult between summer and winter plumages can give very blotchy appearance. Juvenile plumage has darker saddle. At all times bill black, long and fine, and legs and feet red brown.

adult, summer plumage

adult, summer plumage

juvenile

Flight light and erratic, with frequent dips to surface of water.

adult

first autumn

Breeding plumage bird has black head, neck and body, upperwings greyer and show bright silver-white wing coverts. Underwing shows black coverts and pale-grey flight feathers. Rump, vent and tail white. In winter, grey above and white below, with white collar and white rump contrasting with grey tail. Bill short and pointed, crimson when breeding, otherwise black. Legs and feet bright red in summer, darker in winter. Juvenile similar to winter adult but with darker, mottled brown back forming saddle.

juvenile

LEFT:
summer adults
BELOW:
summer adult

WHITE-WINGED BLACK TERN
Chlidonias leucopterus

THE NATURAL MARSHES and alkaline pools among the vast grasslands of Poland and Hungary are the White-winged Black Tern's favoured breeding areas. Birds arrive in mid-May from wintering grounds in Africa to begin building their floating nests. They find their food in and around the breeding lakes, sometimes quartering adjacent rivers in typical buoyant and erratic flight. During migration the birds occasionally occur north of their usual range; a few adults are seen annually in spring in northwest Europe, with juveniles occurring in autumn.

BIRD FACTS

VOICE Call is a sharp churring 'keer'; shorter alarm notes

LENGTH 20–23cm

WINGSPAN 63–67cm

WEIGHT 56–80g

HABITAT Natural flooded grasslands and swamps

NEST Heap of floating, partly submerged waterweed with shallow depression

EGGS 2–3; oval, glossy, cream with large blackish blotches

FOOD Mainly aquatic or terrestrial invertebrates; some fish and amphibians

Relatively bulky size invites confusion with sea tern, but has shorter, less forked tail. Summer adult has jet-black crown and nape, contrasting with white lower face. Neck and rest of upperparts uniform grey, including rump and uppertail. Below white face underparts become dark slate grey, darkest on flanks. Vent and undertail coverts white. Upperwing grey, underwing coverts white. In winter much more like sea tern, with grey upperparts and white underparts. Bill dark crimson-red in summer adult but black in winter and juvenile. Legs and feet red at all times. Juvenile resembles winter adult, with dark brown back and pale grey upperwing, giving saddle effect.

WHISKERED TERN
Chlidonias hybridus

THE WHISKERED TERN is found more southerly in Europe than the Black Tern, requiring a warmer climate than that species. The Camargue, in southern France, is a typical habitat. Here the terns nest semi-colonially, building floating nests from vegetation stirred up by wild horses, and often foraging on adjacent flooded rice paddies. The species overwinters in tropical Africa and Asia.

BIRD FACTS

VOICE Loud croaking and cawing 'krrerch'; sharper alarm call

LENGTH 23–25cm

WINGSPAN 74–78cm

WEIGHT 80–90g

HABITAT Clear water, lakes and marshes with floating vegetation

NEST Cone-shaped raft of vegetation, anchored to submerged plant

EGGS 2–3; oval, glossy, pale-blue or grey, spotted and blotched brown

FOOD Insects and their larvae; some small fish, amphibians

juvenile

breeding adult

SANDWICH TERN

Sterna sandvicensis

SANDWICH TERN COLONIES require access to shallow, sheltered waters, usually over sand for fishing, and birds will travel a considerable distance to feeding grounds from where they nest or roost. Nest sites are mostly on offshore islands or calcareous spits with short vegetation in which to place the actual scrape; the birds tend to relocate from one year to the next as the nesting area is often unstable. Sandwich Terns are one of northwest Europe's first summer migrants, appearing at the end of March. They are highly sensitive to disturbance when breeding and benefit greatly from artificial protection measures.

Large and pale tern with long bill and head. Tail short but deeply forked. Wings long and narrow. In breeding season, Sandwich Tern has jet black cap with shaggy crest to rear. Back and upperwing very pale grey with silvery flight feathers. Rump and tail white. Underparts bright white. In winter, forehead becomes white and cap is mottled. At all times, adult has black bill with yellow tip, and black legs and feet. Juvenile resembles winter adult, but has shorter all-black bill and blackish flecking on upperwing and back.

non-breeding adult

BIRD FACTS

VOICE Distinct disyllabic 'keerr-ink'; shorter, sharp alarm note

LENGTH 36–41cm

WINGSPAN 95–105cm

WEIGHT 225–285g

HABITAT Low-lying coasts with access to shallow, sandy-bottomed waters

NEST Shallow, unlined scrape on shingle or amongst vegetation

EGGS 1–2; glossy, creamy white, variably marked with dark brown

FOOD Mainly surface-dwelling marine fish, especially sand-eels

Loses black forehead by late summer and acquires dusky wedge on outerwing through wear.

breeding adult

Deep, disyllabic call and bright white plumage allow easy identification.

breeding adult

DID YOU KNOW?

Most Sandwich Terns migrate to West African coasts for the winter; the Black Sea population only moves to the southern Mediterranean.

nesting adults

Comparable in size to Sandwich Tern but has bulkier outline with heavier, more direct flight. In breeding season, has black crown reaching low down nape; white hindneck, face and underparts. Back, rump and tail ash grey. Upperwing pearl-grey with duskier primaries towards tip. Underwing white except for dusky wedge near tip. Winter adult loses black cap but retains black mask. At all times in adult, bill black, thick and blunt, and legs and feet black. Juvenile darker than winter adult, with grey feathers of back and shoulders smudged brown; legs and feet red-brown.

GULL-BILLED TERN

breeding adult

Gelochelidon nilotica

THE GULL-BILLED TERN is more catholic in its choice of colony sites than other terns and is less dependent on close proximity to water. From its overwintering grounds south of the region it returns north in spring, arriving at European breeding sites in late April; it is during this period of spring migration that individuals very occasionally arrive as vagrants in northwest Europe. The Gull-billed Tern will forage over damp agricultural land, but it can also be seen fishing in coastal lagoons. It can survive in a wide range of man-managed habitats.

breeding adult

BIRD FACTS

VOICE Loud, deep, trisyllabic grating call
LENGTH 35–38cm
WINGSPAN 100–115cm
WEIGHT 190–280g
HABITAT Lowland coasts and deltas; inland to lakes rivers and marshes
NEST Shallow depression in soil, close to grassy tuft or other object; lined with vegetation
EGGS 1–4; smooth, pale yellow-buff, speckled black-brown
FOOD Wide range of small mammals, bird chicks, amphibians, fish and insects

breeding adult

DID YOU KNOW?

Great care is needed to distinguish this species from Sandwich Tern; thick bill and harsh, grating call are best identification features.

breeding adult

CASPIAN TERN

Sterna caspia

THE IMPRESSIVE-LOOKING Caspian Tern is not common in Europe, being mainly restricted to the Baltic coasts. Breeding birds arrive in late April and forage for fish on large, sheltered waters, travelling some distance from the nest in order to do so. The Caspian Tern is a strong flier, often seen at higher altitudes than other terns, and looks very gull-like in flight. Like all sea terns, Caspian Terns are migratory, moving south for the winter. Migration begins in late summer and it is often in August that wandering individuals turn up on western European coasts. However, the Caspian Tern seldom stays long and its unpredictability makes it a difficult bird to see.

BIRD FACTS

VOICE Utters loud, deep, barking notes with short, sharp alarm call
LENGTH 47–54cm
WINGSPAN 130–145cm
WEIGHT 600–750g
HABITAT Sheltered continental coasts with rocky islets, sand dunes, spits
NEST Shallow unlined depression on ground, in the open
EGGS 1–3; smooth, cream, speckled dark brown-black
FOOD Mainly fish; occasionally invertebrates

DID YOU KNOW?

The Caspian Tern is shy at its breeding grounds and tends to choose more isolated locations in Europe to avoid disturbance.

IDENTIFICATION

Huge gull-sized tern with massive bill, round body, blunt wings and short tail. In breeding season, crown and shaggy nape black, and hindneck, face and underparts white. Back and upperwing silvery grey, darker towards wingtip. Underwing has large dusky patch at tip. Rump and tail whitish, sometimes with grey cast. In winter, cap more mottled with black speckling extending on to face; wings become darker with wear. Massive dagger bill is bright coral red in summer, more orange in winter with dark tip. Legs and feet black at all times. Juvenile has mottled black cap extending on to face, and irregular brown flecking on back.

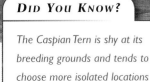

breeding adult

COMMON TERN

Sterna hirundo

COMMON TERNS ARE widespread throughout Europe in summer, returning to their nesting colonies in April, and, although tied to water, they are the least exclusively marine of all the sea terns. Nests can be some distance from feeding locations but the birds are well able to cope with any necessary commuting. Like all sea terns, Common Terns are migratory, with the majority of the European birds overwintering in the tropical seas off West Africa. A useful identification feature to separate them from the Arctic Tern on migration is the dark wedge on the outerwing, formed by non-moulted older primary feathers.

BIRD FACTS

VOICE Utters harsh rasping and emphatic 'keey-yah' call; also short, sharp alarm

LENGTH 31–35cm

WINGSPAN 77–98cm

WEIGHT 90–150g

HABITAT Along coasts and on inland fresh waters, sometimes on artificial platforms

NEST Shallow depression lined with available material

EGGS 1–3; buff, variably tinted with green or blue, spotted and lined with black-brown

FOOD Fish, crustaceans

breeding adult

Legs very short but longer than Arctic Tern's; dark outer primaries visible when bird is standing.

Birds have easy, buoyant flight, slower than gulls.

DID YOU KNOW?

Common Terns select breeding locations on small, rocky islands or sandy shores; they will also nest on inland lakes or reservoirs, where they often choose artificial platforms.

breeding adult

breeding adult

IDENTIFICATION

Often seen with Black-headed Gulls, but are fractionally shorter, with narrower, more pointed wings and long forked tail. Very similar to Arctic Tern, but with larger bill and head, stouter body and shorter tail; legs longer than Arctic Tern's. Summer adult has jet-black cap, pearl-grey upperparts with darker grey outer primaries and white rump and tail. Underparts white. In winter, adult has white forehead and mottled black cap. At all times adult has red, black-tipped bill, and red legs and feet. Juvenile is like winter adult but with ginger-brown mottling to back and forewing, and pale orange bill with black tip.

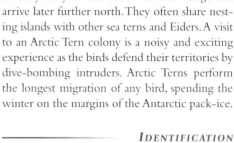

ARCTIC TERN

Sterna paradisaea

ARCTIC TERN COLONIES are mainly confined to coasts, where grassy islands are favoured, but in Norway and Russia birds will move inland along rivers to find ice-free nesting grounds. Arctic Terns return to their colonies in early May in the south of their range but arrive later further north. They often share nesting islands with other sea terns and Eiders. A visit to an Arctic Tern colony is a noisy and exciting experience as the birds defend their territories by dive-bombing intruders. Arctic Terns perform the longest migration of any bird, spending the winter on the margins of the Antarctic pack-ice.

BIRD FACTS

VOICE Utters shrill, nasal, grating notes and short, sharp alarm call; colonies very noisy

LENGTH 33–35cm

WINGSPAN 75–85cm

WEIGHT 87–119g

HABITAT Inshore and offshore waters with grass-covered islets; sometimes inland along rivers

NEST Shallow, unlined scrape

EGGS 1–3; pale buff, variously spotted and scrawled dark brown

FOOD Marine fish, crustaceans, insects

IDENTIFICATION

Difficult to separate from the Common Tern, but has shorter bill and head, longer tail and much shorter legs. Summer adult pale blue-grey above, white below but with dusky grey wash on breast and belly. Rump and tail bright white. Jet-black cap, white cheeks and blood-red bill. White flight feathers, translucent from below, lack dark markings of Common Tern. Winter birds, not seen in region, have crown speckled white. Legs and feet coral-red in summer, darker in winter. Juvenile has white forehead, marked black cap and is pale grey above, lacking brown tints of other juvenile sea terns.

breeding adult

ABOVE: *Breeding adult*

BELOW: *Breeding adult*

LEFT AND BELOW: *breeding adult*

Shorter head and bill and longer tail give Arctic Tern subtly different flight shape from Common Tern.

ROSEATE TERN

breeding adult

Sterna dougallii

BIRD FACTS

VOICE Calls include distinct rasping 'aakh' and whistled 'chewit'

LENGTH 33–38cm

WINGSPAN 72–80cm

WEIGHT 100–130g

HABITAT Maritime coasts with low rocky islets, sand dunes

NEST Shallow, unlined scrape under vegetation or in shelter of rock

EGGS 1–2; smooth, pale cream with black-brown spots and scrawls at broad end

FOOD Mainly small marine fish

BRITAIN AND IRELAND are the most important areas in Europe for Roseate Terns and they breed there in small colonies on offshore islands close to shallow, sheltered bays where they can fish. There are a few pairs in northwest France and a healthy population on the Azores, but they are very rare throughout Europe as a whole. Roseate Terns are the most marine of the European sea terns and their autumn migration takes them swiftly down to the tropical coasts of West Africa; they are very rarely seen inland. They can be identified at migration points by their very white appearance and long tail.

IDENTIFICATION

Similar to the Common Tern but has shorter wings and longer tail, giving slimmer appearance. In breeding season, adult has narrow, jet-black cap on crown and nape. Lower face, rump and tail white. Upperparts have blue-grey wash, paler than in Common Tern. Underparts washed with strong pink. Flight feathers pale silvery grey and translucent from below. Winter adult loses rosy wash and forehead becomes white. Long, narrow, black bill with red base seen at all times in adults. Legs and feet coral red in summer, dull red in winter. Juvenile has heavy brown spotting on upperparts, reminiscent of young Sandwich Tern.

Medium-sized, pale sea tern with long, flowing tail streamers; elegant in summer plumage.

ABOVE AND BELOW: Breeding adult

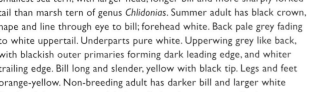

Smallest sea tern, with larger head, longer bill and more sharply forked tail than marsh tern of genus *Chlidonias*. Summer adult has black crown, nape and line through eye to bill; forehead white. Back pale grey fading to white uppertail. Underparts pure white. Upperwing grey like back, with blackish outer primaries forming dark leading edge, and whiter trailing edge. Bill long and slender, yellow with black tip. Legs and feet orange-yellow. Non-breeding adult has darker bill and larger white forehead than summer adult. Juvenile has browner-grey feathers on back and upperwing.

BELOW: Breeding adult; BELOW RIGHT: courting pair.

LITTLE TERN
Sterna albifrons

IN BRITAIN LITTLE TERNS are exclusively coastal, but elsewhere in Europe they are found along major rivers and around lakes as well as on the seashore. They arrive in Europe in April, when they can be seen fishing just offshore and can be heard courting noisily during their fluttering flight. They leave during September for their overwintering grounds in West Africa, where the first-year birds spend a whole year before joining the northern migrants. Little Terns suffer from competition with humans for fine sandy beaches, and their survival here depends on direct protection from disturbance.

BIRD FACTS

VOICE Rasping and churring 'kierr-ink' call; also shorter distinctive 'kik'

LENGTH 22–24cm

WINGSPAN 48–55cm

WEIGHT 50–60g

HABITAT Coastal or riverine strips of bare shingle, sand with shallow lagoons, inlets

NEST Shallow, unlined scrape in sand or gravel

EGGS 1–3; smooth, pale cream with dark spots, blotches and occasional streaks

FOOD Small fish, crustaceans, insects

Short, yellow legs and yellow bill with small black tip unique.

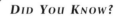

DID YOU KNOW?

Little Terns' size, narrow wings and bright, white appearance make identification easy.

LEFT: Breeding adult BELOW: nesting bird.

PUFFIN

Fratercula arctica

THE PUFFIN IS a locally abundant North Atlantic seabird breeding in large colonies on offshore islands and isolated mainland cliffs. Puffins return to their clifftop colonies in March in the south of their range, but not until May in the north. They prefer to excavate nesting burrows on sloping terraces of peaty turf above coastal cliffs, where colonies become very large. Displaying pairs make their strange growling and creaking calls as they stand bill to bill at the burrow entrance. Puffins swim and dive expertly to catch fish. In the open sea they are less vulnerable to oiling than some species, but their breeding success can be affected by human fishing activities.

Smaller than Guillemot and Razorbill, with obvious deep, colourful bill making head appear large. Has black upperparts and white underparts in all plumages, smartest in breeding adult, duller in juvenile. Summer adult has grey face and triangular bill, coloured bright red, blue-grey and yellow. Brightness of bill much reduced in winter. Red eye has surround of blue-grey horny appendages. Back, upperwing, rump and tail black. Underwing grey, rest of underparts white. Legs and feet bright orange. Juvenile has flesh-coloured feet and small, blackish bill, thinner than adult's.

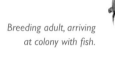

Breeding adult, arriving at colony with fish.

BIRD FACTS

VOICE Least vocal of the auks; creaking, growling and grunting calls heard in breeding season only

LENGTH 27cm

WINGSPAN 47–63cm

WEIGHT 370–450g

HABITAT Breeding colonies on sloping sea cliffs; open sea outside breeding season

NEST Shallow burrow under boulder or in natural crevice

EGGS 1; dull white, sometimes with purplish-brown markings

FOOD Marine fish; some crustaceans

DID YOU KNOW?

The large, powerful bill is slightly hooked to help the bird hold slippery prey; the bright colouring is lost in the winter.

summer adult

TOP RIGHT:
Off-duty bird resting on cliff.
BOTTOM RIGHT:
Breeding adult at burrow entrance.

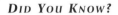

newly hatched chick

four-week-old chick

six-week-old-chick

immature, first winter

adult, winter

adult, summer

RAZORBILL

Alca torda

RAZORBILLS NEST ON sea cliffs and among boulders on the coasts of northern Europe, where they are sometimes found in mixed colonies with their commoner relative, the Guillemot. Britain and Ireland are very important for this species, holding half the world population. Returning from the winter in the open sea, Razorbills occupy their cliff ledges in April. They are noisy and quarrelsome at nesting colonies and their lack of manoeuvrability in the air causes many territorial disputes on landing. Razorbills are most at home in the sea, diving and swimming underwater, using feet and open wings for propulsion when chasing fish.

BIRD FACTS

VOICE Various growling calls

LENGTH 37–39cm

WINGSPAN 63–68cm

WEIGHT 600–800g

HABITAT Breeds on sea cliffs and boulders of undercliff; overwinters inshore or on open sea

NEST In cliff crevice, among boulders or in burrow entrance; rarely on open ledge

EGGS 1; pale brown or greenish; spotted and scribbled with dark brown

FOOD Mainly fish; some invertebrates

IDENTIFICATION

Size of Guillemot, with head, neck, back, upperwings and tail jet black in summer; underparts bright white. In winter throat and upper breast become dirty white and upperparts greyer. Breeding adult has deep, heavy black bill with neat white line across middle, and a white line connecting base of bill to eye, white on bill and eyeline duller in winter. Legs and feet black. Juvenile smaller than adult, browner and with bulbous bill.

ABOVE: *Lacking maneouvrability and ungainly in the air, Razorbills are in their true element underwater.*

BELOW: *The chick loses its white down by 15 days, and leaves for the sea two days later; at this stage it cannot fly.*

DID YOU KNOW?

The distinctive square-ended bill gives the Razorbill its name.

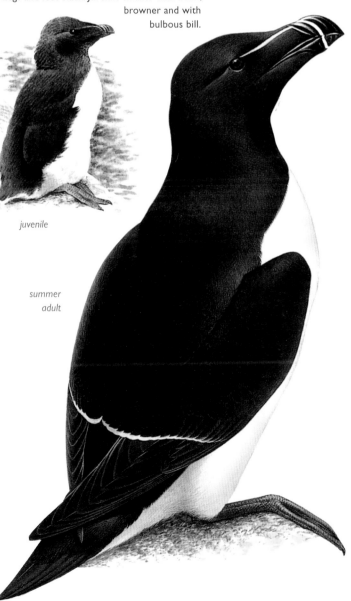

juvenile

summer adult

GUILLEMOT

Uria aalge

Distinguished from Razorbill in flight by dagger-like bill and longer neck.

GUILLEMOTS ARE FOUND around the coasts of northwestern Europe in densely packed cliff-ledge colonies, often numbering tens of thousands of birds. Winter attendance at the breeding cliffs is not uncommon, but it is March when the masses start to assemble on ledges. Guillemots are strong fliers but lack agility, so precision landing at the nest site often requires more than one attempt, and cliff bays can be alive with circling birds. Guillemots catch fish by diving underwater in pursuit of their quarry, sometimes crashing through the surface into shoals spotted from the air.

Longer-bodied and shorter-tailed than Razorbill. In summer, head, neck and upperparts dark brown, underparts mainly white. Flanks streaked with brown. White line across closed wing formed by white tips to secondaries. Dark furrow behind eye; this feature is white and extends around eye in so-called bridled form, giving spectacled appearance. In winter, cheeks and neck white, upperparts greyer. At all times in adult birds, bill black, long and tapering, and legs and feet dark blue-grey. Juvenile has plumage like winter adult but smaller bill.

bridled form

BIRD FACTS

VOICE Growling and guttural rolling calls

LENGTH 38–41cm

WINGSPAN 64–70cm

WEIGHT 500–800g

HABITAT Breeds on rocky sea cliffs and stacks; overwinters in marine offshore and inshore waters

NEST None; eggs laid in gravelly crevice or on ledge

EGGS 1; pointed, oval, roughened, blue-green to white heavily blotched with dark scribbles

FOOD Mainly fish; some invertebrates

Winter adult; note dark line running back from eye.

ABOVE: *bridled and ordinary forms*

DID YOU KNOW?

Both Britain and Ireland are Guillemot strongholds; the more northerly birds tend to have darker summer plumage.

summer adult

The bridled form shows white spectacle round eye.

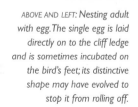

ABOVE AND LEFT: *Nesting adult with egg. The single egg is laid directly on to the cliff ledge and is sometimes incubated on the bird's feet; its distinctive shape may have evolved to stop it from rolling off.*

BRÜNNICH'S GUILLEMOT

Uria lomvia

Slightly larger and bulkier than Guillemot, with heavier bill and thicker head and neck. Plumage very similar to Guillemot. In summer adult has darker brown-black upperparts than Guillemot and white underparts; lacks brown flank streaks, and white breast meets brown-black throat in a sharp point. In winter upperparts retain blackish cast; white from throat extends onto face only below eye, not above as well, as seen in Guillemot. At all times adult has black, deep and strong bill, with white lower edge to upper mandible extending from base to mid-point. Legs and feet are brown to front, black to rear. Juvenile is smaller than winter adult, which it resembles in plumage except for mottled throat.

COLONIES OF BRÜNNICH'S Guillemot are confined to high Arctic islands and coastal sea cliffs, with concentrations in Svalbard, Jan Mayen Island and Iceland. The birds avoid areas of permanent pack-ice, preferring circulating, cold, open water, which supports an abundance of plankton. Brünnich's Guillemots return to their colony sites, which they often share with Guillemots, in April. Nesting ledges face the open sea so that the fledgelings can glide safely down to the water. Winter ice formation forces Brünnich's Guillemots to be migratory, though dispersal is confined mainly to northern Arctic waters.

BIRD FACTS

VOICE Utters growling and hoarse crowing calls
LENGTH 39–43cm
WINGSPAN 65–73cm
WEIGHT 750–1,080g
HABITAT Breeds on Arctic sea cliffs and steep boulder slopes; open Arctic waters in winter
NEST None; egg laid on cliff ledge or rested on feet
EGGS 1; pointed, oval, roughened, grey with dark blotches and scribbles
FOOD Mainly fish; some invertebrates

Summer adult has distinctive white gape streak.

breeding adult

winter adult

BLACK GUILLEMOT

Cepphus grylle

Medium-sized auk with round body, smallish head and paddle-shaped wings. Strikingly different plumage patterns in summer and winter. Summer adult uniform dark chocolate brown except for large, white, oval patch on both upperwing and underwing coverts. In winter appears much whiter with back speckled grey and white; head, neck and underparts dirty white. Wing retains summer pattern. At all times, adult has sharply pointed black bill with vivid orange inside, and bright red legs and feet. Juvenile resembles winter adult but with upperparts and flanks more darkly mottled.

NOT AS INTENSELY colonial as the other auks, Black Guillemots select nesting sites in natural rock holes or crevices, often among boulders at the base of sea cliffs. They return to their breeding areas in May, when small groups can easily be seen sitting on the sea below the cliffs making their thin whistling calls. Black Guillemots are bottom feeders and so require shallow waters all year round. Winter dispersal is undertaken only where necessary to avoid sea ice. Around Britain birds stay on inshore waters and can often be seen either singly or in small groups around harbours and estuaries during the winter months.

BIRD FACTS

VOICE Utters a thin, shrill whistle
LENGTH 30–32cm
WINGSPAN 52–58cm
WEIGHT 340–450g
HABITAT Breeds on sea cliffs and maritime boulder slopes; overwinters in shallow coastal seas
NEST Natural holes and crevices in boulder scree
EGGS 1–2; oval, matt white-buff, spotted or blotched red-brown
FOOD Marine fish and crustaceans

ABOVE: breeding adult

winter adult

The bright gape is usually only seen during courtship displays.

breeding adult

breeding adult

Bright white wing patches clearly visible in flight; flies fast and low over water.

Nesting among boulders has made Black Guillemots vulnerable to predation by introduced North American mink.

LITTLE AUK
Alle alle

LITTLE AUKS ARE the most northerly distributed of the auk family, breeding in colonies numbering millions of individuals on high Arctic islands. In spring, Little Auks congregate on melting pack-ice just offshore from their breeding cliffs. They can endure severe weather, with nesting sites sometimes still snow-covered at the time of egg laying in late June or July. After breeding, Little Auks stay in cold northern waters unless forced south by late autumn storms. When the storms are particularly severe birds can be driven inland and tired individuals may be seen almost anywhere.

BIRD FACTS

VOICE Twittering trills uttered at breeding colonies; whinnying alarm call in flight

LENGTH 18cm

WINGSPAN 40–48cm

WEIGHT 140–170g

HABITAT Breeds on Arctic mountain and cliff scree slopes; cold open sea in winter

NEST Shallow layer of pebbles, hidden in rock crevices

EGGS 1; pale greenish-blue

FOOD Mainly planktonic crustaceans

winter plumage

Flies with very fast wingbeats; underwing paler than Puffin's.

breeding adult

On the water the short, plump neck and almost bill-less profile are striking.

winter adult

IDENTIFICATION

Size of Starling, with smart black and white plumage showing narrow white lines on shoulder and white tips to secondaries, visible when wings closed. Bill very small and black. Body short and stubby with neckless appearance. Summer adult has black head, neck and breast. In winter, throat and breast white. Rest of upperparts black, underparts white. Juvenile similar to adult but browner.

Little Auk colony on Spitzbergen.

FERAL PIGEON *The continuing encroachment of the feral form is the greatest threat to the Rock Dove's survival.*

area of true Rock Dove

ROCK DOVE
Columba livia

THE ROCK DOVE must be the best-known European bird due to the abundant populations of so-called Feral Pigeons that inhabit our towns and cities. As a naturally wild species it is much harder to see because its choice of habitat takes it into wilderness areas where the lack of trees discourages its competitors. Feral populations became established following a long history of domestication by humans, and it is difficult now to distinguish between wholly wild populations and those augmented by town birds that have returned to their ancestral haunts. Truly wild Rock Doves are shy, fast-flying birds, and are very wary of predators.

BIRD FACTS

VOICE Various moaning, cooing calls
LENGTH 31–34cm
WINGSPAN 63–70cm
WEIGHT 238–370g
HABITAT Oceanic coasts and rocky areas; inland amongst open country; feral in towns
NEST Loose cup of roots, stems and other vegetation, on ledge
EGGS 2; smooth and glossy, white
FOOD Cereal and weed seeds; green leaves and buds; insects

As its name suggests, the Rock Dove prefers rocky habitats – in northwestern Europe this often means exposed sea cliffs and offshore islands.

ROCK DOVE

IDENTIFICATION

Much smaller than Woodpigeon. Adult is medium-sized, blue-grey pigeon with two obvious black bars across rear half of innerwing; plumage relieved on nape, neck and upper breast by green-purple gloss. Back, scapulars and innerwing paler ash-grey, tail with broad brownish-black terminal band. Bright white underwing coverts and lower back seen in flight. Bill lead-coloured, off-white at base. Legs and feet dull to bright red. Juvenile like adult but duller, except for sharing bright white on lower back.

Black wingbars obvious in flight.

IDENTIFICATION

Largest pigeon in Europe. Adult easily identified by blue-grey plumage with white neck patch, white wing crescents and black terminal band to longish, full tail. Sides and back of neck glossy green with purple sheen. Breast warm mauve-pink. In flight, adult's white wing crescents very obvious; also shows blackish primaries with white outer webs sometimes showing as pale panel. Bill is reddish with yellow tip and off-white patch at base. Pale yellowish eye. Legs mauve-pink. Juvenile much duller than adult; lacks white neck patch.

DID YOU KNOW?

Over the last hundred years or so Woodpigeons have expanded their range northwards through Britain and Scandinavia; this is linked to the increase in agricultural production and the easy availability of winter food.

From a distance, overall impression is of a grey bird, but at closer range browner back and pink breast discernible.

WOODPIGEON
Columba palumbus

THE WOODPIGEON IS a powerful flier able to employ fast jinks and swerves to avoid predators, and its undulating, wing-clapping display is well known. When alighting it invariably raises and lowers its tail, a characteristic that aids long-distance identification. Woodpigeons are catholic in their choice of habitats and are adaptable to change, which has allowed them to colonise most of Europe. The presence of woodland is one of their major requirements and often woodland edges bordering agricultural land are favoured; they are also common in urban areas, where they inhabit parks and tree-lined streets. In western Europe the population is mainly resident.

BIRD FACTS

VOICE Multisyllabic cooing, with emphasis on second note
LENGTH 40–42cm
WINGSPAN 75–80cm
WEIGHT 460–570g
HABITAT Woodland and scrub; agricultural fields next to woods in winter
NEST Flimsy platform of twigs, usually high in tree
EGGS 1–2; glossy, white
FOOD Mainly plant material including roots; occasionally insects

White crescent on wing and adult's neck patches diagnostic.

STOCK DOVE

Columba oenas

Upperwings have darker edges; two small bars visible close to body.

STOCK DOVES ARE found mostly in the lowlands, although they will venture into the uplands where suitable habitats occur. Their nests are usually sited in tree-holes, often the old cavities once used by Black Woodpeckers, and breeding birds are unobtrusive and would be easily overlooked were it not for the male's distinctive call. In western Europe and Scandinavia Stock Doves are migratory, spending the winter months in warmer countries such as Spain. They are resident particularly in Britain, where feeding flocks in winter fields are easily seen.

BIRD FACTS

VOICE Disyllabic, warm, cooing 'oo-look'; also growling calls at nest

LENGTH 32–34cm

WINGSPAN 63–69cm

WEIGHT 263–335g

HABITAT Border of woodland and open country

NEST Hole in tree, cliff or building; slight lining of twigs and grass

EGGS 2; glossy, creamy white

FOOD Seeds, green leaves, buds and flowers; occasionally invertebrates

adult

Adult plumage mainly grey. Head and underbody bluer and sides of neck have glossy green sheen. Upper breast has warm pink wash. Grey tail has broad black terminal band. Bill grey-buff, off-white at base. In flight, upperwing shows paler grey central panel and twin black bars on tertials. Eye brown with grey orbital ring. Legs bright pinkish-red. Juvenile browner and duller than adult, lacking any green sheen.

adult

adult

Flight action faster than Woodpigeon's.

Medium-sized, blue-grey pigeon, slightly smaller than Rock Dove, which it resembles except that it never has any white in its plumage at any age.

COLLARED DOVE

Streptopelia decaocto

adult

COLLARED DOVES EXPANDED north and west into Europe very quickly from 1930 onwards, reaching Britain in the 1950s and Norway in the 1960s. This spread is continuing with movements to Russia in the northeast. The speed of colonisation has relied on the ready availability of food, which Collared Doves find on arable farms and processing plants where there is an abundant supply of grain. In winter, birds congregate in very large feeding flocks, and they will readily enter buildings in search of grain. Despite such new-found abundance, Collared Doves are not as yet seriously threatened by predators or persecution from farming interests.

BIRD FACTS

VOICE Repeated, penetrating, unmusical cooing

LENGTH 31–33cm

WINGSPAN 170–240cm

WEIGHT 150–200g

HABITAT Mixed habitats of gardens, farms, orchards and town avenues

NEST Rough platform of twigs and roots, in tree

EGGS 1–2; glossy, white

FOOD Cereal grain and other seeds; fruits

DID YOU KNOW?

In western Europe Collared Doves favour mixed habitats such as gardens, orchards and parks, where they readily use buildings and wires for perching.

IDENTIFICATION

Larger than Turtle Dove, with longer tail and uniform pale, sandy grey plumage. Adult has pale-grey crown. Face, neck and breast pinkish-buff, fading to cream on belly and undertail coverts. Narrow, white-edged black half-collar. Back, scapulars and smaller wing coverts sandy grey-brown. Greater coverts and secondaries show grey panel next to darker, dusky primaries. Underwing coverts white. Uppertail brown with whitish tips to outer feathers. Broad, white terminal band to undertail. Bill black. Eye dark red with pale orbital ring. Legs and feet mauve-red. Juvenile duller than adult, lacking black half-collar.

adult

Flight action is fast, with clipped wingbeats.

adult

Smaller and slighter than Collared Dove. Adult has blue-grey crown with face, neck and breast warm pink. Patch of narrow black and white lines on neck. Back and rump brown with indistinct dark flecking. Closed wing has dappled pattern with black-centred, rich brown feathers. In flight, shows blue-grey greater coverts and dusky flight feathers. Complicated tail pattern of white-tipped black feathers, except for central pair, which are wholly brown. Undertail black, rimmed white, contrasting with cream underparts. Dark bill with pale tip. Yellow eye with crimson orbital ring. Legs reddish. Juvenile duller, lacking neck patch.

adult

TURTLE DOVE
Streptopelia turtur

THE TURTLE DOVE with its deep, purring, cooing song is a quintessential summer bird of Europe. The species is distributed widely across Europe but its dislike of cold, wet weather keeps it away from the most northern latitudes and from mountain ranges. As with most pigeons, the Turtle Dove is a woodland edge species preferring open country with mature vegetation; its liking for concealment within dense vegetation can make it hard to see. It requires the close proximity of croplands and scrub where it can find a good supply of food. Turtle Doves are migratory and spend the winter in sub-Saharan Africa.

Small, slim dove with thin neck, protruding round head and deep chest; has comparatively long, wedge-tipped tail and swept-back wings.

adult

adult

adult

BIRD FACTS

VOICE Deep, purring 'coo'

LENGTH 26–28cm

WINGSPAN 47–53cm

WEIGHT 100–170g

HABITAT Warm woodlands, open scrub, orchards and parks

NEST Flimsy platform of small twigs, in hedge or small tree

EGGS 1–2; glossy white

FOOD Seeds and fruits of weeds and cereals

Similar in size to Collared Dove but with longer tail. Adult male has slate-grey head, breast and upperparts. Underparts, from lower breast to undertail coverts, white with close, narrow blackish barring forming pattern of transverse lines across underbody. Upperwing darker grey-black, underwing paler. Darker tail feathers tipped and spotted white. Female similar to male but browner with buff breast band; occasional form has grey replaced with rufous, barred black. Decurved bill has yellow base with darker tip. Legs and feet yellow. Juvenile similar to rufous female but differs in having barred throat, white nape and white edges and tips to dark feathers.

CUCKOO
Cuculus canorus

THE CUCKOO'S SILHOUETTE in flight can resemble a small falcon or hawk; however, a prolonged view will reveal that the Cuckoo has a distinctive rowing flight action. The Cuckoo is most often seen in open scrub and woodland, though the abundance of its host species in upland grasslands and reedbeds will attract it to these habitats too. It has many host species and will commonly lay a single egg in each nest of the Dunnock, Reed Warbler or Meadow Pipit. The Cuckoo is migratory, with European adults flying off to Africa in July; mysteriously, juveniles, which follow several weeks later, know without any contact with parents where to go for the winter.

Unlike falcon or hawk, Cuckoo has weak flight action with rapid wingbeats not raised above the horizontal; wings are pointed.

Juvenile (LEFT) rufous with pale nape patch. Has a squeaking hunger call; it is fed by its 'parent' even when it is already quite well grown.

adult

BIRD FACTS

VOICE Familiar male call 'cu-coo'; female makes repeated bubbling notes

LENGTH 32–34cm

WINGSPAN 55–60cm

WEIGHT 100–130g

HABITAT Woodland, scrub, parkland and open uplands

NEST Eggs laid in host species' nests, mainly Meadow Pipit, Dunnock and Reed Warbler

EGGS Average 9; smooth, glossy, very variable, resembling host species' eggs

FOOD Insects, mainly hairy caterpillars and beetles

GREAT SPOTTED CUCKOO

Clamator glandarius

THE GREAT SPOTTED Cuckoo feeds mainly on caterpillars, which it searches for by hopping along the ground with its tail raised. The prey is taken to a nearby perch, where the irritant hairs are removed by wiping on a branch before the caterpillar is eaten. This parasitic species lays single eggs in each of up to 18 host nests. The European population is migratory, leaving breeding areas in July for overwintering grounds in Africa. In early spring birds returning north sometimes overshoot, so vagrant individuals can appear in northern Europe.

This impressive bird is strikingly patterned, has a long tail and perches prominently.

BIRD FACTS

VOICE Loud harsh rasping calls and double 'kioc-kioc'

LENGTH 38–40cm

WINGSPAN 58–61cm

WEIGHT 140–190g

HABITAT Warm Mediterranean scrub; open woodland

NEST Eggs laid in host nest, usually crows

EGGS Up to 18; smooth, pale green-blue, spotted red-brown mimicking host

FOOD Hairy caterpillars and other insects

Much larger than Cuckoo, with crest, broader wings and tail. Adult has blue-grey crested crown; upper face and neck blackish-brown. Rest of upperparts dusky brown with prominent white tips to scapulars, underwing coverts and long graduated tail. Chin, throat, foreneck and breast have warm orange-buff wash; rest of underparts off-white. Underwing coverts cream. Longish, stout, grey-black bill. Red eyering. Brown-grey legs and feet. Juvenile recalls bright adult but lacks crest; whole of crown dark brown. Light tips to feathers are cream not white, and bright chestnut primaries conspicuous in flight.

Juvenile unmistakable in flight, with black cap, chestnut primaries and adult's disproportionately long tail.

juvenile

adult

adult

BLACK-BELLIED
SANDGROUSE

BLACK-BELLIED SANDGROUSE

Pterocles orientalis

THE BLACK-BELLIED SANDGROUSE is the larger of the two European species of sandgrouse and is found mainly in Spain and Turkey. Nesting birds are well camouflaged and usually nervous of people, so the species is most often seen flying in pairs or small parties. It flies great distances to water at dusk and dawn, when larger flocks are on the move, and its evocative bubbling calls echo across the plains. This wary bird will circle a watering hole many times before landing to drink.

adult

BIRD FACTS

VOICE Musical cluckings and low bubbling notes, heard mostly in flight

LENGTH 33–35cm

WINGSPAN 70–73cm

WEIGHT 350–550g

HABITAT Flat plains on sandy soils, steppes

NEST Unlined depression on gravelly ground, sometimes with pebble surround

EGGS 2–3; glossy, buff or greenish-grey, heavily marked with brown and purple

FOOD Mainly seeds

Heavy-bodied, pigeon-like bird with short, pointed tail and broad, pointed wings. Male head, neck and breast grey with chestnut and black half collar on foreneck. Grey breast separated from black belly by narrow black and white bands. Back and upperwing ochre-yellow with blackish flecking. Flight feathers grey-black. Underwing shows black flight feathers and white coverts. Pointed tail barred yellow and black. Female and juvenile are duller than male; breast is spotted.

PIN-TAILED SANDGROUSE

Pterocles alchata

IN EUROPE, THE Pin-tailed Sandgrouse is confined to the warm, arid steppes of Spain, Portugal and Turkey, with a northerly outlying population on the stony Crau plain, adjacent to the Camargue in southern France. Like all sandgrouse it often flies in large flocks, when its rapidly beating whistling wings draw attention, and the distinctive chattering flight call can be heard. Access to fresh water is essential in such arid conditions.

adult

BIRD FACTS

VOICE Noisy and distinctive repeated 'chata-chata' flight call

LENGTH 31–39cm

WINGSPAN 54–65cm

WEIGHT 230–290g

HABITAT Warm arid Mediterranean steppes, dried-out marshes

NEST Shallow unlined depression on ground

EGGS 2–3; glossy, buff with brown and grey blotches and speckles

FOOD Seeds, shoots, green leaves

Both sexes have brown bill, white feathered legs and grey feet. Male has chestnut face, black throat, black margins to chestnut breast band; underbody and underwings white. Back and upperwing have greenish marbling, white-edged maroon wing coverts and black-barred yellow rump. Dark tail streamers. Female similar to male but with crown and nape streaked black, more yellow, less chestnut and more fine black barring on upperparts. Juvenile resembles dull female.

Smaller than Tawny Owl but with longer, narrower wings. Adult from south and west European race has warm, vermiculated yellowish-brown upperparts contrasting with clear silver-white underparts. Crown, nape, back and rump warm yellowish-brown with soft grey mottling and rows of tiny blackish spots. Coverts on closed wing similar; in flight shows warm-buff flight and tail feathers with dark-brown barring. Face has complete heart-shaped white facial disc with dark rusty eye pits and black eyes. Underparts, including feathered legs, silky white. Feet grey-brown. Bill pinkish. Adult from central European race has buff body underparts and underwing coverts. Similar in other respects to white-breasted race. Juvenile resembles adult as soon as down is lost.

adult

adult

dark-breasted adult

adult

BARN OWL
Tyto alba

BARN OWLS ARE found in many countries around the world, preferring mild, middle latitudes without extreme weather conditions. A hunting Barn Owl is a beautiful sight, with its slow, buoyant flight, wavering direction, hovering and swift plunges into the undergrowth for prey. Not strictly nocturnal, this owl can be seen in the half-light of winter afternoons, patrolling silently along hedgerows next to country lanes. The European population is in decline and factors known to be affecting numbers are the reduction in traditional farming systems and the increasing use of pesticides.

BIRD FACTS

VOICE Screeching, whistling and snoring notes in breeding season

LENGTH 33–35cm

WINGSPAN 85–93cm

WEIGHT 240–360g

HABITAT Open lowlands with small woods, hedges and fields; upland grasslands and heaths

NEST In hole of tree or building; on bare wood or artificial platform

EGGS 4–7; smooth, not glossy, white

FOOD Small mammals; fewer small birds and amphibians

adult

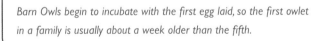

adult

DID YOU KNOW?

Barn Owls begin to incubate with the first egg laid, so the first owlet in a family is usually about a week older than the fifth.

TAWNY OWL
Strix aluco

BIRD FACTS

VOICE Classic melodious hoot 'huit-houuu'; common call 'ke-wick'

LENGTH 37–39cm

WINGSPAN 95–100cm

WEIGHT 350–600g

HABITAT Deciduous or mixed woodlands, forest and parks in towns

NEST Hole in tree or building, occasionally in old nest of Magpie or squirrel

EGGS 2–5; smooth, glossy white

FOOD Wide range of small mammals; birds, amphibians, earthworms and insects

IN NORTHWEST EUROPE the Tawny Owl is the most likely owl to be encountered by the casual observer, as the adaptability of the species makes it tolerant of humans. The Tawny Owl is a nocturnal species and night-time viewing can lead to difficulties with identification. In car headlights it often appears paler than it really is and care is needed to note the large-headed, round-bodied appearance and its flapping and gliding flight. This owl is resident throughout much of its range, taking advantage of good conditions for breeding as early in the year as February, even quite far north in its range.

adult

juvenile

The Tawny Owl may be mobbed by smaller birds, giving away its presence.

adult

Looks bulky in flight, with big head, short tail and broad wings.

adult

In daylight the Tawny Owl's neat, rounded appearance and pale spots on the closed wing make identification straightforward.

IDENTIFICATION

Medium-sized, broad-winged owl with large, rounded head and no ear tufts. Mottled, barred and streaked plumage varies from rufous-brown to grey-brown. Greyish facial disc bordered blackish with white eyebrows, lores and sides to chin. Eyes large and black. Crown, neck and back brown, boldy streaked with black. Prominent line of white-spotted scapulars. Flight feathers softly barred dark brown. Underwing buff-brown. Underparts greyer and usually paler with uniform blackish streaks. Bill yellowish-grey. Legs and feet buff, feathered; claws grey. Juvenile similar to adult, once down has been lost.

Adult with Bank Vole prey.

adult

adults

GREAT GREY OWL
Strix nebulosa

THE GREAT GREY OWL often hunts by day, using forest glades, bogs and adjacent open moorlands. Mature forests of pine and fir provide it with nesting sites, although recently in Finland Great Grey Owls have used artificial nesting platforms. Great Grey Owls are easily capable of catching prey in snow, listening for small mammals moving underneath before plunging with open talons through the surface onto the prey beneath. Although usually a sedentary species, the Great Grey Owl can become nomadic in response to fluctuating populations of prey mammals. Its survival depends also on the availability of tall, mature forest habitat.

IDENTIFICATION

Large, round head, long wings and tail. Adult plumage dark brown-black and white, appearing grey at distance. Head, back, rump and tail are pale grey, profusely streaked and barred dark brown. Dark blotching on back. Indistinct rows of pale spots on scapulars and coverts. Closed wing is brown, heavily streaked and barred blackish. Facial disc striking, with concentric fine black and grey barring, bright white eyebrows, lores, moustache and chin. Bright-yellow eye and bill. Underbody pale grey, heavily streaked dark brown. Juvenile like adult once down is lost.

BIRD FACTS

VOICE Deep, muffled, pumping hoots with squealing and growling alarm notes

LENGTH 65–70cm

WINGSPAN 135–160cm

WEIGHT 500–1,000g

HABITAT Dense, mature boreal pine, fir forests and adjacent moorland

NEST In old tree nest of other raptor; occasionally on ground

EGGS 3–6; smooth, slightly glossy white

FOOD Mainly small voles, shrews and birds

Great Grey Owl is a huge owl and could be mistaken for an Eagle Owl or Ural Owl; it is proportionately longer-winged than either species, slimmer-bodied than Eagle Owl and shows less barring on wings than Ural Owl.

URAL OWL
Strix uralensis

IN SUMMER, THE Ural Owl hunts along forest fringes and in glades, either from tree-stump perches or in searching flight. In winter it moves towards villages or farms, where more open habitats and cultivation can provide an easier source of food. The Ural Owl can be mistaken for a Short-eared Owl or even a Goshawk when its long tail is evident in flight. However, it is heavier and more purposeful than the Short-eared Owl, with broader wings and greyer plumage.

IDENTIFICATION

Larger than Tawny Owl, with longer tail. Adult plumage pale grey. Head, neck, back and underbody pale grey with uniform pattern of dark brown streaks. Circular, pale brownish-grey facial disc neatly outlined in dark brown. Eyes blackish-brown. Edges of scapulars white, forming distinct rows of pale spots down back. Wings grey with warmer brown tones to broadly barred flight feathers. Underwing contrastingly marked with whitish, black-tipped coverts and dark-brown barred flight feathers. Tail grey with broad, dark-brown bands. Bill yellow. Legs and feet feathered, buff-grey. Juvenile similar to adult once fully fledged.

BIRD FACTS

VOICE Deep hoot of three di- or trisyllabic notes; also harsh croaks

LENGTH 60–62cm

WINGSPAN 125–135cm

WEIGHT 500–1,000g

HABITAT Temperate forests of Europe with glades; also overwinters in parks and around villages

NEST Hole in tree, top of stump or old nest of raptor or crow; rarely on rocky ground

EGGS 2–4; smooth, white

FOOD Mainly mammals and birds up to size of Woodpigeon

adults

The survival of this sedentary species is dependent on the availability of a year-round feeding territory and, in central Europe, undisturbed woodland habitat.

LONG-EARED OWL

Asio otus

THE LONG-EARED OWL is distributed widely throughout Europe wherever there are trees. It is less dependent on forests than some other owls and is often found in mixed agricultural areas where there are small woodland copses or riverine trees. It can also colonise the conifer plantations of uplands in northwest Europe. Adults usually hunt at night, spending the day in dense vegetation, where they are difficult to detect. This is a migratory species in the north of its range, moving to southern Europe in the winter. Long-eared Owls roost communally in winter, often in thick scrub; if found, the birds are hard to disturb.

Smaller than Tawny Owl, though appears tall and thin when alarmed. Adult plumage ground colour is rufous-brown on upperparts, only slightly paler on underparts. Most feathers fringed pale buff. Crown, neck and back streaked and barred with black. Closed wing shows white shoulder and white covert spots. Flight feathers are rich orange, barred blackish. Facial disc warm orange-buff divided by point of grey crown and white eyebrows. Prominent, blackish, pale-fringed ear tufts. Eyes bright orange. Bill grey. Underparts buff-brown with heavy, blackish arrowhead streaks. Belly and undertail unstreaked. Legs and feet feathered, buff; claws grey. Juvenile similar to adult but with closer and less regular barring.

adult

BIRD FACTS

VOICE Quiet, but far-carrying, repeated 'oo' notes; young like squeaking gate

LENGTH 35–37cm

WINGSPAN 90–100cm

WEIGHT 300–350g

HABITAT Woodland copses and scrub with open habitats for hunting

NEST In old tree nest, usually of crows

EGGS 3–5; smooth, slightly glossy, white

FOOD Usually small rodents; some birds, larger mammals and shrews

adult

The ear tufts are erect when the owl is alarmed.

adult

adult

The tufts are lowered and the facial expression is quite different when the bird is relaxed.

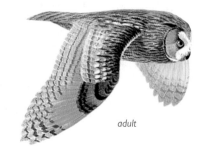

adult

adult

SHORT-EARED OWL

Asio flammeus

THE SHORT-EARED OWL can be identified by its long, narrow wings, buoyant flight and horizontal posture when perched. It will feed both by day and at night, and, unusually for an owl, it does not require the presence of trees. However, in Britain it takes advantage of the early growth conifer plantations, where they replace traditional moorland habitats. Northern populations are migratory, mostly overwintering in the southern part of the breeding range. Coastal marshes are favoured in winter, when it is possible to see several birds at the same place quartering the marsh in typical buoyant, floating flight.

BIRD FACTS

VOICE Low-pitched hollow 'hoo-hoo-hoo' series of notes; hissing and rasping calls at nest

LENGTH 37–39cm

WINGSPAN 95–110cm

WEIGHT 260–425g

HABITAT Open country, moorlands, rough grazing, sand dunes, marshes

NEST Shallow scrape on ground, roughly lined with vegetation

EGGS 4–8; smooth, white

FOOD Mainly small voles but will also take birds and other mammals

adults

adult

Ear tufts are very small and seldom seen.

Nesting adult with chick.

Always nests on ground in thick cover.

adult

IDENTIFICATION

Long-winged owl with fairly small head, often confused with Long-eared Owl. Adult plumage yellowish-buff, heavily streaked with black. Head and neck buff with bold, dark streaks. Back so heavily streaked it appears mostly blackish. Rump paler with fewer streaks. Tail yellowish-buff, broadly barred dark brown. Striking facial disc surrounded by heavy black spotting. Pale-buff cheeks and reversed white brackets between yellow eyes sunk in blackish pits. Underbody clearer, warm buff with lighter streaks. In flight, wing shows dark carpal patch and dark tip. Bill grey. Legs and feet feathered, buff. Juvenile similar to adult but with broader, pale tail-tip.

1st winter

adult

EAGLE OWL

Bubo bubo

THE EAGLE OWL'S direct and purposeful flight action is similar to that of a Buzzard, so care is needed to identify it when it is flying away from the observer; it is the only large owl with ear tufts. The Eagle Owl is a bird of wilderness areas, uncluttered by human impact and free from disturbance; it is thus absent from most of the industrialised northwest. It nests where it can have an unobscured view of approaching danger. Most of the day is spent perched motionless, but active hunting begins at sunset, or earlier when there is a chick to feed.

Largest European owl; barrel-shaped with prominent ear tufts. Adult plumage usually warm brown, heavily marked on upperparts with thick, black streaks and spots. Flight feathers barred black. Paler brown underparts have black droplets on breast; narrower streaks and fine dark bars on belly and flanks. Head has laterally flattened blackish ear tufts and well-marked pale-grey facial disc with bright orange eyes. Chin and throat show furry, whitish ruff. In flight the dark leading edge to wing contrasts with yellowish flight feathers, barred blackish. Feathered legs and feet. Bill black. Juvenile paler and fluffier than adult, lacking ear tufts, and has more completely barred underparts.

The Eagle Owl is a truly impressive bird when seen standing on a cliff ledge or when flying down prey in a fast glide.

adult

adult

adult

SNOWY OWL

Bubo scandiaca

THE SNOWY OWL requires huge expanses of tundra in which to select its nest site, usually on a low hummock with good visibility all around. In Europe it is a rare breeding bird, with fluctuating numbers in Scandinavia and a more stable population in northern Russia. The adult does not tolerate disturbance from humans and spends long periods watching over the nest or scanning for intruders. In flight it is an active hunter and is surprisingly swift in its chase and falcon-like capture of prey. Snowy Owls are irruptive: when lemming populations are low, large numbers are forced to move from the normal range in search of food, especially in winter.

Mainly white owl with relatively small, round head and long, rounded wings. Golden-yellow eyes sunk in dusky pits. Bill black. Legs and feet densely feathered, white with black claws. Adult male almost entirely creamy white. Occasional small, dark-brown spots on underwing coverts hardly noticeable. Adult female ground colour is white but heavily spotted and chevronned dark brown over whole of upperparts and most of underbody. Pure white face and centre of breast stand out. Juvenile has dark-grey head and body; rest of plumage like adult female.

adult male

adult male   *adult female*

adult female

Very large, essentially white owl, exceeded in size among European owls only by Eagle Owl.

Small, dark owl with longish legs. Adult upperparts dark brown-grey, spotted and flecked with white. Crown and nape closely spotted white. Back more uniform dark brown with whitish fringes to lower neck feathers, scapulars and coverts, creating pale lines. Tail has four pale-brown bars. Facial disc buff-grey, more rectangular than round, with prominent pale eyebrows and yellow eyes. Underparts paler buff-grey with gorget of heavy streaks on upper breast, finely streaked on belly and flanks. Bill grey-brown. Legs feathered buff-white; feet brown. Juvenile similar to adult but paler; plumage is more uniform with less streaking and spotting.

adult

LITTLE OWL

Athene noctua

THE LITTLE OWL is widely distributed across Europe, and is a bird of open country. A common requirement of the species in all its diverse habitats is the abundance of perches from which the birds can hunt prey and watch for danger. The Little Owl's flight action is distinctive, with woodpecker-like bounding undulations, but it can be difficult to follow as it flies close to the ground before swooping up to perch. The species usually nests in tree-holes, and it is usual to see one parent perched on guard near the nest. When alarmed it will bob up and down, giving hissing and barking calls.

BIRD FACTS

VOICE Hollow, rising whistle, sometimes repeated in crescendo; chattering warning call

LENGTH 21–23cm

WINGSPAN 54–58cm

WEIGHT 140–225g

HABITAT Lowland agricultural habitats in west; more arid rocky gorges and plains in east

NEST Hole in tree or building, or crevice in cliff

EGGS 2–5; smooth, matt white

FOOD Mainly insects; some small mammals and birds

DID YOU KNOW?

Little Owls are fairly easy to see because of their willingness to perch in the open; they are most active around dawn and dusk.

adult

pair at nest

An upright posture is adopted when the bird is alarmed.

adult

adult

SCOPS OWL

Otus scops

THE SCOPS OWL is a nocturnal, arboreal species, which hunts in the open and thus requires secluded perches for daytime roosting and plenty of open varied habitats in which to find prey. Where mixed open woodland is unavailable, this owl will select managed orchards, olive groves, parks and farmland landscapes. It can also be found in many southern European towns, where it frequents tree-lined boulevards and city squares. The Scops Owl advertises its presence at night with its penetrating and repetitive whistling call, but actually sighting the bird is difficult. European Scops Owls are migratory, moving south of the Sahara for the winter.

IDENTIFICATION

Small, large-headed owl with slender body and fairly long wings. Adult seen with either brown-grey or rufous upperparts; both have blackish streaks, bars and delicate pattern of vermiculations. Scapulars show as prominent line of black-tipped white feathers. Facial disc with incomplete blackish-brown border, mainly on sides. Shape accentuated by prominent streaked ear tufts, which are often flattened sideways. Paler brown to buffish-white underparts with dark-brown streaks and vermiculations. Outer flight feathers broadly barred buff. Underwing paler buff. Bill blue-black. Eye yellow. Legs feathered, buff; feet grey. Juvenile inseparable from adult.

adult

adult

adult

With its excellent camouflage and habit of roosting during the day in mature trees and bushes, the Scops Owl is very hard to see.

BIRD FACTS

VOICE Repeated, short, human-like whistle, reminiscent of slow time signal pips

LENGTH 19–20cm

WINGSPAN 53–63cm

WEIGHT 80–120g

HABITAT Warm, dry lowlands in open mixed woodland; parks with old hollow trees

NEST In hole of tree, building or nest box; occasionally in old nest of crow

EGGS 4–5; smooth and glossy white

FOOD Mainly insects; a few small birds, reptiles and mammals

PYGMY OWL

Glaucidium passerinum

The combination of stern expression, white barred tail and absence of pale, spotted scapulars allows separation from Tengmalm's Owl.

THE PYGMY OWL'S fast, undulating, almost urgent flight is reminiscent of a small woodpecker, and when perching it often waves its tail up and down or sits with it cocked like a flycatcher. It is the prey of larger raptors and owls, and so chooses the deep forest interior with large, old trees to provide nest holes. It favours open areas for hunting, such as clearings and woodland meadows. The preferred diet of the Pygmy Owl is small birds, which it pursues actively and relentlessly mostly during the day. It also hunts small mammals at dusk and dawn.

IDENTIFICATION

Tiny, small-headed owl, roughly size of Hawfinch. No real facial disc but curved rows of brown and buff spotting and white eyebrows and white sides to chin neatly frame face. Adult has dark-brown upperparts, spotted and barred with whitish-buff. Shows two whitish curves back to back on nape, and buff-spotted brown crown. Throat and sides of breast brown, barred black. Rest of underparts white, streaked blackish, extending up centre of breast. Relatively long narrow tail, brown with white barring. White bars on brown flight feathers. Eyes yellow. Legs and toes feathered, white. Juvenile similar to adult but duskier, with less pale spotting and barring.

adult

Adult with Blue Tit prey.

BIRD FACTS

VOICE Monotonous, fluty, repeated whistle; various hissing notes

LENGTH 16–17cm

WINGSPAN 34–35cm

WEIGHT 50–70g

HABITAT Taiga and montane coniferous forest

NEST In tree-hole, often old nest of woodpecker; will use nest box

EGGS 4–7; smooth, slightly glossy, white

FOOD Small mammals and small birds

adult

Smallish, dark owl with large, square head and longish tail. Adult upperparts dark brown with copious white spotting on crown, and fewer, larger spots on nape and back. Broad white edges to scapulars show as pale braces. Wing coverts and flight feathers dark brown, finely spotted with white. Tail dark brown with rows of tiny white spots. Squarish grey facial disc outlined in black. Yellow eyes set in dark pits. Underparts pale greyish-white, spotted with light brown. Bill yellowish-grey. Legs and feet feathered, white. Part-fledged juvenile dark chocolate brown with white eyebrows and moustache; white spotting on wings. Similar to adult in other respects.

Range of Tengmalm's Owl overlaps with smaller Pygmy Owl, with which it can be confused.

adult

TENGMALM'S OWL
Aegolius funereus

IN THE NORTH, Tengmalm's Owl has a preference for spruce and birch forests where these border open moor-lands, but in central Europe montane mixed forests of fir and beech are preferred. In these woodlands it uses old Black Woodpecker nesting holes to raise its young. Tengmalm's Owl can be difficult to observe and it can be confused with other small owls. It is a vora-cious hunter of mammals and small birds, and can be very manoeuvrable in pursuit amongst the dense stands of trees. Tengmalm's Owl is resident in central Europe, though wandering juveniles may make short movements out of the main range.

Adult at entrance to nest hole.

adult

Similar in size and shape to Sparrowhawk, with proportionately smaller head, slimmer body and longer tail than other owls.

The Hawk Owl has a fierce expression that reflects its voracity as a predator of small mammals and birds; it is also an aggressive defender of its nest, repeatedly attacking intruders.

adult

HAWK OWL
Surnia ulula

RUSSIA CONTAINS HUGE areas of suitable habitat for Hawk Owls, but they also breed in Scandinavia, where they move into more southerly habitats in periodic population irruptions. In tundra forest this species chooses clearings surrounded by trees, often using broken-topped stumps from which to watch for prey. The Hawk Owl could easily be mistak-en for a Sparrowhawk in flight. However, it in-tersperses direct flight with bursts of undulating, bounding flaps and glides, and it usually approaches a perch with a fast upward sweep. Hawk Owls are nomadic, following fluctuating small mammal populations.

IDENTIFICATION

Adult has strongly patterned blackish and pale-grey plumage. Crown, nape and back blackish-brown, spotted white. Large whitish shoulder patch. Closed wing dark brown with few white spots. Flight feathers dark with whitish bars. Rump pale, barred blackish. Long, dark-brown tail narrowly barred pale grey. Face whitish with broad, blackish, curved borders to facial disc. Breast and belly very pale grey, narrowly barred blackish. Wings short and pointed. Eyes striking pale yellow. Bill yellow-horn. Legs and feet feathered white. Juvenile paler and fluffier than adult, with more barring; other characteristics similar to adult.

OWLS **181**

NIGHTJAR

Caprimulgus europaeus

BIRD FACTS

VOICE Monotonous whirring 'churr'; disyllabic 'kwa-eek' note

LENGTH 26–28cm

WINGSPAN 57–64cm

WEIGHT 65–100g

HABITAT Dry, open conifer woods, scrub, sandy heaths and semi-deserts

NEST Shallow, unlined scrape on ground

EGGS 2; glossy, cream, spotted and blotched with yellow or dark brown

FOOD Insects, mainly moths and beetles, taken aerially

THE NIGHTJAR IS nocturnal and more likely to be heard than seen. The song is distinctive, far-carrying but difficult to locate exactly. When not hunting moths at night the birds spend most of their time sitting on the ground, where their plumage renders them almost completely invisible when motionless. At dusk on warm summer evenings it is possible to see the dimly lit shapes of flying Nightjars in courting displays, when males use spectacular wing-clapping to advertise themselves.

adult male

TOP: adult male; BOTTOM: nesting female

DID YOU KNOW?

The Nightjar is a summer visitor to Europe; it is thought the entire population overwinters in sub-Saharan Africa.

IDENTIFICATION

Shape similar to small falcon or Cuckoo. Adult plumage dark grey and rufous-brown with heavy black barring and delicate pattern of vermiculations. Head, nape, back and rump grey, lightly streaked with black. Long, grey tail, barred black outer feathers tipped white in male, buff in female. Scapulars and coverts edged silvery white, showing as pale lines. In flight, rufous-brown flight feathers heavily barred black, showing white patch near wingtip in male, buff patch in female. Underparts brown, finely barred black, becoming rufous towards undertail. White moustache. Bill very short; black with wide gape. Juvenile resembles pale adult female, but lacks wing and tail spots.

female

male

Adult has mostly rufous-brown plumage with complex variegated markings. Greyish crown, brown back, rump and tail variously streaked black. Pale-buff tips to scapulars and coverts create pale lines across closed wing. Warm rufous-pink collar and throat relieved by narrow, white moustache and broad, white spots to side of chin. Underparts pale rufous-brown with narrow, black bars and greyish band across breast. In flight, both male and female show white wing spots and long white patches on outertail feathers. Juvenile resembles dull adult with more buff plumage.

Adult female with chick.

RED-NECKED NIGHTJAR
Caprimulgus ruficollis

THE RED-NECKED NIGHTJAR prefers open habitats with bare patches of dry, sandy soil and scattered trees to use as song-posts. The stone pine woods of the Coto Doñana in Spain are typical of the preferred habitat, but the birds will also use arid hillsides with dwarf vegetation. The Red-necked Nightjar is mainly nocturnal and its song, which is repeated continuously for long periods, can be the best clue to its presence. The species is migratory, breeding between May and August and overwintering in West Africa.

Larger than Nightjar, with longer wings and tail and large head.

male

female

BIRD FACTS

VOICE Repetitive, low-pitched, double knocking 'cut-oc, cut-oc'

LENGTH 30–32cm

WINGSPAN 65–68cm

WEIGHT 65–70g

HABITAT Stone pine woods; plantations with open, sandy ground

NEST Shallow, unlined scrape on ground

EGGS 2; fairly glossy, grey-white, marbled and blotched yellow-brown

FOOD Insects, mainly moths

adult

ALPINE SWIFT
Apus melba

THE ALPINE SWIFT is common and well distributed across all of southern Europe. The underlying habitat is not of great significance, but it does use air currents generated by landscape features and so prefers hilly areas. It is an impressive bird to watch, with its powerful, fast flight, easy glides and chattering call. At first glance, distant birds can appear like small falcons. The Alpine Swift is migratory and in winter can be seen in many African countries. Its return north in the spring regularly results in individuals being seen much further north in Europe than the breeding range.

IDENTIFICATION

Much larger than its European relatives, with bulky body and long, broad, crescent-shaped wings. Upperparts warm sandy brown, appearing paler when pale margins to fresh feathers are evident. Black patch in front of eye noticeable at close range. Chin and throat white. Broad, sandy-brown breast band. Lower breast, belly and flanks are white. Underwing brown with darker brown flight feathers showing above and below wing. White chin hard to see but large white belly patch obvious. Juvenile shows more prominent white tips to brown feathers than adult.

adult

BIRD FACTS

VOICE Loud, shrill, chattering call during breeding season

LENGTH 20–22cm

WINGSPAN 34–60cm

WEIGHT 80–120g

HABITAT Aerial over southern European mountains, coasts and open country

NEST Shallow cup of straw and feathers, cemented with saliva, on ledge in building or cliff

EGGS 3; smooth, matt white

FOOD Moderate-sized airborne spiders and insects

DID YOU KNOW?

Close views of Alpine Swifts can be obtained by watching from the tops of sea cliffs or rocky gorges; as the birds pass by their wings make an audible swishing sound.

SWIFT

Apus apus

THE SWIFT IS entirely aerial except for nesting. In northern latitudes abundant insect food is available only in the short summer months, so Swifts are migratory, overwintering in sub-Saharan Africa; they arrive in Europe in early May and are gone again by late August, raising young quickly on a rich protein diet of airborne insects. Nestlings are able to enter torpor to endure fluctuations in food supply when wet conditions reduce the adults' ability to catch prey. When a fledgling takes flight for the first time it is likely to remain on the wing for the next couple of years, feeding and sleeping in flight.

Medium-sized, all-brown swift, with small white throat patch. Very similar in size and shape to Pallid Swift, but wings slightly narrower and tail more noticeably forked. Greyish forehead visible at extremely close range. In bright sunlight pale upper surface to flight feathers. Powerful rapid flight with winnowing wings. Juvenile bird essentially indistinguishable from adult, showing long, crescent-shaped wings, short, forked tail and all-dark plumage.

BIRD FACTS

VOICE Shrill screaming whistle in breeding season

LENGTH 16–17cm

WINGSPAN 42–48cm

WEIGHT 35–50g

HABITAT Aerial; usually in and around towns and villages

NEST Shallow cup of vegetation and feathers, cemented with saliva, in roof space or under eaves

EGGS 2–3; smooth, matt white

FOOD Flying insects; airborne spiders

The Swift's familiar crescent shape is ideal for rapid sustained flight.

adult

juvenile

Parties make screaming calls as they fly together.

adult

nesting adult

Similar in size to Swift but subtle differences in shape and colouring are important for identification. A slightly bulkier bird than the Swift overall, particularly noticeable in broader wings and shorter, more rounded tail forks. Adult and juvenile essentially indistinguishable. Plumage brown with pale margins to feathers creating sandy effect in good light. Forehead greyish-white. Slightly darker brown saddle on back contrasts with paler rump and upper surface to wings. Prominent white throat patch. Underbody pale sandy brown caused by pale margins to most feathers.

PALLID SWIFT

Apus pallidus

THE WARM, SUNNY, coastal Mediterranean towns are where Pallid Swifts look most at home. Bright sunlight and a dark background assist in definite identification, allowing the pale sandy colour to be seen well. Pallid Swifts are migratory, though the more reliable climate in southern Europe allows them to have two broods of young before departing as late as September for African overwintering areas. They return north again in April and it is at this time that individuals may get caught up with flocks of common swifts and arrive as very rare vagrants in northern Europe.

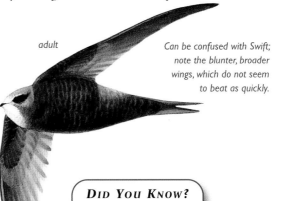

adult

Can be confused with Swift; note the blunter, broader wings, which do not seem to beat as quickly.

BIRD FACTS

VOICE Screaming whistle in breeding season, deeper than swift
LENGTH 16–17cm
WINGSPAN 42–46cm
WEIGHT 35–45g
HABITAT Mediterranean zone, around towns, villages and coasts
NEST Shallow cup of vegetation and feathers, cemented with saliva, in dry, rocky area, building or cliff crevice
EGGS 2–3; smooth, matt white
FOOD Flying insects

DID YOU KNOW?

Pallid Swifts prefer dry, rocky areas, and will nest in old town churches and other large traditional buildings; alternatively they will select sea cliffs, where the nest can be sited in a natural crevice.

WHITE-RUMPED SWIFT

Apus caffer

WHITE-RUMPED SWIFT Very fluttery flight, lacking power of larger relatives.

THE WHITE-RUMPED SWIFT has only recently been found in Europe, where it is confined to the southern tip of Spain. This Iberian population is remarkable in its behaviour as a nest-parasite, using the nests of the Red-rumped Swallow in which to lay its eggs. These sites are usually under rocky outcrops in the midst of farmland, over which the birds forage. The White-rumped Swift consorts with swallows and martins more than other swifts. It is believed to be migratory, but very little is known about its movements and individuals have been recorded as present in December.

BIRD FACTS

VOICE Whistle beginning as chatter, merging into trill
LENGTH 14cm
WINGSPAN 34–36cm
WEIGHT 20–28g
HABITAT Rocky habitats; in vicinity of coastal towns in southern Spain
NEST In Spain, in nests of Red-rumped Swallow
EGGS 2; smooth, matt white
FOOD Airborne insects and spiders

IDENTIFICATION

Smallish, slim-bodied swift with long, deeply forked tail and dark plumage. Adult has mainly blue-black colour to body and wings, with noticeable narrow, bright white band across upper rump. Greyish crown and line over eye, small whitish chin and silvery sheen to underwing flight feathers, visible at close range. Long, narrow wings give distinctive silhouette. Juvenile shows more whitish tips to body feathers than adult and less blue-black sheen to dull, dark plumage.

LITTLE SWIFT

Apus affinis

LITTLE SWIFT

LITTLE SWIFT

THE LITTLE SWIFT is sometimes suspected of breeding in southern Spain and is observed on a scarce but regular basis feeding over coastal marshes in the southern Iberian peninsula. Elsewhere in Europe, Little Swifts occur as rare vagrants, mostly in late autumn, and have been reported as far away as Britain and Sweden. The small size, square-ended tail and conspicuous white rump of the Little Swift allow it to be readily identified. It hawks for insects like other swifts and often glides on stiffly held wings, but unlike its relatives it intersperses this flight pattern with bouts of fluttering flight that can appear almost bat-like.

IDENTIFICATION

Small compact swift. Recalls House Martin in plumage details but easily recognised as a swift species by silhouette. Sexes similar. Adult has dark sooty-brown plumage except for square, white rump and white throat; forehead greyish. Tail relatively short and square-ended. Juvenile similar to adult but plumage not as dark.

BIRD FACTS

VOICE High-pitched screaming call uttered in flight
LENGTH 12cm
WINGSPAN 34–35cm
WEIGHT 25–30g
HABITAT Nests in buildings and on cliffs; otherwise entirely aerial
NEST Almost spherical construction of plant material held together with saliva; may also use old nest of House Martin or Red-rumped Swallow
EGGS 2–3; white
FOOD aerial insects

KINGFISHER

Alcedo atthis

KINGFISHERS NEED SMALL, sheltered bodies of water that contain areas of undisturbed clear water for fishing, where the birds can see fish from a suitable perch before plunge-diving for capture. In the breeding season sandy banks above water are necessary for excavating the nesting tunnel. Kingfishers are fairly secretive and wary birds, and can be difficult to spot despite their bright plumage. The shrill whistling call and arrow-like flight low across the water are often all that the observer sees.

Small kingfisher with long bill and relatively large head. Adult has crown, nape, moustache and all upperparts bright blue, tone varying with light and viewing angle. Pale sheen on back. Crown and wing coverts have pale blue spotting. Scapulars, flight feathers and tip of tail darker blackish-blue. Face, underbody and underwing coverts rich orange-chestnut, paler on throat and centre of belly. White spots in front of eye, on side of neck and under chin. Long dagger-shaped bill, all black in male, with reddish base in female. Legs and feet coral red. Juvenile lacks brilliance of adult, and has greener upperparts and bluish-grey breast. Legs dull orange.

BIRD FACTS

VOICE Song comprises Starling-like bubbling whistles; also plaintive chattering whistle calls

LENGTH 16–17cm

WINGSPAN 24–26cm

WEIGHT 35–45g

HABITAT Streams, rivers and lakes with surrounding vegetation

NEST Tunnel in clay or gravel bank of stream; pit usually above water

EGGS 6–7; almost round, smooth, glossy white

FOOD Mainly small freshwater fish; some aquatic insects and crustaceans

After a successful dive, prey is carried to a nearby perch where it is killed and swallowed.

The male presents the female with a fish during the courtship display.

DID YOU KNOW?

If there is no suitable perch, the Kingfisher will hover for several seconds with rapid wingbeats before plunging after prey.

WHITE-BREASTED KINGFISHER

Halcyon smyrnensis

THE WHITE-BREASTED KINGFISHER'S main range extends across the Indian subcontinent and Southeast Asia. Its distribution continues westwards into the Middle East and the species occurs sparingly in southern Turkey. White-breasted Kingfishers favour perches that are 1–3m above water. Extended periods of time are spent simply watching for fishing opportunities, but the birds will also take terrestrial prey such as insects and lizards from river banks and dry land. Nesting burrows are usually sited close to areas of good feeding and can be more than a metre long.

IDENTIFICATION

A beautifully marked, distinctive kingfisher. Sexes similar. Adult has striking white throat and chest, and chestnut head, neck, breast and underparts. Back, tail and wings iridescent blue except for black tips to primaries and black and chestnut wing coverts. Bill proportionately massive and bright red; legs and feet bright red. Juvenile similar to adult but duller.

PIED KINGFISHER

Ceryle rudis

THE PIED KINGFISHER is a widespread tropical species; in Europe, it is restricted to the southern coasts of Turkey. It is essentially resident throughout its range, but it is a rare, regular winter visitor to Cyprus. Pied Kingfishers are entirely dependent on water for feeding and can be found along almost any fish-rich stretch of water. Like other kingfishers, they spend long periods of time perched on overhanging branches, scanning the water below. Prior to actually diving after fish, they habitually hover in mid-air before plunging down.

IDENTIFICATION

Distinctive and well-marked kingfisher. Adult male has striking black and white marbled upperparts. Underparts essentially white except for two black breast bands. Adult female similar to adult male but has one, not two, black breast bands. Juvenile similar to adult female but has chest band grey not black. All birds have black bill and feet.

PIED KINGFISHER

WHITE-BREASTED KINGFISHER

Adult's bright colouring is distinctive.

HOOPOE

Upupa epops

THE HOOPOE SPENDS a lot of time on the ground catching insects, walking with a rather short, pigeon-like gait. The hoopoe chooses dry, warm, open landscapes with some bare sandy ground and trees or other surfaces for perching. It requires a good supply of large insects and their pupae for food, sometimes using its long bill to probe into the ground. The young are usually raised in a tree-hole nest, often in an orchard, but the bird will use nest boxes. European Hoopoes are migratory, overwintering in Africa; on returning to Europe early in the spring, some birds overshoot the normal range to reach more northern and western countries.

IDENTIFICATION

Adult has head, neck, back and underbody pale brownish-pink, with warmer pinkish shade on breast. Long erectile crest of pink feathers, tipped with white and black. White crescent on rump. At rest, transverse black and creamy-white barring crosses wings and shoulders, the foremost bar being pale orange. Tail black with wavy white band near base. Undertail coverts whitish. In flight, primaries are black with single white crescent near tips. Long, slender, decurved bill, black with pinkish base. Legs and feet black. Juvenile duller than adult, with dingy cream barring and shorter bill.

adult

DID YOU KNOW?

In flight, looks strikingly black and white; on the ground, however, it can be surprisingly difficult to spot, especially on broken terrain.

adult

Similar to Jay in size and colour but slimmer when perched; crest is only raised when bird is alarmed.

Disproportionately large, rounded wings show well in flight; Hoopoe has erratic, bounding flight action, reminiscent of a giant butterfly.

adult

When disturbed, Hoopoe freezes and will not rise until approached very closely.

BLUE-CHEEKED BEE-EATER

Merops superciliosus

THE BLUE-CHEEKED BEE-EATER occurs as a breeding species in northwest Africa and locally from the Middle East to northwest India; small numbers also breed in southeast Turkey. It is a very rare vagrant to Europe, mainly appearing in late spring. Although superficially similar in outline to European Bee-eater, this species should present few identification problems when seen well. Like other bee-eaters, Blue-cheeked Bee-eaters spend considerable periods of time perched on prominent branches from which passing flying insects can easily be spotted.

IDENTIFICATION

Attractive bee-eater. Sexes similar. Adult mainly green with bluish rump and lower back, and rusty-red underwing. Head markings distinctive. Has black eyestripe and white forehead grading to sky blue supercilium. Cheeks sky blue and throat yellow, grading to orange-red. Tail streamers extremely long, at least twice length of those of European Bee-eater. Juvenile similar to adult but plumage duller and tail streamers much shorter.

adult

adult

Slim, long-winged bird with distinctive flight silhouette and multicoloured plumage. Adult has chestnut crown, nape and back shading to yellowish-brown on scapulars and rump. Uppertail dark shiny green, duller below with central two feathers darker and elongated. Wing coverts chestnut, surrounded with bluish-green. Flight feathers shiny blue, dark-tipped. Whitish forehead and narrow pale blue supercilium. Black eye-mask and black border to bright yellow throat. Underparts pale turquoise-blue. Underwing orange with darker tipped flight feathers. Long, slim, black decurved bill. Eyes reddish. Legs and feet brownish-black. Juvenile resembles dull adult but greener on back and wings.

adult

adult

BEE-EATER
Merops apiaster

THE BEE-EATER BREEDS in warm, sunny open landscapes in the drier parts of Europe. Sandy or clay banks are required for colonial nesting tunnels. Bee-eaters are migratory, returning to Europe from their African overwintering areas in April and May. During the spring rush to reach breeding areas they regularly overshoot their normal range and can often be seen in northwest Europe. In such circumstances they occasionally stay to breed, accounting for the historical expansion and contraction of the species' range.

BIRD FACTS

VOICE Liquid bubbling 'pruupp'

LENGTH 27–29cm

WINGSPAN 44–49cm

WEIGHT 45–75g

HABITAT Warm open habitats with mixed agriculture; clumps of trees, often near rivers

NEST Colonial tunnels in vertical or sloping sandy bank

EGGS 6–7; smooth, glossy, pinkish-white

FOOD Flying insects, preferably bees and wasps

The Bee-eater prefers to be in close proximity to water, which ensures an abundant supply of large insects such as dragonflies; it goes after them with a typical slow glide.

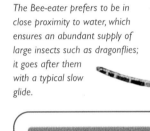

adult

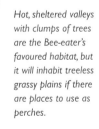

adult

Hot, sheltered valleys with clumps of trees are the Bee-eater's favoured habitat, but it will inhabit treeless grassy plains if there are places to use as perches.

adult

ROLLER
Coracias garrulus

THE ROLLER IS a spectacular bird of warm, dry southern and central European lowland habitats. Its favoured habitat is open old forest with healthy clearings and adjacent grasslands. Stands of riverine poplars are chosen in large areas of otherwise tree-less grasslands, such as in the pusztas of Hungary and Poland. The species migrates to Africa for the winter and it is at migration times that wanderers can be encountered well north of the usual range. The Roller uses the old nest holes of other species, particularly woodpeckers, to nest in. It also perches in trees to locate and drop down onto prey. It is an easy bird to find within its range as it habitually perches prominently along roadside wires.

Large crow-like bird, with very brightly coloured plumage. In flight, upperwing shows two-tone blue coverts and blackish flight feathers. Underwing shows pale blue coverts and blue black-tipped flight feathers. Adult has head, neck and underbody pale green-blue. Forehead and chin whitish, with narrow black eye-mask. Back chestnut, rump purple-blue. Shoulder iridescent cobalt blue with pale green-blue coverts and blue-black flight feathers. Tail blue-black with pale greenish outer webs and dark tips to feathers. Strong, decurved and slightly hook-tipped black bill. Legs and feet black. Juvenile has similar pattern to adult, but all colours duller.

BIRD FACTS

VOICE Rasping, accelerating rattle; harsh, short contact call

LENGTH 30–32cm

WINGSPAN 66–73cm

WEIGHT 110–160g

HABITAT Warm continental lowlands, old open forest, heaths and grasslands

NEST Hole in tree; less often in building or amongst rocks

EGGS 3–5; smooth, glossy white

FOOD Mainly large insects; also small mammals, nestling birds, amphibians and reptiles

adult

adult

DID YOU KNOW?

In the breeding season the male performs an acrobatic mating dance, where he dives rapidly towards the ground with half-rolls, like a Lapwing.

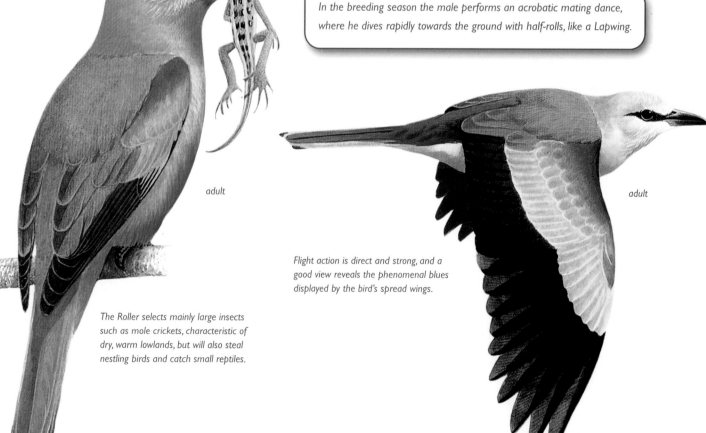

adult

adult

The Roller selects mainly large insects such as mole crickets, characteristic of dry, warm lowlands, but will also steal nestling birds and catch small reptiles.

Flight action is direct and strong, and a good view reveals the phenomenal blues displayed by the bird's spread wings.

Colourful and distinctive bird with a long-tailed outline in flight. Sexes similar. Adult male has mainly green plumage but dark flight feathers are noticeable on the wing. Has red bill and eyering, and pinkish neck ring, dark-bordered towards lower margin. Adult female is similar but lacks markings on neck or throat.

male

RIGHT: With its neck stretched, the pink elements of this male's neck 'ring' are obvious; the species is sometimes called Rose-ringed Parakeet.

female

male

RING-NECKED PARAKEET
Psittacula krameri

THE RING-NECKED PARAKEET is an established alien species (its natural range is Asia and Africa) and a rather bizarre addition to the European list. A feral population (escapees from captivity and their progeny), numbering many hundreds of birds, is now established in parts of the region. The suburban western fringes of London are a stronghold for the Ring-necked Parakeet, and it looks particularly incongruous when seen flying over the M4 or against the bleak backdrop of industrial complexes that fringe Heathrow Airport.

BIRD FACTS

VOICE Announces its presence (including in flight) with loud, squawking calls
LENGTH 27–43cm
WINGSPAN 42–48cm
WEIGHT 95–140g
HABITAT Open woodland, suburbs and parks
NEST Cavity in tree, often an old woodpecker hole, often 5m or more above the ground
EGGS 3–4; white and rather rounded
FOOD Wide variety of food items including fruits, flowers and food from bird tables

DID YOU KNOW?

Several other populations have become established in the wild across Europe of this and other species of parrot and parakeet.

DID YOU KNOW?

The nest hole is usually situated in a tree branch rather than on the main trunk.

adult

Similar in size to Nightingale but longer and slimmer, with plumage recalling Nightjar.

WRYNECK
Jynx torquilla

THE WRYNECK NEEDS open, warm, sunny habitats, often with bare sandy ground where it can easily find ants on which to feed. It nests in trees, but does not drum or excavate a nest hole, instead using the old site of another species. It is unobtrusive during the breeding season, when the only clue to its presence may be its quiet, ringing call. The Wryneck flies with a low, direct flight and its camouflaged plumage makes it difficult to detect. Some Wrynecks are migratory, the northern birds overwintering in Africa. Populations in southern Europe are only partially migratory, with birds present in Spain all year.

BIRD FACTS

VOICE High-pitched, ringing 'pee-pee-pee', like small falcon
LENGTH 16–17cm
WINGSPAN 25–27cm
WEIGHT 30–40g
HABITAT Lowland woodland fringes, orchards, parks and large gardens
NEST Natural or artificial hole in tree, wall or bank
EGGS 7–10; smooth, matt white
FOOD Principally ants, with some other insects; includes berries on migration

adult

adult

adult

IDENTIFICATION

At a distance, adult appears mottled grey and brown; at close range very finely marked. Grey crown, sides to mantle and back bordered by black scapular stripe, which connects on side of neck with elongated black eyestripe. Wings brown with heavy dark barring and vermiculation. Long, grey full tail has transverse black bars. Throat and upper breast yellowish with short black bars. Lower breast and belly creamy white with dark spots. Bill, legs and feet pale brown. Juvenile slightly paler than adult, with less barring.

GREEN WOODPECKER

Picus viridis

ALTHOUGH IT IS traditionally a forest species, the Green Woodpecker has adapted to the loss of this type of habitat and is now also found in more open terrain with trees. Its preferred food is ants, and where they are abundant in old pastures and sandy heaths the Green Woodpecker feeds exclusively on the ground. It uses its strong bill to dig into the ants' nest and its long sticky tongue picks up adults, larvae and pupae alike. The Green Woodpecker is difficult to observe because of its shy nature, particularly at the nest, where the only clue to its presence may be an occasional glimpse of the adult silently slipping away with its heavy undulating flight. More generally heard than seen, this bird has a ringing, laughing call, which is responsible for its local name, the yaffle.

A large, bulky woodpecker. Adult male has red crown extending on to nape; he has black face patch with red moustachial stripe set in black. Upperparts bright green with bright yellow rump and brown-black primaries, barred cream. Tail dark greenish-grey with faint cream spotting. Rear of face, sides of neck and underparts pale, clear yellow except for darker barring on flanks. Bill grey with yellowish lower mandible. Legs and feet grey. Adult female similar to male but has smaller black face patch and lacks red moustache. Juvenile plumage pattern similar to adult but colours dulled by white spotting and barring on upperparts; dark bars on underparts.

BIRD FACTS

VOICE Ringing laugh known as a yaffle; alarm call is a short 'kyack'

LENGTH 31–33cm

WINGSPAN 40–42cm

WEIGHT 180–220g

HABITAT Open, broad-leaved, lowland forest with clearings; parks, gardens and heaths

NEST Excavated hole in tree

EGGS 5–7; smooth, glossy white

FOOD Almost exclusively adult and pupal ants; occasional seeds and fruit

juvenile

adult female

adult male

adult female

adult male

Red centre of the male's moustachial streak hard to see in poor light.

DID YOU KNOW?

Signs of Green Woodpecker attacks can often be seen on forest anthills.

Adult male has grey head marked only with red forecrown and narrow black moustache above whitish throat. Back, scapulars and wing coverts pale but intense green. Rump yellow. Breast and underbody pale grey. Tail greenish. Folded flight feathers brownish-black, barred with white. In flight, upperwing shows an even green colour, except for dark brown-grey primaries conspicuously barred white. Underwing dark grey, barred white. Bill dark grey, yellowish towards base. Female has no red on crown and is similar to but duller than male. Legs and feet of both sexes grey. Juvenile browner and scruffier than adult.

Smaller than Green Woodpecker, with less robust bill.

adult male

adult female

GREY-HEADED WOODPECKER

Picus canus

THE GREY-HEADED WOODPECKER is found across the middle latitudes of Europe wherever woodland is plentiful. It reaches higher altitudes in the mountains than its close relative, the Green Woodpecker, and selects coniferous forests, mainly of larch. Nest holes are excavated in mature trees. Both species are predominantly ant-feeders and spend much of their time on the ground; however, the Grey-headed Woodpecker is a less specialised feeder, eating other insects gleaned from tree trunks or walls, and in winter it will visit garden bird tables. Like most woodpeckers this species is resident in Europe, although there is some evidence of irruptive behaviour when individuals can be seen outside the normal range.

adult male

BIRD FACTS

VOICE Short drumming; repeated fluty whistles slowing and descending in pitch
LENGTH 25–26cm
WINGSPAN 38–40cm
WEIGHT 100–150g
HABITAT Open deciduous woods and riverine carr; montane larch woods in central Europe
NEST Excavated tree-hole; lined with wood chips
EGGS 7–9; smooth, glossy white
FOOD Mainly ants and other insects; some seeds and fruit

Largest European woodpecker, half the size again of the Green Woodpecker. Adult male glossy black with scarlet forehead and long crown. Adult female browner and lacking plumage gloss, with red on crown restricted to small patch above nape. Massive, grey-brown, chisel-like bill with darkish tip. Legs and feet dark grey. Juvenile resembles adult, but with grey chin and red on crown less extensive or sometimes absent.

adult female

adult male

adult male

Large trees are required for nest sites, and the Black Woodpecker's ability to excavate living wood creates many opportunities for other hole-nesting species.

BLACK WOODPECKER

Dryocopus martius

THE BLACK WOODPECKER's noisy and showy behaviour makes it easy to track down. When foraging on trees it climbs with very pronounced bounds, using its massive bill to chisel rapidly into even healthy wood. Its flight is irregular, with periods of closed wings causing non-rhythmical bounds, but the overall impression is of a fast-flying crow dodging through the tall trees. The Black Woodpecker does not readily tolerate the close proximity of humans and its reliance on mature old-growth forest makes it vulnerable to habitat destruction by commercial forestry activities.

adult male

BIRD FACTS

VOICE Loud, far-carrying drumming; loud, melodious, repeated notes – often in flight
LENGTH 45–47cm
WINGSPAN 64–68cm
WEIGHT 260–360g
HABITAT Mature northern taiga; southern montane deciduous forests with mature tall trees
NEST Excavated hole in tree or telegraph post
EGGS 4–6; smooth, glossy white
FOOD All life cycle stages of ants and wood-boring beetles; occasional fruit and birds' eggs

GREAT SPOTTED WOODPECKER

Dendrocopos major

THIS IS THE commonest woodpecker in the region, and the most adaptable with regard to habitat. This species exhibits racial differences across the continent: the British race is smaller, with less clean plumage than its mainland Europe counterparts; it is also generally sedentary. Races in northern coniferous forests show irruptive behaviour. The Great Spotted Woodpecker gleans food from cracks and holes in the timber and excavates rotten wood to search for beetles. It is largely resident in Europe and begins breeding activity quite early in the year. A new nest hole is excavated each year.

Blackbird-sized, strong-billed pied woodpecker. Upperparts almost wholly black, relieved by large white scapular patches, lines of white spots across flight feathers and white barring on outertail feathers. Adult male has crimson nape patch, absent in female. Face, including eyering, mainly white with black moustache connecting with black nape and with black extension bar on to sides of breast. Enclosed white patch on sides of neck. Underparts creamy white with pinkish-red vent area and 'trousers'. Bill, legs and feet dark grey. Juvenile has black-bordered red crown, dirty-white underparts and less distinct white barring on wings than adult.

BIRD FACTS

VOICE Loud drumming; call is a sharp 'tchicc' and short rattle of similar notes

LENGTH 22–23cm

WINGSPAN 34–39cm

WEIGHT 70–100g

HABITAT Adaptable to various habitats with trees; prefers open, mature, deciduous woods

NEST Excavated hole in tree

EGGS 4–7; smooth, glossy white

FOOD Mainly insects; some seeds; occasional birds' eggs and nestlings

DID YOU KNOW?

The loud drumming made by the repetitive striking of the Great Spotted Woodpecker's bill on hollow trees can be heard in European woods from early January.

Male at nest.

female (LEFT) and juvenile (RIGHT)

adult male

adult male

adult female

Similar to Great Spotted Woodpecker. Adult has generally black upperparts and white underparts. On face, black moustachial line turns up and back, but stops before joining with back of neck, giving more open-looking white face than Great Spotted Woodpecker's. Male has red nape. Bolder white barring on wings but tail almost completely black – lacking white bars as on outer feathers of Great Spotted Woodpecker; vent paler pink than that species. Bill, legs and feet dark grey. Juvenile similar to adult but has red crown and flank streaks.

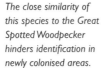

The close similarity of this species to the Great Spotted Woodpecker hinders identification in newly colonised areas.

SYRIAN WOODPECKER

Dendrocopos syriacus

THE SYRIAN WOODPECKER spread northwestwards into central Europe during the 20th century; it replaces its close relative, the Great Spotted Woodpecker, in the warmer, drier, open lowland habitats of the Balkans. It is less attracted to large stands of forest and can be found mainly in orchards, parks, avenues and riverine woods. The Syrian Woodpecker is one of three pied species in Europe with white shoulder patches, so care is needed with identification. Its unmarked face is often difficult to be sure of, but it has a soft contact call and a very long drumming bout.

adult male

adult male   *adult female*

BIRD FACTS

VOICE Long, loud drumming; call soft, short 'chjuck'
LENGTH 22–23cm
WINGSPAN 34–39cm
WEIGHT 70–80g
HABITAT Warm, open landscapes with scattered trees; orchards and parks
NEST Excavated hole in tree
EGGS 4–7; smooth, glossy white
FOOD Mainly insects; also fruit and nuts

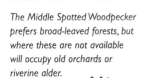

adult

The Middle Spotted Woodpecker prefers broad-leaved forests, but where these are not available will occupy old orchards or riverine alder.

MIDDLE SPOTTED WOODPECKER

Dendrocopos medius

THE STRONGHOLD OF the Middle Spotted Woodpecker is the hornbeam-oak forests of mainland central Europe. It prefers old stands of forest, particularly where traditional woodland management has resulted in a mosaic of coppiced undershrubs and large standard trees. Plenty of dying timber is important for excavating nest sites and food. It is significantly smaller than the Great Spotted Woodpecker, and its delicate bill cannot exert the same power in excavating healthy hardwoods, so the two species can coexist in similar habitats, utilising different parts of the woodland.

adult

BIRD FACTS

VOICE Drumming rare; far-carrying Jay-like 'quahh'; contact call soft and short
LENGTH 20–22cm
WINGSPAN 33–34cm
WEIGHT 55–80g
HABITAT Mixed deciduous woods of hornbeam and oak, parkland elms and riverine alder
NEST Excavated hole in decayed tree
EGGS 4–7; smooth, glossy white
FOOD Almost exclusively insects; occasional seeds

IDENTIFICATION

adult

Smaller, less cleanly marked version of Great Spotted Woodpecker. Adult male has red crown, which is shorter and duller in female. Remainder of upperparts black with white scapular patches (smaller than on Great Spotted Woodpecker), white barring across flight feathers and white outertail feathers, barred black. Face white with black moustachial border not connecting with black on nape. Downward extension of moustache onto sides of throat gives way to black streaking, extending down flanks. White chin and throat shading to dirty yellowish breast. Belly and vent pinkish. Bill, legs and feet grey. Juvenile similar to adult but duller, with less contrast and fewer flank streaks.

LESSER SPOTTED WOODPECKER

Dendrocopos minor

adult male

VOICE Quiet, high-pitched drumming; soft whistling 'pee-pee-pee', repeated up to 20 times

LENGTH 14–15cm

WINGSPAN 25–27cm

WEIGHT 20–30g

HABITAT Open, broad-leaved woodland; riverine alders, parks, orchards and tree-lined avenues

NEST Excavated tree hole, often on underside of branch

EGGS 4–6; smooth, glossy white

FOOD Almost exclusively insects and their larvae

THE LESSER SPOTTED Woodpecker does not need large trees, as foraging and nesting usually take place in smaller side branches and along twigs in the canopy. The bird's behaviour, small size and un-obtrusiveness make it difficult to spot. With its fluttery, buoyant flight, the Lesser Spotted Woodpecker is more like a passerine than its larg-er relatives, and is often found up among the high-est branches. When feeding it creeps along thin twigs and investigates dead wood with a barely audible tapping. The best clues to its presence are the weak, but ringing, repeated whistles and, in early spring, quiet but fairly long drumming bouts.

IDENTIFICATION

Smallest pied woodpecker, about size of Nuthatch. Adult upperparts predominantly black with heavy white barring across back and wings; black tail with outer feathers barred white. Male has short red crown; white in female. Rear of crown black. Buff-white face above black moustache curving upwards around ear coverts, with downward-extending bar. Underparts buffish-white, streaked black on flanks, with black spots on undertail coverts. No red around vent. Bill, legs and feet grey. Juvenile similar to adult, but with browner and more streaked and spotted underparts.

Distinguished from Great Spotted Woodpecker by small size and absence of white patches on wings.

adult male

adult male

This tiny woodpecker avoids dense stands of mature forest, particularly conifers.

adult male

WHITE-BACKED WOODPECKER

Dendrocopos leucotos

BIRD FACTS

VOICE Long, loud accelerating drumming. Low, quiet 'kjuck' and other hoarse squeaks

LENGTH 24–26cm

WINGSPAN 38–40cm

WEIGHT 100–120g

HABITAT Extensive deciduous or mixed forests

NEST Excavated hole, usually in rotten tree

EGGS 3–5; smooth, glossy white

FOOD Mainly insects, particularly beetle larvae; nuts and berries

THE WHITE-BACKED WOODPECK-ER is the largest pied woodpecker in Europe. It requires large tracts of relatively undisturbed old-growth forest with a high proportion of dead and decaying timber. In the north it can find these conditions in swampy coniferous forest, but further south the steep montane beech and fir forests are favoured, such as those in the mountain national parks of Hungary and Slovakia. Identification of this species should be straightforward, especially if seen in flight, when the white back and wing-barring is obvious. Clues to its presence are the long and accelerating bouts of loud drumming.

adult male

The white back, which gives this species its name, is not obvious until the bird is in flight.

IDENTIFICATION

Large pied woodpecker. Adult upperparts predominantly black with heavy white barring across wings, and white lower back and rump. Black tail has barred white outer feathers. Male crown red, extending slightly on to nape; female crown black. White face with black moustachial stripe turning up, but not connecting with black nape, and extending down to break into heavy black streaks covering sides of breast and flanks. Chin and throat white. Breast pale-buff, lower belly and vent bright pink-red. Bill, legs and feet grey. Juvenile similar to adult but has black streaks intermixed with red crown, greyish flanks and less red around vent.

adult male

THREE-TOED WOODPECKER

Picoides tridactylus

BIRD FACTS

VOICE Long, rattling drumming; contact call soft, longish 'gjug'

LENGTH 21–22cm

WINGSPAN 32–35cm

WEIGHT 60–75g

HABITAT Northern, dense, moist, coniferous forests; central montane steep-slope spruce forests

NEST Excavated hole in dead or dying conifer

EGGS 3–5; smooth, glossy white

FOOD Insects, mainly adults and larvae of wood-boring beetles; also drinks sap

adult male

THERE ARE TWO geographically separate races of Three-toed Woodpecker in Europe; the majority belong to a northern boreal and Arctic sub-species, with a less common Alpine race in the mountains of central Europe. The northern race of Three-toed Woodpecker is the only true Arctic European woodpeck-er and is also a more exclusively conifer for-est dweller than other species. This wood-pecker is a tame species, but is unobtrusive in its habits, being less flighty and not as energetic a feeder as some species. Although insect larvae are important in its diet, Three-toed Woodpeckers regularly ring spruce trees with holes to extract sap. The bird's calls and drummings can be quite soft. This species is mainly a sedentary European resident but northern populations can be irruptive. In the central European mountains it is sedentary and stays put even during harsh winters.

adult male

Medium-sized woodpecker with black and white plumage, differently patterned from other pied woodpeckers and lacking red.

IDENTIFICATION

Adult of northern race has black nape, face and moustache with white rear supercilium and white stripe under ear coverts. Back and rump white with ragged black border. Wings and tail black with narrow, white barring on flight feathers and outertail feathers. Underparts buff-white with grey barring on sides of breast and flanks and black-spotted undertail coverts. Male has yellow crown; this black with white flecks in female. Alpine race darker, with less white on back and heavier markings on underparts. Bill, legs and feet grey. Juveniles of both races greyer on underparts than respective adults.

SHORE LARK

Eremophila alpestris

BIRD FACTS

VOICE Subdued twittering song of thin musical notes

LENGTH 14–17cm

WINGSPAN 30–35cm

WEIGHT 30–45g

HABITAT Sub-Arctic or Arctic lowland tundra or montane plains; on coasts in winter

NEST Unlined depression on ground; usually sheltered under stone or tussock

EGGS 2–4; smooth, greenish-white spotted with pale brown

FOOD Insects and seeds in summer; seeds in winter

IN SWEDEN AND Finland the Shore Lark breeds in the driest stony areas of tundra, where the dominant sparse vegetation is lichen. In the southern mountains it chooses similar habitats on the bare upland plateaux. It is often difficult to spot on the ground, using stones and vegetation to hide its progress when feeding. Its thin song is mostly delivered from the ground. The most northern Shore Larks are migratory, and in winter are found among sand dunes and salt marshes along the North Sea coasts of western Europe. With its distinctive appearance and habitat preferences, the Shore Lark is unlikely to be confused with any other species in Europe.

Adult male has pale yellow face and throat with black forecrown and black mask curving down below eye. Black gorget across upper-breast. Reddish-brown rear crown and nape with tufted black feathers on sides of crown forming 'horns'. Facial markings made more striking by abrasion through winter into spring. Rest of upperparts warm brown, heavily mottled with black. Tail black with brown centre and white outer feathers. Lower breast and belly white with pinkish-brown wash and faint black streaking on flanks. Adult female is duller and more heavily streaked than male. In both sexes bill grey, and legs and feet black. Juvenile recalls adult but is speckled and lacks face pattern.

winter adult

Smaller and slimmer than Skylark, with crouched appearance when seen on ground.

Flight appears strong and powerful, with bounding action between flaps.

summer adult

Smaller and slighter than Skylark, though plumage superficially similar with buff upperparts, heavily streaked blackish. Adult has face well marked with bold white supercilia meeting on nape, and dark brown surround to warm buff cheeks. Hindneck and rump pale whitish-buff. Head has small crest at rear of crown. Closed wing shows black and white bar at wing bend. Tail short and dark, with white spots at tip. Underparts buff-white with necklace of prominent black streaks. Fine bill, dark grey-brown with paler base. Legs and feet pink. Juvenile similar to adult but has less well-marked face and white spotting on upperparts.

WOODLARK

Lullula arborea

THE WOODLARK PREFERS habitats often found where heathland meets woodland edge. Here the ground is usually well drained, with low vegetation cover for nesting and trees for perching. In winter, birds will often move onto adjacent fallow farmland. Overall the Woodlark resembles the Skylark; however, the short tail and blunt wings make the Woodlark look quite different in flight, with a hesitant fluttering action. It has a beautiful fluty song, which can be heard in the early spring. In central Europe, Woodlarks are migratory, but the maritime populations, such as in southern England, are mainly resident.

BIRD FACTS

VOICE Flight-song is a beautiful descending series of rich, mellow, fluty whistles

LENGTH 15cm

WINGSPAN 27–30cm

WEIGHT 25–35g

HABITAT Warm, dry, sandy lowlands with heathland vegetation and scattered trees

NEST Deep depression in the ground in sheltered position under bush; lined with vegetation

EGGS 3–5; smooth, fairly glossy, olive-white spotted and blotched brown at broad end

FOOD Insects in breeding season; mainly seeds at other times

adult

adult

In flight shows very short tail and more rounded wings than skylark.

juvenile

adult

DID YOU KNOW?

On the ground, the bright face and black and white wing markings are good features to look for.

CRESTED LARK

Galerida cristata

THE CRESTED LARK prefers warm, open plains with low vegetation and is most at home in grassland or cultivated areas with some bare ground. It is able to take advantage of human-modified habitats and can be found on urban waste ground, airfields and gravel pits. In Spain it occupies traditional low-intensity cereal fields. The Crested Lark has a shorter, weaker song than the Thekla Lark, and is a ground-dwelling bird. This species is largely resident in Europe, but it is possible that juvenile Crested Larks wander at migration times.

BIRD FACTS

VOICE Song from ground or in flight is loud with fluty whistles and mimicry

LENGTH 17cm

WINGSPAN 29–38cm

WEIGHT 40–50g

HABITAT Open, dry plains with low vegetation; artificial habitats such as waste ground

NEST Shallow depression on ground; roughly lined with grass

EGGS 3–5; off-white, smooth and glossy with fine buff-brown speckles

FOOD Seeds, leaves, shoots and roots; some insects

adult

adult

IDENTIFICATION

Bulky, Skylark-sized bird with long bill, spiky crest, deep chest and upright stance. In flight it looks compact with broad wings and short tail. Adult plumage ground-coloured, sandy-buff on upperparts and underparts. Blackish streaking most obvious on crown, including crest and back, and on chest and flanks. Face strikingly marked with cream supercilium and eyering forming spectacle; also neat black moustachial and malar stripes. Dark tail with buff outer feathers. Underwing coverts bright orange-buff. Longish dark grey-brown bill. Legs and feet flesh coloured. Juvenile has shorter crest than adult, darker upperparts with white speckling and whiter underparts.

adult

adult

DID YOU KNOW?

The Thekla Lark is difficult to separate from the Crested Lark where the ranges overlap, but the practised observer will learn to associate it with different habitats.

adult

Song is longer and louder than Crested Lark's, with rich, fluty whistles, but do not rely solely on this for identification.

adult

THEKLA LARK
Galerida theklae

IN EUROPE, THEKLA Larks are closely associated with Mediterranean habitats and there is considerable overlap in Spain with their close relatives, Crested Larks. The Thekla Lark prefers complex habitats with open soil, trees and bushes, walls, cereal fields and river valleys. It enjoys hilly and rocky locations, especially where habitats have been over-grazed or where farmland has been abandoned. On the Mediterranean islands it is found along the coasts and favours sand dunes. Close attention to plumage details is needed to separate this species from the Crested Lark.

IDENTIFICATION

Same size as Crested Lark but slighter build, shorter bill and fuller fan-shaped crest are all useful identification features. Adult upperparts greyish-brown; underparts show greyer chest and whiter belly. Distinct blackish streaks on crown, whole of neck and back. Rump rufous. Finely streaked throat. Heavy black spotting on greyish-brown chest extends on to flanks. In flight, underwing appears dull grey-brown. Bill grey-brown with paler base. Legs and feet flesh-coloured. Juvenile similar to adult but has shorter crest and upperparts speckled with white; almost inseparable from juvenile Crested Lark.

BIRD FACTS

VOICE Loud, fluty song with whistled notes and mimicry, alarm-call is a repeated fluting whistle
LENGTH 17cm
WINGSPAN 28–32cm
WEIGHT 25–40g
HABITAT Mediterranean mixed habitats of forest edge, scrub and cultivated plains
NEST Shallow depression on ground; roughly lined with vegetation
EGGS 3–4; smooth, glossy, off-white with brown speckling
FOOD Insects and seeds

IDENTIFICATION

Larger than Skylark with broader wings, short tail and heavy bill. Adult has crown, nape, back and wings buff-brown with blackish feather centres forming streaks. Warm brown face with creamy supercilium and narrow eyering. Dark brown tail with white outer feathers. Underparts creamy white with blackish patches on sides of breast and warm yellowish wash, spotted black extending down on to flanks. In flight, shows white trailing edge to wings and black underwing. Bill grey-brown with dark tip. Legs and feet pale brown. Juvenile similar to adult but more speckled on upperparts and throat and lacking clear blackish patches on breast.

CALANDRA LARK
Melanocorypha calandra

THE CALANDRA LARK's heavy bill, long legs and bulky body are all helpful in identification. The wings are broad and give the bird a powerful and direct flight action; they are very dark underneath, which is another useful pointer for identification. It sings in flight, whether hovering at a great height like a Skylark or simply undertaking a low-level, flapping sortie. This lark is mainly resident in Europe, though the large winter flocks may wander nomadically in search of food, gathering on cultivated land to feed on winter-sown grain.

Can run strongly on the ground and will perch prominently on bushes in the open.

adult

adult

adult

adult

BIRD FACTS

VOICE Loud, rich fluty song interspersed with grating notes; shrill buzzing contact call
LENGTH 18–19cm
WINGSPAN 34–42cm
WEIGHT 50–70g
HABITAT Grassland steppes of lowland plains and upland plateaux; in cultivated fields
NEST Shallow depression on ground under tussock; lined with grass and softer vegetation
EGGS 4–5; slightly glossy, white, spotted and blotched dark brown and purple
FOOD Mainly insects in summer; seeds and shoots in winter

SKYLARK

Alauda arvensis

BIRD FACTS

VOICE Loud melodious warbling flight-song; call is a liquid rippling 'chirropp'

LENGTH 18–19cm

WINGSPAN 30–36cm

WEIGHT 30–50g

HABITAT Grasslands in lowlands and uplands; cultivated fields

NEST Shallow depression amongst growing grass; lined with vegetation

EGGS 3–5; smooth, glossy greyish-white, spotted brown

FOOD Insects in summer; at other times mixed with seeds, grains, flowers and roots

TRADITIONALLY A SPECIES of steppe grassland, the Skylark has adapted to a variety of habitats; it does not require trees as it feeds and nests exclusively on the ground. The Skylark's familiar song is delivered while the bird maintains a fluttering position high in the sky. In the northeast of its European range the Skylark is migratory, increasing the resident populations of western Europe in winter. Large flocks can often be seen moving ahead of snow in late autumn and early winter. Skylark numbers are declining, probably as a result of pesticide use and intensive cereal production; unimproved grassland is its favoured habitat.

DID YOU KNOW?

In winter, Skylarks from northern Europe move south and gather in feeding flocks that may number several hundred birds.

Short-distance flight is fluttery; over longer distances flight action is strong and undulating.

Smaller than Song Thrush, with a stout bill that distinguishes it from pipits. Sexes similar. Adult upperparts buff, streaked blackish-brown. Crown well streaked, with short crest prominent only when erect. Pale buff supercilium and surround to dull buff cheeks. Closed wing shows blackish buff-edged coverts forming wingbars. Tail blackish-brown with white edges. In flight, wings show clear white trailing edge. Underparts buff-white with heavy streaking across breast and flanks. Bill grey-brown. Legs and feet pale brown. Juvenile recalls adult but has heavily speckled white on upperparts with black drop-shaped markings on breast.

adult

adult

adult

One of Europe's commonest larks, the Skylark does not require such warm and dry conditions as many of its relatives.

adult

adult

adult

SHORT-TOED LARK

Calandrella brachydactyla

THE SHORT-TOED LARK feeds unobtrusively on the ground, often making use of ruts and vegetation to obscure its presence. It can be confused with its close relative, the Lesser Short-toed Lark, but has long tertials that cover the wing point at rest and a cleaner-looking breast. The Short-toed Lark's song is a plaintive, persistent series of mellow whistles. This species is migratory, overwintering in Africa. During the autumn passage, juvenile birds sometimes exhibit reverse migration and head north instead of south.

IDENTIFICATION

Smaller and paler than Skylark, with compact body, neat finch-like bill and no crest. Adult upperparts sandy-buff, lightly streaked dull brown. Crown warm rufous-brown. Off-white supercilium contrasts with brown cheeks. Closed wing shows line of blackish-centred coverts with pale buff margins. Pale buff rump contrasts with blackish tail with white edges. Underparts clear white with faint sandy wash across breast and darker brown patches on breast sides. Bill grey-brown with yellow base. Legs and feet brown. Juvenile similar to adult but more obviously speckled on upperparts and has gorget of dark streaks across upper breast.

adult

BIRD FACTS

VOICE Song from ground or in flight is shrill, jingling and melodious with swallow-like twittering
LENGTH 13–14cm
WINGSPAN 25–30cm
WEIGHT 20–30g
HABITAT Dry, open steppes on plains and undulating landscapes; often in fields in winter
NEST Shallow depression on ground; lined with vegetation, soft seeds and down
EGGS 3–5; smooth, glossy, whitish, spotted and blotched brown and purple
FOOD Insects and seeds in summer; seeds only in winter

LESSER SHORT-TOED LARK

Calandrella rufescens

THE LESSER SHORT-TOED Lark favours more open, sandy ground than the Short-toed Lark. Separation from that species is tricky. Note Lesser Short-toed's prominent wing point, streaked breast and pale forehead. The jangling song is an important feature. The species is sedentary.

IDENTIFICATION

More heavily streaked upperparts and chest than Short-toed, with long wing point and tiny bill. Adult upperparts rufous-brown with blackish feather centres, particularly on crown and mantle. Pale cream supercilia frame brown face and meet across pale forehead. Underparts buffish with brown wash on chest, and gorget of black streaks extending to flanks. Wings brown with pale feather edgings; three primaries project at rest. Bill pale grey-brown with darker tip. Legs and feet yellowish. Juvenile similar to adult but more speckled.

BIRD FACTS

VOICE Long, continuous and melodious song in flight; quite loud, rippling alarm call
LENGTH 13–14cm
WINGSPAN 24–32cm
WEIGHT 20–25g
HABITAT Continental steppes and semi-deserts, especially sandy ground with low shrubs
NEST Shallow scrape on ground, sheltered by tussock and lined with vegetation
EGGS 3–5; smooth, glossy, variable whitish, yellowish or buff, spotted with brown
FOOD Mainly insects in summer; seeds at other times

DUPONT'S LARK

Chersophilus duponti

DUPONT'S LARK HAS very precise habitat requirements that restrict its range. It is remarkably reluctant to fly, preferring instead to run. Clumps of vegetation are used for nesting and concealment. It is one of the most difficult species to see in Europe. Dupont's Lark's beautiful, mournful flight song is usually heard just before dawn.

IDENTIFICATION

Smaller than Skylark with long bill and no crest. Adult upperparts brown, heavily streaked with blackish-brown. Face well marked with long buff-white supercilium and eye-ring forming spectacle; pale grey half-collar surrounds brown cheeks. Mantle, scapular and wing feathers are edged buff, giving scaly effect. Underparts white with heavy black spotting across chest and streaking down flanks. Long, decurved grey-brown bill. Long, brownish-white legs. Juvenile similar to adult but upperparts less streaked; pale feather edges create scaly look.

adult

adult

BIRD FACTS

VOICE Song beautiful mixture of fluty notes and finch-like twittering
LENGTH 18cm
WINGSPAN 26–31cm
WEIGHT 35–45g
HABITAT Dry, open, Mediterranean steppes with sparse vegetation; cereal fields in winter
NEST Scrape on ground, hidden under bush or rock; sparsely lined with vegetation
EGGS 3–4; smooth, glossy pinkish-white, densely spotted red-brown
FOOD Mainly insects and seeds

SWALLOW

Hirundo rustica

THE SWALLOW IS found throughout nearly the whole of Europe, and is absent only from Arctic latitudes, desert regions and the highest mountain areas. It prefers to hawk for insects over old pasture, agricultural crops, along hedges, woodland edge and over water, and is often found in the vicinity of villages, which provide nesting sites in old buildings and wires and roofs on which to perch. The Swallow is migratory, overwintering in the southern half of Africa. It is the traditional harbinger of summer, returning by the middle of April and advertising its presence with its pleasant, warbling song.

Classic swallow shape with small bill and long, forked tail streamers. Adult upperparts and breast band shiny blue-black. Forehead, chin and most of throat above breast band rich rufous-red. Underparts, including underwing coverts and long undertail coverts, buff-white, with black undersurfaces of flight feathers and black underside to tail. When spread, tail shows white spots towards the tips of all but outermost feathers, which are elongated into streamers. Female has shorter streamers than male. Bill and feet black. Juvenile similar to adult but has less shiny plumage, paler head, mottled breast band and shorter forked tail.

BIRD FACTS

VOICE Song is a pleasant warble with some rattling notes; alarm call is a loud, short 'chit'

LENGTH 17–19cm

WINGSPAN 32–35cm

WEIGHT 16–24g

HABITAT Aerial above pasture, open water, villages and farms

NEST Cup of mud attached to ledge against building; lined with feathers

EGGS 4–5; elongated, oval, smooth, glossy white, lightly speckled with red-brown

FOOD Flying insects, particularly flies

adult male

male

Long tail streamers and steady, gliding flight make this species easy to identify.

The mud and straw nest is usually built in recesses inside buildings or under bridges.

male

Juvenile begging for food from adult male.

adult male

RED-RUMPED SWALLOW
Hirundo daurica

THE RED-RUMPED SWALLOW is a very attractive member of the swallow family, but care is required to identify it when seen from a distance. It is structurally similar to the Swallow and shares some plumage characteristics and flight behaviour with the House Martin. Identification is further complicated by the occurrence of hybrids involving all three species. It enjoys rocky upland habitats, particularly warm gorges where it can hawk for insects above a river in hot, sheltered conditions. It nests in natural crevices and rocky hollows and occasionally on artificial constructions, particularly underneath old stone bridges. The Red-rumped Swallow is migratory, and overshooting birds are sometimes seen in northwest Europe during spring migration.

Note rich buff band on nape and mostly rufous face with neat blue-black cap.

IDENTIFICATION

Sexes similar. Adult has crown, mantle, scapulars and upperwing coverts blue-black, not as shiny as Swallow. Wings and tail brown-black, including undertail coverts, which gives effect of whole tail having been dipped in black paint. Broad, pale chestnut band across nape, and chestnut lower back shading to buff rump. Forehead and cheeks speckled rufous-buff. Underparts buff, faintly streaked black. Underwing coverts buff, contrasting with blackish flight feathers. Bill black. Legs and feet brown-black. Juvenile duller than adult, with much shorter tail streamers.

adult male

Similar in size to Swallow but bulkier, with blunter tail streamers turned inwards.

Adult male collecting mud.

BIRD FACTS

VOICE Quiet, twittering, chattering song; short, descending, whistling alarm note
LENGTH 16–17cm
WINGSPAN 32–34cm
WEIGHT 20–28g
HABITAT Aerial over meadows and pasture, open water and villages; in warm latitudes
NEST Mud pellets in bowl shape with extended entrance tunnel attached under overhang
EGGS 4–5; long, smooth, glossy white with some delicate red-brown speckling
FOOD Aerial insects; may take prey from ground in bad weather

IDENTIFICATION

Heavier and more bulky than Sand Martin, with broad wings, almost unforked tail and uniform dusky plumage. Adult upperparts dusky brown-grey. Underparts dark buff with smoky tone. Underwing coverts blackish. At close range buff throat is speckled with dark brown. Lateral tail coverts show pale chevrons. In flight white spots are visible towards tips of tail feathers. Bill black. Legs and feet dark brown. Juvenile similar to adult but has warmer plumage tones, with paler throat.

adult

Unlikely to be confused with any other species in Europe, but at first glance may look like a small Swift, especially as it tends to glide in flight; lacks Sand Martin's brown chest band.

adult

CRAG MARTIN
Ptyonoprogne rupestris

THE CRAG MARTIN prefers sheltered valleys, warmed by the southern summer sun. As for most aerial feeders the underlying habitat is not especially important, but the Crag Martin does hunt low down over fast-flowing water. It has a graceful, slow flight, repeatedly quartering along the same sheltered crag or cliff. This is not a wholly migratory species, which is unusual for a European hirundine. There is altitudinal movement in the winter and some birds stay in southern Europe, particularly in the west. Northern birds generally migrate to North Africa for the winter.

BIRD FACTS

VOICE Quiet, but persistent, guttural twittering song. Short, single-note contact call
LENGTH 14cm
WINGSPAN 32–34cm
WEIGHT 20–25g
HABITAT Mountainous regions and river valleys and gorges with exposed rock faces; coasts in winter
NEST Half-cup of mud under overhang or in short tunnel on cliff; lined with feathers
EGGS 3–5; long, slightly glossy white, delicately spotted reddish at broad end
FOOD Small aerial insects

SAND MARTIN

Riparia riparia

THE SAND MARTIN is a common bird around bodies of water, particularly if there are nearby sandy banks for its colonial nest tunnels. It will also use artificial nest holes, such as drainpipes in walls, so colonies can be found along city rivers and around coastal harbours. Sand Martins are wholly migratory, with the European population over-wintering in Africa south of the Sahara. Before departure for the winter quarters, large flocks gather over lakes and reservoirs. In early spring the Sand Martin is often one of the first migrants to return, sometimes being seen in March.

Smallest hirundine in Europe, with short, slightly forked tail. Adult has whole of upperparts, including flight and tail feathers, dark greyish-brown, often with sandy tone. Brown extends down onto cheeks and broad band across breast, with light brown smudges on flanks. Rest of underparts white. Underwing dusky brown. Throat often speckled or shaded with brown. Black bill, legs and feet. Juvenile similar to adult but upperparts less uniform with pale fringes to feathers.

juvenile

BIRD FACTS

VOICE Harsh, twittering, quiet song; harsh, grating, single-syllable contact call

LENGTH 12cm

WINGSPAN 27–29cm

WEIGHT 10–17g

HABITAT Aerial, in vicinity of sandy banks and near to water

NEST Excavated hole in river bank or sand-cliff; cup of feathers and grass

EGGS 4–6; fairly glossy, smooth, white

FOOD Small airborne insects and spiders

DID YOU KNOW?

Birds are hard to detect against a sandy background, but can often be seen perching on wires, branches or even the ground.

adult

Has rather fluttery flight action.

adult

Plumage distinctive when seen well: pattern of clear white underparts separated by brown breast band is diagnostic.

Adult at nest burrow entrance.

Short and stubby hirundine with large head and noticeably forked short tail. Summer adult has dark blue-black upperparts, except for prominent white rump. Underbody from chin to vent clear white in male, slightly dirty white in female. Dull grey underwing coverts and dusky grey undersurfaces to flight and tail feathers. Winter adult has white underparts mottled or smudged with brown, and is less smart. Bill black. Legs feathered white, and feet flesh-pink. Juvenile is duller greyish-black on upperparts than adult, with some white mottling on nape.

adults

adult

HOUSE MARTIN

Delichon urbica

THE HOUSE MARTIN'S association with human habitats has made its range extensive throughout Europe. It takes its prey of insects aerially, usually at higher altitudes than its relatives, and its habit of foraging high in the sky means that birds go unnoticed except where they actually nest, although in bad weather foraging birds are often forced lower and can be seen hawking for insects over water. House Martins nest in loose colonies and, once a building is chosen, many nests are built in the eaves and walls sheltered by the roof. The species is migratory, overwintering in the southern half of Africa.

BIRD FACTS

VOICE Soft, sweet twittering song; long, trill alarm call

LENGTH 12.5cm

WINGSPAN 26–29cm

WEIGHT 16–23g

HABITAT Usually in high air-space above towns, villages and occasionally coastal cliffs

NEST Half-cup of mud pellets and feathers, attached to vertical surface, usually a building

EGGS 3–5; smooth, glossy white, occasionally finely marked red-brown

FOOD Flying insects

adult

Flight is a mixture of long gliding bouts and rapidly fluttering wingbeats with sudden swoops and changes of direction.

adult

TREE PIPIT

Anthus trivialis

BIRD FACTS

VOICE Loud, rich song starting with rattle, ending in descending piping notes; loud 'tseeep' call

LENGTH 15cm

WINGSPAN 25–27cm

WEIGHT 18–28g

HABITAT Mosaic of open grassland or heath and woodland edge or forestry plantations

NEST On ground; shallow cup of grass, leaves and moss with lining of fine grass and hair

EGGS 2–6; smooth, glossy, very variable in colour and markings

FOOD Insects; some plant material in winter

THE TREE PIPIT feeds and nests on the ground but requires trees for look-outs and song-posts. It also likes parkland and heathland in the early stages of woodland colonisation and will use young conifer plantations. The Tree Pipit can be difficult to identify because of its similarity to other pipits; however, its flight song is distinctive – a finch-like chatter as it ascends from its tree-top perch and a series of decelerating piping notes while descending. Tree Pipits are wholly migratory, and it is likely that all but the most eastern of Europe's birds move to Africa for the winter.

Smart pipit with clear markings. Adult head, nape, back and wings warm buff-brown with black streaks on back. Face well marked with yellowish supercilium and eyering, and brown eyestripe. Cream margins and tips to blackish-brown wing feathers give closed wing a striking pattern. Rump unstreaked. Tail dark brown with white edges. Chin and throat buffish-white, warmer yellowish on breast and flanks with bold brown-black spotting. Belly and undertail coverts buff-white. Bill dark grey-brown with pale flesh-coloured base. Legs and feet flesh-pink. The hind claw (see photo below) is distinctly shorter than Meadow and other ground-dwelling pipits. Juvenile very similar to adult, with buffer ground colour and more streaking.

BELOW AND BELOW RIGHT: adult

displaying adult

Very clean-looking bird with warm buffish-yellow tones and upright stance.

adult

Adult head, nape, back and wings have variable ground colour of greenish-olive to dark buff-brown, with blackish streaks prominent on crown and back. Mantle sometimes shows pair of indistinct buffish braces. Face shows thin, off-white supercilium. Rump brighter, usually olive-brown, faintly streaked. Underparts greyish-white to olive with chest band of narrow blackish spots and streaks extending on to flanks. Bill grey-brown. Legs pinkish-buff. Juvenile has heavier streaking on upperparts than adult, and cleaner, brighter, pale margins to wing feathers; underparts warmer yellowish-olive.

adult

MEADOW PIPIT

Anthus pratensis

ALTHOUGH CLEARLY A pipit, specific identification of this species can be difficult, but its numbers and voice are a help to the observer. Its most usual call is a thin repeated 'tsip' note uttered as the bird escapes in a bounding flight from any disturbance. In the mountains of southern Europe it does not extend to the high altitudes occupied by its relative the Water Pipit, but in Britain it is an abundant bird on the highest moorlands. Northern and eastern populations are migratory and augment those further west in Europe. Meadow Pipits can be seen in winter in southern Europe, when flocks congregate on inland pasture or coastal salt-marshes.

BIRD FACTS

VOICE Flight-song comprises thin whistling calls ending in descending scale; thin quiet 'tsip' call

LENGTH 14.5cm

WINGSPAN 22–25cm

WEIGHT 14–24g

HABITAT Open, completely vegetated landscapes, particularly grasslands, bogs and tundra

NEST Cup of grasses, lined with hair, concealed under vegetation

EGGS 3–5; smooth, glossy, variable grey to reddish; spotted, mottled or streaked blackish

FOOD Mainly invertebrates; some plant seeds in winter

adult

DID YOU KNOW?

Sings in flight and parachutes to earth while delivering a fluty, descending flourish to end the song.

adult

Tail dark brown with white edges.

adult

ROCK PIPIT

Anthus petrosus

Overall dark plumage creates rather dull appearance.

THE ROCK PIPIT is now treated as the specific coastal replacement of the Water Pipit; formerly, both were regarded as races of a single species. It is not strikingly patterned, but draws attention to itself by its very bold and noisy behaviour, and can often be seen in open habitats along the shore. Most Rock Pipits are sedentary, particularly where they breed along ice-free coasts, but some northern populations do move considerable distances. During the breeding season, Rock Pipits favour cliffs and slopes within sight of the sea, nesting in rock crevices. Outside the breeding season, they favour beaches where small groups hunt for insects and sandhoppers.

BIRD FACTS

VOICE Song is an accelerating series of loud, full, rattling notes; alarm call is a loud, metallic 'tsup'

LENGTH 16–17cm

WINGSPAN 22–27cm

WEIGHT 22–26g

HABITAT Rocky sea cliffs and also coasts; salt-marshes in winter

NEST Cup of grasses and seaweed; hidden under overhanging bank in vegetation

EGGS 4–6; smooth, glossy grey-white, heavily spotted olive-brown

FOOD Mainly insects; occasional seeds

Underparts sometimes so heavily streaked that they look as dark as upperparts.

IDENTIFICATION

Larger and darker than Meadow Pipit, with strong bill and legs. Adult upperparts dark olive-grey with blackish mottled streaking. Pale-buff supercilium and pale-grey wingbars and tertial edgings relieve rather drab appearance. Tail dark brown with dirty-buff edges. Underparts creamy buff to darkish olive, with variable amounts of streaking across breast and on flanks. Some birds are so heavily streaked on underbody as to appear fairly uniform on upperparts and underparts. In winter paler birds become much darker with more blackish streaking. Bill dark grey-brown. Legs dull brown-grey. Juvenile similar to adult but appears more mottled.

TOP AND ABOVE: **summer adult**; BELOW: **winter adult**

WATER PIPIT

Anthus spinoletta

THE WATER PIPIT was long considered the same species as the Rock Pipit, but recently it has been given its own specific status. It is common in the Pyrenees, the Alps, the Apennines and the higher mountain ranges of central and eastern Europe. In winter it moves altitudinally, occupying lower slopes and valleys, usually in wet and boggy areas. The more eastern breeding birds migrate further, and it is probably these individuals that occasionally overwinter on the coasts and estuaries of western Europe close to Rock Pipits. Both have strong flight and loud calls, which should aid identification.

BIRD FACTS

VOICE Melodious, abandoned, twinkling song; contact call is a full, almost grating 'tseep'

LENGTH 17–18cm

WINGSPAN 23–28cm

WEIGHT 20–28g

HABITAT Montane short grasslands and heaths; lowland wetlands in winter

NEST Cup of grass and leaves; hidden under overhanging vegetation or bank

EGGS 4–6; smooth, glossy grey-white, heavily marked brown-grey

FOOD Mainly insects; some seeds and other plant material, including algae

IDENTIFICATION

Medium-sized pipit, less streaked in summer than other pipits. Summer adult has grey-brown upperparts, brownest on back and closed wing. Prominent double wingbar formed by pale grey margins and tips to wing coverts, and panel caused by pale edgings to tertials gives strong pattern to closed wing. Tail brown-black with outer edges white. Underbody dull white with pinkish wash on breast. Winter adult loses grey cast to upperparts, and pink wash from breast becomes browner with streaked underparts. Bill dark grey-brown. Legs and feet dark brown-grey. Juvenile similar to winter adult but with cleaner appearance.

RED-THROATED PIPIT

Anthus cervinus

THE RED-THROATED PIPIT chooses open habitats north of the forest belt, preferring willow and birch swamps, where trees are widely spaced. It often creeps slowly through low vegetation, keeping very close to the ground, and can be hard to flush. Probably the best opportunity for seeing it in Europe is during the autumn or spring passage when vagrants appear along coastal migration watch-points south and west of their normal range. They often migrate with flocks of Meadow Pipits, which provide a useful comparison.

BIRD FACTS

VOICE Loud twittering and whistling song with bubbling trill; call is a loud, thin, buzzing note

LENGTH 15cm

WINGSPAN 25–27cm

WEIGHT 17–24g

HABITAT Arctic and sub-Arctic mossy tundra and swamps; muddy grazed pastures in winter

NEST Mossy hollow under shrub; lined with grass, hair and feathers

EGGS 5–6; smooth, glossy, variable grey to pinkish-olive with red-brown speckling or blotching

FOOD Insects; small water snails; some seeds

IDENTIFICATION

Smallish, short-tailed, stripy pipit with markedly different summer and winter plumage. Breeding adult has dark-brown upperparts, heavily streaked with black. Mantle often shows pale-buff braces. Yellowish-buff margins to blackish wing coverts show as double wingbars. Buff margins to tertials are distinct, contrasting with dark, heavily streaked rump. Tail dark with white edges. Face and chin plain pinkish-buff. Breast and flanks warm reddish-buff; flanks streaked black. Rest of underbody paler buff. Winter adult and juvenile more black and white than summer adult, with heavily streaked chest; reddish wash to face and throat absent. In all plumages, bill dark grey-brown with pinkish base, and legs and feet yellowish-buff.

WATER PIPIT
spring adult

RED-THROATED PIPIT
BELOW: juvenile; RIGHT: autumn adult

RED-THROATED PIPIT
Reddish wash on underparts and very streaky appearance make Red-throated Pipit easy to identify in breeding season.

spring adult

RED-THROATED PIPIT *spring adult*

TAWNY PIPIT

Anthus campestris

BIRD FACTS

VOICE Monotonous song of metallic repeated phrases; alarm call like House Sparrow 'cherrup'

LENGTH 16.5cm

WINGSPAN 25–28cm

WEIGHT 22–28g

HABITAT Sunny, dry, sandy ground with scant vegetation; grasslands and coastal dunes

NEST On ground, under tussock; cup of grasses and leaves lined with finer material and hair

EGGS 4–5; smooth, glossy, whitish, heavily marked with purplish-brown blotches

FOOD Mainly insects; some seeds in winter

THE TAWNY PIPIT is a bird of warm, dry lowlands, selecting sandy habitats, where it is well camouflaged. It prefers scant vegetation with bare ground in between clumps, so it can run easily when searching for its prey or when avoiding danger. Adult Tawny Pipits are usually distinctive, with their unstreaked appearance and horizontal running gait reminiscent of a wagtail, but juveniles are more problematic and their streaked appearance allows confusion with some of the rarer members of the family.

spring adult

spring adult

Long, slim pipit, size of Yellow Wagtail. Adult has crown, mantle, scapulars and rump sandy ochre, mottled with dark brown on all but rump. Closed wing darker sandy brown with noticeable line of dark spots formed by blackish coverts with pale tips. Tail brown with pale-cream edges. Face pale with long, cream supercilium and narrow, black lores and moustachial stripe. Chest and flanks sandy buff, usually unstreaked; rest of underbody whiter. Longish fine bill, brown with buff-pink base. Spindly legs and feet yellowish with long hind-claw. Juvenile much more streaked than adult, with some streaking on breast.

The largest pipit breeding in Europe, the Tawny Pipit is found in sandy habitats.

spring adult

WHITE WAGTAIL

Motacilla alba alba

BIRD FACTS

VOICE Song is a twittering warble; call is a shrill 'tchissick'

LENGTH 18cm

WINGSPAN 25–30cm

WEIGHT 19–27g

HABITAT Farmland, wetlands, open country

NEST Grass and moss construction placed in holes in walls, ivy-covered banks, buildings, etc.

EGGS 5–6; pale grey with speckles

FOOD Invertebrates and seeds

AS A BREEDING species, the White Wagtail is the most common and widespread wagtail in Europe. In western and southern Europe the species is generally a year-round resident, while in the north and east of its breeding range it is a migrant. Like other wagtails, the White Wagtail is constantly active in its search for invertebrate prey. In some plumages, notably juvenile, White Wagtails are very difficult to distinguish from Pied Wagtails. A close look at the lower back and rump, which are always grey in the White Wagtail and black in the Pied Wagtail, is needed for certain identification.

adult male

IDENTIFICATION

Breeding male has black cap and nape and black throat and upper breast. Back and rump grey, not black as on Pied Wagtail. Underparts white. Blackish wings show two white wingbars. Tail long and black with white outer feathers; constantly pumped up and down. On non-breeding male black on underparts is confined to upper breast band; plumage somewhat grubby but otherwise similar to breeding male's. Breeding female similar to male, but markings less well defined. In winter loses black cap, and face grubby. Juvenile similar to non-breeding female.

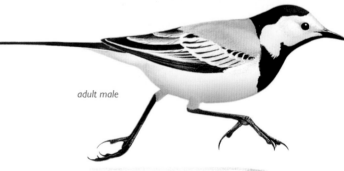

adult male

Adult male in summer has black on crown, nape, chin and upper breast. Back, wings and tail black except for white fringes and tips to wings and white outertail feathers. Adult female in summer similar to male but with greyer back. Black throat absent in non-breeding adults, leaving narrow black breast band. Juvenile recalls non-breeding female but has dusky brown tinge to plumage, and buff fringes to wing feathers.

PIED WAGTAIL

Motacilla alba yarrellii

THE PIED WAGTAIL is the British and Irish race of the White Wagtail, and the striking plumage, active habits and bounding flight with loud calls all draw attention to it. Separating Pied Wagtails from other races of White Wagtail in anything but adult male plumage can be difficult, and juveniles could be confused with juvenile Yellow Wagtails of some races. Pied Wagtails prefer open areas, except for roosting, when reedbeds are often used. The easy availability of insects around human habitation has enabled this species to live close to people.

BIRD FACTS

VOICE Song is a hurried warbling twitter; main contact call loud 'chissik'

LENGTH 18cm

WINGSPAN 25–30cm

WEIGHT 17–26g

HABITAT Mainly waterside habitats and bare areas created by human activity

NEST Cup of twigs and grass lined with moss and hair; in natural or artificial crevice

EGGS 5–6; smooth, glossy bluish-white, finely speckled grey-brown

FOOD Small invertebrates

Differs from White Wagtail in having black, not grey, mantle and rump.

DID YOU KNOW?

Pied Wagtails often gather together in large, communal roosts, partly for safety, partly for warmth.

juvenile

adult male

adult male

adult female

Resembles slim black and white pipit with fast running action and wagging tail.

adult male

GREY WAGTAIL

Motacilla cinerea

RIGHT: Summer
adult male

THE GREY WAGTAIL prefers fast-flowing rivers and streams and is found in upland regions of Europe, where it swoops and darts above streams in short sallies for insects, or stands on a rock in the water with the rear of the body appearing to move up and down with the wagging tail. Grey Wagtails usually nest in a waterside crevice, and a dislodged brick under a bridge is a common site; they will also sometimes use other man-made structures. The Grey Wagtail is partially migratory, with some birds staying throughout the winter, and others moving to more southerly parts of the European range. Northern birds may reach North Africa.

BIRD FACTS

VOICE Song is a series of shrill elements, getting louder; usual contact call is a shrill 'tchee'

LENGTH 18–19cm

WINGSPAN 25–27cm

WEIGHT 15–22g

HABITAT Running fresh water, particularly upland streams with rocky margins

NEST In hole or crevice, usually above water; cup of grass, roots and twigs lined with moss

EGGS 4–6; smooth, glossy creamy-buff, faintly marked grey

FOOD Mainly insects and spiders; some small fish and tadpoles

IDENTIFICATION

Adult male has grey upperparts with olive-yellow rump. White supercilium and submoustachial stripe, contrasting with black bib. Closed wing shows yellowish-white fringes to tertials and inner secondaries; main flight feathers blackish. Underbody lemon yellow with greyish flanks. Female and non-breeding male show reduced black bib or white throat; underparts buffer. Legs and feet flesh-coloured in all birds and bill greyish-black. Juvenile resembles non-breeding adult but with buff fringes to wing feathers.

ABOVE: *adult male*

winter female

adult male

adult male

Long, slim wagtail with a very long black tail with white outer feathers.

adult male

In flight, upperwing shows white bar; underwing greyish with white centre.

adult male

YELLOW WAGTAIL

Motacilla flava

THE YELLOW WAGTAIL is widely distributed across lowland Europe. The species is represented in Europe by a spectrum of different geographical races that are mainly separable in adult male plumages, and are distinct enough to have earned them separate vernacular names. In the breeding season it favours wet meadows with grazing animals and can be found in large numbers where this traditional agricultural management is still practised. Yellow Wagtails are migratory and often one of the first species to arrive in Europe in spring. Their distinctive flight call often announces their arrival on coastal marshes in late March or early April.

BIRD FACTS

VOICE Song is a rhythmic series of twittering notes; usual call is shrill 'pseeep'

LENGTH 17cm

WINGSPAN 23–27cm

WEIGHT 15–20g

HABITAT Lowland wetlands, particularly water meadows, salt-marshes and dune slacks

NEST Cup of grass leaves and stems; in shallow scrape on ground

EGGS 4–6; smooth, glossy buff-white, densely spotted with brown

FOOD Small invertebrates

ABOVE AND LEFT: male
BELOW: female

IDENTIFICATION

Adult males of the various geographical races separable in breeding plumage (see illustrations below). Females and juveniles duller yellow than males, with more uniform olive-buff plumage tones; geographical races essentially inseparable in field.

male

Smallest, most compact European wagtail, with pipit-like silhouette.

Adult males of all races have greenish-yellow mantle, greyish-green wings with whitish-yellow fringes to coverts and tertials, and dark greyish tail with outer feathers.

male

Adult male of race iberiae (Spanish Wagtail) shows blue-grey head, white supercilium and throat and black cheeks; breeds on Iberian peninsula.

Adult male of race thunbergi (Grey-headed Wagtail) shows slate-grey head, dark cheeks, white moustache and yellow throat; breeds in northeast Europe and Russia.

Adult male of race flava (Blue-headed Wagtail) shows blue-grey head, white supercilium and moustache, dark cheeks and yellowish throat; breeds across Central Europe and Scandinavia.

Adult male of race cinereocapilla (Ashy-headed Wagtail) shows blue-grey head, black cheeks and white throat; breeds in Italy.

Adult male of race feldegg (Black-headed Wagtail) shows entirely black head and yellow throat; breeds in southeast Europe and the Balkans.

WAXWING

Bombycilla garrulus

DURING THE BREEDING season, Waxwings favour nesting sites among old stunted conifers, often festooned with hanging lichens; they are largely insectivorous at this time, catching flying insects in sallies from a perch. In winter they disperse to the south and west, sometimes showing irruptive behaviour with large numbers moving to find food. At this time Waxwings can often be seen in cities in western Europe, where they feed on berry-laden trees and shrubs in gardens and parks. When it is observed under ideal conditions, the Waxwing is unmistakable, but at some distance in winter a flock in silhouette may be taken for a flock of Starlings.

Adult plumage basically warm pinkish buff-brown with small areas of black and striking colours. Head has fluffy backward-pointing crest. Brown shades into chestnut around face, and pinkish on neck, breast and flanks. Narrow black eyestripe and wide black bib. Grey rump. Blackish tail has broad, yellow tip. Belly yellowish, contrasting with orange-brown vent. Closed wing shows remarkable pattern of white tips to primary coverts and secondaries with waxy red appendages. Dark primaries have white and yellow margins. Bill and legs black. Juvenile duller than adult, without rich plumage tones and wing decoration.

In winter, Waxwings are often indifferent to human presence as they gorge themselves on rowan or hawthorn berries.

female

male

male

Female tends to have less intense black bib than male and fewer red waxy tips to secondaries.

Size and proportions of Starling, with similar flight action.

First-winter bird lacks white at tips of inner webs of primaries.

Adult has rufous-brown upperparts with paler buff-brown underparts, barred all over. Supercilium narrow and creamy, and throat pale buff. Closed wing shows lines of white barring on short, dark primaries. Undertail coverts and flanks also show some buffy-white barring. Bill long, thin and slightly decurved, dark grey-brown with yellowish lower mandible. Legs light brown. Juvenile like adult, but with even warmer brown tones to plumage.

WREN
Troglodytes troglodytes

THE WREN IS usually found in scrub or rank herbage, close to ground level where it forages for insects and spiders, creeping and flitting among the stems. It is often very difficult to locate, as it stays in thick cover, but on occasions it advertises its presence by engaging aggressively with neighbours or even birds of other species. Male birds build a series of nests with which to tempt the female. Once she has chosen the best, the others are left unused. In winter, Wrens often survive extremely cold nights by roosting communally in tightly packed clumps, either in substantial cracks in tree bark or in nest boxes.

BIRD FACTS

VOICE Powerful, shrill, trilling song; ticking alarm call

LENGTH 9–10cm

WINGSPAN 13–17cm

WEIGHT 7–12g

HABITAT Wide variety of habitats which offer some cover

NEST Dome of leaves, grass and moss lined with hair; in crevice, usually near ground

EGGS 5–8; smooth, glossy white, occasionally speckled blackish at broad end

FOOD Mainly insects and spiders; occasional fruits and seeds

adult

adult

Probably shortest bird in Europe when holding short tail erect.

adult

In flight, whole appearance is of warm-brown, round, whirring, bee-like bird.

adult

DIPPER

Cinclus cinclus

THE DIPPER IS found erratically throughout the continent, breeding exclusively along fast-flowing streams and rivers. Dippers rear their young in a concealed nest, usually under a river bank. They are often seen perching on rocks in midstream, bobbing in characteristic fashion, then suddenly disappearing underwater. They swim and walk along the bottom of the river against the current, foraging and identifying prey by touch. Most European populations are resident, moving to lower valleys in winter, but some northern birds are partial migrants. Eggs are laid at any time between March and June.

BIRD FACTS

VOICE Song is a pleasing rippling warble of mellow whistles; sharp 'tzit' call

LENGTH 18cm

WINGSPAN 26–30cm

WEIGHT 50–70g

HABITAT Fast-flowing, rocky streams and rivers, usually in mountains; lower altitude in winter

NEST Dome of moss and grass; in hole or crevice in stream bank

EGGS 4–5; smooth, glossy white

FOOD Large, mainly aquatic invertebrates; some worms and small fish

Adult has dark-brown head and neck. Rest of upperparts, wings and tail very dark slate with blackish feather margins, giving mottled effect. Chin, throat and breast bright white. British and central European birds have reddish-brown belly grading to blackish-brown on rear of underparts. Birds from northern Europe have uniformly blackish-brown belly and rear of underparts. Underwing black-brown. Juvenile has all dark-slate upperparts, mottled by black feather margins. Underparts white, heavily mottled, spotted and barred with dusky feather tips. All ages show white eyelid when blinking and black-brown bill and legs.

Adult northern European bird, showing uniformly dark belly and rear of underparts.

DID YOU KNOW?

Resembles a small, rotund thrush with short, rounded wings and cocked tail; British race has chestnut patch on anterior margin of dark underparts.

juvenile

adults, British race

DUNNOCK

Prunella modularis

MOST ACCENTORS ARE mountain birds, and the Dunnock's habitat preferences were probably originally similar – in the Alps it chooses cool, damp coniferous forest with plenty of glades surrounded by scrub. In western Europe it is less fussy and has colonised a wide variety of lowland habitats, including parks and gardens. The Dunnock is unobtrusive for much of the year, creeping along close to the ground, twitching its wings and tail nervously. It has a complicated breeding strategy, with both males and females often having multiple partners.

IDENTIFICATION

Size of House Sparrow but slimmer. Adult head, neck, throat and breast slate grey with brown streaks on crown and greyish-white streaks on face. Mantle, scapulars and wing coverts rich brown, streaked with black. Closed wing dark with buff fringes forming wingbar. Rump unstreaked dull brown, tail blackish-brown. Slate-grey of breast shades into brown on flanks, and to whitish-grey on belly. Eye noticeably red-brown. Short, fine bill blackish with pale-brown base. Legs pinkish-brown.

BIRD FACTS

VOICE Song is a weak, truncated warble; call is a sharp 'tzchik'

LENGTH 14.5cm

WINGSPAN 19–21cm

WEIGHT 15–25g

HABITAT Natural scrub in northern and upland coniferous forest; secondary scrub in western Europe

NEST Substantial cup of plant material lined with wool, hair and feathers, in bush or hedge

EGGS 4–6; smooth, glossy blue with reddish spotting

FOOD Mainly insects; seeds in winter

DID YOU KNOW?

The lively, warbling song is often delivered from an exposed perch.

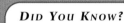

adults

adults

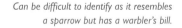

Can be difficult to identify as it resembles a sparrow but has a warbler's bill.

adult

adults

ALPINE ACCENTOR

Prunella collaris

THE ALPINE ACCENTOR is restricted in Europe to the highest mountain ranges of the central continent, preferring exposed but sunny short Alpine grasslands and boulder fields. It feeds and nests on the ground and chooses habitats without any tall vegetation. Alpine Accentors often sing from the top of boulders and rocks. In winter they sometimes descend to valleys and lower slopes, often around villages or ski installations, where they can become very tame. In southern Europe birds regularly choose lower, arid habitats in winter.

Adult head, breast and belly ash-grey with brownish tinge in some lights. Chin whitish with neat black speckling. Mantle grey-brown with heavy black-brown streaking. Rump grey and uppertail coverts rufous, streaked black. Tail dark brown, tipped white. Closed wing patterned with black, white-tipped coverts forming noticeable panel against rufous-edged secondaries and dark primaries. Underwing mottled rufous and grey. Flanks boldly streaked and blotched chestnut. Undertail coverts have black and white arrowhead barring. Bill black with yellow base. Legs red-brown. Juvenile like adult but duller and scaly.

adult

Bulky passerine recalling small lark.

adult

BIRD FACTS

VOICE Musical chattering warble; ventriloquial rippling call

LENGTH 18cm

WINGSPAN 30–33cm

WEIGHT 33–43g

HABITAT Montane habitats above tree-line

NEST In crevice amongst rocks; inner cup of moss and feathers surrounded by grass and stems

EGGS 3–4; smooth, glossy pale blue

FOOD Mainly insects with some spiders, earthworms, snails and plant seeds

RUFOUS BUSH ROBIN

Cercotrichas galactotes

THE RUFOUS BUSH Robin is likely to be first seen in flight, when it appears dashing and fluttering like a large warbler. However, when it is seen perched its similarities with chats are obvious; it cocks its long tail over its body, droops its wings and bobs its head. It looks odd in silhouette, with its long legs completing the picture, and is often visible perched on top of a bush delivering its song. On the ground the bird takes large hops, jerking its tail each time. European Rufous Bush Robins are migratory, overwintering in Africa south of the Sahara, and only return to their breeding areas in late May.

adult

Size of large warbler but with long, graduated tail.

adult

BIRD FACTS

VOICE Song is a jerky Robin-like warble; contact and alarm calls are short 'tsip' notes

LENGTH 15cm

WINGSPAN 22–27cm

WEIGHT 21–26g

HABITAT Southern steppes with planted scrub; also trees, parks, orange groves and gardens

NEST In low, thick bush; untidy collection of twigs and grasses lined with hair and feathers

EGGS 4–5; pale grey, tinged bluish, heavily marked with purplish-brown spots and streaks

FOOD Large insects and earthworms; some fruit

IDENTIFICATION

Adult Iberian race has rufous-brown upperparts and wings with brighter rump and bright reddish-chestnut tail, tipped black and white. Head shows long, cream supercilium and eyering, brown eyestripe and paler cheeks. On closed wing the pale-tipped coverts show as two wingbars. Chin and throat whitish, with rest of underbody sandy pink, brightest on breast and flanks; southeast European race greyer. All birds have strong bill, which is grey-brown with pale base. Legs and feet brown. Juvenile very similar to adult but has lightly speckled throat and breast.

adult

ROBIN
Erithacus rubecula

ROBINS CHOOSE SHADY habitats, usually with moist ground in which they can easily forage; they tend to stay away from open, dry and sunny locations. In Britain, in particular, they have become popular because they have adapted to living close to humans in gardens and parks. Robins feed on insects, worms and other invertebrates, and will often accompany gardeners in search of creatures disturbed by their activities. Both adult males and females use song to defend exclusive territories from each other during autumn and winter; the autumn song can sound very melancholy. Juveniles are not so easily identified and care should be taken not to confuse them with other young chats. This species is a partial migrant, with northern populations moving into the southern breeding range for the winter.

IDENTIFICATION

Small, round chat with large head. Sexes similar. Adult has olive-brown upperparts and tail. Often shows short, narrow wingbar formed by buff tips to greater coverts. Orange-red forehead, surround to eye, forecheeks, chin, throat and breast. Brown upperparts separated from orange face and chest by band of soft blue-grey. Flanks warm buff, belly and undertail coverts white. Bill dark brown and legs brown. Juvenile very different from adult, with brown upperparts and buff underparts all copiously spotted with pale buff.

BIRD FACTS

VOICE Both sexes sing series of mellow whistled warbles; call is a sharp 'tic'
LENGTH 14cm
WINGSPAN 20–22cm
WEIGHT 13–23g
HABITAT Shady, undisturbed coniferous and broad-leaved woodland; also gardens and town parks
NEST In natural or artificial hollow; base of dead leaves, cup of moss, grass and leaves
EGGS 4–6; white with reddish speckling and spotting giving rusty appearance
FOOD Invertebrates, especially beetles; some fruit and seeds in autumn and winter

DID YOU KNOW?

In the north of their range, Robins favour coniferous forests, while further south they prefer broad-leaved woodlands or even gardens and parks.

juvenile

juvenile

adult

BLUETHROAT

Luscinia svecica

IN THE NORTH of its range the Bluethroat prefers wooded tundra with marshy glades, often among spruce, willow or juniper for nesting; further south it usually selects thick scrub by water, though in Mediterranean latitudes it lives in broom scrub on open, sunny hillsides. The red-spotted form is found in Scandinavia and Russia (northeast), while those south of the Baltic are mainly white-spotted. Birds from some mountain ranges in central Spain are unspotted. In autumn, when non-breeding birds can be seen on passage, their behaviour is skulking; a glimpse of the chestnut patch on the tail is a good identification clue. The majority of European Bluethroats overwinter in the African and Asian tropics, but some birds overwinter on the Mediterranean. The northward passage in spring allows observers in Britain to see occasional Bluethroats further north and west of their breeding range.

BIRD FACTS

VOICE Song mimics other species in loud, short, warbling phrases; contact call 'chuck'

LENGTH 14cm

WINGSPAN 20–23cm

WEIGHT 15–25g

HABITAT Moist, wooded tundra with glades and scrub near water

NEST Concealed amongst thick ground vegetation; cup of plant material lined with hair

EGGS 5–6; smooth, slightly glossy pale bluish-green, finely marked red-brown, looking rusty

FOOD Mainly insects; some seeds and fruits

Adults of both sexes have buffish supercilium bordered by black above and brownish cheeks below. Tail dark brown with orange-chestnut base to outer feathers. Breeding male has metallic blue throat and upper breast with either a reddish or white central spot, depending on race; the spot is sometimes absent in some races. Blue throat is bordered below by narrow black, white and chestnut bands. Underbody off-white with greyish flanks. Non-breeding adult has pale throat and otherwise more subdued colours than breeding male. Female lacks male's blue throat; note dark 'moustache' and 'necklace'. Grey-brown bill and ochre-brown legs in both sexes. Juvenile spotted with pale buff, assuming female-like plumage in autumn.

adult male

Adult male is easily identified in breeding plumage, when male shows distinctive blue throat, mostly with either a red or a white spot.

Adult male, red-spotted form, displaying.

juvenile

DID YOU KNOW?

Adult female usually lacks male's throat pattern but has black moustache joining brown-black necklace.

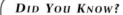

autumn male

Adult has fairly uniform russet-brown upperparts with warmer tone to rump and uppertail coverts, and bright chestnut-brown tail with dark central feathers. Head has uniform brown face with buff eyering. Closed wing shows darker brown-centred flight feathers. Underparts are dull cream-white with brownish suffusion across breast and down flanks. Vent and undertail coverts brighter cream-buff. Bill dark grey-brown with pale base. Legs pale brown or flesh. Juvenile is very speckled, but when this plumage is lost, looks like adult with buff tips to wing coverts and tertials.

NIGHTINGALE
Luscinia megarhynchos

IN EUROPE THE Nightingale is the more westerly counterpart of the Thrush Nightingale, but prefers warmer climates and is less restricted to lowland valleys near water, often inhabiting dry, sunny hillsides on sandy soils. Woodland scrub is its preferred habitat. Traditional woodland management, where oak standards and hazel coppice are encouraged, has provided one suitable habitat in parts of Europe. It also chooses invasive scrub on chalky hillsides and Alpine meadows, and it is these more open habitats that allow the species to live around the Mediterranean. The Nightingale probably has the best-known song of any European bird.

BIRD FACTS

VOICE Beautiful, mellow, musical and varied song, with pure whistles and rattles

LENGTH 16.5cm

WINGSPAN 23–26cm

WEIGHT 20–28g

HABITAT Scrub in woodland, along rivers or on dry, sunny hillsides

NEST On or near ground; bulky loose cup of plant material, lined with fine grasses and feathers

EGGS 4–5; pale blue, finely speckled and mottled red-brown

FOOD Mainly terrestrial insects, spiders, woodlice, snails and earthworms; berries in autumn

The long, broad tail with its bright chestnut colouring is the most obvious feature as the bird disappears into cover.

adult

juvenile

DID YOU KNOW?

Confusion with the Thrush Nightingale is easy when trying to identify this species by sight, but the more russet-toned plumage, brighter tail and cleaner underparts are all useful features.

adults

BIRD FACTS

Voice Beautiful, long and varied warble with deep 'tchock' notes and rattles

Length 16.5cm

Wingspan 24–27cm

Weight 25–32g

Habitat Open woodland and thicket scrub, often along rivers; also orchards and parks

Nest On ground; loose cup of grass and leaves, lined with hair

Eggs 4–5; variable buff, olive or greenish-blue with reddish and white marks

Food Woodland floor invertebrates; fruits and seeds in autumn

THRUSH NIGHTINGALE

Luscinia luscinia

THE THRUSH NIGHTINGALE and the Nightingale are very similar species in Europe and great care is needed in their identification. The Thrush Nightingale is more definitely a lowland plains species and likes proximity to water. Nesting occurs in deep shade and cover. Identification by sight depends on prolonged views in good light, when plumage tone, the contrast between the warm brown tail and the rest of the upperparts, and the mottled chest are all important features. The songs of the two species are different but care is needed to detect the differences.

adult

DID YOU KNOW?

The Thrush Nightingale is wholly migratory in Europe, overwintering in East Africa.

IDENTIFICATION

Resembles a small thrush. Very difficult to separate from Nightingale on sight alone. Adult has dark olivaceous-brown upperparts with warmer brown uppertail coverts and dull rufous-brown tail. Underparts dull whitish-grey with clean throat bordered by brown malar stripe and breast. Chest and flanks mottled dusky brown. Bill dark grey-brown with pale base to lower mandible. Legs brown. Juvenile appears darker, with contrasting pale spots on tips of tertials and wing coverts. Legs pale flesh.

The rich and varied song with solemn, pealing bell-like notes, clipped phrases and rasping notes lacks only the crescendo elements of Nightingale's song.

adult

adult

BIRD FACTS

Voice Song is loud and mimetic, unlike other wheatears; call is 'tchok', 'click' and 'dweet'

Length 16.5cm

Wingspan 27–31cm

Weight 25–32g

Habitat Bare hillsides and dry plains, all with sparse vegetation

Nest Among stones, in holes or burrows; cup of plant materials, with softer lining

Eggs 4–5; pale blue, with reddish-brown speckles mostly at larger end

Food Invertebrates, especially ants and beetles

ISABELLINE WHEATEAR

Oenanthe isabellina

The Isabelline Wheatear's stance is more upright than that of other wheatears, its long legs making it look as though it is on stilts.

IDENTIFICATION OF THIS pale wheatear, which lacks a clear plumage pattern, is difficult. These subtle differences from other wheatear species should be noted: longer bill; rather shorter, broader tail with wider black tail band and shorter vertical bar; limited face pattern; larger wing and tail area with a more powerful and less flitting flight action; and it glides well. The male's territorial song differs from all other wheatears'; it is loud and amazingly rich in mimicry of other birds and sounds, so the bird has been called 'the nightingale of the desert'. It feeds by making quick dashes along the ground after its prey.

IDENTIFICATION

Largest and palest wheatear in the region. Sexes similar. Less contrast between upperparts and underparts than in other wheatears. Generally pale sandy brown above and buffish-white below, with brown wings showing broad creamy fringes to coverts and secondaries. Dirty-white supercilium, black lores and eyes. Tail white with broad, black terminal band and less noticeable vertical bar. Bill and legs long and black. Hard to distinguish from some female wheatears. Juvenile paler than adult but otherwise similar.

adult

adult

adult

Male black except for white rump and tail coverts, white tail with end marked by upside-down 'T', the end bar being narrower than the Northern Wheatear's. Black underwings contrast with greyish-white in fringes of flight feathers. Female separable at close range; more sooty brown than black, especially on face and underparts when feathers are worn. Bill and legs black in both sexes. Juvenile similar to female.

adult

BLACK WHEATEAR
Oenanthe leucura

THE BLACK WHEATEAR is generally a sedentary bird. It is less solitary than most other wheatears, and three to five commonly feed together. They are territorial, probably pair for life and, although shy and wary, are actually more approachable in the breeding season, from mid-March in southern Spain. The Black Wheatear's nest is a remarkable construction: it has to be in a hole big enough to contain a foundation of stones built by both male and female. Favourite sites are used for several years; one was recorded to contain around 9,300 stones and covered 2sq m of a cave floor.

adult

BIRD FACTS

VOICE Call is a distinctive 'pee-pee-pee'; song is a quiet mixture of warbles and chatter
LENGTH 18cm
WINGSPAN 26–29cm
WEIGHT 38–42g
HABITAT Gorges and rock-strewn places, quarries and screes
NEST In a hole; bulky cup of grass and leaves, lined with wool and feathers
EGGS 3–6; very pale blue, sparsely spotted reddish-brown at larger end
FOOD Mainly insects, including large beetles

DID YOU KNOW?

The males are easily spotted from February onwards, when they perform the song-flight, rising up like a pipit and singing a more melodious song than most wheatears before gliding to a perch.

Adult male has black face and throat linked by black feathering to black wings. Crown, nape and underparts essentially white. Superficially similar to black-throated form of Black-eared Wheatear. Tail pattern also similar to that of Black-eared Wheatear: white with black central feathers and trailing edge. Males in autumn and winter have pale-brown feather edges and so white elements of plumage look buff and black elements look greyish. Adult female has dark grey-brown head, throat and upperparts; underparts grubby white. During winter months pale feather margins reduce contrast in plumage. Bill and legs dark in all birds.

1st winter

male

PIED WHEATEAR
Oenanthe pleschanka

AT THE WESTERN edge of its range, the Pied Wheatear has a toe-hold in Europe, having bred in Turkey and the former Yugoslavia and nesting on a regular, if local, basis in Bulgaria. It occurs in small numbers on migration in the eastern Mediterranean, and as a rare vagrant further north and west. Unfortunately most of these extralimital records refer to first-autumn birds, which are easily confused with immature Northern Wheatears. The species overwinters in East Africa.

BIRD FACTS

VOICE Calls include a sharp 'tchek'; song includes rattling, buzzing and warbling phrases
LENGTH 14–15cm
WINGSPAN 26–27cm
WEIGHT 18–20g
HABITAT Stony hillsides and broken ground
NEST Grassy nest constucted in hole or under boulder
EGGS 4–5; pale blue
FOOD Mainly insects and other invertebrates

female

CYPRUS PIED WHEATEAR

Oenanthe cypriaca

BIRD FACTS

VOICE Song is a continuous series of buzzing, sawing notes; various clicking calls

LENGTH 14cm

WINGSPAN 23–25cm

WEIGHT 15–20g

HABITAT Open, stony, arid areas and fallow fields

NEST In hole in bank or under rock; grass cup lined with wool or hair

EGGS 4–6; smooth, glossy, pale bluish-green, spotted and speckled red-brown

FOOD Mainly insects, with some worms and snails; berries in autumn

PREVIOUSLY AUTHORITIES THOUGHT the Cyprus Pied Wheatear was a race of the Pied Wheatear. It has now been elevated to species status. Because it occurs on an island where the only other wheatears are migrants or overwintering species, identification of the species in summer should present few problems, especially as it is so numerous. This species is migratory, overwintering in northeast Africa, and returning to Cyprus from late March.

IDENTIFICATION

Adult male has white crown and nape. Face, chin to upper breast, neck, back and wings black. Rump and uppertail coverts white. Tail white with black central feathers; all feathers black-tipped. Underparts from lower breast to undertail coverts black and flight feathers dusky. After autumn moult, plumage is browner with little contrast; breeding plumage acquired by wear. Female resembles dull male with dark olive-brown crown contrasting with pale-buff supercilium and nape. Juvenile dark with pale-spotted upperparts.

BLACK-EARED WHEATEAR

Oenanthe hispanica

BIRD FACTS

VOICE Song is a rich warble interspersed with scratchy, buzzing phrases

LENGTH 14.5cm

WINGSPAN 25–27cm

WEIGHT 15–20g

HABITAT Warm Mediterranean and steppe open habitats with dry stony ground

NEST Cup of grass and moss, lined with hair; on ground under rock or bush

EGGS 4–5; smooth, glossy pale blue, finely marked red-brown at broad end

FOOD Mainly insects; some snails and berries, particularly in autumn

THE ADULT MALE Black-eared Wheatear is one of the smartest passerines in Europe; females and juveniles are not so easy to identify and can resemble other wheatears. The more richly coloured *O. h. hispanica* occurs in the west of the range while the paler race, *O. h. melanoleuca*, is found in areas of the eastern Mediterranean. The whole European population overwinters across northern tropical Africa.

IDENTIFICATION

Males of both black- and pale-throated forms have sandy-buff crown, nape, mantle and underbody. Tail white with black inverted 'T' caused by black central feathers and narrow black tips. Forehead and supercilium creamy white. Throat either black or sandy as underbody. Underwing coverts black, contrasting with grey flight feathers. In autumn fresh buff feather margins reduce contrast between black and sandy plumage. Females of both races recall male but lack strong head pattern. Bill and legs black in both sexes. Juvenile resembles female but has buff spotted underparts and scaly, brown breast.

CYPRUS PIED WHEATEAR *male*

CYPRUS PIED WHEATEAR *male*

BLACK-EARED WHEATEAR *female, eastern race.*

BLACK-EARED WHEATEAR
Adult male, black-throated form.

1st autumn male

BLACK-EARED WHEATEAR
ABOVE: Adult male, pale-throated form.

RIGHT: Male of black-throated western form; both forms have black face and wings and white rump.

Adult male has diagnostic grey crown and back, white supercilium, black mask through eye widening over cheek, and black wings; chin to breast pink-buff, rest of underparts white. Rump, uppertail coverts and tail white, the last with tip marked by broad, black upside-down 'T'. Adult female similarly patterned but wings, crown, cheek patch and back all brown-toned. Underparts usually buffer. Juvenile has dark upperparts with scaly appearance, and pale underparts with darker crescent-shaped markings. In many plumages similar to other wheatears; identification is best done by noting tail pattern and length, face pattern and colour tones of body plumage. This is the only wheatear breeding in north and northwest Europe.

NORTHERN WHEATEAR

Oenanthe oenanthe

THE NORTHERN WHEATEAR is the most widespread and best-known species of wheatear. This bouncy, ground-loving bird is found in a variety of open habitats from the Arctic to the Mediterranean, from sea level to over 3,000m. It overwinters in Africa, and is often the first song-bird to arrive in northwest Europe in spring, commonly appearing in March. Autumn migration is protracted, from August to October. In its breeding territory the male Northern Wheatear is a conspicuous bird on lowland grassland, but is well camouflaged among the rocks of hillsides. The Northern Wheatear is solitary on its breeding grounds but forms small flocks at coastal stopovers on migration. It is a wary bird; when disturbed it bobs its whole body, and if pressed dashes away low, showing its striking tail pattern.

BIRD FACTS

VOICE Song is an energetic, short warble; call is 'chak'; alarm call is 'weet-chak, chak'.

LENGTH 14.5–15.5cm

WINGSPAN 26–32cm

WEIGHT 22–28g

HABITAT Open, very diverse habitats; Arctic tundra, sand dunes, cliff-tops, moors, mountains

NEST In hole in rock or wall, or rabbit burrow; loose cup of grass and moss, lined with grass and wool

EGGS 5–6; very pale blue, unmarked

FOOD Mainly insects; also spiders, snails and earthworms; berries in autumn

juvenile

Male (RIGHT) easily identified; female (FAR RIGHT) and first-winter birds similar to other wheatears.

adult male

adult male

adult male

adult male, Greenland race

adult male

227

STONECHAT

Saxicola torquata

THE STONECHAT REQUIRES substantial vegetation cover, so shuns bare areas and steppes that have only extensive grass cover. Where it does occur the Stonechat will tolerate many different habitats, often on the edge of agriculture where there are scattered scrub, fences and walls. Stonechats are resident over much of their European range, but the most northern and eastern populations escape the cold by moving south within Europe.

female

BIRD FACTS

VOICE Shrill and fairly monotonous series of short, scratchy and whistled phrases; call is a harsh 'tchack'

LENGTH 12.5cm

WINGSPAN 18–21cm

WEIGHT 13–18g

HABITAT Dry, scrubby areas, particularly heaths and sand dunes; also young plantations

NEST Loose cup of dry stems and leaves lined with hair, feathers and wool; hidden near ground

EGGS 4–6; smooth, glossy pale blue to greenish-blue, variably marked reddish

FOOD Invertebrates; also seeds in winter

Adult male has dark-brown head and throat, with isolated white patches on sides of neck. Mantle and scapulars evenly dark brown. White rump streaked blackish. Closed wing shows white panel on coverts. Breast and flanks orange, shading to greyish-white on centre of belly and undertail coverts. Underwing dark. Adult female upperparts mottled brownish, and white areas replaced by buff. Juvenile greyer and heavily spotted, resembling bright but uniform buffish female by first autumn.

male

male

Smaller than Robin, with shorter, more rounded wings than Whinchat.

WHINCHAT

Saxicola rubetra

THE WHINCHAT OCCURS most widely to the north and east of its close family relative, the Stonechat. A bird of the open country, it is found in tall grass, bracken or annual herbs, often on dry, stony ground. Confusion with identification can arise between the juveniles of this species and the Stonechat, because young Whinchats do not display some of the adult plumage characteristics. The buff supercilium, usually present behind the eye, buff fringes to upperparts and pale underparts are useful pointers. Whinchats migrate to Africa, south of the Sahara, for the winter.

BIRD FACTS

VOICE Song is a long series of short units, varied with fluty and scratchy phrases; call is a harsh 'tzec'

LENGTH 12.5cm

WINGSPAN 21–24cm

WEIGHT 14–22g

HABITAT Open grassland and scrub, particularly hay meadows; bracken on hills

NEST On ground; cup of leaves and grasses, lined with fine stems, hair and moss

EGGS 4–7; smooth, glossy pale blue, finely speckled red-brown

FOOD Mainly invertebrates; some seeds

IDENTIFICATION

Smaller than Robin. Adult male has black-brown head with long, broad, white supercilium reaching nape, and similar white border to cheek, upturned at rear. Back dark brown with heavy blackish streaking. Rump paler with rufous tinge. Wing coverts black with bold, white bar extending onto tertials. Flight feathers brown-black with white bases to outer primaries. Tail black with white sides to base. Underbody uniform warm orange. Adult female similarly patterned to male but duller. Bill and legs black in both sexes. Juvenile recalls female but not as distinct; has buff underparts and less clear pattern to face.

male

female

male

male

female

female

Both sexes show distinctive white supercilium, but female (RIGHT) lacks black face mask of male (LEFT).

Slimmer than Robin, with longer wings and tail. Adult male has white forehead and supercilium. Crown and back blue-grey. Wings blackish-brown with buffish fringes and tips to feathers. Rump, uppertail coverts and tail bright chestnut with dark-brown central feathers. Face, throat and upper breast black, contrasting with orange-red lower breast and flanks. Belly white and undertail coverts orange-red. Underwing coverts pale chestnut. Female plumage greyish-brown, darker on upperparts than underbody. White throat and eyering; chestnut tail. Bill and legs black in both sexes. Juvenile has tail like adult but rest of plumage speckled buff and brown.

REDSTART

Phoenicurus phoenicurus

BIRD FACTS

VOICE Melancholy song with sweet and rattling phrases; contact call is a soft 'tchuk'
LENGTH 14cm
WINGSPAN 20–24cm
WEIGHT 11–20g
HABITAT Open, broad-leaved woodland and parkland or heaths, well-treed farmland
NEST In tree-hole or nest box; cup of grasses and moss, lined with hair and feathers
EGGS 5–7; smooth, glossy pale blue
FOOD Mainly insects; fruit in autumn

THE REDSTART INHABITS fairly shady, wooded habitats with old trees, walls or banks to provide nest holes. Regular perches are often used as starting points for fly-catching or ground foraging sorties. The Redstart's behaviour accentuates the smart plumage, with prominent perching and shivering of the reddish tail. Migrants are often quite shy and skulking, dashing away into cover, displaying the bright tail as they swoop up to a hidden perch. Females and young birds may be difficult to separate from the Black Redstart, but the Redstart is paler fawn and has a neat, pale eyering. Redstarts migrate to tropical Africa for the winter.

male

male

female

Female (ABOVE) duller than male (LEFT) but retains chestnut tail coloration.

male

BLACK REDSTART

Phoenicurus ochruros

BIRD FACTS

VOICE Song is a quick, scratchy warble; contact call 'sit'
LENGTH 14.5cm
WINGSPAN 23–26cm
WEIGHT 14–20g
HABITAT Open, rocky and stony habitats in mountains; also wasteland and buildings in cities
NEST On ledge or in crevice; loose cup of plant material, lined with hair and feathers
EGGS 4–6; smooth, glossy, pale blue to white
FOOD Invertebrates and fruit

THE BLACK REDSTART is a common bird throughout much of Europe. Its preferred habitat is open, rocky and craggy terrain, often in mountain regions. However, it has adapted to nesting in holes and crevices on buildings, and so has evolved into more of a village and city bird in some regions of Europe. Females and juveniles require careful separation from common Redstarts but always look much more uniformly dusky. The flight silhouette is compact and resembles a slim Robin. Black Redstarts overwinter mainly in the southern part of the breeding range, around the Mediterranean.

IDENTIFICATION

In spring, adult male has dusky slate head, back, wing coverts and black face and breast. Wings brown-black with off-white panel. Centre of belly greyish-white, vent and undertail coverts orange. Rump and tail are chestnut with central tail feathers and tips dark brown. After fresh moult in autumn, plumage colours are muted by pale feather edgings, and wing panel is brighter white. For description of female, see caption. Bill and legs black in both sexes. Juvenile resembles speckled female.

LEFT: female; ABOVE: male

Male is blackest on face and breast.

male

Female has dull, grey-brown body plumage with orange areas less bright than on male, and buff wing panel.

female

ROCK THRUSH

Monticola saxatilis

male

THE ROCK THRUSH is a very shy and solitary bird in its breeding grounds, seeking cover among the rocks when disturbed – it is more likely to be heard than seen. The male's fluting, melodious song is often given in flight; he sings as he ascends, then suddenly plummets and rises again singing, finally coming to perch using a 'parachute-descent' with wings and tail outspread. All males are mimics and song-flights always include an imitation of the Chaffinch's song. The Rock Thrush ranges widely in search of food in the breeding season, often coming down to hayfields and farmland. The species overwinters in sub-Saharan Africa.

male

BIRD FACTS

VOICE Song is a mellow, flute-like warble; call is 'chack, chack'

LENGTH 18.5cm

WINGSPAN 33–37cm

WEIGHT 48–58g

HABITAT Sunny, dry, stony terraces with scattered trees

NEST In a hole under rocks or in wall; cup of plant material, lined with finer grass

EGGS 4–5; pale blue, usually unmarked

FOOD Mostly large insects, especially beetles, grasshoppers and caterpillars

IDENTIFICATION

Adult summer male unmistakable, with slate-blue head and throat, white back, blue rump and brownish-black wings. Uppertail coverts, tail, underparts and underwing orange; striking in flight. In winter male appears more scaly owing to pale feather fringes. Adult female resembles non-breeding male but lacks blue in plumage. Head, throat and back mottled brown and buff. Lacks male's white patch on back. Underparts buff with brown, crescent-shaped markings. Tail orange. Bill and legs of both sexes dark brown. Juvenile similar to female but even more strongly marked.

Resembles large wheatear, with erect posture and characteristically wagging tail.

female

BLUE ROCK THRUSH

male

Monticola solitarius

SOME EUROPEAN BLUE Rock Thrushes are resident; most are migrants, or at least disperse from their breeding grounds in winter. They are territorial and shy, and may be best observed when the male is singing. The usual song period is from March to May, but some song may be heard through the summer. The male sings mostly in the mornings and evenings; he characteristically performs in flight with spread wings and tail, moving from one exposed perch to another in the morning, and from a solitary perch in the evenings. On the perch he flicks his wings as he sings, in the manner of a Starling.

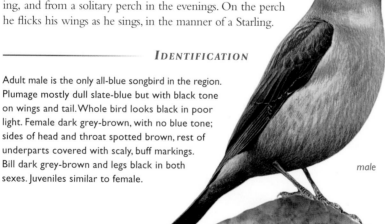

BIRD FACTS

VOICE Call and alarm deep 'tak, tak'; song loud and melodious, of simple phrases

LENGTH 20cm

WINGSPAN 33–37cm

WEIGHT 50–60g

HABITAT Rocky coastlines, rocky mountain valleys, big buildings

NEST Loosely made cup of grass and moss, lined with finer material in a hollow in rocks

EGGS 4–5; very pale blue, usually unmarked

FOOD Mainly invertebrates; also lizards, small snakes, seeds and fruits in autumn

IDENTIFICATION

Adult male is the only all-blue songbird in the region. Plumage mostly dull slate-blue but with black tone on wings and tail. Whole bird looks black in poor light. Female dark grey-brown, with no blue tone; sides of head and throat spotted brown, rest of underparts covered with scaly, buff markings. Bill dark grey-brown and legs black in both sexes. Juveniles similar to female.

Larger than any wheatear and nearly as big as a Redwing, but stockily built.

male

female

Male is only small all-black bird in Europe with bright golden-yellow bill and long, broad tail. Black is glossy but not iridescent. Orange-yellow eyelids form an eyering. Legs dark brown. Immature male's bill is dark grey-brown, turning golden through the first winter, and plumage is dull black. Female head and body dark brown. Underparts often have rufous tone and dark thrush-like mottling on breast; some birds more marked than others. Legs dark brown and in parts of northwest bill dark but yellow at base of lower mandible. Juvenile like female, but more rufous and more spotted below.

Female is much darker than Song Thrush.

BLACKBIRD
Turdus merula

THE BLACKBIRD is basically a woodland bird but inhabits many places, from wooded mountain sides to city centres. Northern populations are migrants, moving to the south and west of the breeding range; others are resident. The Blackbird does not suffer as badly in cold winters as other thrushes. It hunts in leaf litter, flicking material aside with its bill or scratching like a hen to seek invertebrates. It also forages in meadows and lawns for worms, which it can find at the rate of one or two a minute. It can even dig through 5 to 7cm of snow. The Blackbird commonly rears two to three broods a year.

BIRD FACTS

VOICE Call sounds like 'see'; alarm is a shrill chatter; song is a variety of flute-like, musical phrases
LENGTH 24–25cm
WINGSPAN 34–38.5cm
WEIGHT 95–110g
HABITAT In most places where trees are present, but also on moors and in towns
NEST Stoutly built cup of grass and leaves, lined with mud, then with finer grass
EGGS 4–5; light blue, usually profusely speckled and mottled reddish-brown
FOOD Insects, earthworms; wild fruits in autumn and winter

Adult male unlikely to be confused with any other bird.

Juvenile more spotted than female.

Bright white breast crescent and grey wing-panel obvious on adult male.

RING OUZEL
Turdus torquatus

THE RING OUZEL has a somewhat restricted breeding range in Europe, preferring wild and remote upland areas for nesting. Ring Ouzels arrive on breeding territory early in the season, and are often present by mid-April. They leave again by August and September, most European birds overwintering around the Mediterranean region, with a few crossing to North Africa. During the winter months they favour open, stony slopes, reminiscent of their breeding habitat. Ring Ouzels can be difficult to see. If undisturbed, males will sit out on rocks and sing, but if alarmed they skulk.

male

Flight pattern recalls that of other thrushes, although it is noticeably deep-winged and powerful.

male

male

female

BIRD FACTS

VOICE Song simple and fluty; chattering alarm call
LENGTH 24cm
WINGSPAN 38–42cm
WEIGHT 95–130g
HABITAT Mountains and moorland; winters on Mediterranean slopes
NEST Woven grass and leaves among boulders
EGGS 4–5; dark speckled on bluish-green background
FOOD Mainly invertebrates; berries and fruit in autumn

IDENTIFICATION

Male has blackish plumage with pale fringes to feathers on wings and underparts. Conspicuous white crescent on breast is diagnostic. Legs dark flesh in colour, and bill yellow with black tip. Female has brownish plumage, with more noticeable pale fringes to feathering giving scaly appearance. Pale crescent of female has dark feather edging. Juvenile is similar to female but crescent band is usually faint. Closed wings of both sexes show pale panel.

REDWING

Turdus iliacus

THE REDWING IS the smallest of the common European thrushes. The species is mostly migratory, many millions of birds moving to western and southern Europe for the winter. In hard weather it gets driven into city parks and gardens, and may suffer mass mortality. Redwings are usually first noticed in northwest Europe in early October. They migrate at night in loose flocks, often with other thrushes, their quiet but penetrating calls keeping the flock together. In winter, Redwings roost together in flocks of several hundred in shrubberies and evergreens. When disturbed, a flock will fly to the tops of the nearest trees.

Plumage recalls Song Thrush but adult recognisable by red flanks and long, creamy supercilium contrasting with dark-brown cheeks and brown crown. Sexes alike. Dark-brown streak runs from base of bill. Breast yellowish-buff on sides, dark-brown streaks spreading out to form a gorget. Undertail coverts white. Belly white, streaked with lighter brown on side. Underwing chestnut-red. Bill blackish-brown. Legs yellowish or flesh-brown. Juvenile recalls adult but shows darker streaking and spotting with buffish wash to face and flanks.

In flight, tawny-red underwing is diagnostic.

Adult upperparts uniformly dark warm brown, darkest on flight feathers.

FIELDFARE

Turdus pilaris

THE FIELDFARE BREEDS widely and commonly across northern Europe. Northern and eastern populations are migratory, although birds reach southern Europe only in the hardest winters. Emigration from Scandinavia is linked to the success or failure of the rowan crop. In winter, large, roving flocks feed on open ground or in fruiting hedgerows and trees, and many hundreds roost together. The Fieldfare breeds most commonly in colonies of up to 40 to 50 pairs; all feeding by the colony is done on neutral ground away from the nest site. It is a noisy, aggressive bird at nest sites and in defence of a winter food source.

Adults of both sexes have slate-grey head, nape and rump contrasting with chestnut back and black tail. Throat and breast golden-brown, streaked black. Bill yellow on breeding male; has dusky tip and culmen in winter male, females in all plumages and juveniles. Juvenile plumage recalls Mistle Thrush but shows pale streaks on back.

On ground, shows upright stance and hopping run typical of all thrushes.

Large thrush with unmistakable plumage pattern. Combination of white underwing, grey rump and black tail diagnostic.

Sexes similar. Adults have warm-brown upperparts. Rump and uppertail coverts more olive, crown and tail with a rufous tone. Indistinctly marked face has whitish eyering, pale-cream moustachial stripe and blackish-brown streak from base of bill, which contrasts with white throat. Underparts white with golden-brown wash on sides of breast and flanks, breast marked with blackish-brown spots that fade out on belly; spots arranged more in streaks than random spots of Mistle Thrush. Underwing coverts and axillaries golden-buff. Bill blackish-brown; legs pale flesh. Juvenile similar to adult but with pale streaks on back.

This juvenile shows the long-legged, upright stance typical of all ground-feeding thrushes.

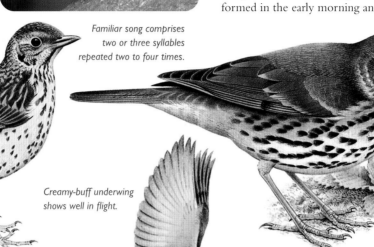

Familiar song comprises two or three syllables repeated two to four times.

Creamy-buff underwing shows well in flight.

SONG THRUSH
Turdus philomelos

MANY SONG THRUSH populations are resident, but northern birds are migratory, with more birds migrating in bad weather. The Song Thrush is found wherever grassland and nearby trees and bushes provide a plentiful supply of invertebrate food. It has a characteristic way of eating snails, beating them on hard ground or a stone to break the shells. The Song Thrush is more solitary and shy than other thrushes. Its song is a succession of musical phrases, each phrase repeated from two to four times; the song period often begins in November, but peaks in March and April. Most song is performed in the early morning and late evening.

BIRD FACTS

VOICE Call 'tsip'; alarm rattle 'tic-tic-tic'; song loud, repetitive, musical
LENGTH 23cm
WINGSPAN 33–36cm
WEIGHT 65–85g
HABITAT Parks, woods, hedges, even in towns and cities
NEST Well-shaped cup of grass, with unique, smooth inner lining of wood pulp or mud
EGGS 4–6; bright, light blue, sparingly spotted with black
FOOD Wide variety of invertebrates; snails; fruit in autumn and winter

Sexes similar. Adult recalls Song Thrush but is larger, with whitish underparts covered with large, wedge-shaped black spots; flanks and breast marked with buff. Upperparts and wings greyish-brown with conspicuous greyish-white fringes to tertials and wing coverts. Tail grey-brown with diagnostic white tips to outer feathers noticeable when bird flies away. White underwing striking in distinctive, powerful flight; it closes its wings after each burst of wingbeats but the flight path is still direct, not undulating. Upright stance on ground emphasised by long tail. Juvenile similar to adult but spotted white on head, mantle and wing coverts.

Gleaming white underwing obvious in flight.

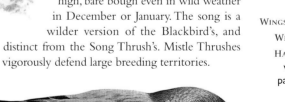

MISTLE THRUSH
Turdus viscivorus

THE MISTLE THRUSH breeds widely across the region, but is comparatively scarce in Norway and southeast Europe. Birds in the south of the range are mostly sedentary but northern and eastern populations move south and west in the winter months. They form small flocks in late summer, prior to dispersal, many becoming nomadic rather than migratory. The Mistle Thrush tends to sing from a high, bare bough even in wild weather in December or January. The song is a wilder version of the Blackbird's, and distinct from the Song Thrush's. Mistle Thrushes vigorously defend large breeding territories.

BIRD FACTS

VOICE Call harsh, distinctive rattle; song loud, short, fluty phrases
LENGTH 27cm
WINGSPAN 42–47.5cm
WEIGHT 100–130g
HABITAT Orchards, woods, farmland, parks and gardens
NEST Bulky cup of plant materials, lined with fine grass, in a tree-fork
EGGS 4–5; pale blue or pale greenish, with reddish and purplish blotches
FOOD Wide variety of invertebrates; berries in autumn and winter

Overall appearance very grey when compared to Song Thrush.

Juvenile shows white spotting on back and wings.

BIRD FACTS

VOICE Call is a sharp 'chip'; song is very distinctive, loud and abrupt

LENGTH 13.5cm

WINGSPAN 15–19cm

WEIGHT 9.9–15.9g

HABITAT Bushy places giving shelter by swamps, watersides, marshes

NEST Untidy outer shell of dead leaves and grass; deep inner cup with fine lining

EGGS 4; bright chestnut or deep brick red

FOOD Chiefly insects, adults and larvae; also spiders and worms

CETTI'S WARBLER

Cettia cetti

Song has been described as loudest song among small European birds.

CETTI'S WARBLER is unusual for several reasons: most passerines have 12 tail feathers but Cetti's has only 10; it lays red eggs; the males are often polygynous, mating with two to four females, and they take little part in rearing the young. However, it is the song that is the most distinctive feature: a sudden explosion of sound, usually 2.5 to 5 seconds long, composed of clear-cut, rhythmic phrases, which may be rendered as 'CHE–che-weechoo-weechoo-wechoo-wee'. Each male has an individual song pattern that birdwatchers can learn to recognise.

IDENTIFICATION

Sexes similar but male larger and heavier than female. Adult upperparts and wings uniform chestnut brown. Face broken only by off-white eyering and short, grey supercilium. Chin and central underparts off-white, rest grey-brown or darker brown, especially on flanks and undertail coverts; dull-white tips of undertail coverts usually obvious when bird cocks its tail in excitement. Bill short and fine, dark brown. Legs strong, brown-flesh. Juvenile similar to adult.

BIRD FACTS

VOICE Call is persistent 'zip'. Song is high-pitched, sharp 'tsip-tsip- ...' or 'zit-zit- ...'

LENGTH 10cm

WINGSPAN 12–14.5cm

WEIGHT 8–11g

HABITAT Rough, grassy plains, grain fields, marshes, rice fields

NEST Deep and pear-shaped, with opening at top; made of fine grass bound with cobweb

EGGS 4–6, variable; white or pale blue, with or without coloured specks

FOOD Small insects and larvae, some as large as grasshoppers

FAN-TAILED WARBLER

Cisticola juncidis

THE FAN-TAILED WARBLER is a skulking bird, but inquisitive, and may be seen perching on grass stems, sometimes with its feet on separate stems, or in flight. The male's song-flight is long and undulating, each bounce synchronised with the song-note 'zit'. The songster covers 300–400m or more and utters over 100 song-notes. The male is polygynous, often mating with four females. He builds on average six nests in a season lasting from April to September. He builds the outer shell while the female lines the nest, lays the eggs and rears the young with no help from her mate.

IDENTIFICATION

Adult has warm buff upperparts streaked blackish-brown on crown, mantle and wings. Nape, rump and uppertail coverts almost unstreaked. Paler face has short, creamy supercilium and pale circle around eye. Breast and flanks buff. Tail brown with underside marked with black sub-terminal band and white tip. Bill brown above and grey below, with dark tip on breeding male and flesh-pink tip on other males and females. Juvenile similar to adult female.

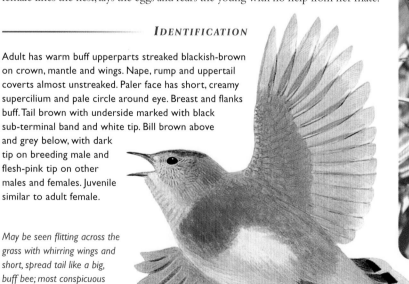

May be seen flitting across the grass with whirring wings and short, spread tail like a big, buff bee; most conspicuous on male's song-flight.

Chin, throat, belly and undertail coverts white.

Mouse-like bird in its movements, preferring to run and creep rather than fly if disturbed.

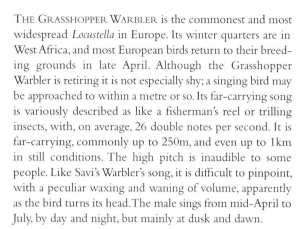

GRASSHOPPER WARBLER
Locustella naevia

THE GRASSHOPPER WARBLER is the commonest and most widespread *Locustella* in Europe. Its winter quarters are in West Africa, and most European birds return to their breeding grounds in late April. Although the Grasshopper Warbler is retiring it is not especially shy; a singing bird may be approached to within a metre or so. Its far-carrying song is variously described as like a fisherman's reel or trilling insects, with, on average, 26 double notes per second. It is far-carrying, commonly up to 250m, and even up to 1km in still conditions. The high pitch is inaudible to some people. Like Savi's Warbler's song, it is difficult to pinpoint, with a peculiar waxing and waning of volume, apparently as the bird turns its head. The male sings from mid-April to July, by day and night, but mainly at dusk and dawn.

IDENTIFICATION

Small, uniformly coloured warbler. Adult upperparts olive-brown, spotted and streaked with dark brown from crown to rump. Wings darker brown with buff to reddish fringes to feathers, visible at close range. Streaks on rump fade out on reddish-brown uppertail coverts. Tail reddish-brown, softly barred darker. Underparts mostly buff, but almost white on chin, throat and centre of breast and belly. Undertail coverts streaked with brown. Bill blackish brown with bright-yellow base. Legs pale, yellowish brown to pink. Sexes alike. Juvenile very similar to adult.

Longest uninterrupted song timed at 110 minutes.

GRASSHOPPER WARBLER

RIVER WARBLER
Locustella fluviatilis

THE RIVER WARBLER is a bird of central and eastern Europe, though it has spread westwards since the 1950s; it favours areas of very dense vegetation up to 2m tall among trees, such as bogs, carr, damp forest clearings and abandoned orchards. It is a summer visitor to Europe. Breeding starts in late May and the birds leave for Africa early, in late July or August. The River Warbler is a skulking bird, feeding in dense cover, so it is difficult to observe. Unusually for a warbler, it obtains its food as it runs about in the thick grass, nettles and fallen leaves. Its calls are confusingly like those of several other species, so the best chance of a sighting is to watch a male singing from its exposed perch. The slow, throbbing song consists of clearly separated disyllabic notes, 'chuff-chuff, chuff-chuff', delivered at a rate of about seven pairs a second, sounding like a distant steam engine, bush-cricket or cicada. A distant bird is hard to locate.

IDENTIFICATION

Unstreaked small-to medium-sized warbler. Upperparts, wings and tail olive-brown, darker on uppertail coverts and tail, slightly greyer on head and back. Underparts dull white with olive-brown wash on flanks and sides of breast. Undertail coverts long, to tip of tail, buff-brown with broad, white tips. Bill dark brown with pale base. Legs flesh to brown. Sexes similar but female greyer above. Juvenile similar to adult.

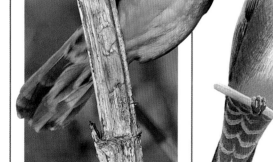

GRASSHOPPER WARBLER

RIVER WARBLER *Combination of unstreaked upperparts and faint mottling on chest is best distinguishing feature.*

SAVI'S WARBLER
Locustella luscinioides

SAVI'S WARBLER IS a bird of unbroken swamps and reedbeds, and the nest site can usually only be approached by wading. Its preference for this type of habitat gives the species a very fragmented distribution from Spain across central and eastern Europe. In the past 40 years it has expanded its range north and west on the continent, recolonising England in 1960; it is now one of Britain's rarest breeding birds. Males return to the reedbeds from Africa in mid-April and set up territories about 12 days before the females arrive. Their reeling songs can, with practice, be recognised as different from those of other *Locustella* warblers, but they are remarkably like that of Roesel's Bush-cricket! Savi's Warbler is less shy than other *Locustella* warblers with reeling songs, and regularly climbs to a prominent perch to sing. It often sings through the night.

BIRD FACTS

VOICE Call 'pit'; alarm sharper rattle; song accelerating ticking sound

LENGTH 14cm

WINGSPAN 18–21cm

WEIGHT 13–17g

HABITAT Reedy swamps and fens, overgrown fringes of lakes

NEST Loose outer cup of waterside plants; firm inner cup, lined with finer fibres

EGGS 4–5; white, densely speckled with shades of brown, mostly at larger end

FOOD Adult and larval flies, butterflies and moths, bugs, spiders and beetles

Similar to other plain warblers. Sexes similar. Adult distinguished by dark, unstreaked, reddish-brown head and upperparts, with faint, buff supercilium fading out behind the eye. Underparts brownish-white with rufous-brown along sides of breast and flanks to undertail coverts. Wings and tail uniform reddish-brown like upperparts. Tail broad and graduated towards the tip. Bill dark grey-brown. Legs pale brown. Juvenile similar to adult.

SAVI'S WARBLER
Bird turns its head as it sings, making its position very difficult to pinpoint.

AQUATIC WARBLER
Very similar to Sedge and Moustached Warblers, but with sharp crown stripe.

MOUSTACHED WARBLER (BELOW)
The southerly counterpart of the Sedge Warbler, the Moustached Warbler prefers emergent vegtation over water, where its large feet and claws enable it to move easily among the reed stems when searching for food.

When nervous, Moustached Warbler has a habit of cocking its tail slightly upwards.

Aquatic Warblers are rare but regular passage migrants to northwest Europe in the autumn.

MOUSTACHED WARBLER
Acrocephalus melanopogon

THE MOUSTACHED WARBLER has a scattered distribution across southern Europe, being dependent on suitable wetland habitats, such as in the Camargue, the River Danube and Albufera Marsh on Mallorca. It is mostly sedentary but northerly populations migrate south and winter on the northern and eastern fringes of the Mediterranean. It is noted for skulking, but it can be approached closely on occasions. The song is richly varied and is notably different from the Sedge Warbler's. It includes a diagnostic, introductory series of low, pure notes, 'tu-tu-tu-tu', a crescendo recalling a Nightingale followed by a scratchy warble.

BIRD FACTS

VOICE Call is a soft 't-rrrt'; alarm is 'churr'; song is a distinctive musical medley

LENGTH 12–13cm

WINGSPAN 15–16.5cm

WEIGHT 10–12g

HABITAT Swamps of sedges, reeds and reedmace

NEST Deep cup, loosely made of plant material, lined with reed flowers and feathers

EGGS 3–4; white, with light-olive mottling all over

FOOD Almost wholly arthropods, especially small beetles

IDENTIFICATION

Similar to Aquatic and Sedge Warblers, but separable with care; note the head pattern, upperparts, duller wings, behaviour and diagnostic song. Sexes similar. Adult and juvenile have nape and mantle rufous brown, nape unmarked but mantle streaked black. Unstreaked rump almost same colour as dark-brown tail. Wings olive-brown with paler feathers. Underparts whitish with rusty flanks, vent and sides to breast. Head has distinctive pattern of blackish crown and broad, white supercilium – square-ended behind eye – highlighted by dusky lore and eyestripe.

AQUATIC WARBLER
Acrocephalus paludicola

THE AQUATIC WARBLER is a summer visitor to lowland marshes, mostly in eastern Europe. Its distribution has probably always been broken because of its preferred habitat and it is now one of Europe's rarest passerines. There are less than 20,000 pairs globally, most of which breed in Europe. The Aquatic Warbler is a difficult bird to watch because of its love of low, dense cover. However, it can be drawn into the open by imitating its call, and the male can be watched on his breeding territory during his song-flights between mid-May and mid-July. Peak song periods are before sunrise and at dusk. Males are polygamous and do not help at the nest.

IDENTIFICATION

Sexes similar. Adult upperparts more sandy than Sedge Warbler's, with long, dark-brown streaks highlighted by paler stripes. Rump rusty, streaked with brown. Underparts creamy buff, becoming whiter with wear, with fine, brown streaks on side of breast and on flanks. Head pattern diagnostic: pale-buff crown stripe and supercilium, separated by dark-brown stripe at side of crown; supercilium highlighted by brown eyestripe from behind eye. Tail is dark with tawny fringes and pointed feathers. Bill dark brown and legs orange-yellow. Juvenile is brighter than adult.

BIRD FACTS

VOICE Call is a harsh 'churr'; song incorporates short rattles, with some fluty notes

LENGTH 13cm

WINGSPAN 16.5–19.5cm

WEIGHT 9–15g

HABITAT Marshes of sedge and iris, with low vegetation

NEST Well-shaped cup of grasses and cobwebs, lined with feathers; low down

EGGS 5–6; pale buff with darker mottling

FOOD Mostly insects, from small dragonflies to small flies

Adult upperparts and head strongly marked. Shows olive-brown nape, mantle and scapulars with dark streaks. Rump tawny and unstreaked, tail dark brown. Wings buff-brown with lighter edges to tertials and greater coverts. Underparts off-white, washed whitest on throat and belly, more rufous on flanks. Head has black-streaked crown and long, creamy white supercilium above dusky olive lores. Bill blackish, paler at base; legs greyish. Juvenile separable from adult by creamier supercilium, yellower underparts and distinct brown spots across breast.

SEDGE WARBLER

Acrocephalus schoenobaenus

THE SEDGE WARBLER is the most common and widespread *Acrocephalus* warbler in Europe; it is also the easiest to observe. The species favours low vegetation in moist habitats from the high Arctic to the edge of the Mediterranean zone. It is a summer visitor to the region and is common from May to August. In Britain, and in many other parts of its range, the Sedge Warbler has undergone a decline in breeding numbers; this is thought to be because of poor survival in drought conditions on its overwintering grounds in Africa.

BIRD FACTS

VOICE Call 'tuc'; alarm 'churr'; song is a loud and varied mix of harsh and musical notes

LENGTH 13cm

WINGSPAN 17–21cm

WEIGHT 9.5–13.6g

HABITAT Reedbeds and other lush vegetation near water

NEST Low in herbage; loose outer shell of grass, sedge etc., lined with soft materials

EGGS 5–6; pale greenish, profusely speckled olive or buff, often covering the egg

FOOD Chiefly insects, from aphids to dragonflies; also spiders

DID YOU KNOW?

Inquisitive birds often sidle up vertical stems to investigate an intruder or noise.

Sedge Warblers are territorial in winter and summer, defending feeding and breeding areas.

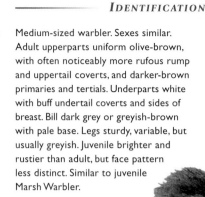

REED WARBLER

Acrocephalus scirpaceus

THE REED WARBLER is a skulking but not especially shy bird of reedbeds. It is common and widespread throughout much of Europe, wherever suitable habitats occur. A summer visitor to the region, the entire population overwinters in Africa. The Reed Warbler is closely, but not exclusively, associated with reedbeds; it will also breed in other vegetation such as willowherb, and recently in crops of rape. Its large footspan is an adaptation allowing it to move easily through a forest of vertical plant stems. This species is at risk be-cause its habitat is in constant danger of being drained for development.

BIRD FACTS

VOICE Call 'churr-churr'; alarm harsher; song low, guttural churring, with long phrases

LENGTH 13cm

WINGSPAN 18–21cm

WEIGHT 10–13g

HABITAT Edges of reedbeds with strong stems, and nearby vegetation

NEST Deep cup of grass and flower heads woven round several reed stems

EGGS 4; pale green, blotched and speckled olive, usually at larger end

FOOD Chiefly insects, especially flies; also spiders, small snails

DID YOU KNOW?

This very agile bird clings to reed stems with both feet, or to adjacent stems; moves up and down in jerks, or hops from one plant to another.

IDENTIFICATION

Medium-sized warbler. Sexes similar. Adult upperparts uniform olive-brown, with often noticeably more rufous rump and uppertail coverts, and darker-brown primaries and tertials. Underparts white with buff undertail coverts and sides of breast. Bill dark grey or greyish-brown with pale base. Legs sturdy, variable, but usually greyish. Juvenile brighter and rustier than adult, but face pattern less distinct. Similar to juvenile Marsh Warbler.

RIGHT AND BELOW: adults

MARSH WARBLER

Fuller-bodied and heavier than Reed Warbler, with slightly shorter bill and more rounded crown.

Acrocephalus palustris

THE MARSH WARBLER is a summer visitor to Europe, overwintering in southeast Africa. It arrives in northwest Europe in late May and leaves early: most birds leave by the end of August. Males may spend 12 to 15 hours a day singing on arrival at a breeding site. The song is an outstanding war-bling, lively chatter, with a remarkable amount of mimicry and variety of tones and pitches, sung by day and night. Some songs may be 90 per cent mimicry, all learned in the bird's first year. At least 99 European and 113 African species' calls have been recognised in Marsh Warbler songs. An average repertoire may contain 76 species, 45 African and 31 European.

BIRD FACTS

VOICE Call 'tchuc'; alarm 'chirrr'; prolonged, very musical song

LENGTH 13cm

WINGSPAN 18–21cm

WEIGHT 11–16g

HABITAT Dense low vegetation, osier beds, other rank vegetation

NEST Untidy nest of plant fibres, fixed by 'handles' to plant stems

EGGS 4–5; very pale blue or green, bold spots of olive-green and grey

FOOD Chiefly insects and spiders; some snails and berries

DID YOU KNOW?

Sings in an upright posture, often raising and fanning wings.

IDENTIFICATION

Medium-sized warbler, very hard to separate from Reed and Blyth's Reed Warblers (latter breeds from Baltic eastwards). Sexes similar. Adult usually has more olive-brown upperparts than Reed Warbler and lacks rufous rump. Has short, wide-based bill, round head, long wings showing eight to nine primary tips, pear-shaped or pot-bellied appearance and long undertail coverts. Less agile than Reed Warbler. Juvenile similar to adult.

Similar in appearance to Reed Warbler but clearly larger, with longer, stouter bill. Adult upperparts warm olive-brown, crown darker, rump fawnier, wing coverts edged rufous. Shows creamy supercilium, dusky eyestripe and pale-cream eyering. Underparts mainly creamy buff but more buff on flanks, and chin and throat off-white. Bill grey-brown, with bright pinkish base to lower mandible. Legs pale brown. Singing bird reveals bright orange-yellow mouth. Female tends to be brighter above and less white below than male. Sexes otherwise similar. Juvenile similar to adult.

Large warbler, nearly as big as a small thrush.

GREAT REED WARBLER

Acrocephalus arundinaceus

THE GREAT REED Warbler breeds widely across Europe from Iberia to Russia, mostly in the lowlands. It is a summer visitor, arriving from mid-April onwards; European birds overwinter in Africa south of the Sahara. Great Reed Warblers are territorial; good habitats often have high populations with contiguous territories. Many of the clusters are known to be formed by polygynous males with as many as three females; these males do not help with nest building or incubation. The male Great Reed Warbler sings more or less throughout the day, from arrival until a mate is found, and thereafter again if he attempts to attract another female. The song is well known for its remarkable volume and great variety of pitch and tone; it may carry as far as 1km.

BIRD FACTS

VOICE Call 'chak'; alarm harsh chatter; song very loud, harsh 'churrs' and rattles
LENGTH 19–20cm
WINGSPAN 25–29cm
WEIGHT 25–33g
HABITAT Mostly lowland in aquatic vegetation, especially dense reedbeds
NEST Mostly in thick reeds; deep cup of plant material, attached to six or so stems of common reed
EGGS Usually 4–5; pale green or blue, spotted dark brown, olive
FOOD Mainly insects, but also spiders, snails and small frogs

ICTERINE WARBLER

Hippolais icterina

THE ICTERINE WARBLER is a robust bird with a dramatic song, and is the northeastern counterpart of the Melodious Warbler. This warbler is a summer visitor; the entire population overwinters in Africa, arriving back in Europe from late April to June. The male defends his territory passionately at the start of the season, driving rivals and other species away with song, bill-snapping and even fights. The Icterine Warbler does not sing much after pairing, but until then its vigorous, varied, musical song is a splendid feature of central and eastern European countryside. The nest is said to be the finest built by any warbler. The species is generally shy and retiring on passage.

Medium-sized warbler, with long bill accentuated by rather flat crown and long wings reaching at least to end of uppertail coverts. Sexes similar. Adult basically green above and yellow below. Area between bill and below eye yellow, giving a pale-faced effect. Wings have distinct pale panel formed by yellow edges to dark-olive tertials and secondaries. Legs bright blue-grey. Late-summer adults in worn plumage are browner above and whiter below. Juveniles usually flushed with yellow.

BIRD FACTS

VOICE Call 'tec' and, in spring, diagnostic 'deeteroo', song loud and mimetic
LENGTH 13.5cm
WINGSPAN 20.5–24cm
WEIGHT 11–16g
HABITAT Mainly sunny wooded lowlands, cultivated lands and gardens, even in towns
NEST Deep, well-made cup in fork, 1–4m up; made of plant fibres, lined with hair, fur and feathers
EGGS 4–5; pale purplish-pink, sparingly spotted with black
FOOD Chiefly adult and larval insects; butterflies, grasshoppers, beetles; various fruits

BIRD FACTS

VOICE Call 'tack';
alarm repeated ticking;
song high-pitched, rapid,
scratchy warble

LENGTH 12–13.5cm

WINGSPAN 18–21cm

WEIGHT 8–16g

HABITAT Shrubs,
orchards, gardens,
palm groves, lowlands
and bushy hills

NEST Well-built
cup of twigs and
grass, lined with finer
materials, in tree or
bush

EGGS 3–4; pale
grey-white, sparingly
spotted with black

FOOD Chiefly insects,
to size of grasshoppers
and dragonflies; some
fruit

EASTERN OLIVACEOUS WARBLER

Nondescript bird sings its simple, repetitive song from thick cover.

Hippolais pallida

HIPPOLAIS WARBLERS CAN be extremely difficult to identify and this species, being the least marked of the genus, causes the most problems; in many respects it resembles Reed and Marsh Warblers. It is a summer visitor to the eastern Mediterranean, breeding from May onwards; it winters in Africa. Eastern Olivaceous Warblers favour a range of habitats and are not especially shy, but their dull appearance and preference for shrubby places can make observation tricky. Males are very vocal and territorial in the breeding season.

IDENTIFICATION

Medium-sized warbler. Sexes are similar; adults and juveniles are similar. Plumage recalls Garden Warbler: dull grey-brown above, creamy white below with pale buff wash on sides of breast and flanks; yellowish wash sometimes seen in spring. Note dull white supercilium, pale lores and square-ended tail. Face dominated by flat crown, rather long, prominent bill and dark eye with whitish eyering. Rump washed buff, faintly distinct from tail. Wings short relative to body size. Legs very variable, brown to bluish-grey.

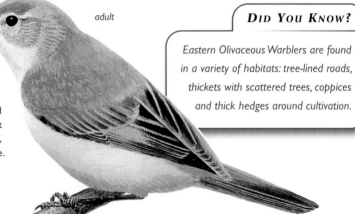

adult

DID YOU KNOW?

Eastern Olivaceous Warblers are found in a variety of habitats: tree-lined roads, thickets with scattered trees, coppices and thick hedges around cultivation.

BIRD FACTS

VOICE Call 'hooeet';
alarm harsh 'tchurrrr';
song sustained, varied
and musical

LENGTH 13cm

WINGSPAN 17.5–20cm

WEIGHT 10–13g

HABITAT Principally
on wooded lowlands,
often near water

NEST Deep cup in
a fork 1–2m above
ground; of plant fibres,
lined with roots, hair
and feathers

EGGS 3–5, usually 4;
light purplish-pink,
sparsely spotted
and streaked black

FOOD Adult and larval
insects; fruit in autumn

MELODIOUS WARBLER

Hippolais polyglotta

THE MELODIOUS WARBLER is the western counterpart of the Icterine Warbler, and like its relative is a summer visitor to Europe, overwintering in West Africa. It is a very vocal bird at the start of the breeding season in late April, and several pairs may nest close together. The male's song, a prolonged warble, may last from 7 to 13 seconds, and carries for up to 70m. The Melodious Warbler feeds restlessly in shrubs and trees using a round-winged, fluttering action, often moving abruptly, or stretching its neck to reach an insect. When moving through foliage in search of insects it can appear clumsy.

IDENTIFICATION

Medium-sized, long-billed warbler. Sexes similar. Adult upperparts brownish-green (less bright than Icterine), underparts rich yellow. Wings and tail olive-brown; wings without pale wing panel (*cf* Icterine). Head round-crowned, brownish-green with yellow supercilium from bill to just behind eye, which has yellow eyering. Late-summer adults in worn plumage are bleached and appear dun-coloured above and whitish below. Juvenile in fresh plumage sometimes bright yellow or yellowish-green.

adult

adult

adult

WESTERN OLIVACEOUS WARBLER

Hippolais opaca

SIMILAR TO EASTERN Olivaceous and the two were treated as conspecific until recently. Separable on structural and plumage details (Western has stouter bill and warmer brown upperparts than Eastern). Also separated geographically (you are most unlikely to see the two species together). A summer visitor to Iberia and North Africa, it breeds from May onwards and favours dense scrub. Males are vocal and territorial but birds often sing from cover and are tricky to see well.

BIRD FACTS

VOICE Call 'tack'; alarm repeated ticking; song high-pitched, rapid, scratchy warble

LENGTH 12–13.5cm

WINGSPAN 18–21cm

WEIGHT 8–16g

HABITAT Shrubs, orchards, gardens, palm groves, lowlands and bushy hills

NEST Well-built cup of twigs and grass, lined with finer materials, in tree or bush

EGGS 3–4; pale grey-white, sparingly spotted with black

FOOD Chiefly insects, to size of grasshoppers and dragonflies; some fruit

IDENTIFICATION

Medium-sized warbler. Sexes are similar; adults and juveniles are similar. Plumage recalls Garden Warbler: dull brown above, creamy white below with pale buff wash on sides of breast and flanks; yellowish wash sometimes seen in spring. Note dull white supercilium, pale lores and square-ended tail. Face dominated by flat crown, rather long, prominent bill and dark eye with whitish eyering. Rump washed buff, faintly distinct from tail.

OLIVE-TREE WARBLER

Hippolais olivetorum

THE OLIVE-TREE WARBLER is an arboreal species, favouring oak woods, orchards and olive groves; in Greece and Bulgaria it is found in bushier places on hillsides and in vineyards. It overwinters in Africa and arrives back in its breeding areas in early May. Though it is not a numerous species, it forms neighbourhood groups and so is locally common. The Olive-tree Warbler is a more skulking, secretive species than other *Hippolais* warblers, feeding mostly in the canopy of the trees.

IDENTIFICATION

Large, greyish, long-winged warbler with dagger-like bill. Sexes similar. Adult upperparts and wings brownish-grey, with whitish edges to greater coverts, secondaries and tertials, forming wing panel. Has buff-white supercilium and whitish eyering. Bill's large size accentuated by long, flat crown. Tail grey with white edges. Underparts dirty white with grey wash on breast, flanks and neck. Late summer plumage looks duller and wing panel is obscured. Juvenile as adult but upperparts more olive.

BIRD FACTS

VOICE Call 'tuc'; song distinctly lower-pitched and slower than its relatives'

LENGTH 15cm

WINGSPAN 24–26cm

WEIGHT 15–20g

HABITAT Coastal, insular, open-canopy woods, groves and orchards

NEST Deep, well-made cup of plant materials and cobwebs, up to 3m from ground

EGGS Usually 4; very pale pink, with sparse black markings

FOOD Presumably insects and their larvae; some fruit

TOP: male; INSET: juvenile; ABOVE; female

Recalls small Whitethroat or Subalpine Warbler without moustache but with striking white eyering.

SPECTACLED WARBLER

Sylvia conspicillata

SPECTACLED WARBLERS ARE summer visitors to most of their southern European breeding range, overwintering in northwest Africa; eastern birds are mostly resident, however, with some moving south to the Nile and Eilat. The Spectacled Warbler is typically shy and skulking but, like a Whitethroat, it scolds intruders from a prominent perch, cocking its tail and showing off its white out-ertail feathers. Once alarmed it dives for cover and stays there. Good views are best had by watching a singing male, either on a perch or in his song-flight.

IDENTIFICATION

Adult male grey to sandy brown above with striking orange edges to wing feathers forming glowing patch. Black tail clearly edged white. Underparts pink except for white chin, grey throat and buffish-grey head, which in some lights appears black between bill and below eye. Female browner on head and upperparts than male with no black on face; underparts less pink, more buff. Chin white. Female looks more like Whitethroat than male. Juvenile similar to female but with buffish suffusion to plumage.

BIRD FACTS

VOICE Call high 'tseet'; song short, sweet, rapid, variable warble

LENGTH 12.5cm

WINGSPAN 13.5–17cm

WEIGHT 8–11g

HABITAT In low scrub and rough ground beside cultivation; also in glasswort in wet lowlands with salt-laden soils

NEST Neat cup of grass, leaves and roots, lined with wool, hair and fine roots

EGGS 4–5; very pale greenish- or buffish-white, finely spotted olive or greenish

FOOD Mainly invertebrates, including grasshoppers, flies and spiders; some autumn fruit

DARTFORD WARBLER

Sylvia undata

THE DARTFORD WARBLER is easy to separate from all other warblers except Marmora's and Balearic. It is a skulking bird and patience is needed to see it well. Its flight is weak; damp, windy days drive it out of sight until the weather changes. Fine, sunny mornings are the best times to see a male clearly, perched on a bush, with tail cocked and singing his scratchy song. In the south, this is a common bird of the maquis, but in the northwest of its range it is typical of lowland heath. It is mostly sedentary, although some juveniles disperse southwards in winter.

male

BIRD FACTS

VOICE Call 'tuc' and grating alarm 'tchirrr'; song musical chatter, some liquid notes

LENGTH 12.5cm

WINGSPAN 13–18.5cm

WEIGHT 8.5–10g

HABITAT Low, dense cover on coastal scrub, heathland or maquis

NEST Low down; cup of grass, wool, plant down with soft, fine lining

EGGS 4; usually white, tinged green or grey, finely speckled brown

FOOD Exclusively invertebrates in Britain; occasionally autumn fruits elsewhere

DID YOU KNOW?

The Dartford Warbler is emblematic of southern English heathlands – its favoured habitat. Its fate is inextricably linked to that of these fragile heathlands themselves.

Male Dartford Warblers often sing from exposed perches in early spring, providing the best opportunities for observing the species well.

male

female

IDENTIFICATION

Adult male is dark slaty brown above with greyer head, and wine-red below. Wings almost uniformly brownish-black. Tail grey-black with narrow, white edges. Throat white-spotted in fresh plumage but spots wear off by June or July. Bill dark brown. Legs brownish-yellow. Eye and eyering orange to red. Female duller than male. Juveniles are browner on upperparts and may be all grey below.

MARMORA'S WARBLER

Sylvia sarda

MARMORA'S WARBLER IS confined in the breeding season to the western Mediterranean islands between Corsica and Pantelleria (southwest of Sicily). Some birds migrate to northwest Africa in winter. Marmora's Warbler is found in the lowest vegetation layer, and, unusually for a warbler, it spends up to one-third of its time on the ground. It often sings from the top of bushes or in a song-flight, which is a steady ascent to between 4 and 7m, followed by a dive to cover.

IDENTIFICATION

Adult male dull blue-grey above and below. Wings and tail dull black, latter with dusky-white edges, often not noticeable. Legs yellow-brown. Female's plumage drabber and browner than male's. Juvenile even browner than female with dull-yellow eyes.

BIRD FACTS

VOICE Call explosive 'crrip' or 'tsig'; song weak, high-pitched warble

LENGTH 12cm

WINGSPAN 13–17.5cm

WEIGHT 9–12g

HABITAT Heath and low scrub on dry hillsides and coastal slopes

NEST Cup of dry plant pieces, cobwebs and wool, with finer lining

EGGS 3–5; white or greyish-white, spotted grey and reddish-brown

FOOD Chiefly small insects

BALEARIC WARBLER

Sylvia balearica

TINY, SKULKING WARBLER, restricted to Balearic islands (except Menorca) where it is resident. Formerly considered to be conspecific with Marmora's but now treated as a separate species. Easiest to see in spring when territorial males sometimes sing from exposed perches.

BALEARIC WARBLER
male

MARMORA'S WARBLER
Darkest warbler in region, very like Dartford in build and actions but with slightly shorter tail.

adult male

IDENTIFICATION

Adult male is mostly dull blue-grey but with whiter throat than on Marmora's. Legs are orange and eye is orange-red. Female is duller than male with overall more brown tone to plumage. Juvenile is similar to female but browner and with dull yellow eyes.

BIRD FACTS

VOICE Call is a soft, nasal 'tsrrk'; song is a rapid, slightly harsh warble

LENGTH 12cm

WINGSPAN 13–17.5cm

WEIGHT 9–12g

HABITAT Low Mediterranean scrub

NEST Cup of dry plant material

EGGS 3–5; white and lightly spotted

FOOD Mainly small insects

SARDINIAN WARBLER male

SARDINIAN WARBLER

Sylvia melanocephala

THE SARDINIAN WARBLER breeds throughout much of the Mediterranean basin, occurring mainly in coastal regions; it is more widespread inland in Iberia and Italy. Mainland and northern populations migrate to North Africa and the eastern Mediterranean; island and coastal populations are mostly sedentary. The Sardinian Warbler spends much of its time in thick cover but appears frequently in the open. Its song is more tuneful than the Whitethroat's, but uttered similarly from a perch or in flight. The male is quarrelsome, noisily chasing rivals.

IDENTIFICATION

Adult male has black hood extending well below eyes to lores and ear coverts; sharp division between cap and pure white chin and upper throat. Steep forehead helps to accentuate red eye and eyering. Rest of upperparts grey; rest of underparts off-white, fading to grey on flanks. Bill buffish-brown with black tip. Legs reddish. Wings blackish with feathers edged grey. Tail black, edged white. Female has same pattern on head as adult male but black replaced by dusky grey. Upperparts dirty brown; underparts and breast pinkish-brown, flanks dull brown; otherwise white. Juvenile similar to female.

Like male, female has red eye and eyering; dark-brown tail has same white edges as male's.

Adult male distinctive but needs some care at first to separate from other black-headed warblers.

BIRD FACTS

VOICE Harsh alarm rattle; 'treek, treek' call; song rapid medley, harsh and musical

LENGTH 13.5cm

WINGSPAN 15–18cm

WEIGHT 11–14g

HABITAT From scanty undergrowth, scattered shrubs and thickets to open woodland

NEST Low down; cup-shaped, of grass, cobwebs and plant down, lined with grass and hair

EGGS 3–4, variable; whitish or tinted background, finely speckled with buffs and greys

FOOD Chiefly insects; fruit in autumn and winter; fruit all year in south

SUBALPINE WARBLER
Sylvia cantillans

THE SUBALPINE WARBLER is a summer visitor to the region, overwintering in Africa; it is a rare but almost annual visitor to northwest Europe, most often in spring. This warbler is most often seen in garigue where broom, cistus and fragrant shrubs bloom, and in thorny maquis; it also occurs among holm oaks, on sunny hillsides and in bushy ravines. The male usually sings from cover but is conspicuous when he sings from a perch or in flight.

IDENTIFICATION

Adult male has pale blue-grey upperparts, dark pink-chestnut breast and unmarked throat, and conspicuous white 'moustache'. Rest of underparts and belly white, undertail coverts buff. Wings and tail dark grey-brown with pale-grey fringes to wing feathers and white outertail feathers. Bill blackish-brown, legs yellowish-brown. Rich red eye in red eyering. Adult female is pale grey-brown above, with clear but duller moustache. Underparts pinkish-buff; white area more extensive than on male and wings browner. Juvenile has washed-out colours but usually a hint of a white 'moustache'. Often hard to separate this species from Spectacled Warbler in autumn.

BIRD FACTS

VOICE Call 'tec'; alarm oft-repeated 'tec'; song like Whitethroat's, but more musical

LENGTH 12cm

WINGSPAN 15–19cm

WEIGHT 9.2–13g

HABITAT Woodland glades, thickets, stream banks

NEST In low shrub; cup of dry grass and plant down, with finer lining

EGGS 3–5; white or palely tinted, variably speckled and mottled

FOOD Adult and larval insects; fruit in late summer and autumn

CYPRUS WARBLER
Sylvia melanothorax

AS A BREEDING bird, the Cyprus Warbler is entirely restricted to Cyprus; it is, however, widespread and common in suitable habitats, especially in coastal maquis, although it tends to be shy and skulking. Most birds seem to be resident, but some migrate (to Egypt and Sinai), so the bird is less common in winter. Breeding grounds above 1,000m are vacated outside the breeding season. Resident birds are believed to hold territories all year, and overwintering birds at Eilat have been observed defending territories too.

IDENTIFICATION

Adult male easily separated from other *Sylvia* warblers by black and white mottled underparts, from chin to undertail coverts, and pale fringes to innerwing feathers. Pronounced white moustache. Black tail with white edges contrasts with grey mantle, back and rump. Yellow to chestnut eye in yellowish to red eyering. Female similar to male but much duller and browner; moustachial stripe dull white. Eye and eyering duller than male's. Juvenile similar to female but markings on throat less pronounced; difficult to distinguish from juvenile Sardinian Warbler.

BIRD FACTS

VOICE Call is a grating 'tchek'; song vigorous rattle of high and low notes

LENGTH 13.5cm

WINGSPAN 15–18cm

WEIGHT 10–15g

HABITAT Maquis scrub, especially among *Cistus*; also scrub forest edge

NEST In low scrub; cup of leaves, grass, juniper bark, lined with grass and hair

EGGS 4–5; very pale green, spotted with olive-brown and violet-grey

FOOD Mainly invertebrates; little is known in detail

male

CYPRUS WARBLER
Bill buffish-yellow and legs vary from flesh-yellow to reddish-brown.

SUBALPINE WARBLER
female

female

SUBALPINE WARBLER
male

Robust warbler resembling a large Blackcap but easily distinguished by white outertail feathers and adult's pale yellow-white eyes. Adult male has dark cap extending to lores and ear coverts. Nape and upperparts grey-brown; wings and tail dusky brown. Pale-grey fringes to tertials and larger coverts. Underparts basically white but with pinkish flush on breast in breeding season. Bill long, blackish. Female closely resembles male but duller with more grey on upperparts. Juvenile even browner than female and lacks adults' dark head.

1st autumn

ORPHEAN WARBLER

Sylvia hortensis

BASICALLY A MEDITERRANEAN bird, the Orphean Warbler is a summer visitor to the region, occurring from May to August and overwintering in sub-Saharan Africa. It is a vagrant to northwest Europe, including Britain. Although not a shy bird, it is not necessarily easily observed because it spends much of its time searching the upper foliage of thickets for food. The Orphean Warbler prefers trees and larger bushes to lower vegetation, and the male sings from the cover of bushes and small trees rather than on song-flights. In defence of its young the Orphean Warbler has been seen to lure an intruder away by pretending to be disabled.

BIRD FACTS

VOICE Call 'tac, tac' or 'trrrr' alarm; song pleasant, thrush-like warble

LENGTH 15cm

WINGSPAN 20–25cm

WEIGHT 20–27g

HABITAT Stunted open forest and scrub on hillsides; also orange and olive groves, and gardens

NEST Loosely made; thin twigs, grass and cobwebs, lined with finer roots, grass and hair

EGGS 4–5; white or faint bluish-white, sparingly marked with spots of several colours

FOOD Chiefly invertebrates, as big as grasshoppers and stick insects; autumn fruits

adult

Legs grey or grey-brown.

adult

Adult male has forehead, crown, lores, chin, throat and upper breast black, relieved by bright-red eye and eyering and conspicuous white moustache. Rest of upperparts grey and underparts greyish-white, greyer on flanks and whiter on belly. Tail black with white outer feathers. Bill quite long, blackish with paler, yellowish base to lower mandible. Female and juvenile duller and browner than adult male, with most showing faint impression of male's head markings.

male

RÜPPELL'S WARBLER

Sylvia rueppellii

RÜPPELL'S WARBLER IS a summer visitor to its eastern Mediterranean breeding range, overwintering in northeast Africa. There is a marked passage in spring and autumn through Egypt, and it is quite common in Cyprus in spring. Rüppell's Warbler has a splendid song-flight, with the bird rising to a height of 10 to 20m on a zigzag path with fully extended, slowly flapping wings, followed by a parachute descent on outspread wings like a pipit. Males arrive before the females and half-build several speculative nests to attract the female.

BIRD FACTS

VOICE Hard 'tak, tak', song rapid, chattering, with some call notes and pure tones

LENGTH 14cm

WINGSPAN 18–21cm

WEIGHT 12–16g

HABITAT Thorny scrub, maquis, on rocky slopes and in gullies; also undergrowth in old woods

NEST A neat cup of grasses, lined with plant fibres, in a bush

EGGS 4–5; white tinged with green, profusely speckled, sometimes appearing olive all over

FOOD Adult and larval insects; autumn fruits

Wings mainly black with striking whitish fringes and tips to tertials.

female

male

BARRED WARBLER

Sylvia nisoria

BIRD FACTS

VOICE Call harsh 'charr'; song short, rich warble with harsh call notes mixed in

LENGTH 15.5cm

WINGSPAN 23–27cm

WEIGHT 23–26g

HABITAT Often thorn thickets, riverine woodland or orchards

NEST In fork of twigs; loosely built of dead grass, lined with fine roots and hair

EGGS Usually 5; pale whitish- or greenish-grey, finely speckled with darker greys

FOOD Insectivorous; fruits and berries in autumn

THE BARRED WARBLER is a summer visitor to Europe, overwintering chiefly in Kenya; it appears annually in northwest Europe in late summer. This is the largest and among the most secretive of the *Sylvia* warblers. The males are best observed when displaying. They perch conspicuously, jerking and fanning their tails, and then sing in flight for 5 to 10 seconds, in an erratic loop above a bush. The song is often preceded by audible wing-clapping. During the breeding season, the Barred Warbler often nests close to the Red-backed Shrike.

RIGHT: adult; BELOW: juvenile; INSET: juvenile

Robust warbler, all plumages of which show pale wingbars, pale-edged tertials and white-tipped tail. Adult male's head, face and upperparts grey. Pale-yellow eye. Wings dark brown-grey with pale bar on greater coverts, less clear bar on median coverts and pale, bright-grey edges and tips to tertials. Underparts dull white from chin to undertail coverts, liberally barred with dark grey-brown crescents, emphasised by white tips. Tail long and broad, dark brown with white edges. Adult female like male but duller and browner above with barring less clear below and paler eye. Juvenile recalls Garden Warbler, being unbarred and dark-eyed.

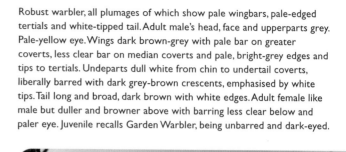

LESSER WHITETHROAT

Sylvia curruca

BIRD FACTS

VOICE Hard 'tack' or 'churr'; song loud rattle often preceded by quiet warble

LENGTH 12.5–13.5cm

WINGSPAN 16.5–20.5cm

WEIGHT 10–13g

HABITAT Woodland edge, thick hedges, shrubberies with thick, dark cover

NEST Low in thick cover; of grass, fine twigs and spiders' cocoons, with finer lining

EGGS 4–6; white, sparingly spotted with olive or buff

FOOD Mainly insects; a few spiders and worms; fruits and berries in summer

A SUMMER VISITOR, the Lesser Whitethroat arrives in the region in late April and early May; peak departures for northern Africa are in late August and early September. It frequents thickets, woodland edge and areas with scattered trees, almost always with thicker cover than the Whitethroat favours. It is an active but skulking bird. The rattling, repetitive element of the song may carry 200m and, at a distance, sounds like the entire song. At close range, however, the observer can hear that the trill is often preceded by a musical, low, varied warble. This complete song is unlike any other warbler's, and could easily be missed.

Adult greyer above and whiter below than Whitethroat and lacks the contrasting rufous wing panel, so upperparts look dull grey-brown and underparts are dull white. Dark face mask formed by black lores and ear coverts against slate-grey on rest of head. Primaries and tail browner and darker than rest of upperparts. Outertail feathers white. Unusually for this genus, sexes similar but when seen side by side, male sometimes has blacker mask and paler pink flush on breast than female.

DID YOU KNOW?

Song is quite unlike Whitethroat's but can be misidentified as that of Cirl Bunting or Bonelli's Warbler.

Adult male has grey cap extending to below eye, whitish eyering and brown eyes. Chin and throat pure white. Breast pale pinkish-buff and rest of underparts white. Upperparts dull brown, suffused with grey in spring plumage. Very distinctive panel on wing formed by rufous edges to wing coverts, secondaries and tertials. Tail dark brown with white outer feathers. Bill buffish-brown with dark tip; legs pale to flesh brown. For description of female and juvenile, see caption.

WHITETHROAT
Sylvia communis

THE WHITETHROAT IS the most widespread *Sylvia* warbler in Europe, and the commonest on farmland. It is a bold bird, often scolding the observer from its vantage point on a bramble or bush with its grating 'charrr'. It is a summer visitor, overwintering in Africa. The males arrive back in Europe as much as two weeks before the females, mostly in mid-April. Autumn migration lasts from mid-July to mid-October. In summer the male's dancing song-flight is an attractive feature of scrubby habitats. He builds several incomplete trial nests, one of which the female may finish.

BIRD FACTS

VOICE Scolding 'charr', sharp 'tac'; song short, rapid, chattery warble

LENGTH 14cm

WINGSPAN 18.5–23cm

WEIGHT 14–17g

HABITAT Most open habitats with thickets and shrubs

NEST In low bushes and nettles; substantial grass cup lined with black hair

EGGS 4–5; with very pale blue or green, very fine markings and speckling

FOOD Mostly insectivorous; currants, raspberries, blackberries and other wild fruits

Prefers sunny breeding sites with bushes and thickets, often on the edge of cultivated land.

adult

juvenile

RIGHT: *adult male*

Female and juvenile (LEFT) similar to male but white throat is duller and rest of plumage browner; bill and leg colour as male's.

adult male

DID YOU KNOW?

Male has rather jerky song-flight, as if being bounced on invisible piece of elastic.

BLACKCAP

Sylvia atricapilla

BIRD FACTS

VOICE Call loud repeated 'tac'; song loud, rich warble, rising in pitch

LENGTH 13cm

WINGSPAN 20–23cm

WEIGHT 15–22g

HABITAT Open woodland and copses with thick undergrowth; in towns

NEST Low down, in bush, briar, nettles; thin, well-made cup of grass, rootlets and cobweb

EGGS Usually 5, variable; mainly white or buff with dark spots

FOOD Many types of insect; fruit and berries, especially in autumn

TO MOST OF Europe the Blackcap is a summer visitor from Africa. Birds from the Mediterranean region are generally resident, however, and small numbers are increasingly overwintering in northwest Europe. The Blackcap is essentially a woodland bird, but it will also nest and overwinter in parks and gardens in towns if there are sufficient trees and undergrowth. Although the cap is diagnostic, the Blackcap could be confused with the Marsh or Willow Tit, or in the south with Orphean or Sardinian Warblers. The song is easily confused with that of the Garden Warbler.

Adult male has diagnostic black forehead and crown (cap) above ash-grey nape and face. Upperparts ashy brown, darker on tail and primaries (although wing coverts and tertials edged paler). Chin, breast and flanks grey, the first two silvery when plumage is fresh; belly and undertail coverts white. Bill dull black, legs slate. Adult female similar to male but cap bright red-brown and upperparts browner. Juvenile very like female but cap duller brown.

Largish warbler, easily identified if seen clearly.

male

female

female

Unlike Marsh Tit's cap, male's black crown only extends as far as eye, not below; red-capped female unmistakable.

male

female

male

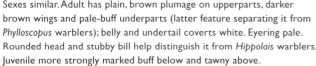

Sexes similar. Adult has plain, brown plumage on upperparts, darker brown wings and pale-buff underparts (latter feature separating it from *Phylloscopus* warblers); belly and undertail coverts white. Eyering pale. Rounded head and stubby bill help distinguish it from *Hippolais* warblers. Juvenile more strongly marked buff below and tawny above.

GARDEN WARBLER

Sylvia borin

THE GARDEN WARBLER is a bird of broad-leaved woodland with thick undergrowth. It is a summer visitor to Europe, over-wintering in Africa. Its skulking habits and the similarity of its song to the Blackcap's mean that it may be a long time before an observer sees one and confirms its identity. Its song is distinguishable from the Blackcap's by its lower, contralto pitch and longer phases. The Garden Warbler avoids competition with the Blackcap, even in overlapping territories, by arriving later, in or about the third week of April; by vertical separation in the habitat (the Blackcap generally feeds higher); and by feeding on different prey.

Song lacks Blackcap's flourish and wider range of pitch, but this is compensated for by greater persistence and richness of sound.

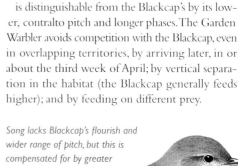

Plainest of the Sylvia warblers and medium- to large-sized.

BIRD FACTS

VOICE Call soft, nasal 'check'; song rich, sustained, flowing warble

LENGTH 14cm

WINGSPAN 20–24.5cm

WEIGHT 19–22g

HABITAT Open deciduous or mixed woodland with thick undergrowth

NEST Substantial, loose cup in low shrub, of dry grass, lined with grass and hair

EGGS 4–5; usually whitish ground colour; markings very variable, like Blackcap's

FOOD Mostly insects and spiders; some fruit and berries

WOOD WARBLER

Phylloscopus sibilatrix

THE WOOD WARBLER arrives on its breeding grounds in early May, appreciably later than most of its relatives; it also leaves earlier at the end of the summer. It overwinters in equatorial Africa. On arrival the male Wood Warbler vigorously defends a territory, and on his courtship flight dodges in and out of the trees like a big dragonfly, until he lands by the female with quivering wings and fanned tail. The male has two strikingly different songs: the first is a repeated note, starting slowly but developing into a passionate trill; the second comprises a series of notes like the call note. He sings as many as 10 or 12 of the first sort to one of the second.

Long wings are not flicked; they droop either side of shortish tail.

adult

Start of the first song form often delivered in flight, but trill invariably comes from a perch.

BIRD FACTS

VOICE Usual call plaintive 'pew, pew'; song in two phases, mainly a trill

LENGTH 12cm

WINGSPAN 19.5–24cm

WEIGHT 8–11g

HABITAT Prefers hilly terrain, and woodland with good canopy (beech and oak especially)

NEST On the ground, with little or no ground cover; domed, of grass and dead leaves

EGGS 6–7; white, heavily marked with reddish- or purplish-brown and greyish spots

FOOD Insects and other invertebrates; some berries occasionally in autumn

The most distinctive *Phylloscopus* warbler; larger than others, with relatively longer wings and shorter tail. Sexes alike. Adult appears to be a three-colour bird: yellowish-green upperparts; bright-yellow supercilium, throat and breast; pure white belly and undertail coverts. Tail, flight feathers and tertials brown, outer edges of first two edged yellowish-green, but tertials edged white or yellowish-white. Bill has dark-brown upper mandible, pale-flesh lower mandible. Legs pale yellowish-brown. Juvenile similar to brightly coloured adult.

BIRD FACTS

VOICE Call plaintive,
disyllabic 'hoo-eet';
song lovely cascade
of pure notes

LENGTH 10.5–11.5cm

WINGSPAN 16.5–22cm

WEIGHT 7–9g

HABITAT Woods,
forests; mostly coppices,
scrub, anywhere with a
few trees

NEST Well hidden on
ground in thick herbage;
domed, of grass, lined
with finer materials

EGGS 6–8; white with
fine speckles of red
or red-brown

FOOD Insectivorous;
mostly flies, but also
bees, beetles, aphids;
young fed on larvae

WILLOW WARBLER

Phylloscopus trochilus

adult

THE WILLOW WARBLER arrives in Europe in April
and leaves generally between July and September.
This is the commonest *Phylloscopus* warbler in the
region and one of the most numerous of Europe's
summer visitors. It overwinters in sub-Saharan
Africa. The male establishes a territory,
aggressively chasing off other males, and
even other species, including songbirds larger than itself. In courtship the
male is very demonstrative, chasing the female,
quivering his wings, and displaying in a 'butterfly flight' with few or no wingbeats. The well-
concealed nest is very hard to find once the
surrounding grass grows.

juvenile

IDENTIFICATION

Delicate little warbler, size of a Blue Tit but slimmer.
Adult olive-green above, yellowish-white below;
has cleaner colours than very similar Chiffchaff.
Has pale-yellow supercilium, brown bill and
orange-brown legs (the latter reliably distinguish
it from Chiffchaff). Adults become browner above
and whiter below during summer from
feather abrasion. Juvenile in autumn has
much yellower supercilium, throat
and breast than adult.

adult

juvenile

*Like Chiffchaff, Willow
Warbler constantly inspects
twigs and foliage for tiny
insects; frequently flicks its
wings and sings while foraging.*

BIRD FACTS

VOICE Call monosyllabic
'hweet, hweet'; song
diagnostic 'chiff-chaff-
chiff'

LENGTH 10–11cm

WINGSPAN 15–21cm

WEIGHT 7–8g

HABITAT Woodland,
but not deep forest or
coniferous plantations;
also copses, hedgerows

NEST A few centimetres
above ground in thick
herbage; domed, of
grass, lined with
feathers

EGGS 4–9, but usually
5–6; white, sparingly
spotted with purple
or purplish-brown

FOOD Almost
exclusively insects

CHIFFCHAFF

Phylloscopus collybita

THE CHIFFCHAFF IS a summer
visitor and usually the first warbler
to arrive; migrants first appear at the
beginning of March, later further east and
north. Autumn migration begins in August and
peaks in September. Most Chiffchaffs overwinter
around the Mediterranean and across sub-Saharan
Africa, although a few overwinter in Britain. The
Chiffchaff is an active bird, flitting among the
foliage and twigs, flicking its wings and tail with
a distinctive sideways movement. The male defends
his territory vigorously. In courtship he follows the
female with quivering wings, calling, or flies towards
her in the so-called 'moth flight'.

IDENTIFICATION

Adult is dull brownish-olive above and dull, pale yellow
below, shading to buff flanks. Browner above and more
buff below than Willow Warbler, with much less yellow
tint (although this is more noticeable on autumn
juveniles). Eastern forms greyer above and whiter
below than western forms, with whitish wingbar not
normally found on western and southern forms.
Otherwise all forms lack distinctive features except for
pale-yellow supercilium, pale eyering, contrasting dark
eyes and dark legs (distinguishing it from Willow
Warbler). Juveniles and first-winter birds have warm-
brown upperparts and underparts yellowish.

IBERIAN CHIFFCHAFF

Phylloscopus ibericus

PREVIOUSLY TREATED AS a subspecies of Chiffchaff, Iberian Chiffchaff
has been elevated to species status. It is brighter yellow overall
than its cousin, particularly on the underparts, and has
a green rump. But the main way of distinguishing the
two is by listening to the voice: rather than a
simple *chiff-chaff*, the male sings a *tsit-tsit-tsit-
tswee-tswee* song. Iberian Chiffchaff is a
summer visitor to uplands in central
Spain and winters in Africa.
Vagrants have turned up as
far north as Britain.

GREENISH WARBLER
Phylloscopus trochiloides

THE GREENISH WARBLER is a summer visitor to the region, arriving from the Indian subcontinent in the second half of May; it is a vagrant to northwestern Europe, with the majority of records coming in early autumn. The Greenish Warbler is always on the move, usually in the forest canopy in summer but lower down in winter. Because it is so like Willow and Arctic Warblers and the Chiffchaff it is very difficult to identify quickly. Careful observation will confirm its distinctive call and song, shape and behaviour, clear wingbar, bright lower mandible, head pattern and dusky legs.

BIRD FACTS

VOICE Call distinctive 'chee-wee', the second note lower; song Wren-like medley

LENGTH 10cm

WINGSPAN 15–21cm

WEIGHT 6–8g

HABITAT Open woodland (coniferous or broad-leaved) copses, overgrown orchards

NEST On the ground in tall herbage; domed, of moss, grass and dead leaves

EGGS 4–6; white

FOOD Almost wholly insects; some, unusually for this genus, picked off the ground

IDENTIFICATION

Small and superficially similar to Willow Warbler. Plumage pale greyish-olive above, dull white below. Shows long, yellowish-white supercilium reaching nearly to the nape (often upturned at the end), dark eyestripe and pale wingbar (in fresh plumage). Bill has pale lower mandible; legs variable shade of brown, distinguishing bird from Arctic Warbler. Juvenile in first-winter plumage similar to adult but sometimes shows faint second wingbar.

ARCTIC WARBLER
Phylloscopus borealis

THE ARCTIC WARBLER is a common breeding bird within its range; it overwinters in southeast Asia. It is also a vagrant to western Europe, with a handful of sightings a year coming after strong easterly winds. Despite its English name, the Arctic Warbler might better be called the sub-Arctic warbler since it does not breed beyond the treeline. At the start of the breeding season, the male's display includes a remarkable wing-rattling as he flies between song-posts. The nest on the ground is usually built into the herbage or under a rotting stump so that only the entrance shows.

IDENTIFICATION

Superficially similar to several other members of the genus *Phylloscopus* (especially Willow and Greenish Warblers, and Chiffchaff) but bulkier in the body. Adult largely greenish above and off-white below. Best features are obvious creamy wingbar and yellowish-white supercilium from bill to nape, often upturned at hind end. Shows dark eyestripe, noticeably pointed brown bill and pale yellowish-brown legs. Juvenile similar to adult but with brighter colours.

BIRD FACTS

VOICE Calls 'tzic' and 'tseep'; song loud, energetic but monotonous trill

LENGTH 10.5–11.5cm

WINGSPAN 16.5–22cm

WEIGHT 8.5–11g

HABITAT Taiga forest, willow and birch forest, often near water or damp ground

NEST On the ground; domed, of moss, dry grass and dead leaves, lined with finer grasses

EGGS 5–6; white, finely and sparsely spotted with light reddish-brown

FOOD Almost wholly insectivorous, especially mosquitoes, ants and insect larvae

GREENISH WARBLER
Small, slim, graceful warbler; continually active.

ARCTIC WARBLER
adult

Robust and active Phylloscopus warbler.

ARCTIC WARBLER
juvenile

EASTERN BONELLI'S WARBLER
adult

Most birds arrive at the breeding grounds by mid-April and the eggs are laid by mid-May.

WESTERN BONELLI'S WARBLER
adult

WESTERN BONELLI'S WARBLER
Phylloscopus bonelli

EASTERN BONELLI'S WARBLER
Phylloscopus orientalis

FORMERLY TREATED AS races of a single species, Western and Eastern Bonelli's Warblers are now considered to be separate species. Although rather similar to look at (there are subtle differences in plumage and voice) they are separated geographically in the breeding season: Westerns breed from Spain and France east to Austria and Italy while Easterns are found mainly in Greece, the Balkans and Turkey. Both species winter in Africa. In the breeding season they are unobtrusive birds of the upper leaf canopy of forests. Listen for the song to detect their presence in any given woodland.

IDENTIFICATION

All birds are overall rather pale. Western has light grey-brown upperparts, washed with pale olive-green. Head and nape often appear particularly pale. Has silky white under and pale yellowish rump. Upper mandible of bill is brown, lower mandible flesh coloured. Legs dull brown. Sexes and ages are similar. Eastern is similar but much paler, greyer and less colourful overall.

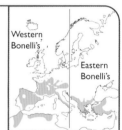

Western Bonelli's

Eastern Bonelli's

BIRD FACTS

VOICE Call 'hu-eet' (Western), 'chirp' (Eastern). Song is a trill in both species, recalling Wood Warbler

LENGTH 11.5cm

WINGSPAN 16–20cm

WEIGHT 7–8g

HABITAT Woods, very often cork oak or pine, usually 700–2,000m above sea level

NEST On the ground; domed, of grasses, lined with finer grass, roots, hair; camouflaged

EGGS Usually 4–6; white, finely and profusely spotted with dark red and purplish-brown

FOOD Insects and a few other invertebrates; young also feed on insects

GOLDCREST

Regulus regulus

BIRD FACTS

VOICE Calls frequently; song repeated double note and trill; all very high pitched

LENGTH 9cm

WINGSPAN 13.5–15.5cm

WEIGHT 4.5–7.5g

HABITAT Coniferous woods for breeding; wanders widely in winter

NEST Hammock of moss, lichens and cobwebs near end of conifer twig

EGGS 7–10; white or pale buff, finely speckled with buff-brown

FOOD Insectivorous; especially springtails, aphids, leafbugs and Lepidoptera larvae

THE GOLDCREST IS resident in much of its range, migrating in winter only from the harshest weather in the far north and east; in winter, numbers in northwest Europe are noticeably increased by immigrants from northern Europe. In the breeding season Goldcrests will inhabit deciduous woods, gardens, cemeteries and parks if there are some suitable conifers, especially when populations are high. In winter small groups often move with tits and treecreepers and are found in pine stands of deciduous woodland as well as conifer forests. Feeding flocks keep up a continuous stream of contact notes (like the song, too high-pitched for some people to hear).

IDENTIFICATION

Tiny: Europe's smallest bird. Adults have dull, greenish upperparts, pale olive-green underparts, darker on the flanks. Wing coverts greenish; paler wing panels and wingbar. Appears to be large-eyed, black on a plain face. Crown of male orange-yellow, lined each side with black, often not noticeable in the field; in display male raises crest to reveal startling orange centre. Crown centre of female yellow. Juvenile lacks adults' crown markings.

male

DID YOU KNOW?

Whilst foraging for food, Goldcrests are often seemingly indifferent to human observers.

male   *female*

FIRECREST

Regulus ignicapillus

BIRD FACTS

VOICE Very high-pitched; 'zit, zit,' call, lower than Goldcrest; song rapid string of calls

LENGTH 9cm

WINGSPAN 13–16cm

WEIGHT 4.5–6.5g

HABITAT Less restricted to conifers than Goldcrest; gardens, scrub, tree heath

NEST Deep cup slung under a twig near end of branch; of moss, lichen and cobwebs

EGGS Usually 7–11, sometimes 12; pinkish-buff colour with very fine red dots

FOOD Arthropods, especially springtails, aphids, spiders; insect larvae

THE FIRECREST IS much less widespread than the Goldcrest, breeding only in more temperate and warmer parts of central and southern Europe. Northern and eastern populations are migratory, moving in winter to the Mediterranean basin and the far southwest. In display the male points his bill towards the bird he is displaying to, thus showing the crest and the startling face pattern of black and white stripes. The Firecrest spends more time in broad-leaved trees than the Goldcrest; in conifers it feeds in less dense branches, moves about more and prefers larger prey. The male holds a larger territory and defends it with a louder, more penetrating song.

IDENTIFICATION

Adult is more brightly coloured than Goldcrest. Most striking feature is striped head: male has golden-orange crown stripe, lined each side with black; crown stripe of female yellow. Both sexes show white supercilium underlined by black eyestripe. Mantle to uppertail coverts bright olive-green, tail darker and browner; all underparts greenish-white. Striking bronze patch on side of neck. Bill black, legs brown. Juvenile plumage shows pale supercilium but crown and shoulder are plain greenish. Immatures acquire adult-like plumage before autumn migration.

male

Greener above and whiter below than Goldcrest, and shows bright-orange shoulder patches.

ABOVE: male; INSET: juvenile

Very similar to Collared and Semi-collared Flycatchers. Breeding male black above and unmarked white below, but black is relieved by white forehead (often divided into two spots), white-edged tertials, which meet white bar on greater wing coverts and white basal half of outertail feathers. From central Europe eastwards males are increasingly grey-brown, not black. After breeding, male moults and black elements of plumage replaced by brown or grey, so white wing panel not so striking. Female resembles non-breeding male but tail and rump not as black. Bill and legs black in all plumages. Juvenile looks like non-breeding adult with buff-spotted crown, mantle and breast.

ABOVE: Adult female has black elements of male's plumage replaced by brown.

male

male

PIED FLYCATCHER

Ficedula hypoleuca

THE PIED FLYCATCHER is a summer visitor, over-wintering in Africa in the forests bordering the Gulf of Guinea. Pied Flycatchers arrive in Europe between mid-April and late May; the males arrive first and choose the nest hole, and sing until they have attracted mates. These visitors leave in August and September, stopping over in southwest Europe before their trans-Saharan flight. Some males successively take two or three mates, each in different territories, but will help to feed only the first brood. After the breeding season, Pied Flycatchers become remarkably secretive as they prepare for migration.

BIRD FACTS

VOICE Call loud 'whit' or 'wee-tic'; alarm 'phweet'; song a rapid sequence of high and low notes
LENGTH 13cm
WINGSPAN 21.5–24cm
WEIGHT 11–15g
HABITAT Deciduous and mixed open woodland; has spread to orchards, gardens
NEST In a tree-hole; loose cup of leaves, grass and bark, lined with finer materials
EGGS 6–7; pale blue, rarely with fine reddish-brown speckles
FOOD Flying and non-flying arthropods, especially bees, flies and beetles

COLLARED FLYCATCHER

Ficedula albicollis

THE COLLARED FLYCATCHER returns to Europe to breed from late April to mid-May. It is a vagrant to northwest Europe. Collared Flycatchers feed mainly in tree canopies. The best chance of finding one in a wood comes with recognising the call and song.

COLLARED FLYCATCHER female

BIRD FACTS

VOICE Call 'seep'; song like Pied Flycatcher's, a series of high and low notes and whistles
LENGTH 13cm
WINGSPAN 22.5–24.5cm
WEIGHT 12–16g
HABITAT Sunny, deciduous woodland and forest, well-timbered parks, orchards
NEST Cup of leaves and grass, lined with fine grass, in a hole in a tree or wall, or a nest box
EGGS 5–7; very pale blue, unmarked
FOOD Flying and non-flying arthropods and their larvae

Very like Pied and Semi-collared Flycatchers; breeding male unmistakable but other plumages hard to separate from these two species. Breeding male white below and black above. Note white forehead, broad white collar, white wing panel from tertials to flight feathers, whitish patch on lower back and rump, and black (or mottled white) outertail feathers. Female, immature and winter male lack collar and have black elements of male's plumage replaced by brown.

COLLARED FLYCATCHER male

SEMI-COLLARED FLYCATCHER

Ficedula semitorquata

THE SEMI-COLLARED is the rarest flycatcher in the region, restricted to oak or hornbeam forest in its main range, and ancient beech forest in Greece. Males arrive at their breeding grounds several days before females and select suitable nest holes.

Breeding male black above and white below; has white patch on forehead. Note white half-collar, white wing panel where tertials meet white-tipped greater coverts and bases to flight feathers. Short white bar on median coverts is not found in other flycatchers. Has greyish lower back and rump, and more extensive white in outertail feathers than Pied or Collared Flycatchers. Female has black elements of male's plumage replaced by grey-brown.

SEMI-COLLARED FLYCATCHER male

BIRD FACTS

VOICE Calls include a loud 'whit'; song a rapid sequence of high and low notes; hard to distinguish from related flycatchers'
LENGTH 13cm
WINGSPAN 23.5–24cm
WEIGHT 13–15g
HABITAT Deciduous forest on mountain slopes up to 2,000m above sea level, and riverine forest
NEST In a tree-hole; cup of dead leaves, grass and moss, lined with finer grass
EGGS 5–6; pale blue, unmarked
FOOD Mainly flying insects

RED-BREASTED FLYCATCHER

Ficedula parva

1st autumn

THE RED-BREASTED FLYCATCHER is a forest bird, preferring tall trees, especially beech in the west of its range. It is a summer visitor, overwintering in Asia, and usually arrives in Europe in early May. It is a rare but annual passage migrant to northwest Europe, first-winter birds being recorded mainly in September and October. The Red-breasted Flycatcher is very agile on the wing, flicking and cocking its tail more than its relatives do. Although it is secretive and unobtrusive for most of the breeding season, the male is more noticeable in May, when he sings in flight, fluttering from perch to perch.

IDENTIFICATION

Adults of both sexes ashy brown above; flanks washed with buff; wings and tail dark brown. Tail has diagnostic long, white patches each side at the base, noticeable in flight and when bird flicks its tail. Male has orange-red chin, throat and upper breast, and looks like diminutive Robin, but female has buff throat and breast. Juvenile is spotted, but retains the white tail patches. First-winter plumage similar to female. In all plumages, dark eye is highlighted by white eyering, more noticeable in the male.

BIRD FACTS

VOICE Call short, harsh 'trrt'; song cadence, descending in pitch

LENGTH 11.5cm

WINGSPAN 18.5–21cm

WEIGHT 9–13g

HABITAT Mixed and deciduous forest with much undergrowth

NEST In tree hollow or hole; small cup of moss, leaves and lichen, lined with hair

EGGS 5–6; whitish, very finely speckled with reddish-brown

FOOD Insects and other invertebrates, mostly in the tree canopy

summer male

male

Male's song is a loud, silvery run of mostly pure notes, reminiscent of Willow Warbler; he only sings until incubation starts.

SPOTTED FLYCATCHER

Muscicapa striata

adult

THIS DRABLY COLOURED flycatcher is the most widespread flycatcher in the region, breeding throughout lowland Europe except where tree cover is absent or where the forest is dense. It is often the last summer visitor to arrive on its breeding territory from Africa, in early May, yet many manage to rear two broods before leaving, usually in August and September. The Spotted Flycatcher obtains most of its food in flight. It uses an open perch from which it sallies forth, sometimes with several twists and turns, before it catches an insect. It often returns to the same branch, where it perches with its characteristic upright stance, legs and feet hardly showing.

IDENTIFICATION

Largest flycatcher in the region and the only one with streaked underparts. Adult has all upperparts, wings and tail grey-brown, appearing unmarked at long range. Sexes similar. Forehead and crown streaked black, outlined in white. Underparts white, washed with brown on side of breast and flanks. At close range, throat, side of breast and flanks show dull-brown streaks. Bill dull grey-brown. Legs brown or black. Juvenile superficially similar to adult but upperparts buffer than adult's; feathers of head, back, rump, lesser and median coverts have pale, round, buff-white spots; underparts not streaked like those of adult but spotted dark brown.

BIRD FACTS

VOICE Call 'tzee-zuk-zuk'; song quiet, short, squeaky

LENGTH 14.5cm

WINGSPAN 23–25.5cm

WEIGHT 14–18g

HABITAT Woodland edge, glades, parks, orchards, gardens

NEST In a tree-fork, crevice or creeper; plant material and twigs, lined with feathers and hair

EGGS 4–5; very pale blue, mottled and blotched reddish and purplish

FOOD Mainly flying insects, especially flies and bees

adult

adult

adult

CRESTED TIT
Lophophanes cristatus

Small tit with backward-pointing black crest, with the feathers tipped white. Sexes similar. Adult has very distinctive face pattern of black line on a white face, running behind eye and around rear of ear coverts; another black line starts at end of crest and runs down side of neck to join black bib. Upperparts buff-brown, wings and tail grey-brown. Bill black, quite long for a small tit. Legs olive-grey. Juvenile has shorter crest than adult but otherwise similar.

THE CRESTED TIT is the only small European bird with a crest. It is a very sedentary bird, only very rarely wandering as far as 50km. The Crested Tit is an undemonstrative tit with a limited vocal repertoire. Most of the work of excavating the nest hole and building the actual nest is done by the female; a new hole is prepared each year, even if it is made in the same stump as last year's hole. Unusually among the tits, the young are not fed extensively on moth larvae, receiving instead many spiders and pine seeds. In common with their relatives, however, Crested Tits store food in autumn for use in winter.

Crest can be very difficult to see, particularly if bird is overhead.

adult

adult

DID YOU KNOW?

The Crested Tit's range is limited by its need for rotten wood in which to excavate its nest hole.

BIRD FACTS

VOICE Call low-pitched purring trill; song makes repeated use of calls
LENGTH 11.5cm
WINGSPAN 17–20cm
WEIGHT 10–12g
HABITAT Pine forest in the north; mixed woods; also in beech or cork oak woods in south
NEST Moss, lined with hair and wool, in an excavated tree-hole
EGGS 6–7; white, spotted and blotched rusty red, usually more at large end
FOOD Insects and spiders; seeds outside breeding season

COAL TIT
Periparus ater

Slightly smaller and shorter-tailed than Blue Tit. Adult has glossy black cap and white cheeks; large, white patch on nape is diagnostic. Cap extends down to level of eye; chin, throat, upper breast black, joined to cap by black collar. Underparts buff, paler towards the centre. Upperparts, wings and tail olive-grey. Median and greater wing coverts have white tips, forming two wingbars. Bill rather fine, black. Legs lead-blue. Sexes similar but female has less extensive bib. Juvenile similar to adult but markings less distinctive.

Distinctive double wingbar is often easier to see than nape patch; at close range wingbars show as separate white spots.

adult

THE COAL TIT is often considered the most typical tit of coniferous woods, but in southern and western Europe it is more often found in mixed and deciduous forest, as well as almost anywhere where there are a few conifers. It readily comes to birdtables in winter and is especially fond of sunflower seeds. The Coal Tit's toes and claws are long and are specially adapted to a life in conifers; it shows greater agility than other tits when foraging in the foliage. When viewed from below it is very like other black-capped tits; from this angle, the extent of the black bib and its calls are the most important features.

adult

adult

BIRD FACTS

VOICE Call piping 'tsee'; song loud and clear 'teechu, teechu, teechu'
LENGTH 11.5cm
WINGSPAN 17–21cm
WEIGHT 9–10g
HABITAT Typically coniferous forest and woodland, but now anywhere with firs, including cemeteries and parks
NEST In hole in tree-stump, tree, wall or rock; of moss, lined with hair and wool
EGGS 8–9; white, finely speckled with red-brown
FOOD Adult and larval insects and spiders; seeds in autumn and winter

LONG-TAILED TIT

Aegithalos caudatus

Tiny-bodied, long-tailed bird, not related to true tits.

THE LONG-TAILED TIT is mainly sedentary, but at times of high populations many irrupt from their breeding grounds. Long-tailed Tits are territorial in the breeding season, after which they are gregarious, forming small flocks of around ten birds. These flocks defend a winter territory against others, and consist of parents, their offspring and helpers related to the male. A flock keeps together with the help of a constant 'conversation' of 'tsirrrup' calls, as its members restlessly hunt for food. The flock roosts communally, in a thick bush, huddled together on one horizontal perch.

——————— *IDENTIFICATION*

Sexes similar. Adult birds from most of Europe have head and underparts whitish, washed with dusky pink on nape, and from belly to undertail coverts; black bands extend from bill, above the eyes to the mantle. Upperparts, wings and tail dull black, with pink scapulars and rump, and white tips and edges to graduated tail feathers. Pink tones wear off. Adult of subspecies from northern and eastern Europe has pure white head and noticeably white-edged tertials and secondaries; birds of southern subspecies have grey backs, darker faces, and little or no pink. Eyering reddish in all birds. Juvenile shorter and darker than adult, with dusky mask and drab upperparts.

Adult of Scandinavian race.

Adult of Western European race.

BIRD FACTS

VOICE Call low, repeated 'tsupp'; alarm trilled 'tsirrrrup'; song rapid repetition of calls

LENGTH 14cm

WINGSPAN 16–19cm

WEIGHT 7–9g

HABITAT Deciduous woodland; for nesting, thick scrub like gorse, bramble or briar

NEST Usually in a thorny bush; domed nest of moss, lichen and feathers

EGGS 8–12; white, unmarked or with minute reddish speckles

FOOD Insects, especially eggs and larvae of butterflies and moths

GREAT TIT

Parus major

adult male

THE GREAT TIT has the widest distribution in the world of all the tits. Birds from western and southern Europe are mostly sedentary but northern and central European birds, at times of high population, irrupt into other parts of Europe. Great Tits forage for food low down more than other tits. Those resident in beech woods may spend as much as 45 per cent of their time on the ground in late autumn searching for beech-mast. By contrast, in an oak wood they may spend 60 per cent of the time on low branches in search of insects. In winter they regularly come to bird tables.

Song is vary varied, often leading to misidentification.

Juveniles look very washed out and have yellow cheeks rather than white.

——————— *IDENTIFICATION*

The largest common tit, with quite a long tail. Adult is basically yellow-green above and yellow below. Wings have black flight feathers, blue-grey coverts and black tertials, tipped white. Shows white wingbar and white outertail feathers. Distinctive head pattern comprises glossy blue-black cap with triangular white cheek patch. Black on chin and throat extends into bold, black stripe down centre of underparts, forming a wide black patch between legs on male, and much narrower one on female. Bill strong and black. Legs blue-grey. Juvenile similar to adult but has sooty crown, browner back, cheeks washed yellow and underparts duller yellow.

adult male

Large size and striking combination of colours make Great Tit unmistakable.

BIRD FACTS

VOICE Call loud 'tink, tink, tink'; song far-carrying 'teacher, teacher, teacher'

LENGTH 14cm

WINGSPAN 22.5–25.5cm

WEIGHT 16–20g

HABITAT Almost anywhere with trees, except coniferous forest; even in cities

NEST In hole in wall or tree, or nest boxes; moss base, cup lined with hair, wool and feathers

EGGS 5–12; white, speckled reddish-brown, larger than Blue Tit's markings

FOOD Great variety of adult and larval insects; spiders; seeds and fruits in winter

Adult is the only European tit with bright-blue crown, bordered with white. Has dark lines from bill through eye, around back of head and around otherwise white cheeks. Upperparts yellowish-green, underparts sulphur-yellow, with small blackish central streak. Wings dark blue with white wingbar. Tail dark grey-blue. Bill short, black. Legs dusky blue. Female very similar to male but colours less bright. Juvenile washed yellow and lacks blue in plumage but similar to adult in other respects.

BLUE TIT
Cyanistes caeruleus

THE BLUE TIT is abundant in most habitats with trees, although it avoids conifers, and outside the breeding season even wanders to reedbeds and clifftops. It tends to feed high up in broad-leaved trees, foraging on twigs, buds and leaves, but will visit bird tables in winter. Blue Tits are inquisitive and agile birds: they tap reed stems to locate hidden prey and open only those stems that contain larvae. They are occasionally known to hang by one foot and grab food with the other and routinely hold hard seeds underfoot and hammer them with their bill; they can also solve bird-table puzzles in order to reach food.

BIRD FACTS

VOICE Call 'tsee-tsee'; alarm 'chirr.r.r'; song tremolo 'tsee-tsee-tsee-tsuhuhuhu'

LENGTH 11.5cm

WINGSPAN 17.5–20cm

WEIGHT 10–12g

HABITAT Anywhere with trees, even inner-city parks and gardens

NEST Hole in tree or wall, nest box; pad of moss, cup lined with hair and fine grass

EGGS 6–16; white with fine, reddish spots

FOOD Chiefly adult and larval insects and spiders; fruits and seeds in winter

Fledglings have same patterning as adults but yellower face.

DID YOU KNOW?

Blue Tits are extremely acrobatic, and unlike Great Tits are light enough to forage at the tips of even the thinnest twigs.

Male glides slowly towards a possible nest site to attract females to it; at other times flight action is fluttery.

DID YOU KNOW?

In Britain Blue Tits sometimes rip open tops of newly delivered milk bottles to drink the cream. They are also known to exploit the nectar in willow catkins and cherry flowers, a rich food source little used by other European birds.

MARSH TIT

Poecile palustris

THE MARSH TIT is separable from the Willow Tit only with difficulty, by noting its glossy black cap, which does not extend as far down the nape, its small bib with well-defined edges, its paler underparts, its lack of a pale wing panel and its quite distinct calls and song. It does not visit bird tables as frequently as other tits, nor does it readily take to a nest box. Marsh Tits pair for life and spend the whole year in the same territory. They sometimes join other tits but rarely stray out of their own territory, even in hard weather.

In Europe, one of four dark-capped tits with similar plumage pattern (*see also* Willow, Siberian and Sombre Tits), though each has clear size and colour differences. Sexes similar. Adult has glossy black cap from bill to nape. Small black chin and centre of throat, rest of face white. Wings, tail and upperparts greyish-brown, with dark-brown centres to tail feathers. Underparts dull white, with pale-buff tinge on flanks and undertail coverts. Bill short and black. Legs dark blue-grey. Juvenile very similar to adult but cap not glossy. Acquires adult plumage by September.

Neck is slimmer and bib neater than on Willow Tit.

BIRD FACTS

VOICE Calls 'pitchoo' and nasal 'ter-char-char-char'; song repetition on one note

LENGTH 11.5cm

WINGSPAN 18–19.5cm

WEIGHT 9–12g

HABITAT Deciduous woodland, especially oak and beech, not marshes

NEST Low, in hole in tree or stump; cup of moss, lined with hair and feathers

EGGS 7–10; white, usually with fine reddish-brown spots at larger end

FOOD Mostly insects and spiders in spring and summer; seeds and nuts in winter

---

WILLOW TIT

Poecile montana

THE WILLOW TIT favours three different habitats in different parts of its range. Conifers are preferred on the slopes of southern mountains while lowland river valleys and overgrown stands of trees on damp ground are chosen at lower altitudes. Northern birch and conifer woodlands are the species' haunt at northern latitudes. The Willow Tit excavates its own nest hole, low in a very soft, rotten stump, generally alder, birch, willow or elder. Willow Tits pair for life, live in the same territory all year round, and in winter are gregarious and will forage with other tits.

Very similar in size and appearance to Marsh Tit, but looks less smart than that species. Adult has black cap extending down to mantle. Black bib quite extensive, with poorly defined borders. Tail is slightly round-ended, not square or slightly forked. Best plumage difference is this species' light patch on secondaries in closed wing (not always conspicuous, however). Scandinavian and central European birds much greyer on back and whiter on face than British birds, which are closest in appearance to Marsh Tit. Juvenile very similar to adult of any given race. Always note call notes as well as plumage details to separate this species from Marsh Tit.

The nest hole is excavated by both male and female but only the female builds the nest.

BIRD FACTS

VOICE Calls 'eez-eez-eez' and characteristic, nasal 'tchay, tchay'; song a single note, repeated lugubriously

LENGTH 11.5cm

WINGSPAN 17–20.5cm

WEIGHT 10–13g

HABITAT Montane, coniferous forest; trees on damp ground; mixed woodland

NEST In hole in rotten tree stump; cup of plant materials, rarely moss, lined with hair

EGGS 6–9; white, variably speckled with red-brown

FOOD Mainly invertebrates in breeding season; seeds and berries at other times

Adult of British race very similar to Marsh Tit; has plumper appearance, duller black cap and buffish flanks.

SOMBRE TIT

Poecile lugubris

ALTHOUGH IT IS as large as a Great Tit and is easy to identify, the Sombre Tit is hard to find because it spends so much time in the foliage of the woods and open forests it inhabits. Its song is not striking, having a repetitive, buzzing quality, but it does have a characteristic call of alarm or excitement, a deep 'churrrr', not unlike a sparrow's alarm. The Sombre Tit comes to ground much less often than other tits and over 90 per cent of its time is spent foraging in the crown of deciduous trees.

Has heavy bill to split large seeds.

adult male

IDENTIFICATION

Dull plumage pattern similar to Marsh Tit's. Adult has sooty black, long cap. Sooty black chin and throat appear as large bib. Cheeks, ear coverts and sides of neck white. Upperpart, wings and tail ashy brown, with distinct greyish-white fringes to tertials and inner secondaries. Underparts dull, creamy white with ash-brown wash on the sides. Bill strong, black. Legs grey. Female similar to male but with less contrasting cap. Juvenile is similar to adult female, with grubby cheeks.

SIBERIAN TIT

Poecile cinctus

THE SIBERIAN TIT is a rather sedentary resident, but juveniles are sometimes nomadic outside the breeding season. In winter it visits the houses of foresters to feed on bird tables and rubbish-tips, and will even land on foresters who are having a meal to pick up crumbs. This tit is territorial, pairs for life, and is gregarious in winter, when small flocks follow the same route each day through the forest. Unusually for a tit, the Siberian Tit does not have a far-carrying song, and it can therefore be hard to find.

Very confiding, even at nest site.

adult male

IDENTIFICATION

Large, often fluffy-looking tit. Sexes alike. Adult and juvenile have sooty-brown cap and nape, with darker line through eye. White face. Large sooty-black bib with broken edge. Upperparts warm brown. Wings dark brown, flight feathers edged with greyish-white, creating strong contrast between wings and back. Tail grey-black with dull-white outer feathers. Breast and belly are dull white, sides of breast and flanks are rusty red. Bill black. Legs grey.

IDENTIFICATION

Smaller than Blue Tit, but with relatively longer tail. Adult has pale-grey head with black mask. Mantle, scapulars and wing coverts chestnut. Flight feathers black, fringed with buff. Back and rump greyish, contrasting with nearly black tail, which has off-white feather margins. Underparts off-white with chestnut smudges on sides of breast and flanks. Bill black. Legs bluish-black. Sexes similar, but female less bright than male. Juvenile lacks black face mask of adult and has cinnamon back.

PENDULINE TIT

Remiz pendulinus

THE PENDULINE TIT is migratory in the north of the range, and resident in the south. The migrants winter in southern Europe within the species' overall breeding range. Adult Penduline Tits are gregarious, active little birds and both adults and juveniles will allow close approach. A family stays together in a flock after breeding and attracts attention with its soft, repeated calls. The Penduline Tit's amazing nest is started by the male, who twists plant fibres into a ring dangling from a forked twig on a tree that hangs over or is near water. Once mated, the pair build a cup, which is then roofed; finally a little tunnel is made for an entrance near the top.

Males build throughout the breeding season as part of a complex mating system: both males and females usually have more than one mate.

Plant fibres of hop and nettle are the main nest materials, woven tightly to a felt-like consistency with plant down and wool.

BEARDED TIT

Panurus biarmicus

THE BEARDED TIT - sometimes referred to as the Bearded Reedling - is very dependent on reedbeds, and is a species that suffers badly in hard winters. Birders often refer to it as a 'pinger' because of its distinctive call. It is very gregarious outside the breeding season and confiding at nesting time. The birds are restless and regularly fly out low over the reeds, with whirring wings and long, waving tail. The birds are not territorial, and nests are often concentrated in one place, leaving large, communal feeding areas. Juveniles form flocks of up to 200 soon after independence.

adult male

adult female

IDENTIFICATION

Short-winged, very long-tailed, unmistakable bird with predominantly tawny russet plumage at all times. Adult male has grey head and striking black 'moustaches' of loose feathers highlighted by white chin and throat. Tail graduated, with white tips to feathers forming ladder effect. Undertail coverts black. Closed wing appears banded: white on outer flight feathers, rufous centre panel, black and white tertials. Stubby yellow bill, orange eye, black legs. Female lacks male's head pattern, is duller and less russet; undertail coverts warm buff but similar to male in other respects. Juvenile resembles female but has obvious black back and wing coverts.

adult male

NUTHATCH

Sitta europaea

THE NUTHATCH is the only widespread member of its family in Europe. It is a resident and very sedentary. Birds pair for life and live in the same territory throughout the year, and most juveniles settle within 10km of where they hatched; all ages are tolerant of humans and regularly visit bird tables in winter. The Nuthatch searches for food on tree-trunks; a seed is fixed in a crevice of bark in a tree and hammered open with blows of its bill. It stores food in the winter in the same way that tits do. Sometimes an observer is attracted to a Nuthatch by hearing the ringing blows high up in a tree.

IDENTIFICATION

Easily recognised by plump body, short tail, long head and woodpecker-like bill. Only male has darker chestnut patch on flanks. Adult upperparts all blue-grey. Cheeks and throat white. Rest of underparts orange-buff merging into orange in birds from central, southern and western Europe but much paler in Scandinavian race. Has white-centred chestnut undertail coverts. Broad, black eyestripe. Outertail feathers black with white subterminal spots. Bill long, pointed, greyish-black. Legs yellowish-brown. Juvenile similar to adult but duller below.

This small, woodpecker-like bird is always on the move.

Scandinavian race adult.

Nuthatches are the only European birds that can move head first down a tree-trunk in search of food.

Western European race adult.

CORSICAN NUTHATCH

Sitta whiteheadi

CORSICAN NUTHATCH

THE CORSICAN NUTHATCH is one of Europe's rarest birds. It is chiefly sedentary, although snow in the mountains will force birds down below 1,000m. Corsican Nuthatches are not shy, and will tolerate human presence provided that their habitat is secure. They feed and move like Nuthatches, and cache seeds of Corsican Pine for the winter. This nuthatch commonly uses the holes of Great Spotted Woodpeckers to nest in, but will also excavate its own in rotten sapwood.

KRÜPER'S NUTHATCH

IDENTIFICATION

Noticeably small nuthatch. Finest bill, longest-looking head and shortest tail of the European nuthatches. Adult essentially grey-blue above, dull white below. Male has head pattern of jet-black crown and long, white supercilium, underlined with long, black eyestripe. Female has black crown replaced by dusky blue. Both sexes show dark primaries. Outertail feathers black with white tips. Bill black, greyish at base. Legs lead-grey. Juvenile similar to adult female but with buff wash to all underparts except throat.

KRÜPER'S NUTHATCH

Sitta krueperi

KRÜPER'S NUTHATCH HAS a limited global range – mainly coastal Turkey and the southern fringes of the Black Sea. In Europe, it is also found on the Greek island of Lesvos. A mainly resident species, it can be easily recognised by its nuthatch profile and striking red chest patch. Outside the breeding season, the species is unobtrusive and rather hard to locate, unless you can recognise its call. In spring, singing males make locating the birds a little less challenging.

IDENTIFICATION

Small nuthatch with an extremely slender bill. Adult male is essentially grey-blue above, with white face and throat and pale blue-grey underparts showing striking red chest patch and reddish undertail coverts; note the dark eyestripe, white supercilium and blackish cap. Female is similar to male but with less intense dark cap and paler chest band. Bill is greyish with dark tip. Legs are lead-grey. Juvenile similar to adult female.

adult

ROCK NUTHATCH

Sitta neumayer

THE ROCK NUTHATCH is a sedentary bird, but in some areas birds retreat down to valleys at the onset of snow, and may be found in wayside shrubs and even in gardens. Rock Nuthatches mostly hunt on the ground and in rock crevices. When feeding, one of the pair will continually break off from foraging to check for predators. They are lively birds and call frequently. The Rock Nuthatch builds an amazing nest under an overhang of rock or in a slight depression on the rock face. This flask-shaped structure is made of mud and animal excrement, built against the rock, with a tunnel-like entrance.

adult

adult

IDENTIFICATION

Similar in appearance to Nuthatch but much paler. Adult is basically blue-grey above from forehead to tail, and dirty white below. Underparts change from white on face and throat, to buff belly; darkest on undertail coverts. Long, broad, black eyestripe separates grey crown and white face. Grey tail is unmarked. Bill black with paler base to lower mandible.

TREECREEPER
Certhia familiaris

BIRD FACTS

VOICE Call thin 'tsiew'; song high-pitched cadence lasting 2.5–3 seconds

LENGTH 12.5cm

WINGSPAN 17.5–21cm

WEIGHT 8.5–10g

HABITAT Predominantly in mature broad-leaved trees, but also conifers

NEST Commonly behind loose tree-bark; cup of grass on twigs, lined with hair

EGGS 5–6; white with fine reddish-brown speckles

FOOD Insects and spiders throughout the year; some winter seeds

THE TREECREEPER is mostly a sedentary bird, but northern populations overwinter further south in the species' breeding range. It is hard to find in the woods because of its camouflaged plumage and high-pitched voice, which is beyond the hearing of many observers. The Treecreeper spirals up and around tree trunks and under branches, and when it has searched up one tree it flies to low down on another. It creeps close to the trunk on its short legs, supported on its tail feathers. Treecreepers are known to roost, sometimes communally, in bark crevices in the winter months.

Sexes alike. At a distance adult appears brown above and silky white below. At close range shows rufous rump, long, white supercilium and white-mottled and streaked back. Complex pattern on wings comprises two pale-buff wingbars on coverts, buff band across secondaries and primaries, and white-spotted tertials. Tail is long and brown with dark shafts; feathers are stiff and pointed, and when spread the tail looks frayed. Bill quite long, gently decurved (rare in European passerines) and dark brown. Legs pale brown. Juvenile very similar to adult but upperparts appear spotted. *See entry for Short-toed Treecreeper, which is almost identical, for details of separation of the two species.*

Underparts can become stained as they drag on bark, moss and lichen, and should not be confused with Short-toed Treecreeper's duller underparts.

Attractive woodland bird; adult has delicately marked brown upperparts and white underparts.

Like Treecreeper, usually solitary outside the breeding season, but will associate with foraging tit flock.

SHORT-TOED TREECREEPER

Certhia brachydactyla

THE SHORT-TOED TREECREEPER is very similar to the Treecreeper to look at and its most reliable field characteristic is its voice. Its calls are louder and less sibilant than its relative's and include a diagnostic, shrill, loud 'tseep', rather like a Dunnock's call. This is used as an alarm or rival-call, either singly or in a series. The song is a rapid, short phrase, lasting a second or so, of about six notes; 'teet-teet-teetero-tit'. Its short duration, loudness, lower pitch, and short and clear introductory notes make it clearly distinguishable from the Treecreeper's song.

IDENTIFICATION

Very similar to Treecreeper and often best distinguished by voice. Sexes alike. Adult is brown above and white below. Compared to Treecreeper, sustained observation should reveal these differences: (a) upperparts and wings are duller, browner and less obviously spotted; (b) dull brown rump; (c) shorter, duller supercilium often not showing in front of eye; (d) breast and rest of underparts washed grey or brown, most noticeably on the flanks; (e) bill usually looks longer and more slender, and bent at tip rather than gently decurved. Juvenile similar to adult but upperparts appear more spotted.

BIRD FACTS

VOICE Call shrill 'zeet', and 'srriih'; song comprises short, loud phrase

LENGTH 12.5cm

WINGSPAN 17–20.5cm

WEIGHT 8.5–11g

HABITAT Tall trees with rugged bark in parks, avenues, orchards, forest edge

NEST Often behind loose bark; like Treecreeper's

EGGS 6–7; white spotted with shades of red chiefly at larger end

FOOD Mainly insect larvae and pupae and spiders throughout the year

---

IDENTIFICATION

Unmistakable. Breeding male upperparts from forehead to uppertail coverts grey. Lower face, throat and upper breast black, shading to dusky grey on rest of underparts. Undertail coverts white-spotted. Large butterfly-like wings. Wing coverts crimson. Flight feathers sooty black with crimson bases. Outer four primaries have grey tips with two white spots behind. Tail black, tipped grey with a white spot on outertail feathers. Male moults between July and September. Tail and flight feathers then look blacker but face and upper breast lose black, becoming white, shading to grey. Legs black at all times. Bill black, needle-like, long and decurved. Female and juvenile similar to non-breeding male.

WALLCREEPER

Tichodroma muraria

WALLCREEPERS ARE OFTEN found near torrents, caves and scree. Some birds are sedentary, but most are short-distance migrants, retreating before the winter snows. The species is a very rare vagrant to northwest Europe. The Wallcreeper looks much bigger in flight than perched because its wings are broad and a third longer than the wings of other species of similar length. It is constantly on the move, flicking its wings as it searches for insects. Wallcreepers move quite fast as they forage, in short flights like jumps, or hopping supported by their wings. They are fairly confiding throughout the year, and will allow careful approach to within 10–20m.

It seems likely that the spectacular crimson coverts and white spots evolved as visual signals, this form of communication being more effective in mountainous terrain than sound.

BIRD FACTS

VOICE Call short chirp; song comprises clear whistles in crescendo, rising in pitch

LENGTH 16.5cm

WINGSPAN 27–32cm

WEIGHT 17–19g

HABITAT Rocky, broken, precipitous mountain terrain, 1,000–2,000m

NEST In a cleft in rock or scree; of moss, grass, roots; lined with hair and wool

EGGS 4–5; white with sparse, fine, deep-red speckles, mostly at large end

FOOD Small insects and spiders found mainly on rock faces

RED-BACKED SHRIKE

Lanius collurio

RED-BACKED SHRIKES ARE summer visitors to Europe, wintering in eastern tropical and southern Africa; sadly, their numbers have declined in many parts of Europe. Most of a shrike's prey is hunted using a 'wait-and-see' strategy from a perch with a good all-round view. When an insect passes by, up to 30m away, the shrike will dive on to it, seize it in its bill, and return to a bush with a characteristic, abrupt sweep upwards to the perch. In the breeding season an average of 34 sorties an hour has been noted. Extra prey is often impaled on thorns and barbed wire to guarantee a food supply.

Adult male has blue-grey crown and nape, chestnut back, blue-grey rump and black tail with white outer feathers. Underparts pinkish-white. Shows narrow, black band across forehead extending into broad, black mask through eye and across ear coverts. Flight feathers, tertials and greater coverts brown-black with chestnut margins. Bill black, distinctly hawk-like with hooked tip. Legs grey-black. Female has rufous-brown upperparts, reddish tail, pale-buff supercilium and cream underparts with brown crescent markings. Juvenile similar to female with close barring and black crescents on upperparts.

BIRD FACTS

VOICE Call harsh 'chack, chack'; song subdued, lengthy, with mimicry

LENGTH 17cm

WINGSPAN 24–27cm

WEIGHT 25–36g

HABITAT Sunny, open terrain with bushes and small trees for lookouts

NEST In a bush, about 1m up; loose cup of plant materials, with compact lining

EGGS 3–7; very variable ground colour with multicoloured spots at larger end

FOOD Mainly insects, especially beetles; some small birds and animals

At rest, frequently fans tail or swings it from side to side.

female

juvenile

male

male

DID YOU KNOW?

Now essentially extinct as breeding bird in Britain and northwest Europe, but may be seen on passage.

Small pied shrike with chestnut rear crown, nape and upper mantle in all adult plumages. Adult male has black forehead, which continues as broad, black patch through eye and ear coverts, and black wings and tail. Shows white outertail feathers, rump (conspicuous in flight), scapulars (forming two oval patches when perched) and underparts. Back grey. Bill short but strong, hook-tipped, black. Legs black. Female similar to male but colours duller and shows chestnut flecks in black forehead, white at base of bill, browner back and variable markings on breast. Juvenile has mostly grey or buff upperparts with pale whitish-buff scapulars, all barred with dark brown. Rump rufous and underparts dull white with many crescent-shaped bars. Whitish supercilium. Wings brownish-black with paler feather edges. Tail brownish-black with white edges.

Adult birds are easily recognised by their black, white and chestnut plumage.

WOODCHAT SHRIKE

juvenile

Lanius senator

THE WOODCHAT SHRIKE is a summer visitor to Europe, overwintering in Africa; it is a rare spring and autumn passage migrant to northwest Europe. Woodchat Shrikes prefer less open perches in trees than other shrikes, from which they drop or glide onto ground-prey or chase flying insects. As with other shrikes, indigestible food such as chitin, hair and bones is regurgitated in small, hard pellets. Woodchat Shrikes are usually paired by the time they arrive in Europe. Males have the best song of all European shrikes: a single bird may include imitations of seven to eight other species.

LEFT AND BELOW: female

BIRD FACTS

VOICE Call 'kiwick, kiwick'; song is a rich sustained warble with mimicry
LENGTH 18cm
WINGSPAN 26–28cm
WEIGHT 30–40g
HABITAT Woodland margins, old orchards, roadsides, maquis
NEST On horizontal tree branch below 5m; strong cup of leafy material, roots, lined
EGGS 5–6; greenish with brown and olive speckles at larger end
FOOD Mainly insects, especially beetles; some small vertebrates

---

adult male

MASKED SHRIKE

Lanius nubicus

THE MASKED SHRIKE has less of a hawk-like bill than other shrikes in Europe. It hunts more from the inside and lower branches of trees, and less from exposed perches; it does, however, employ a similar perch-and-pounce strategy. It is the most agile on the wing of the European shrikes; its actions are then like those of a flycatcher. Although its behaviour often seems to be skulking, the Masked Shrike shows little fear of people when feeding, and has even been known to follow people closely to catch grasshoppers disturbed as they walk through grass.

BIRD FACTS

VOICE Calls hard 'tsr' and reedy 'keer'; song is a vigorous warble
LENGTH 17–18cm
WINGSPAN 24–26.5cm
WEIGHT 20–25g
HABITAT Almost any wooded country, including citrus and olive groves
NEST In tree or dense, thorny bush, mostly above 5m; carefully made
EGGS 4–7; creamy or yellowish, blotched pale grey, speckled brown at larger end
FOOD Insects, especially beetles and grasshoppers; some small birds

DID YOU KNOW?

The Masked Shrike is a summer visitor to its breeding range, overwintering in Africa, south of the Sahara.

IDENTIFICATION

Small shrike, more slightly built than Woodchat Shrike, and with proportionately the longest tail of the region's shrikes. Male distinctively pied: generally black above and white below with reddish-orange flanks. Has white forehead and supercilium, white outertail feathers, white scapulars and broad, white bar across base of primaries. Bill slight, black. Legs black. Female similarly patterned to male but has greyer head, browner wings and less rusty underparts. Juvenile plumage scaly grey-brown; very hard to separate from young Woodchat Shrike but has longer tail and greyer upperparts.

adult male

GREAT GREY SHRIKE

Lanius excubitor

BIRD FACTS

VOICE Call harsh 'sheck, sheck'; song is a quiet, rambling warble with mimicry

LENGTH 24–25cm

WINGSPAN 30–34cm

WEIGHT 60–75g

HABITAT Open country with plenty of bushes and trees

NEST In a tree, usually 3–7m up; bulky nest of twigs and grasses, softly lined

EGGS 4–7; colour variable even in one clutch, heavily blotched with darker colours

FOOD Large insects, especially beetles; small reptiles, birds and mammals

POPULATIONS OF GREAT Grey Shrike are mainly resident from central Europe southwards, but northern birds are migrants, some travelling as far as southern Europe. The species is strongly territorial in summer and winter, and a wintering bird may defend a large territory of 20 hectares or more; the birds tend to return to the same territory in successive winters. Besides hunting by waiting on a perch, the Great Grey Shrike will also hunt like a sparrowhawk, dashing along a hedgerow. Prey on the ground is usually attacked and killed by blows from the bill, but a flying bird is seized with the shrike's feet and carried to the ground to be dispatched. Large prey is impaled on a thorn to be dismembered or cached for later.

IDENTIFICATION

The largest shrike. Northern European adult is tricoloured, with black face mask, wings and tail, grey upperparts and white underparts. Adult has white supercilium, white patch on scapulars, white-edged tail (which is long and graduated) and white, narrow bar across base of primaries. Bill quite long, hooked, black. Legs black. Sexes alike, but female has faint brown barring on breast in winter. Juvenile has brownish-grey upperparts and brownish-white underparts with faint, brown, wavy bars from throat to breast and flanks.

SOUTHERN GREY SHRIKE

Lanius meridionalis

BIRD FACTS

VOICE Call harsh 'sheck, sheck'; song is a quiet, rambling warble with mimicry

LENGTH 24–25cm

WINGSPAN 30–34cm

WEIGHT 50–70g

HABITAT Open country with plenty of bushes and trees

NEST In a tree; bulky nest of twigs and grasses

EGGS 4–7; heavily blotched with darker colours

FOOD Large insects, especially beetles; small reptiles, birds and mammals

SHRIKE CLASSIFICATION IS complex. Formerly treated as a race of Great Grey Shrike, Southern Grey has now been elevated to species status. Birds from southern France and the Iberian Peninsula are mainly resident and have pink-flushed underparts that distinguish them from Great Greys. Birds from North Africa and the Middle East are trickier to tell apart (having grey, not pink, underparts) and migratory Asian birds are considered by some to represent a separate species, Steppe Grey Shrike *L. pallidirostris*. The predatory habits of all birds are similar to those of Great Grey Shrike.

IDENTIFICATION

All adult birds have greyish upperparts (tinged buff in birds from Iberia and southern France) and black face mask, wings and uppertail. Note the narrow white supercilium and whitish throat. Underparts are flushed pinkish-buff in birds from Iberia and southern France, grey in birds from North Africa and Middle East and pale grey in birds from Asia; latter have more extensive white on wing than other Southern Greys or Great Grey. Bill is long, hooked and black and legs are black. Sexes are similar. Juvenile has grey elements of plumage replaced by brownish-grey and grubbier looking underparts; faint barring is often seen on underparts.

GREAT GREY SHRIKE *adult*

SOUTHERN GREY SHRIKE *adult*

GREAT GREY SHRIKE *adult*

GREAT GREY SHRIKE *1st winter*

male

LESSER GREY SHRIKE

Lanius minor

DESPITE ITS SUPERFICIAL similarity to the Great Grey and Southern Grey Shrikes, this species should not be confused for there is little overlap in their distribution. The entire population of this summer visitor overwinters in southern Africa. It is a rare visitor to northwest Europe in spring and autumn. The Lesser Grey is shorter than the Great Grey Shrike, but its proportionately longer wings allow it to chase prey rapidly, glide well, and hover and pounce like a Kestrel. It will use many perches in its breeding territory, each one having a good all-round view and clear sight of the ground, on which it can spot large insects up to 15m away. It rarely caches food.

BIRD FACTS

VOICE Calls variable; song is a soft, musical, chattering ramble with mimicry
LENGTH 20cm
WINGSPAN 32–34.5cm
WEIGHT 45–65g
HABITAT Warm, open country with scattered or grouped bushes and trees
NEST Usually about 5m up in small tree; well-made cup of plant materials, often unlined
EGGS 5–6; pale bluish-green with olive and lavender-grey spots
FOOD Almost wholly insects, especially beetles

IDENTIFICATION

Adult male has broad black band across forehead, over and through eyes and ear coverts. Rest of upperparts blue-grey. Male underparts white, with breast and flanks washed pink. Wings black with broad, white bar across base of primaries. Tail black with wide, white outer edges. Bill black, short and stubby. Legs brown. Female very similar to male but shows grey speckles on forehead, less pink below, and less blue above. Juvenile has black and white patterns of adult on wings and tail but underparts creamy white and upperparts brownish-grey with fine, close, darker brown bars. Face mask reduced to broad, black eyestripe. Bill grey.

Juvenile has creamy-white underparts and a much smaller face mask than adult.

female

ISABELLINE SHRIKE

Lanius isabellinus

Isabelline Shrikes breeds across central Asia and winter in East Africa, southern Arabia and northwest India. Formerly treated as a race of Red-backed Shrike it is now recognised as a species. Identifying immature birds is a problem. Look at the colour of the crown, nape and back (grey-brown in Isabelline but reddish-brown in Red-backed) and the presence or otherwise of scaly feathering on the upperparts (conspicuous in Red-backed but very faint or absent in Isabelline). Isabelline's reddish-brown tail always contrasts with its greyer back while the brown tail of a first-winter Red-backed Shrike is normally the same colour as the upperparts.

Distinctly pale shrike. Note contrast between grey-brown back and reddish-brown lower rump and tail. Adult male has mainly grey-buff upperparts and reddish-brown tail. Underparts whitish but with buff wash to breast and flanks. Head has black mask through eye. Female has more subdued plumage colours than male. First-winter bird (most likely in Europe) similar to female but scaly markings more extensive and present on face as well.

BIRD FACTS

VOICE Calls include a harsh 'tchak'
LENGTH 17–18cm
WINGSPAN 26–27cm
WEIGHT 28–32g
HABITAT Open grassy areas with scrub
NEST Does not breed in region
EGGS Does not breed in region
FOOD Mainly insects

adult

Immature, first-winter plumage.

JAY

Garrulus glandarius

WESTERN AND SOUTHERN European Jays are sedentary, but other populations are irruptive migrants when the acorn crop fails. Jays are commonest in deciduous woodlands but are often inconspicuous except for their loud, raucous screech. Acorns are the Jay's staple winter diet. They are picked from the tree and many are hidden in soil, turf and moss in September and October. One bird can carry up to nine acorns in its gullet and may bury around 4,000–5,000 during the autumn. Their visual memory is good and most acorns eaten in winter are from caches, even from those under snow.

A small crow, the most colourful in Europe. Sexes alike. Adult body pinkish-brown with white rump and undertail coverts, white forehead, crown streaked black, and broad, black moustachial stripe. Wings black with white at base of outermost secondaries forming short bar on closed wings; outer greater coverts, primary coverts and alula have shiny blue bars. Bill dark. Legs pale flesh-brown. Juvenile similar to adult, but plumage duller and crown less streaked.

BIRD FACTS

VOICE Loud, harsh, raucous calls, including 'skaaak skaaak' – far-carrying even in dense woodland

LENGTH 34–35cm

WINGSPAN 52–58cm

WEIGHT 150–180g

HABITAT Fairly dense cover of trees, usually broad-leaved, but also conifers

NEST In tree or bush, close to trunk; foundation of twigs, lined with roots, grass and hair

EGGS 5–7; pale green or blue or olive, speckled brown and olive all over

FOOD Invertebrates, especially beetles and larvae; fruits and seeds, especially acorns

Most likely to be seen flying away from observer, showing rounded wings and striking black and white pattern of rump and tail.

Juvenile has fewer streaks on crown and smaller moustache but closely resembles adult once fully grown.

SIBERIAN JAY
Perisoreus infaustus

THE SIBERIAN JAY is generally a sedentary resident and is very faithful to its chosen territory. It is a secretive bird in the breeding season and is hard to find at this time of the year. Nevertheless, it is not afraid of people and is quite prepared to approach houses or people for scraps, especially outside the breeding season. Siberian Jays pair for life and are territorial throughout the year. The winter feeding territory may be as large as 150 hectares, but the breeding territory is much smaller. The breeding season is early: eggs are regularly laid in early April when everywhere is covered with snow.

BIRD FACTS

VOICE Calls 'tchair', 'kook kook' and 'kij kij'; mewing like buzzard

LENGTH 30–31cm

WINGSPAN 40–46cm

WEIGHT 80–95g

HABITAT Natural, dense coniferous forest

NEST Close to conifer trunk; cup of lichen lined with feathers and hair, on base of twigs

EGGS 3–4; very pale bluish, spotted and blotched grey and olive brown

FOOD Omnivorous all year round, including carrion and scraps

IDENTIFICATION

Smallest member of the crow family in Europe, with proportionately longer tail than Jay and shorter, pointed bill. Adult has sooty-brown crown, nape and upper face. Dense pale-buff bristles at base of bill. Back and underparts brown-grey, becoming foxy red on rump, upper and lowertail coverts and belly. Wings sooty brown with foxy red coverts and bases to flight feathers. Bill and legs black. Sexes similar and juvenile similar to adult.

Red in plumage is diagnostic for a bird of this size.

DID YOU KNOW?

The nest lining of feathers and reindeer hair and the bird's fluffy plumage serve to insulate the Siberian Jay and its eggs against temperatures ranging from −20 to −30°C.

DID YOU KNOW?

Each Nutcracker caches some 100,000 seeds in autumn, and needs 27,000 to survive.

NUTCRACKER

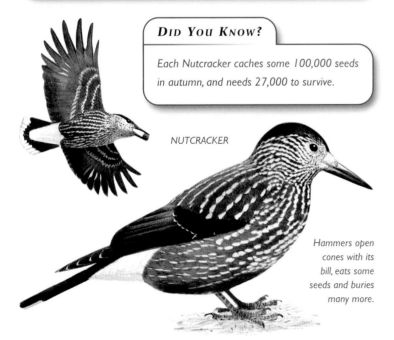

Hammers open cones with its bill, eats some seeds and buries many more.

NUTCRACKER
Nucifraga caryocatactes

THE NUTCRACKER'S DISTRIBUTION is dictated by its food supply; western birds are chiefly resident, but birds from further east are subject to irruptive movements when the conifer seed crop fails. Nutcrackers are secretive in the breeding season, which often begins when snow is still on the ground, but they do favour conspicuous perches in treetops. Irruptive migrants, searching for food, sometimes enter human settlements and become very tame. The survival of Nutcrackers in winter depends on their being able to cache enough food to last from September to May.

BIRD FACTS

VOICE Utters a far-carrying 'kraak'; spring call 'kerr-kerr'; alarm call 'churr'

LENGTH 32cm

WINGSPAN 52–58cm

WEIGHT 150–180g

HABITAT Cool forests of spruce or pine, in northern lowland and southern mountains

NEST Almost always in a conifer; compact, well made, well lined

EGGS 3–4; whitish to deep green, with near-invisible or dense olive and grey spots

FOOD Very dependent on conifer seeds and hazelnuts; some invertebrates

IDENTIFICATION

Sexes alike. Adult body plumage chocolate-brown with teardrop-shaped white spot at tip of most feathers. Forehead and crown very dark brown, nasal bristles and lores creamy white. Wings brown-black, glossed bluish-green, with white spots on lesser and median coverts. Tail brownish-black with blue-green gloss above and feathers tipped white, becoming progressively wider from centre outwards; tail appears mostly dark from above but mostly white from below. Undertail coverts white in contrast to black base of tail and brown body. Bill long and black. Legs black. Juvenile paler than adult, with less well-defined white spots.

MAGPIE

Pica pica

Just prior to the breeding season, Magpies often gather in sizeable groups.

ALTHOUGH THE MAGPIE is predominantly a bird of lightly wooded open country, it has now moved into suburban and urban habitats in several countries. It is widespread throughout Europe except in treeless areas. Adults may spend all their lives in the same territory but first-year birds disperse to find their own territories. The Magpie finds almost all its food on the ground, where it moves in bold steps and hops, with a raised tail. Magpies are gregarious, especially in early spring at the 'great Magpie marriage', a gathering that helps to establish pairs, which strongly defend their territory afterwards. Magpies roost communally; winter roosts may contain over 300 birds.

BIRD FACTS

VOICE Commonest call is a staccato chatter 'chacker chacker chacker chacker'

LENGTH 44–46cm

WINGSPAN 52–60cm

WEIGHT 190–240g

HABITAT Mainly a lowland bird in lightly wooded country

NEST Near top of tree; of twigs, with a roof, lined with mud then softer materials

EGGS 5–7; variable, blue or olive or greenish, heavily speckled olive-brown

FOOD Mostly invertebrates in summer; vertebrates and seeds in winter; also carrion and scraps

IDENTIFICATION

An unmistakable pied bird with a long, graduated tail. Sexes similar. Adult scapulars, belly and flanks white. Rest of plumage black with beautiful iridescence when seen closely in sunlight: purple on most of head and body, green on crown and scapulars, blue-green on wings, and brilliant bronze-green on tail with bands of several shades of purple near tip. Bill and legs black. Juvenile similar to adult but has shorter tail, duller plumage and less iridescence.

fledgling

adult

Long, graduated tail and black and white plumage distinctive even at a distance.

adult

adult

Flies with irregular short bursts of rapid wingbeats.

adult

adult

AZURE-WINGED
MAGPIE

ALPINE CHOUGH
Smart, glossy black plumage; has more Jackdaw-like silhouette than Chough.

adult

AZURE-WINGED MAGPIE
Cyanopica cyanus

IN THE BREEDING SEASON, April to June, the Azure-winged Magpie is secretive and keeps to tree cover much of the time; in a fleeting view it could be confused with the common Magpie. At other times it is noisy and bold. Outside the breeding season a flock, consisting of breeding pairs and their young, defends its territory, forages and roosts together. Pairs are faithful, but in the breeding season non-breeding members of the flock help breeding pairs build their nest and care for their young.

IDENTIFICATION

Small, elegant, long-tailed crow. Adult has forehead, crown and nape velvet black to a line below the eye. Back, rump and uppertail coverts grey-brown. Underparts off-white, with pale tinge of ashy colours on flanks and undertail coverts. Wings azure blue, with inner webs of tertials, greater coverts and primaries black. Tail noticeably graduated, blue above, dark grey below. Bill and legs black. Juvenile similar to adult but plumage duller.

BIRD FACTS

VOICE Main call is a husky whistling 'zhreee', rising at end

LENGTH 34–35cm (nearly half is tail)

WINGSPAN 38–40cm

WEIGHT 70–75g

HABITAT Groups of trees, cork oak and olive groves, pine and eucalyptus plantations

NEST In fork, near the tree crown; of twigs, with mud cup, soft-lined 1cm thick

EGGS 5–7; pale cream to brownish-olive, with sparse brown spots

FOOD Invertebrates, especially beetles, but will scavenge almost anything

adult

ALPINE CHOUGH
Pyrrhocorax graculus

ALPINE CHOUGHS ARE masters of the air. They fly fast and with great skill, manoeuvring near cliffs and in fierce air currents. Their broad, fingered wings and often-fanned tails enable them to twist and turn, spiral and dive with ease. In summer Alpine Choughs feed on the grassland above the tree-line, but in winter they come down to the valleys, into towns, or scavenge at ski resorts. The Alpine Chough is gregarious all year round. It is found in pairs, family parties, or winter flocks that may be as big as 300 birds. Flocks are very vocal throughout the year.

IDENTIFICATION

Adult has all-black plumage with a sheen: blue-green gloss, particularly on wings. Sexes alike. Bill pale yellow. Legs orange. May be distinguished from Chough by its yellow, shorter bill, duller plumage, longer tail, only four separated primaries in flight and straight leading edge to the wings. Juvenile similar to adult.

A small flock in aerial display, calling the diagnostic 'chree', is a memorable sight.

BIRD FACTS

VOICE Calls include a frequent 'chirrish'; in chorus often utters a piercing 'chree'

LENGTH 38cm

WINGSPAN 75–85cm

WEIGHT 190–240g

HABITAT Strictly montane, ranging from tree-line to snow-line

NEST On ledge, crevice in cave, cliff, tunnel, building; bulky mass of twigs, with soft lining

EGGS 3–5; whitish, profusely marked with shades of brown

FOOD Insects from spring to autumn; berries and human scraps in winter

CHOUGH

Pyrrhocorax pyrrhocorax

THE CHOUGH HAS a very fragmented distribution in Europe: it nests in Switzerland as high as 1,500m but is also found on sea cliffs in Britain and Ireland. It is sedentary and rarely leaves its breeding areas. In Britain and elsewhere the Chough has been in decline for many years, probably because of the destruction of traditionally grazed grassland, which supported the Choughs' summer food supply of ants. These and other insects are probed for in the turf using the long bill. Choughs are masterful fliers: they can glide, soar on thermals and perform aerial manoeuvres, all to the accompaniment of many contact calls.

BIRD FACTS

VOICE Common call is a yelping 'cheeow' or 'kiaa'

LENGTH 39–40cm

WINGSPAN 73–90cm

WEIGHT 230–350g

HABITAT Inland crags or coastal cliffs (for nesting) near grassy swards (for feeding)

NEST In crevice in cliff or on ledge in cave; large pile of twigs, lined with wool

EGGS 3–5; very pale buff or green, with small olive and green markings all over

FOOD Soil-living invertebrates; grain; berries in winter

adult

Adult plumage all black; most parts have a blue gloss, although tail, tail coverts and flight feathers have a greener iridescence. Bill red and downcurved. Sexes alike. Juvenile duller than adult, with shorter, orangey bill. Adult Chough separable from adult Alpine Chough by length of bill, shorter tail, about as long as primary tips when bird is standing, five to six primary 'fingers' (in flight), and distinct call.

adult

Glossy plumage is entirely black.

DID YOU KNOW?

Choughs are gregarious even in the breeding season, and small flocks can be seen flying along the cliffs.

adult

DID YOU KNOW?

When a perched bird gives a call it often conspicuously flips its wings and tail to help advertise its presence.

adult

adult

JACKDAW
Corvus monedula

JACKDAWS TEND TO move more outside the breeding season than other members of the crow family and vacate cold, bleak uplands for lowlands in the west. The species has declined in many parts of Europe where its habitat requirements of nest sites near grass grazed by sheep or cattle are poorly met. Jackdaws are very gregarious: they feed together in pairs or small flocks, roost communally at traditional sites (winter flocks may number many hundreds or even thousands), and nest in small colonies. Jackdaws often associate with Rooks on feeding grounds and are given to sudden 'dreads' when the whole flock will fly up in a panic, then break up, circle and drift down again to feed. Jackdaws are wary in the countryside, but quite approachable in towns and villages.

DID YOU KNOW?

The Jackdaw will choose almost any nest site so long as it is a hole – from sea cliffs to old mine shafts and church towers.

IDENTIFICATION

Sexes alike. At a distance adult appears black with grey nape and ear coverts. Close views reveal purple gloss on black crown, some blue gloss on wings and back, and greyish cast on underparts. Eyes of adult pale grey, very distinctive. Bill short and black. Legs black. Juvenile duller than adult, grey patch less contrasting; eyes brown, taking a year to become grey.

juvenile

One of the smallest members of the crow family in Europe.

adult

adult

adult

RAVEN

Corvus corax

BIRD FACTS

VOICE Typical call
is a deep, resonant
'karronk'; also utters
a deep 'prruk' and
'toc-toc-toc'

LENGTH 64cm

WINGSPAN 130–150cm

WEIGHT 900–1,400g

HABITAT From coast
to 3,000m, but not
dense forest, dense
settlement or
cultivation

NEST Usually high
in a tree or on a cliff
ledge; huge pile of
sticks with cup of
wool and hair

EGGS 4–6; light blue
to blue-green, variable
olive and dark-brown
markings

FOOD Much carrion;
seeds and fruit;
scavenges at
settlements;
kills animals
and birds

IN EUROPE RAVENS occur where they can
find eyrie-style nest sites overlooking
a large foraging area. Most Ravens are
sedentary; some may disperse southwards in winter. In flight, overhead, the
Raven's cruciform shape is distinctive.
Ravens are at their most active at the
start of the breeding season (from February onwards), when pairs indulge in
spectacular aerial displays of dives,
tumbles and rolls. Ravens pair for life,
and although solitary in the breeding
season, flocks of 50 to 60 are frequent
at winter roosts and where there are plentiful supplies of food. Nests are often reused, may be very
large, and are built in layers from a base of twigs
and small branches to a cup of wool and hair.

IDENTIFICATION

The largest member of the crow family, one-
third bigger than Rook and Crow, and as big as
a Buzzard. Sexes similar. All-black, iridescent
plumage; purple-blue on wings, reddish-purple
on tail. Shaggy throat feathers and wedge shape
to tip of tail are distinctive. Black bill is massive,
especially deep upper mandible, markedly
curved towards the tip. Legs black. Juvenile
similar to adult.

adult

*Long throat feathers give
bearded appearance; this
and heavy bill help distinguish
Raven from Carrion Crow.*

*A pair defends a large territory of between 7 and 67sq km
(depending on food supply), which may contain two to
seven nest sites that are used irregularly in rotation.*

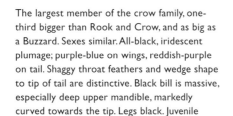

adult

adult

*Large, entirely black crow with
resonant, deep 'prruk, prruk' call.*

DID YOU KNOW?

The Raven's principal food is
carrion, but it will also eat live
small animals and seeds and fruit.

CARRION CROW

Corvus corone

UNTIL RELATIVELY RECENTLY, Carrion and Hooded Crows were considered to be essentially the same species, treated as subspecies separated by geographical range. In 2002 they were 'split' and elevated to separate species status. The all-black Carrion Crow is found in west and northwest Europe. Less gregarious than its cousin the Rook, with which it could conceivably be confused, the Carrion Crow sometimes gathers in flocks for springtime displays and winter roosts, as well as at good food sources such as rubbish tips. Carrion Crows remain paired throughout the year and occupy a range of around 50 hectares.

IDENTIFICATION

Has all-black plumage, bill and legs. Could be confused with juvenile Rook, which lacks adult Rook's whitish face. But note that species' proportionally longer bill. Sexes are similar and juvenile body plumage is brownish-black.

BIRD FACTS

VOICE Call is an abrupt 'kawr', often three together

LENGTH 45–47cm

WINGSPAN 90–100cm

WEIGHT 450–600g

HABITAT Farmland and open country with scattered trees

NEST High in a tree, or a bush if no trees available; substantial nest of twigs with soft lining

EGGS 3–6; light blue or green, variably spotted with olive and brown

FOOD Omnivorous; many invertebrates, much cereal grain, carrion, eggs and nestlings

CARRION CROW can be confused with Rook and Raven, although latter is much bigger, has long throat feathers and noticeably wedge-shaped tail.

Powerful, dagger-like bill can tear flesh with ease.

HOODED CROW

Corvus cornix

THE HOODED CROW is the northern and eastern counterpart of the Carrion Crow, its range extending to Ireland and northern Scotland. Over the years, the Hooded Crow's range has retreated northwards as the Carrion Crow's distribution has expanded. Where the two species overlap (the zone is relatively small) then they interbreed occasionally. Hybrids have intermediate plumage patterns. In many parts of their range, particularly in the north and northwest, Hooded Crows are often easiest to see on coasts, especially in winter. Here, they feed on the seashore and along the strandline.

IDENTIFICATION

Has ashy grey back of neck, mantle, back rump, scapulars, lower breast, belly, flanks, axillaries and undertail coverts. Rest of plumage is black. Bill and legs are black. Both sexes are alike. Juvenile is similar to adult but grey elements of plumage have buffish tinge.

BIRD FACTS

VOICE Call is an abrupt 'kawr', often three together

LENGTH 45–47cm

WINGSPAN 90–100cm

WEIGHT 450–600g

HABITAT Open country, moors and coasts, especially in winter

NEST High in a tree, or a bush or crag if no trees available; substantial nest of twigs with soft lining

EGGS 3–6; light blue or green, variably spotted with olive and brown

FOOD Omnivorous; many invertebrates, much cereal grain, carrion, eggs and nestlings

HOODED CROW has grey back and undersides and grey on innerwing.

LEFT AND RIGHT:
HOODED CROW

ROOK

Corvus frugilegus

Face and chin are pale grey and unfeathered.

BIRD FACTS

VOICE Commonest call is a prolonged 'kaah'

LENGTH 44–46cm

WINGSPAN 81–99cm

WEIGHT 400–500g

HABITAT Wherever tall trees border agricultural land

NEST Colonial; in topmost branches of tree; base of twigs and mud, with soft lining

EGGS 2–6; light blue or green, with specks and blotches of shades of olive

FOOD Especially earthworms and beetles (from pasture) and cereal seed (from arable land)

MANY ROOK POPULATIONS, such as those in Britain and France, are resident; elsewhere Rooks are migrants, especially in cold winters. The Rook is gregarious at all times; after the breeding season family groups join other families for feeding, roosting and migrating. They migrate by day, following valleys and coasts. Winter roosts may be huge, often of thousands of birds. Rooks nest colonially, close together in a 'rookery'. As populations in western Europe have declined, so have the number of nests per colony, but there are still large rookeries across the range; the biggest ever known was around 16,000 nests in Hungary.

IDENTIFICATION

Adult all black except for whitish-grey skin around base of bill, from lower forehead, behind the gape, and on upper throat. Black is iridescent in sunlight with shades of greenish- and reddish-purple. Separable from Carrion Crow by whitish face, steep forehead, narrower bill, more fingered wingtips in flight, round-tipped tail, glossier plumage and loose thigh feathers. Juvenile has black nasal bristles and no bare grey skin.

adult

adult

juvenile

Long, loose thigh feathers give 'baggy trousers' effect.

adult

adult

DID YOU KNOW?

Noise and activity at the rookery peak in early spring, as birds quarrel over territory and males display.

Adult male has bright-yellow head and body, black wings and tail. Head marked by black lores. Black-centred tail has yellow corners. Wings black with short yellow bar across tips of primary coverts. Eye crimson. Bill strong, dark pink. Legs dark grey. Female has yellowish-green body, greenish-brown wings and brownish-black tail with yellow corners. Underparts palest on chin to upper-breast; all underparts streaked dull brown. First-year male is streaked and has bright-yellow plumage replaced by dull olive-yellow. Some mature females appear almost as yellow as male but lores always grey. Juvenile like female but has dark-brown eye and slate-grey bill; takes two years to attain adult plumage.

GOLDEN ORIOLE

Oriolus oriolus

GOLDEN ORIOLES ARE summer visitors to Europe, overwintering in sub-Saharan Africa. Orioles are secretive, arboreal birds and although not abundant, are well known because of the male's far-carrying song. Although the male is unmistakable the female may be confused with the Green Woodpecker, but that is a heavier bird with a dark bill. The Golden Oriole's nest may take the female 6 to 12 days to build on her own. A hammock of plant fibres, tied by 20–40cm long loops of grass to the twigs, first looks like a net, but is filled in with more grasses, feathers, down and wool. It is so well made that it may last, be repaired and used the following year.

DID YOU KNOW?

The Golden Oriole's French name, loriot, well describes its 'lo-lo-loriot' song.

BIRD FACTS

VOICE Call cat-like; alarm rattle; song is a melodious, flute-like whistle

LENGTH 24cm

WINGSPAN 44–47cm

WEIGHT 55–80g

HABITAT Tree-loving but not a forest bird; parks, large gardens, copses, open woods

NEST Slung like a hammock from a fork in a tree

EGGS 3–4; white or cream, with scattered black spots

FOOD Insects, especially large larvae; berries and fruits from late summer onwards

adult female

adult male

adult female

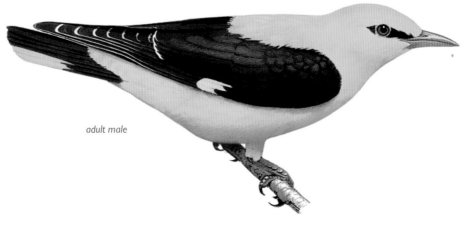

adult male

STARLING

Sturnus vulgaris

BIRD FACTS

VOICE Calls include characteristic 'tsiew', 'tcherr'; song is a lively medley of whistles, gurgles and mimicry

LENGTH 21.5cm

WINGSPAN 37–42cm

WEIGHT 75–85g

HABITAT Almost anywhere; very ready to live with man; needs holes to nest in, open ground to feed on

NEST Hole in a tree, cliff, building or nest box; bulky, grassy base

EGGS 5–7; shades of pale blue

FOOD Mostly insects and larvae in breeding season; also seeds, fruit, nectar

Breeding-plumage male is very glossy and colourful, and beak has blue base.

Song is long, unmusical mixture of trills and rattles, delivered with great energy; many Starlings mimic other birds and mechanical sounds.

STARLINGS FROM NORTHWEST and central Europe are mostly resident, and their numbers are swollen in winter by visitors from northeastern and eastern Europe. The Starling is gregarious throughout the year. Winter roosts in evergreens, reedbeds or on buildings commonly comprise 100,000 or more birds, and they nest in loose colonies. Starlings generally have a direct flight, with a silhouette like a delta-winged fighter, but in summer many will twist and turn high in the sky to catch flying ants. A colony or winter feeding group will suddenly rise in a tight flock, giving a distinctive predator alarm, 'chip chip chip', to mob a raptor.

spring male

IDENTIFICATION

Male in winter has glossy black plumage, with buff tips to feathers of upperparts, buff edges to wing feathers and white tips to feathers of underparts from throat to belly. Bill grey-brown with yellow base. Legs reddish-brown. Eyes brown. Male in summer loses buff and white feather tips, and due to wear the bird looks darker and very glossy, with green, purple, bronze and blue iridescence. Lemon-yellow bill. Female has broader spots in winter than male, keeps some spots all year and is less glossy. Bill has pinkish base in breeding season, eye has a paler ring on the iris. Juvenile looks like a different species with mouse-brown plumage, darker above than below. Shows whitish chin and grey-brown bill. Moults in autumn and attains first-winter plumage similar to adult; bill black.

winter adult

After autumn moult, adult has fresh, creamy tips to body feathers, while wing feathers are edged orange-brown.

winter flock

LEFT AND BELOW: winter adult

Feeding parties on grass have a bustling, jaunty walk and are often quarrelsome.

juvenile

immature, first autumn

immature, first winter

adult, summer

adult, winter

SPOTLESS STARLING

Sturnus unicolor

IN THE WESTERN Mediterranean this starling fills the same niche as its commoner relative, feeding and breeding in a wide variety of habitats, including inner cities. Spotless Starlings commonly feed in similar places to the Starling, and have a similar feeding method, probing into the ground with an open bill to find invertebrates. They are wary at all times, but are more approachable in villages or towns, especially in winter. In Spain, where it is common and increasing in numbers, the Spotless Starling prefers open woodland with easy access to short grass on which to forage and is often found near cattle all the year round.

Winter bird shows
pale tips to
feathers.

Summer adult
has bearded
appearance.

BELOW: summer male

IDENTIFICATION

Male in summer has all-black plumage, glossed purple (not green as in Starling and without pale edges to wing feathers). Feathers of throat are long and bird looks bearded (more so than Starling). Bill pale yellow with bluish-black base. Legs pale pink. In early winter, shows pale tips to feathers on head, mantle and underparts; bill dark. Female similar to male but less glossy; has small, white spots on fresh undertail coverts and pale-yellow margins to larger wing feathers. Juvenile similar to, but darker than, juvenile Starling. First-winters have pale tips to body feathers.

BIRD FACTS

VOICE Similar to Starling, but song louder, especially introductory whistles
LENGTH 21–23cm
WINGSPAN 38–42cm
WEIGHT 80–90g
HABITAT Open woodland, near short grass for foraging; fields and marshes in winter
NEST In hole in tree, building or other nest; foundation of grass and twigs, soft lining
EGGS 4–5; pale blue
FOOD Invertebrates in spring and summer; seeds and fruit at other times

ROSE-COLOURED STARLING

summer
male

Sturnus roseus

THE ROSE-COLOURED STARLING breeds across central Asia, and erratically in Greece, Bulgaria, the former Yugoslavia and the former Czechoslovakia; it mostly overwinters in India. After breeding but before autumn migration, the birds form flocks that wander in search of food. Vagrants seen in northwestern and western Europe mostly occur at this time and are often juveniles; they often spend weeks visiting garden bird feeders with Starlings.

IDENTIFICATION

Adult male's head, crest, neck and upper breast dark with purple sheen. Wings black with greenish sheen and tail and undertail coverts black. Mantle, back, lower breast and belly pink. Pink elements of plumage appear grubby in winter and black lacks sheen. Bill and legs pink. Female like male but plumage duller at all times. Juvenile has essentially pale sandy brown plumage, darkest on wings and tail. Bill yellow and legs pinkish-brown.

BIRD FACTS

VOICE Calls include a thin 'kri'; song varied and twittering
LENGTH 21cm
WINGSPAN 38–40cm
WEIGHT 70–80g
HABITAT Typically arid grassland and semi-desert
NEST Nests colonially in holes in stony cliffs and buildings
EGGS 3–6, pale blue
FOOD Mainly insects but also berries and fruits

juvenile

HOUSE SPARROW

Passer domesticus

male

THE HOUSE SPARROW is widespread and common throughout Europe, although it is almost entirely restricted to habitats close to human habitation. It is generally a sedentary resident, juveniles rarely wandering more than a few kilometres. Birds rapidly become very tame around outlets where food is provided; at open-air cafés they will visit occupied tables and even perch on customers to take food. Most pair for life, and will use a good nest site several years running. This species hybridises with the Spanish Sparrow round the Mediterranean, and stable hybrid populations of 'Italian Sparrows' occur in Italy.

BIRD FACTS

VOICE Calls include familiar 'cheep' or 'chirrp'; song is a succession of chirps

LENGTH 14–15cm

WINGSPAN 24cm

WEIGHT 28–32g

HABITAT Almost invariably associated with human habitation

NEST In a hole, mostly in a man-made structure; loosely made of grass, with softer lining

EGGS 3–5; white or faintly greyish, variably marked in shades of grey and brown

FOOD Principally seeds; household scraps; animal feed; young fed on invertebrates

IDENTIFICATION

Male warm brown above and greyish below, with grey crown, black eyestripe, black bib with broken bottom edge, dull-white cheeks, grey rump, black-brown, square-ended tail and white wingbar. Bill black in breeding season, grey at other times. Legs pink or brown. Female lacks strong plumage pattern. At a distance appears dull brown above and dingy white below. Shows broad, pale-buff supercilium and lighter brown or buff edges to wing feathers. Bill grey, legs pink. Juvenile similar to female.

DID YOU KNOW?

House Sparrows are gregarious, nesting in loose colonies and forming flocks for roosting, feeding and dust-bathing.

female

Adopts perky stance when perched, with chest puffed and tail cocked.

female

male

male

Drab female (BELOW) and juvenile have distinctive pale band over eye.

TREE SPARROW

Passer montanus

In flight, shorter tail and faster flight action distinguish Tree Sparrow from House Sparrow.

TREE SPARROW

IN EUROPE THE Tree Sparrow is much less associated with settlements than its commoner relative, the House Sparrow, and is more shy and retiring. It is particularly fond of lightly wooded farmland, but is an urban bird in the Far East where it is not in competition with the House Sparrow. The Tree Sparrow is a sociable species that forages in flocks with finches and buntings in winter, and in summer breeds in loose colonies. Four or five pairs may nest in the foundations of a heron's or crow's nest. Local populations can be increased by the provision of nest boxes.

IDENTIFICATION

Smaller and more trim than House Sparrow. Sexes alike. Adult distinguished from male House Sparrow by rich, dark-chestnut crown and nape, and whiter cheeks, which almost form a white collar contrasting noticeably with crown and black bib (smaller than House Sparrow's); the cheek shows a conspicuous black patch below and behind the eye. Back and rump yellowish-brown. Tail dark brown. Wings show two pale wingbars. Underparts whitish, palest on belly, and washed buff on flanks. Bill black. Legs pale brown. Juvenile as adult but duller.

BIRD FACTS

VOICE Distinctive, repeated 'chet' or 'teck' is characteristic of birds in flight

LENGTH 14cm

WINGSPAN 20–22cm

WEIGHT 20–24g

HABITAT Small woods, roadside trees, ivy-covered cliffs, parks, wooded suburbs

NEST In hole in tree, earth bank or building; untidy, of plant materials, softly lined

EGGS 4–6; white or pale grey, heavily marked, usually with dark brown

FOOD Seeds and invertebrates, mostly taken on the ground

TREE SPARROW
Unlike House Sparrows, male and female Tree Sparrows share incubation of the eggs.

ROCK SPARROW

Petronia petronia

ROCK SPARROWS ARE sociable birds and form flocks of up to several hundred from late summer to spring. They readily associate with foraging finches, feeding on the ground on seeds throughout the year, on berries in autumn, and on caterpillars and other invertebrates in the breeding season. This is a nervous species and is often the first in a mixed flock to fly up in alarm, though it can become fairly tame in the breeding season. Rock Sparrows generally breed in small, loose colonies, sometimes quite close together, such as in a big cave with many crevices. The males defend a small territory and, once mated, many attempt to get a second mate.

IDENTIFICATION

Adult is superficially like female House Sparrow, but has longer wings, shorter tail and heavier bill. Upperparts and wings dusty brown, heavily streaked with brown-black. Underparts buffish-white, streaked and spotted brown especially on flanks and undertail coverts. Tail dark brown with white terminal spots, which show clearly in flight. Both sexes have distinctive striped head pattern: creamy coloured central crown stripe, dark-brown lateral crown stripes, broad off-white supercilium and dusky ear coverts. Bill large, deep and greyish. Legs brownish-yellow. In spring male has bright-yellow patch on upper breast. Sexes otherwise similar. Juvenile similar to adult female.

BIRD FACTS

VOICE Characteristic call is a nasal 'pey-ee'; song comprises a repetition of calls

LENGTH 14cm

WINGSPAN 28–32cm

WEIGHT 30–35g

HABITAT Treeless terrain with sparse vegetation; sometimes vineyards, olive groves

NEST In a natural hole, a building, in another species' nest hole; untidy, like House Sparrow

EGGS 5–6; white, variably blotched and spotted brown and grey

FOOD Mostly seeds taken on the ground, berries in autumn; feeds young on caterpillars

ROCK SPARROW
Runs around on ground like a pipit rather than hopping and jumping like a House Sparrow.

SPANISH SPARROW

male

Passer hispaniolensis

SPANISH SPARROWS BREED colonially, and outside the breeding season the species is very gregarious. In Spain, in autumn, flocks of up to 4,000 form to forage for food and to roost. Some breeding colonies are huge and closely packed; in these colonies a pair's territory is simply the immediate area around the nest. In southern areas, where the birds are sedentary, the same site may be used every year. Spanish Sparrows often build their nests into those of White Storks, raptors and Crows.

INSET RIGHT: female;
BELOW RIGHT: males

male

BIRD FACTS

VOICE Call distinct, contralto 'chup'; song similar to House Sparrow's but richer

LENGTH 15cm

WINGSPAN 23–26cm

WEIGHT 25–30g

HABITAT Cultivated land, settlements; also arid regions, and woods and thickets

NEST Free-standing on a branch fork; untidy, domed, of grass and straw, with finer lining

EGGS 4–6; white or faintly tinted blue or green, speckled in shades of grey

FOOD Seeds and invertebrates, taken mainly from the ground

IDENTIFICATION

Male has chestnut crown, nape and sides of neck. Black bib extends to unique arrowhead streaks on breast and flanks. White cheeks very noticeable. Short, white, broken supercilium. Mantle and rump grey. Wings brown with two pale wingbars, and tail dark brown. Bill black in breeding season, paler at other times. Legs light brown. Female and juvenile dull brown and dingy white below; almost indistinguishable from equivalent plumages of House Sparrow.

SNOW FINCH

Montifringilla nivalis

ALTHOUGH SUPERFICIALLY SIMILAR to the Snow Bunting, the Snow Finch is not closely related to this species, and has a different geographical range. During the summer months, Snow Finches are found between 2,000m and nearly 3,000m; in winter, however, they may be forced to descend to lower levels in adjacent valleys. Snow Finches are often found in the vicinity of ski-lifts and paths, where they are usually completely tolerant of human presence, on occasion even searching for crumbs; small flocks sometimes aggregate during the winter months. When seen closely, their shuffling and hopping gait recalls that of both Chaffinches and House Sparrows.

DID YOU KNOW?

Snow Finches are birds of mountaintops and Alpine slopes; in Europe they are found in the Pyrenees, Alps and more locally in the Italian Abruzzi Mountains and in the Balkans.

BIRD FACTS

VOICE Sparrow-like song includes Chaffinch-like 'pink'

LENGTH 17cm

WINGSPAN 34–38cm

WEIGHT 35–40g

HABITAT Bare, stony sites, above the tree-line in summer

NEST Grassy nest built in rock crevice

EGGS 4–5; white

FOOD Seeds and invertebrates

IDENTIFICATION

Finch-like member of the sparrow family with considerable amount of white in plumage. Adult has blue-grey head, white underparts and brown mantle. Wings white with black tips, extremely striking in flight. Tail white with black central bar. Male has black bib and dark bill in summer but has yellow bill and loses bib in winter. Female similar to winter male. Juvenile similar to winter male but with dull bill.

Similar to Snow Bunting, but has a quite different range.

male

adult

GOLDFINCH
Carduelis carduelis

NORTHERN GOLDFINCH POPULATIONS are migratory, wintering within the species' breeding range, especially round the Mediterranean. A serious decline in numbers in the 1980s in parts of its range was probably caused by the increasing scarcity of weed seeds, but some recovery has taken place since. Generally the Goldfinch feeds on seeds taken directly from the plant, and birds can often be seen acrobatically extracting thistle seeds or swinging on alder or birch catkins: the relatively long, pointed bill acts like a pair of tweezers. Goldfinches are gregarious outside the breeding season, forming nomadic flocks.

IDENTIFICATION

Adult unmistakable with golden-yellow panel along centre of black wing and head patterned vertically in bands; red from bill to eye, white behind eye, black crown and sides of neck. Sexes similar. Mantle, back, breast band and flanks pale rufous, rump whitish. Tail black. White spots to tips of flight and tail feathers. Bill noticeably pointed, pinkish with dark tip. Legs pale flesh. Juvenile reveals yellow on wings in flight but head and body plumage greyish-brown, spotted and streaked brown until autumn moult.

LEFT: *Young birds lack the adult face pattern on leaving the nest, but acquire it within two months.*

BIRD FACTS

VOICE Call a liquid 'tswitt-witt-witt'; song a characteristic, cheerful tinkling

LENGTH 12cm

WINGSPAN 21–25.5cm

WEIGHT 14–19g

HABITAT Orchards, parks, gardens, scrub, thickets, rough grassland, overgrown sites

NEST Well hidden in outermost twigs of tree; very neat cup of moss and grass, thickly lined

EGGS 4–6; very pale bluish-white, spotted and scrawled reddish or purplish

FOOD Small seeds, especially daisies, dandelions, groundsel, thistles, teasel, burdock

> ### DID YOU KNOW?
>
> *The breeding territory is small, just around the nest, and the pair forages for food up to a kilometre away.*

LEFT: *During the winter months especially, when alternative sources of food are in short supply, teasel seeds are extremely important for Goldfinches.*

CHAFFINCH

Fringilla coelebs

THE CHAFFINCH IS one of the commonest and
most widespread of all birds in western Europe,
breeding wherever there are bushes or trees. Most
birds in northwest Europe are rather sedentary;
other populations are migratory, moving
generally southwest. Spring migration
is in March and April, when flocks
of winter visitors may gather on
farmland where resident males
are already singing and defending
territory. The Chaffinch is gregarious
outside the breeding season. Although
a Chaffinch's song has a generally recognisable form, each male in fact has up to
six song-types; he sings a series of one type
before going on to another.

Male's contrasting plumage
highlighted by pink breast.

male

female

male

IDENTIFICATION

Male very distinctive, with pink face, breast
and belly. Crown, nape, upper mantle blue-
grey; lower mantle chestnut brown.
Greenish rump, white undertail coverts
and black forehead. Tail black with white
outer feathers. Wings black with pale
fringes to flight feathers; shows broad,
white wingbar across tips of greater
coverts, and long, deep, white blaze from
shoulder to scapulars on lesser and
median coverts. Bill blue in breeding
season but dull pinkish-grey at other times.
Legs grey or brown. Female plumage pale
olive-brown above and greyish-white
below; has same diagnostic tail and wing
patterns as male. Bill pinkish-grey and legs
reddish-brown. Juvenile similar to female.

male

DID YOU KNOW?

In continental flocks one sex often
predominates, but flocks of British birds
generally have an equal sex ratio.

female

juvenile

male, September

male, November

male, March

male, May

winter male

In flight, white rump is key identifying feature.

Breeding male's black head and bright breast unmistakable.

summer male

winter male

BRAMBLING
Fringilla montifringilla

IN AUTUMN ALL European Bramblings eventually migrate south and west, but many birds remain in the northeast of their wintering range as long as possible while good stocks of beech-mast last. When these fail they move on, often in huge numbers: several million birds may reach western Europe in hard winters. In winter, at the edge of its range, flocks may contain between a few dozen and several hundred birds, but in central European beech woods there may be hundreds of thousands. In the breeding season, Bramblings forage mainly in trees, feeding on caterpillars. They often associate with Chaffinches and will sometimes visit garden feeding stations.

BIRD FACTS

VOICE Call a wheezy 'tsweep'; song a monotonous, repeated 'dwee'
LENGTH 14cm
WINGSPAN 25–26cm
WEIGHT 20–28g
HABITAT Birch and mixed forest; woodland, and open ground in winter
NEST High in a tree; cup of moss, lichen and grass; lined with feathers, hair and fur
EGGS 5–7; variable, greenish, blue, olive with few or many rusty spots
FOOD Summer diet includes insects as well as seeds; winter diet is mainly seeds

IDENTIFICATION

Identified at all times by buffish-orange breast and shoulder, diagnostic long, white rump and black, slightly forked tail. Breeding male has glossy black head and mantle, orange throat, breast and shoulders; rest of underparts white. Wings black with narrow white bar across tips of greater coverts and white patch below orange shoulder. Bill blue-black. Legs brownish-flesh. In winter, male's head and mantle mottled with brown; bill yellowish with black tip. Female has underparts and wing pattern of male but in washed-out colours. Head has dark-brown crown, greyish nape with brown lateral stripes, buff supercilium and ear-coverts, whitish chin and throat. Bill grey in summer, blue-black in winter. Juvenile as female.

winter female

DID YOU KNOW?

During the winter months, pale tips to feathers acquired in autumn moult gradually wear away and a Brambling's plumage becomes smarter as the winter continues.

winter male

GREENFINCH

Carduelis chloris

THE GREENFINCH IS widespread in Europe from close to the Arctic Circle to the Mediterranean. It is mainly a lowland species closely allied to its habitat of trees and open ground, on which it forages for seeds. Increasingly it has learned to live with man in towns and around farms, especially where cereals and seeds of plants of the cabbage family are found. Most Greenfinches winter southwest of their breeding range. Birds from northwest Europe are partial migrants, tending to move to milder lowland and coastal districts. Greenfinches defend only a small area around the nest, often in neighbourhood groups of four to six pairs, and travel up to 3km to find food. Unlike Chaffinches, Greenfinches even feed their young on seeds. A striking feature of spring and summer is the male Greenfinch's erratic, circular song-flight on slow wingbeats that do not seem strong enough to keep him airborne. At a bird table, dominant birds will get most of the food, quarrels are frequent and birds low down the pecking order will wait or fly off to find other food. Garden fruits like rose-hips and cotoneaster are nibbled to get the seeds, leaving the broken flesh on the plant.

Male is striking olive-green and yellow, darker olive above and yellower below. Tail and flight feathers brown-black, with brilliant yellow fringes to primaries (forming bold patch on bottom edge of folded wing), and brilliant yellow on bases of outer four pairs of tail feathers. Underwing yellow. Yellow patterns very noticeable in flight. Tail short, distinctly forked. Bill stout, conical, pale flesh. Legs pale flesh. Female similar to male but duller overall, with indistinct streaks on crown and mantle. Juvenile even duller than female and more distinctly streaked above and below.

BIRD FACTS

VOICE Call loud nasal 'tsweee'; flight call rapid twitter; song strong, twittering trill

LENGTH 15 cm

WINGSPAN 25–27cm

WEIGHT 25–30g

HABITAT Densely leafed trees in woodland edge, orchards, parks, graveyards, gardens

NEST In fork of dense bush or small tree; bulky cup of grass, moss and twigs; soft lining

EGGS 4–6; greyish- or bluish-white, sparsely spotted red, purple, black

FOOD Fairly large seeds of wide variety of plants, taken on bush or ground

adult male

adult female

adult female

juvenile

DID YOU KNOW?

Winter flocks will stay at a food source until it is exhausted.

Adult male has brighter colouring than adult female.

female

DID YOU KNOW?

Winter flocks are nomadic, and ringing has shown that many birds overwinter in different areas of Europe in successive years, although a few may be faithful to a previously used site.

BELOW: winter female

SISKIN

Carduelis spinus

THE SISKIN BREEDS widely in Scandinavia and eastern Europe, and has spread in Britain and western Europe thanks to afforestation. Most populations are migratory, moving south and west outside the breeding season. Siskins are particularly fond of spruce, alder and birch seeds, which they extract with their tweezer-like bills. They feed mostly in the trees, hanging acrobatically onto cones and twigs, and using both bill and foot to reach for and hold food. They have also learned to feed on peanuts at garden bird tables, a habit that began in southeast England and is now widespread.

BIRD FACTS

VOICE Calls include 'dluee' and 'tsüü', often given in flight; song a sweet twitter with wheezy ending
LENGTH 12cm
WINGSPAN 20–23cm
WEIGHT 12–15g
HABITAT Especially coniferous forest; alders, birches by streams; gardens in winter
NEST High in outer twigs of conifer; cup of conifer twigs, grass and moss; lined with hair and wool
EGGS 3–5; bluish with dark purplish or brown spots over reddish blotches
FOOD Seeds, especially of spruce, alder, birch, and herbs; peanuts

IDENTIFICATION

Both sexes have black wings with a broad, yellow wingbar across tips of greater coverts and inner primaries. Adult male green above and yellow below, with diagnostic black forehead, crown and chin. Tail forked, black, edged along basal two-thirds with brilliant yellow. Belly and undertail coverts white, the latter streaked black. Tapered, pointed bill, yellowish. Legs dark brown. Female lacks male's black crown. Breast yellow, rest of underparts white, streaked black. Yellow on wings and tail patterned like male but less obvious. Juvenile similar to female but browner and more streaked.

male

DID YOU KNOW?

Peanuts at bird tables are particularly welcome in early spring, when the alder seed crop is exhausted.

LEFT: winter male
BELOW: summer male

BIRD FACTS

VOICE Trilling, unmusical song delivered in flight; utters fast 'chuchuchuh-uh' call

LENGTH 13–14cm

WINGSPAN 20–25cm

WEIGHT 10–13g

HABITAT Favours birch and alder woodland; will also nest in conifer plantations and forests

NEST Twig and grass construction, usually high in tree

EGGS 4–5; blue, spotted and streaked

FOOD Mainly seeds

LESSER REDPOLL

Carduelis cabaret

LESSER REDPOLLS ARE perhaps easiest to see in the winter when they gather in flocks, and the trees in which they feed have lost their leaves. Favouring alder and birches, the seeds of which they relish, winter flocks often associate with Siskins as well as Common Redpolls; their calls are often the first clue to their presence. Lesser Redpolls breed across Britain and Ireland and in countries bordering the North Sea, from France to southern Norway, and also in the Alps. Although some birds may be resident within their range year-round, many move south outside the breeding season, often in response to deteriorating weather or food shortages.

male

female

male

female

IDENTIFICATION

Plumage variable but generally has brown, streaked upperparts, pale underparts streaked on flanks, and streaked rump; shows two white wingbars. Male has black chin, red forecrown and narrow band of white running from base of forecrown above eye; shows pinkish flush to breast, most apparent in breeding season. Female similar to male but shows less extensive red on forecrown, base of which is black not white, and lacks pink flush to breast. Bill short, triangular in profile, and yellowish with curved culmen in all birds. Juvenile similar to female but lacks red on forecrown.

BIRD FACTS

VOICE Trilling, unmusical song delivered in flight; utters fast, rattling 'chuchuchuh-uh' call

LENGTH 14cm

WINGSPAN 23cm

WEIGHT 14g

HABITAT Birch forests in summer, birch, willows and alder in winter

NEST Twig and grass construction, usually high in tree

EGGS 4–5; blue, spotted and streaked

FOOD Mainly seeds; some invertebrates in summer

COMMON REDPOLL

Carduelis flammea

SUBTLE PLUMAGE AND vocal differences exist between Common Redpoll and its Lesser cousin, and the two do not interbreed where their ranges overlap. Common Redpoll is found in birch forests of northern Europe in the breeding season. In winter, flocks move south in response to weather or food shortages and small numbers reach Britain.

IDENTIFICATION

Plumage variable and overall similar to Lesser Redpoll but overall paler and greyer. Some pale birds are similar to Arctic but note Common's streaked rump and stouter bill. All birds show two white wingbars. Male has black chin, red forecrown and pink-flushed breast, most obvious in breeding season. Female has less extensive red on forecrown. Bill is short, triangular and yellowish with curved culmen. Juvenile lacks red on forecrown.

ARCTIC REDPOLL

Carduelis hornemanni

ARCTIC REDPOLLS OFTEN only move south from their Arctic breeding grounds in the severest of winter weather. To distinguish Arctic from a pale Common Redpoll is a challenge. The diagnostic rump (unstreaked in Arctic, streaked in Common) is often hard to see but the small, stubby and feather fringed bill is a good pointer to identifying Arctic Redpoll.

IDENTIFICATION

Similar to other redpolls but typically paler, in some races almost white. Rumps of adult birds unstreaked. Bill triangular and yellowish with straight, not curved, culmen. Male has pale buffish-brown upperparts and pale, white underparts with faintly streaked flanks. In breeding season may have pink flush on breast. Shows black bib and red forecrown. Female similar to male but darker.

adult male

BIRD FACTS

VOICE Chattering flight call similar to Redpoll's but slower

LENGTH 13–14cm

WINGSPAN 21–27cm

WEIGHT 12–14g

HABITAT Breeds on Arctic tundra; in winter, most remain in northern latitudes

NEST Twig and grass construction, usually in dwarf willow scrub

EGGS 4–5; pale blue with dark markings

FOOD Mainly seeds of birch, alder and willow

Male has chestnut mantle, scapulars and wing coverts. Wings and tail dark brown with white edges to some flight and tail feathers, showing as indistinct wingbar on perched bird and as greyish patches in flight. Bill greyish-brown and head grey except for crimson forehead. Bill greyish. Legs dark brown. Female lacks male's crimson breast and forehead. Brown back streaked darker than on male and underparts streaked buff-brown. Like male, female shows distinctive whitish wing and tail patches. Juvenile similar to female but more heavily streaked, so shows less contrast between upperparts and underparts. Wing and tail patches indistinct.

male

male

female

Breeding birds perch very openly on the tops of low bushes.

LINNET
Carduelis cannabina

THE LINNET EATS almost exclusively seeds, its favourites being the seeds of chickweed, persicaria, fat-hen and charlock. The increase in cultivation of oil-seed rape has proved to be a help to the Linnet, which feeds on it avidly, and 'set-aside' fields are providing more weed seeds. Even so, the population in many parts of Europe is probably still around 50 per cent below numbers in the 1960s and 1970s. Linnets often form large winter flocks for feeding, roosting and migrating. In the summer they breed in neighbourhood groups of between two and several dozen pairs, with nests only a few metres apart.

male

BIRD FACTS

VOICE Alarm call 'tsooeet'; flight call 'tihtihtihtit'; song a musical, soft warbling twitter

LENGTH 13.5cm

WINGSPAN 21–25cm

WEIGHT 15–20g

HABITAT Scrub, heath, hedges, vineyards, maquis, uncultivated fields

NEST Low in thick, often thorny, bush; cup of twigs, grass; lined with hair and wool

EGGS 4–6; very pale blue with reddish blotches under pink and purplish spots

FOOD Almost completely seeds

ABOVE: summer male
INSET: juvenile

non-breeding adult

TWITE
Carduelis flavirostris

ALTHOUGH TWITES LOOK very much like Linnets or redpolls, their choice of habitat and distinctive alarm and contact calls should help to identify them. The Twite is gregarious outside the breeding season and often winters on saltmarshes or on coastal grassland. The birds in Britain are described as a separate subspecies, and are considered to be in special need of conservation. In many parts of its range, and especially in Britain, the Twite has declined recently, probably because of overgrazing and afforestation of its moorland breeding grounds.

IDENTIFICATION

Adult is liable to be confused with female or juvenile Linnet but plumage is generally darker, more tawny above and more heavily streaked below; the ground colour is warm buff. Shows white wing patches and tail sides but these features less noticeable than on Linnet. Sexes similar but male has rose-pink rump, that of female being same colour as mantle. Both sexes have yellow bill in winter but grey bill in summer. Juvenile similar to winter adult.

summer male

Pink rump prominent in flight; shows very little white on wings.

BIRD FACTS

VOICE Call nasal 'chweek'; constant twitter in flight; song hoarse and twanging

LENGTH 14cm

WINGSPAN 22–24cm

WEIGHT 13–16.6g

HABITAT Almost treeless countryside in cool and often rainy climate

NEST Close to ground in herbage or crevice; deep cup of twigs and bracken; warmly lined

EGGS 4–6; blue, with spots, speckles and scrawls of reddish- or purplish-brown

FOOD Small seeds gathered on the ground

BULLFINCH

Pyrrhula pyrrhula

RATHER A SHY and retiring species, the Bullfinch is heard more often than it is seen: its soft, piping calls carry a surprising distance through the undergrowth. In areas where fruit trees are grown commercially Bullfinches have a bad reputation, since they are extremely fond of the nutritious developing buds that appear in spring. In more natural habitats, Bullfinches can survive perfectly well on nature's harvest, ash-keys in particular being an important source of food from autumn through to early spring. Insects are eaten by adult birds as well, but feature particularly as an appreciable part of the macerated food fed to the young in the nest.

A dumpy finch with a stubby, black bill and conspicuous white rump, seen in flight. Male has black cap, blue-grey nape and mantle, and pinkish-red underparts, except for white undertail feathering; hue of red underparts distinctly different from other birds found in same habitats. Wings black with broad white wingbar; tail black. Female has similar patterning to male but more sombre, muted colours, appearing pinkish-buff. Juvenile similar to female but lacks black cap.

BIRD FACTS

VOICE Call is a distinctive, low piping 'teu'

LENGTH 15cm

WINGSPAN 25cm

WEIGHT 21–27g

HABITAT Undergrowth near woodland edge, hedgerows and gardens

NEST Twig platform, built in deep cover

EGGS 4–5; clear greenish-blue

FOOD Buds, berries and seeds; some invertebrates

RIGHT: *male*
FAR RIGHT: *female*

male

female

White rump shows well in flight.

SERIN

Serinus serinus

ORIGINALLY A MEDITERRANEAN species, the Serin spread north during the 19th century. It is vulnerable to cold, wet weather, however, and so northern populations migrate south to winter within the species' breeding range. Outside the breeding season Serins form small flocks, but often migrate in their hundreds. Serins sing throughout the year. Small, post-breeding flocks keep up a continuous jingling, chirping twitter, while a breeding male sings from a high perch on a tree or telegraph line, or in a spectacular song-flight in an erratic course with slow, deep wingbeats; he may sing all day when the female is building the nest.

DID YOU KNOW?

Breeding birds defend small territories, may form neighbourhood groups and are often very tame; the density of these groups varies markedly from a few pairs to over a hundred pairs per square kilometre.

BIRD FACTS

VOICE Call a distinctive 'tirrilillit'; song a rapid succession of chirps, jingles and twitters

LENGTH 11.5cm

WINGSPAN 20–23cm

WEIGHT 11–13g

HABITAT Forest edge, clearings, parkland, orchards, vineyards, gardens

NEST Often in conifer or fruit tree; small cup of stalks, moss and lichen; thick, soft lining

EGGS 3–4; bluish-white, sparsely spotted and streaked rusty, mostly at large end

FOOD Mostly small seeds from plants such as the daisy and cabbage families and catkins

male

IDENTIFICATION

A tiny finch, as small as a Blue Tit. Male is streaky, greenish-brown above with bright-yellow head, breast and rump. Male's blackish-brown wings have pale fringes to wing coverts showing as pale wingbars. Tail deeply forked. Black eye looks beady on yellow face. Stubby grey bill. Legs brown. Female has same basic pattern as male, but browner above with duller yellow parts. Juvenile resembles dull female. Confusion with female or juvenile Siskin likely, but distinguished by small bill, narrow wingbars and uniformly streaked underparts.

female

male

Corsican Finch range

CITRIL FINCH

Serinus citrinella

CORSICAN FINCH

Serinus corsicana

HAWFINCH
male

THE CITRIL FINCH is a high altitude species found in the mountain ranges of southern Europe during the summer months, some birds moving to lower elevations in winter. Formerly regarded as a subspecies of Citril Finch, the Corsican Finch has been elevated to species status. It is resident on Corsica and Sardinia and breeds from sea level to above the tree line, nesting in bushes of tree heathers and brooms. Within their ranges (and given their altitudinal preferences) both species favour mown meadows, waste ground and gardens outside the breeding season and are gregarious, forming flocks.

IDENTIFICATION

Citril Finch adult is mainly yellow-green with slate-grey nape and sides to neck, yellow rump and unstreaked underparts. Tail and wings black, latter with yellowish-green wingbars. Bill greyish with dark tip. Legs brownish. Female similar to male but duller. Juvenile buffish brown above, pale buff below, streaked on crown, mantle and underparts. Corsican Finch is similar but adult's back is streaked brown.

BIRD FACTS

VOICE Call a metallic 'chwick'; flight call 'didididid'; song a fast tinkling twitter

LENGTH 12cm

WINGSPAN 23–24cm

WEIGHT 11.5–13g

HABITAT Woodland, especially spruce bordering alpine meadows at 700–3,000m (Citril Finch); wide range of woodland and scrub (Corsican Finch)

NEST Almost always in a conifer; cup of grass, roots, lined with hair, feathers and wool

EGGS 3–5; pale blue, sparsely marked at large end with reddish spots

FOOD Small and medium-sized seeds, including grass seeds

CITRIL FINCH

CORSICAN FINCH

HAWFINCH
male

Easily recognised by profile and white band on wings.

HAWFINCH female

HAWFINCH

Coccothraustes coccothraustes

THROUGHOUT MUCH OF their range, Hawfinches go undetected because of their shy nature and habit of favouring dense foliage in tall trees during the breeding season. They are widespread in central and southern Europe although, in the west of their range, their precise distribution is rather patchy; in Britain they occur as far north as southern Scotland. Hawfinches are generally resident but birds from the east of the range migrate south and west in autumn. They are perhaps easiest to see during the winter months, when the leaves are off the trees and their distinctive profile is recognisable even in silhouette. Small flocks sometimes gather in good feeding areas, the seeds of hornbeam being perhaps their favourite food; areas of parkland or coppice planted with this species are well worth investigating. During the summer months, insects, particularly caterpillars, become an important part of the diet.

IDENTIFICATION

Large and unmistakable finch with distinctive profile, both when perched and in flight. Bill proportionately massive and triangular in outline. Bird looks top-heavy and large-headed when perched; in flight shows a considerable amount of white and looks short-tailed with proportionately large head and neck. Male has mainly orange-buff and pinkish-buff plumage. Shows black around base of bill and on bib. Mantle reddish-brown and wings dark but showing broad, white band on coverts. Undertail feathering and tip of tail white. Female similar but with duller colours. Juvenile has brownish plumage and spotted underparts.

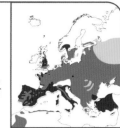

BIRD FACTS

VOICE Loud, robin-like 'tic' call

LENGTH 18cm

WINGSPAN 29–33cm

WEIGHT 48–62g

HABITAT Mixed woodlands, mainly deciduous

NEST Twig construction built in tree

EGGS 4–6; bluish-green, spotted

FOOD Large seeds and fruit stones; some insects in breeding season

HAWFINCH
male

HAWFINCH
male

HAWFINCH male

DID YOU KNOW?

Because of its huge bill, the Hawfinch is the only European bird that can successfully tackle hard-cased hornbeam seeds, and it can also crack open cherry stones.

CROSSBILL

Loxia curvirostra

Dumpy finch with robust bill; mandible tips cross.

UNLIKE ITS NEAR relatives, the Crossbill is widespread through-out much of Europe wherever suitable habitats occur. Its bill is superbly adapted for extracting seeds from the cones of conifers, particularly spruce trees, and in this choice of food it has no bird competitors. Although generally sedentary, Crossbills will often make post-breeding forays, presumably in search of new feeding and nesting areas. In years when the conifer seed crop fails, flocks make long irruptive journeys, sometimes covering hundreds of kilometres.

BIRD FACTS

VOICE Loud, persistent 'chip chip' flight call; song comprises trilling notes followed by Greenfinch-like calls

LENGTH 17cm

WINGSPAN 27–30cm

WEIGHT 34–38g

HABITAT Conifer forests, mainly pine and spruce

NEST Twig platform, built near trunk of tree

EGGS 4; off-white with bold spots

FOOD Conifer seeds, especially spruce

IDENTIFICATION

Adult male has mainly bright-red plumage except for the dark wings. Adult female is green except for the dark wings. Juvenile has brown, heavily streaked plumage; sometimes shows faint wingbars but these much less conspicuous than on juvenile Two-barred Crossbill.

male

female

ABOVE: *female*
BELOW: *male*

Out of range, could easily be confused with small-billed Parrot Crossbill or large-billed Crossbill. Bill is heavy with tips of mandibles overlapping. Adult male has bright-red plumage, except for darker wings. Adult female has green plumage except for darker wings. Juvenile has grey-brown, heavily streaked plumage with same bill shape as adult.

adult male

Has larger, blunter bill than Crossbill.

SCOTTISH CROSSBILL

Loxia scotica

ONCE CONSIDERED TO be a race of Common Crossbill, the Scottish Crossbill has now been elevated to species status. This makes it the only bird that is endemic to Britain: that is, it occurs nowhere else in the world. Its fate is inextricably linked to that of the remaining forest stands of Scots pine: the shape of the Scottish Crossbill's bill has evolved specifically for this tree. All crossbills make regular visits to water to drink: trackside pools are frequently used, affording the observer good views of these rather confiding birds.

DID YOU KNOW?

The Scottish Crossbill is the only British bird that is unique to our islands – it occurs nowhere else in the world and so we have a special responsibility to ensure its long-term survival.

BIRD FACTS

VOICE Loud 'chip chip' flight call; song includes trilling and Greenfinch-like notes

LENGTH 16cm

WINGSPAN 28–30cm

WEIGHT 40–46g

HABITAT Conifer forests

NEST Twig platform, usually close to tree trunk

EGGS 4; off-white with bold spots

FOOD Conifer seeds, mainly Scots pine

PARROT CROSSBILL

Loxia pytyopsittacus

PARROT CROSSBILLS ARE usually sedentary but in years when the pine seed crop fails they sometimes irrupt in search of new sources of food. Small flocks sometimes reach east England. Parrot Crossbills spend much of their time feeding on pine cones in trees. They will also feed on fallen seeds on the ground.

BIRD FACTS

VOICE Utters 'chip chip' flight call, lower pitch than Crossbill's; song comprises Greenfinch-like elements, lower pitch than Crossbill's

LENGTH 17.5cm

WINGSPAN 32cm

WEIGHT 48–62g

HABITAT Conifer forests, mainly pine

NEST Twig platform, built close to tree trunk

EGGS 3–4; pale yellowish-green with brown markings

FOOD Mainly pine seeds

IDENTIFICATION

Superficially very similar to Crossbill. Generally shows larger and heavier bill, the mandible tips of which cross but cannot be seen to project in silhouette. Head and neck also appear proportionately larger. Male has red plumage with dark wings. Female has yellowish-green plumage with dark wings. Juvenile has grey-brown, streaked plumage.

adult male

PARROT CROSSBILL
Most bulky and heavy-billed crossbill.

adult male

TWO-BARRED CROSSBILL

Loxia leucoptera

WHILE SUPPLIES OF larch seeds (the favoured food) last, Two-barred Crossbills are residents within their range. In some years the cone crop fails, forcing them to tackle other conifer species and berry sources and if conditions are particularly severe flocks irrupt in search of food. In August 2008, unprecedented numbers reached Scotland from across the North Sea.

IDENTIFICATION

Adults of both sexes distinguished by relatively long, slender bill with overlapping mandible tips and two striking white wingbars. Male has pinkish-red plumage, while that of female is yellowish-green. Juvenile shows double wingbars but has grey-brown, streaked plumage and lacks adult's white tips to tertial feathers.

TWO-BARRED CROSSBILL
White wingbars impressive at rest and in flight.

juvenile

BIRD FACTS

VOICE Rattling and buzzing song; utters chattering call in flight; occasionally toy trumpet call heard

LENGTH 15cm

WINGSPAN 26–29cm

WEIGHT 29–34g

HABITAT Conifer forests, especially larch

NEST Twig platform, built close to trunk of conifer

EGGS 3–5; pale bluish-white with faint markings

FOOD Mainly larch seeds but sometimes seeds of other conifers or berries

COMMON ROSEFINCH

Carpodacus erythrinus

COMMON ROSEFINCHES ARE summer visitors to Europe, present from May to September; the winter months are spent in the Indian subcontinent and parts of Southeast Asia. Even where they are common, Common Rosefinches can be difficult to see. Although not especially shy, they are rather unobtrusive and spend considerable periods of time either feeding or just resting in cover; their usual reaction when alarmed is to retreat into dense foliage. When seen in the open, the birds appear slightly ungainly as they clamber among the twigs and leaves. The majority of birds seen are either immatures or females, with rather nondescript plumage.

Female (RIGHT) much duller than male (BELOW).

The breeding male's smart colours are a fitting complement to his tuneful song, which contains elements reminiscent of the Golden Oriole.

IDENTIFICATION

Medium-sized finch with large, stubby bill; all ages and plumages show two pale wingbars. Mature adult male distinctive with red head, breast and rump; wings brown with wingbars tinged pink and underparts white. Immature male and adult male in winter have less intense colour. Female and juvenile have undistinguished brown plumage with underparts pale and streaked.

DID YOU KNOW?

The breeding range of the Common Rosefinch spread west during the late 20th century, and it now nests in significant numbers as far west as southern Scandinavia.

PINE GROSBEAK

Pinicola enucleator

PINE GROSBEAKS ARE generally rather sedentary and move little throughout the year. In some winters, however, they range further south, and from time to time irruptions occur south and west of the usual range. They feed on the ground, where they hop and walk, and among branches, where their progress can be rather cumbersome. They are seldom particularly numerous, however, so finding this species can be something of a challenge. Pine Grosbeaks are adapted to make best use of the often meagre supplies of food in their environment. In spring they favour the growing shoots of trees such as birch; in summer they feast on bilberries, other fruits and some insects. The winter months are spent foraging for fallen seeds and the persisting berries of trees such as rowan.

DID YOU KNOW?

Although unobtrusive, Pine Grosbeaks are not shy and can often yield very good views when found.

IDENTIFICATION

Comparatively large, dumpy finch with large head and stout bill. Both sexes show two conspicuous pale wingbars, those of male tinged pink. Wings of both sexes appear dark grey and show grey feathering on undertail and lower belly. In flight, tail looks relatively long. Adult male has pinkish-red plumage, while that of adult female is mainly greenish-yellow. First-year male and female resemble dull version of adult female. Juvenile plumage is dull grey-brown.

adult male

1st winter

Large, dumpy bunting with rather plain plumage. Bill large and pinkish and dark eye proportionately large. Upperparts buffish-brown and heavily streaked. Underparts whitish and also heavily streaked, particularly on breast. Often flies on fluttering wings and with legs dangling. Sexes similar, and juvenile similar to adult.

Flies short distances with legs dangling, on fluttering wings.

CORN BUNTING
Emberiza calandra

BIRD FACTS

A LOCALLY COMMON bird of farmland, the Corn Bunting occurs throughout most of mainland Europe as far north as the Baltic coast, being absent only from some of the larger mountain ranges. Throughout most of their range, Corn Buntings are year-round residents, birds gathering in flocks during the winter months; in the far northeast, however, the species is a summer migrant. The song of the Corn Bunting has been likened to jangling keys; birds sing with head thrown back from a wire fence or exposed branch, and the sound is a familiar one in parts of Europe. Were it not for this unique and diagnostic song, however, the species might be more tricky to identify since it lacks any really distinctive features.

VOICE Song a unique, discordant jangling; flight call a low-pitched, loud 'kwit' or 'quilp kwit-it'

LENGTH 18cm

WINGSPAN 26–32cm

WEIGHT 44–54g

HABITAT Farmland with hedgerows

NEST Large, loose construction of coarse grasses, often in a scrape on the ground

EGGS 3–5; usually pale with bold, dark, scribbles and blotches

FOOD Seeds and invertebrates

Modern, intensive agriculture has caused a catastrophic decline in numbers and range.

juvenile

DID YOU KNOW?

The male's distinctive song is one of the most characteristic sounds of agricultural land in southern Europe.

Both males and females are promiscuous, mating with several partners.

YELLOWHAMMER
Emberiza citrinella

IN MUCH OF western Europe, Yellowhammers are rather sedentary; birds from upland regions and from the north and east of their range are migratory, however, moving south and west in September and October. During the breeding season, males frequently announce their presence by singing from the top of a bush or an exposed branch. They often continue to sing well into the summer, long after other songbirds have become silent. When disturbed, a bird will often make a long, circular flight, returning to a point close to where it took off. Outside the breeding season, Yellowhammers tend to gather in small flocks, especially in areas of good feeding such as grain spills or newly ploughed fields. At this time, they sometimes mix with other species, such as Corn Buntings, Reed Buntings and Chaffinches.

BIRD FACTS

VOICE Chirping song, often rendered in English as 'a little bit of bread and no cheese'; rasping call

LENGTH 16.5cm

WINGSPAN 23–29cm

WEIGHT 25–30g

HABITAT Farmland, heaths, scrub

NEST Bulky platform of grass and straw, low down or on ground in clump of grass

EGGS 3–5; pale with dark 'scribbling' and spots

FOOD Cereal and grass seeds; invertebrates during summer months

IDENTIFICATION

Male in summer is attractive, with mostly lemon-yellow plumage on head and underparts. Plumage often has suffusion of chestnut forming breast band and chestnut on wings, mantle and rump; bright, unstreaked rump striking in flight. In winter male's plumage is duller, the feathers having greyish-green tips. Female much duller than male in all plumages and with stronger facial stripes. Juvenile similar to female but with extensive streaking on head and breast in particular.

TOP: *male*; ABOVE: *female*

male

Breeding male much more colourful than female and non-breeding birds.

male

female

ABOVE: *males*

CIRL BUNTING

Emberiza cirlus

RESIDENT THROUGHOUT THE year within its European range, the Cirl Bunting is primarily a bird of warm climates, whose range includes most of southern Europe. In western Europe it is more widespread, reaching its northern limit in southwest England, where about 700 pairs are confined mostly to Devon. Although generally retiring in nature, Cirl Buntings are sometimes conspicuous in early spring, when the male sings his Lesser Whitethroat-like rattling song from a prominent perch. The song period often continues, off and on, well into late summer, although the frequency at which it is performed gradually diminshes. The Cirl Bunting's soft, penetrating 'ssi' call gives a clue to their identity, but perhaps the most diagnostic feature for juveniles and females is the greenish rump seen in flight.

IDENTIFICATION

Adult male has striking head pattern with black throat and black through eye. Underparts mainly yellow but shows greenish and chestnut breast band. Upperparts mostly chestnut but rump grey-green. Female lacks male's bold head markings and rest of plumage is washed-out version of his. Juvenile similar to female but plumage generally buffish-brown.

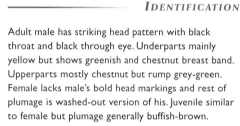

juvenile

male

female

Female distinguished by olive-green rump and buff breast with neat streaks.

IDENTIFICATION

Rather slim, elongated bunting. Adult male has yellowish head and grey-buff underparts. Upperparts are grey-brown overall with streaks on mantle. Note the two pale wingbars. Adult female is similar but plumage colours are much less intense. Juvenile is brown above, pale below and heavily streaked all over.

CINEREOUS BUNTING

Emberiza cineracea

THE CINEREOUS BUNTING has an extremely limited global range with isolated populations scattered from Iran to western Turkey; it also breeds on the Greek island of Lesvos. The species' rather muted colours matches the colour of the boulders and vegetation of its favoured habitat rather well. The best opportunities for observation come shortly after their arrival on breeding grounds, from winter quarters in northeast Africa and the Arabian Peninsula. Males sometimes sing atop a prominent boulder or a treetop.

singing male

male

BLACK-HEADED BUNTING

Emberiza melanocephala

INVARIABLY ASSOCIATED WITH hot, dry regions, the Black-headed Bunting is common in lowland mainland areas in the eastern Mediterranean between May and August; thereafter, it migrates to the Indian subcontinent. With their distinctive song and habit of singing from an exposed perch, male Black-headed Buntings are usually easy to locate at the start of the breeding season. Despite their coloration, feeding birds are unobtrusive, however, and are often found foraging on the ground. Seeds are an important part of the diet but, during the breeding season in particular, insects and spiders are also favoured items of food, especially for nestlings.

Comparatively large bunting with robust, grey bill. Male unmistakable with black head, bright-yellow underparts, yellow sides to neck and chestnut back; wings and tail dark. Female has much more subdued colours, head being greyish-brown. Underparts very pale dirty yellow, and back shows hint of male's chestnut colour. Juvenile superficially resembles Corn Bunting; has rather plain, buffish-brown plumage with streaking on crown and back.

juvenile

male

female

BIRD FACTS

VOICE Song comprises initial harsh phrases followed by series of notes with tinny ring; flight call a sharp 'tsit'

LENGTH 17cm

WINGSPAN 26–29cm

WEIGHT 26–30g

HABITAT Olive groves, orchards and maquis

NEST Low down in dense vegetation

EGGS 4–5; pale green with brown speckles and streaks

FOOD Mainly seeds and invertebrates

YELLOW-BREASTED BUNTING

Emberiza aureola

THE YELLOW-BREASTED BUNTING's main breeding range is central Asia; in Europe a few hundred pairs nest in Finland, where it is present from late May to August. It winters in Southeast Asia and is a rare vagrant to northwest Europe, in autumn. Feeding birds and passage migrants are unobtrusive but territorial males in spring often perch on exposed branches and are keen songsters.

BIRD FACTS

VOICE Jingling song recalling that of Ortolan Bunting; call a sharp 'tsee'

LENGTH 14cm

WINGSPAN 22–24cm

WEIGHT 21–24g

HABITAT Flooded woodland and wetland scrub

NEST On ground, usually in grass tussock

EGGS 4–5; greenish with purple markings

FOOD Seeds and invertebrates

IDENTIFICATION

Mature summer male has black face and chestnut cap, nape, back and breast band. Underparts and partial throat band yellow; shows white on undertail and two white wingbars. First-summer male has incomplete markings on head. Female has striped head with white throat and white stripe above and behind eye. Underparts pale yellow, and upperparts streaked brown; wing-bars less conspicuous. Juvenile has buffish-brown plumage, broad pale super-cilium and dark brown streaked rump.

LITTLE BUNTING

Emberiza pusilla

THE SMALLEST MEMBER of the bunting family in the region, the Little Bunting nests in Finland and northern Norway. It is present in its breeding range from May to August; most winter in eastern Asia. In northwest Europe, Little Buntings are mainly rare autumn passage migrants. Periodically birds will perch in nearby shrubs or bushes, usually if alarmed by some apparent danger on the ground.

BIRD FACTS

VOICE Song a series of sharp phrases; call a metallic 'tik'

LENGTH 13cm

WINGSPAN 20–22cm

WEIGHT 13–18g

HABITAT Favours swampy forests during breeding season

NEST On ground, in tussock of grass

EGGS 4–6; pale green with dark speckles and streaks

FOOD Seeds and invertebrates

IDENTIFICATION

Recalls non-breeding Reed Bunting but smaller; has finer bill with straight culmen. Breeding male has rusty-brown head with buff supercilium and black stripe above eye defining rusty crown stripe. Shows thin, dark stripe running from behind eye and around ear coverts; small pale spot conspicuous on otherwise rusty-brown ear coverts. Underparts white, streaked on breast and flanks, and upperparts streaked brown. Female, non-breeding male and juvenile similar to breeding male but with subdued colours.

Breeding male has distinctive black and white head; all ages show long, notched tail.

When perched, flicks tail and wings nervously, and calls incessantly.

REED BUNTING

Emberiza schoeniclus

THE REED BUNTING nests throughout northern and central mainland Europe, being a resident in the west but a summer visitor in the north and east; these migratory populations move south and west in autumn. Although somewhat subdued, the call of the Reed Bunting, once learned, is distinctive. During the breeding season, males in particular often perch on prominent twigs or barbed wire fences, affording excellent views to the observer as they sing their tirelessly repetitive songs. During the winter, when birds sometimes form small flocks and mix with other species, they can, however, be easy to overlook. In some parts of their range, notably Britain, Reed Buntings visit gardens and bird feeders in the winter.

BIRD FACTS

VOICE Song a short series of chinking phrases; call a thin 'seep'

LENGTH 15–16cm

WINGSPAN 21–27cm

WEIGHT 18–21g

HABITAT Favours wetland habitats, but sometimes found in drier terrain

NEST Usually on ground, among vegetation

EGGS 4–5; pale bluish-grey with dark spots and scratches

FOOD Invertebrates and seeds

IDENTIFICATION

In breeding season male is distinctive, with black bill and black head. White on underparts extends around nape as narrow collar and as moustachial stripes to base of bill. Back brown with dark streaking and rump greyish. In non-breeding male, pale feather tips on head make black elements of plumage appear brownish. Female has stripy-headed appearance with black 'moustache' being prominent; plumage otherwise similar to that of male. Juvenile similar to female but with even less distinct markings on head.

When flushed, may rise up high before diving back into cover; flight action rather jerky.

White outertail feathers prominent in all plumages.

Female has complex, stripy head pattern; juvenile similar but generally more streaked.

juvenile

Upperparts rather sparrow-like, but overall brighter and more contrasting; call is quite different.

RUSTIC BUNTING

Emberiza rustica

THE RUSTIC BUNTING reaches the western limit of its worldwide breeding range in Scandinavia; it is present there from May to August, birds then migrating to their overwintering grounds in southern Asia and Japan. In northwest Europe, Rustic Buntings occur as rare passage migrants, mainly in September and October. During the breeding season, Rustic Buntings favour damp, boggy woodland with ground vegetation that often includes bog moss and bilberry. They are usually fairly tolerant of human intruders in their territories; feeding on the ground or perched in trees, they allow good views to be obtained. If a Rustic Bunting feels threatened, it usually starts to flick its tail and raise its crown feathers before flying off.

adult male

BIRD FACTS

VOICE Song a ringing 'see-see-see-see'; call a sharp 'tik'

LENGTH 15cm

WINGSPAN 21–25cm

WEIGHT 18–21g

HABITAT Breeds in northern woodlands

NEST On ground, usually among moss or grasses

EGGS 4–5; pale bluish-white with olive-grey streaks and speckles

FOOD Invertebrates and seeds

IDENTIFICATION

A well-marked bunting. In some plumages, superficially similar to Reed Bunting, but has proportionately longer bill with straight, not curved, culmen; in all plumages, has pale spots on otherwise dark ear coverts. Male in breeding plumage has bold black and white stripes on head, which has rather peaked appearance. Has rusty chestnut nape, back and breast band with chestnut streaks on flanks and white underparts. In breeding plumage, female similar to male but black on head replaced by brown.

immature

immature

ROCK BUNTING

Emberiza cia

THE ROCK BUNTING invariably favours stony or rocky ground – ideally on sunny, south-facing slopes. In much of its range it is sedentary and a year-round resident, but birds that breed in colder, more mountainous districts show some degree of altitudinal migration in the winter. Rock Buntings are usually relatively easy to see in southern Europe since suitable habitats are often provided by the broken ground found beside roads in the region. Terraced vineyards and stony arable land are also favoured. Outside the breeding season small flocks sometimes gather and occasionally mix with other bunting species.

BIRD FACTS

VOICE Male has Dunnock-like song; calls include a sharp 'tsee'

LENGTH 16cm

WINGSPAN 22–27cm

WEIGHT 23–25g

HABITAT Sunny slopes with broken ground

NEST Grass and moss, built in bush or rock crevice

EGGS 4–5; pale bluish-white with dark streaking

FOOD Seeds and insects

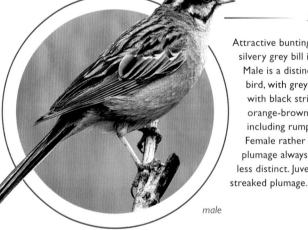

male

IDENTIFICATION

Attractive bunting with triangular, silvery grey bill in all plumages. Male is a distinctive and attractive bird, with grey head boldly marked with black stripes. Underparts orange-brown and upperparts, including rump, reddish-brown. Female rather similar to male but plumage always washed-out and less distinct. Juvenile has brown, streaked plumage.

Characteristically feeds on broken ground, searching for seeds and insects, but progress usually remarkably slow.

male

juvenile

female

CRETZSCHMAR'S BUNTING

Emberiza caesia

A well marked, colourful bunting, superficially rather similar to Ortolan, with reddish bill and legs. Male has blue-grey head with reddish-orange 'moustache' stripes and throat; eyering buffish. Underparts reddish-orange and back and wings reddish-brown. Female similar to male but with more subdued colours and some streaking on head. Juvenile very similar to juvenile Ortolan but plumage has reddish, not sandy-olive, tone.

CRETZSCHMAR'S BUNTING is present in warm Mediterranean habitats from April to September; stray migrant birds are very rare outside their normal range. The species is usually tolerant of humans, but it can be difficult to find since it spends a great deal of time feeding unobtrusively on the ground, and, when alarmed, retreats to the cover of ground vegetation. The species is most easily confused with the Ortolan Bunting; the warmer, reddish plumage of Cretzschmar's, particularly evident on the underparts, throat and 'moustache' stripes, is the best feature for sure identification.

male

male

male

BIRD FACTS

VOICE Song a ringing 'tsee-tsee-tsee'; flight call a sharp 'chit'

LENGTH 16cm

WINGSPAN 23–26cm

WEIGHT 20–23g

HABITAT Dry, sunny slopes

NEST On ground, usually among rocks or vegetation

EGGS 4–5; pale bluish-white with dark speckles and streaks

FOOD Invertebrates and seeds

female

ORTOLAN BUNTING

Emberiza hortulana

THE ORTOLAN BUNTING is in its European breeding range from May to September; it overwinters in sub-Saharan Africa. Its choice of breeding habitat is unusually catholic but it generally favours comparatively sunny, dry regions. Ortolan Buntings are typically rather unobtrusive birds that feed on the ground. On migration they are often found in ploughed or harvested fields.

Attractive bunting with rather subdued colours and pinkish bill and legs. Male has greenish-grey head with pale-yellowish eyering, 'moustache' markings and throat. Underparts orange-red and upperparts mostly reddish-brown. Female has less intense colours on head than male and streaking on breast, but otherwise similar. Juvenile has mostly sandy brown plumage.

male

juvenile

BIRD FACTS

VOICE Male has ringing 'see-see-see-see' song; 'chip' flight call

LENGTH 16cm

WINGSPAN 23–28cm

WEIGHT 20–25g

HABITAT Variety of habitats, including agricultural land and rocky slopes

NEST Grass and moss construction, in dense vegetation

EGGS 4–5; pale blue with dark blotches and speckles

FOOD Invertebrates and seeds

SNOW BUNTING

Plectrophenax nivalis

IN EUROPE THE Snow Bunting nests commonly in Scandinavia and Iceland, and rarely but regularly in Scotland. In winter its range is more extensive and it is widespread in northwest Europe from October to March; it is also found in a broad band from central eastern Europe across Asia. Flocks of Snow Buntings can resemble snowflakes: one moment the birds will be feeding unobtrusively on the ground; the next they are in the air, their wings and tails a blizzard of flashing white. Birds on migration in autumn are often confiding and even later in the winter the birds afford closer views than many other passerines. On the ground Snow Buntings usually adopt a rather horizontal stance and run as if powered by clockwork.

Breeding-plumage male unmistakable, with striking black and white plumage and black bill. Breeding female has white plumage tinged with orange-buff wash and black elements of male's plumage replaced by brown. Bill dark. In autumn and winter, plumage of adults and juveniles rather variable but back and nape usually appear orange-brown. Often shows buffish-orange on cap and cheeks and as breast band. Underparts always white and bill yellow. In flight shows considerable amount of white on wings and tail in all plumages.

BIRD FACTS

VOICE Song a rapid trilling, sung either from perch or in flight; tinkling calls

LENGTH 16cm

WINGSPAN 32–38cm

WEIGHT 30–40g

HABITAT Breeds on Arctic tundra; in winter, on grassland, often coastal

NEST In rock crevice

EGGS 4–6; off-white, blotched brown

FOOD Seeds and invertebrates

ABOVE: juvenile; BELOW: summer male

RIGHT: 1st winter
FAR RIGHT: Breeding male sings sweet, musical song during short display flight.

Plumage of winter birds variable but bill always yellow.

winter male

LAPLAND BUNTING

Calcarius lapponicus

IN EUROPE THE Lapland Bunting breeds in northern Scandinavia. In winter most Eurasian birds are found in central Asia; in Europe the species is most reliably seen in the northwest, mostly in countries bordering the North Sea. The stunted tundra vegetation and the boldness of the bird's plumage often make the Lapland Bunting conspicuous and easy to see in the breeding season. In winter, feeding flocks are unobtrusive and it is often hard to get good views. As they feed in stubble fields or coastal grassland, views are often confined to their backs and heads. When alarmed, the flock will take to the air, where flight calls and wing patterns offer the best clues to their identity. Lone migrants in autumn are sometimes approachable.

BIRD FACTS

VOICE Calls include dry, quick rattle, 'tik-ik-ik-it' and liquid 'tew'; song is a rapid trill, sung either from perch or in flight

LENGTH 15.5cm

WINGSPAN 26–28cm

WEIGHT 25–28g

HABITAT Nests on Arctic tundra; on migration seen on coasts; in winter favours open, often cultivated land, sometimes coasts

NEST In tussock of grass

EGGS 4–5; variable but often pale green with dark markings

FOOD Mainly seeds but invertebrates important during breeding season

On ground, crouches low and runs quickly and jerkily through stubble like clockwork toy.

IDENTIFICATION

Male in breeding season unmistakable. Head has striking black, white and chestnut markings and black-tipped yellow bill. Underparts white and back brown with bold streaks. Female in breeding season similar to male but has black on face replaced by worn-looking brown feathering. Both male and female non-breeding birds lose bold markings on head but usually retain hint of chestnut on nape; chestnut wing coverts bordered by two white wingbars are good features for identification. Juvenile recalls winter female but lacks chestnut on nape. Gait of Lapland Bunting is like Snow Bunting's: crouches low and runs rather quickly and jerkily like clockwork toy.

winter birds

SNOW GOOSE *Anser caerulescens* LENGTH: 70–75cm

Annual visitor to northwest Europe from North America, mainly in winter; also escapes from captivity. Seen in two colour phases. Adult white phase is pure white except for black primaries and greyish upperwing primary coverts. Adult blue phase is a mixture of blue-grey and white.

SNOW GOOSE

BAR-HEADED GOOSE *Anser indicus* LENGTH: 70–80cm

Regular escape from captivity, seen amongst flocks of wild geese. Adult has mainly pale grey-brown plumage on body. Head white except for two dark, transverse bars on crown. Neck dark brown with bold white stripe down side. Bill and legs orange-yellow.

BAR-HEADED GOOSE

RING-NECKED DUCK *Aythya collaris* LENGTH: 42cm

Annual visitor to northwest Europe from North America, mostly in winter. Similar to Tufted Duck. Male has blackish head, neck, breast and back; crown is peaked; greyish flanks separated from black breast by white vertical stripe. Female is brown with pale 'spectacle' around eye.

RING-NECKED DUCK

LESSER SCAUP *Aythya affinis* LENGTH: 42cm

Annual visitor to northwest Europe from North America, mostly in winter. Similar to Greater Scaup but smaller; smaller bill has only small black tip. Has peaked, not rounded, head. Female and juvenile are grey-brown, palest on flanks with pale spot at base of bill.

LESSER SCAUP

SURF SCOTER *Melanitta perspicillata* LENGTH: 50cm

Vagrant to northwest Europe from North America, mostly in winter. Has large, flat-topped head; large bill continues slope of forehead. Male is black except for white patches on nape and forehead and diagnostic bill pattern. Female and juvenile are brown with pale patches on head.

SURF SCOTER

AMERICAN WIGEON *Anas americana* LENGTH: 50cm

Annual visitor to northwest Europe from North America, mainly in winter. Similar to Wigeon. Adult male has yellow crown, green mask, pinkish-grey mantle and pinkish-buff underparts. Female and juvenile have reddish-brown flanks with mottled brown back; greyish head has dark eye patch.

AMERICAN WIGEON

BLUE-WINGED TEAL *Anas discors* LENGTH: 39cm

Annual visitor to northwest Europe from North America. Male has blue-grey head and white crescent in front of eye; body plumage is mottled brown with dark spots. Female, eclipse male and juvenile are mottled grey-brown (recalling Teal) with white patch at base of bill.

BLUE-WINGED TEAL

BLACK DUCK *Anas rubripes* LENGTH: 57cm

Annual visitor to northwest Europe from North America. Large, robust dabbling duck. Recalls female Mallard. Male has chocolate-brown body with paler feather edges, and paler grey-brown head; legs are orange. Female and juvenile are similar but with olive bill and brown legs.

BLACK DUCK

GREEN-WINGED TEAL *Anas carolinensis* LENGTH: 34–38cm

Annual visitor to western Europe from North America, mainly in winter. Tiny dabbling duck, similar to Teal. Male is similar to male Teal but with white vertical stripe at front of flanks. Female and juvenile have mottled brown plumage; indistinguishable from female Teal.

GREEN-WINGED TEAL

WOOD DUCK *Aix sponsa* LENGTH: 40–50cm

Frequent escape from wildfowl collections. Male unmistakable and showy, with red bill and green head showing white stripes. Deep red breast has vertical white stripe; flanks buff and back dark. Female similar to female Mandarin with white 'spectacle' around eye.

WOOD DUCK

STELLER'S EIDER *Polysticta stelleri* LENGTH: 43–47cm

Present all year in north Norway; rare winter visitor to Baltic, typically among Eider flocks. Mature adult male has unmistakable combination of plumage and proportions. Female has dark brown plumage; bill size and head outline are similar to male.

STELLER'S EIDER

PIED-BILLED GREBE *Podilymbus podiceps* LENGTH: 32–35cm

Rare vagrant to Europe from North America, mainly in winter. Small, dumpy grebe. Tail short with powder-puff of white undertail feathers. Adult is grey-brown, darker above than below. Bill is marked with striking black band in breeding season only.

PIED-BILLED GREBE

WILSON'S STORM-PETREL *Oceanites oceanicus* LENGTH: 16–18cm

Antarctic breeder, found from Bay of Biscay to Isles of Scilly in summer months. Similar to European Storm-petrel: mainly sooty black with white rump. Yellow-webbed feet project beyond square-ended tail in flight; this feature is diagnostic.

MADEIRAN STORM-PETREL

Oceanodroma castro LENGTH: 20cm

Breeds on remote Madeiran islands, otherwise seen at sea, north to Bay of Biscay. Very similar to Wilson's and European Storm-petrels. Dark upperwings show only faint pale band across secondary coverts. Tail is slightly forked.

MADEIRAN STORM-PETREL

WILSON'S STORM-PETREL

MACARONESIAN SHEARWATER

BLACK-BROWED ALBATROSS

Diomedea melanophris WINGSPAN: 220–240cm

Rare visitor to European Atlantic waters from southern oceans. Glides on stiffly held wings. Upperwings and mantle are dark. Body white except for black 'eyebrow' line above eye and darkish tail feathers. Bill long and yellowish.

BLACK-BROWED ALBATROSS

MACARONESIAN SHEARWATER *Puffinus baroli* LENGTH: 27–28cm

Nests on island sea cliffs; otherwise always at sea. Rarely seen north of Spanish coast. Flight is fast and fluttering. Smaller than similar Manx Shearwater with proportionately shorter wings. Adult has white underparts including underwing. Upperparts are blackish-brown.

AMERICAN BITTERN *Botaurus lentiginosus* LENGTH: 70–80cm

Very rare vagrant to western Europe from North America. Similar to Bittern. Adult has brown, streaked plumage. White throat has reddish-brown streaks. Cap reddish-brown (blackish in Bittern). Has black flight feathers (brown in Bittern).

AMERICAN
BITTREN

PALLID HARRIER
male

CREAM-COLOURED COURSER

adult

PALLID HARRIER

Circus macrourus LENGTH: 44–46cm

Central Asian breeding species; winters in Africa. Migrant through eastern Europe, rare further west. Similar to Montagu's and Hen Harriers. Adult male is very pale grey with small black wingtips. Adult female is similar to female Montagu's Harrier.

SOCIABLE PLOVER

CREAM-COLOURED COURSER *Cursorius cursor*
LENGTH: 23cm

Breeds in North African and Middle Eastern deserts; rare vagrant elsewhere. Adult has pinkish-buff plumage, striking head pattern and dark underwing. Juvenile is similar but with scaly markings on upperparts and breast, and indistinct head pattern.

SOCIABLE PLOVER *Vanellus gregarius* LENGTH: 28cm

Rare vagrant to Europe, mainly autumn and winter, from Asian breeding grounds. Breeding adult is grey-buff with striking head pattern and dark belly. Winter adult has white belly; head pattern less distinct. Juvenile recalls scaly-looking winter adult.

BELOW: SPUR-WINGED PLOVER *adult*

WHITE-TAILED PLOVER

Vanellus leucurus LENGTH: 28cm

Rare vagrant to Europe from Asia. Adult pinkish-buff, palest on face and belly with greyish-buff cap and red eyering; legs yellow, bill dark. Colours are less intense in winter than summer. White rump and tail striking in flight. Juvenile has scaly-looking mantle.

SPUR-WINGED PLOVER

Vanellus spinosus LENGTH: 25–27cm.

Scarce breeder in southeast Europe and Middle East. Adult has mainly black and white underparts and buff wing coverts and back. Face and shoulders are white. In flight, mostly white underwing contrasts with black primary tips and belly.

WHITE-TAILED
PLOVER *adult*

GREATER SAND PLOVER

Charadrius leschenaultii LENGTH: 24cm

Migrant in eastern Mediterranean, rare vagrant elsewhere. Breeding adult is mainly sandy brown above and white below, with red chest band, white face and dark eye patch. Male is brighter than female. Winter adult recalls large-billed Kentish Plover.

GREATER SAND PLOVER
adult male

CASPIAN
PLOVER

CASPIAN PLOVER *Charadrius asiaticus* LENGTH: 19cm

Very rare Asian vagrant to Europe, mainly in spring. Breeding male has dark-grey cap, white face and throat, dark ear coverts, brown back, brick-red chest band and white underparts. Other plumages are duller with less well-defined chest band.

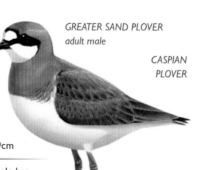

KILLDEER *Charadrius vociferus* LENGTH: 24cm

Rare vagrant to western Europe from North America. Recalls outsized Ringed Plover with longer body and legs; has two black chest bands; tail extends beyond wingtips at rest. Winter adult and juvenile have pale margins to upperpart feathers.

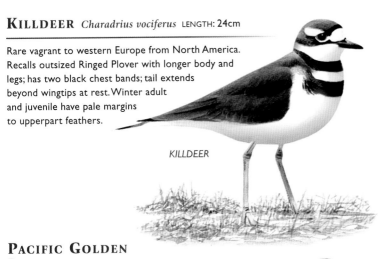

KILLDEER

PACIFIC GOLDEN PLOVER *Pluvialis fulva* LENGTH: 24cm

Rare vagrant to western Europe from Siberia. Similar to European Golden Plover but with pale grey (not white) on underwing, more slender body; has longer legs than American Golden Plover and less black on underside in breeding plumage.

PACIFIC GOLDEN PLOVER

SHARP-TAILED SANDPIPER
Calidris acuminata LENGTH: 18cm

Rare vagrant to Europe from Siberia. All birds have brown upperparts, pale underparts, brown cap and ear coverts and broad, pale supercilium; breeding plumage adult has streaks on throat and arrow markings on flanks and undertail.

SHARP-TAILED SANDPIPER

LEAST SANDPIPER *Calidris minutilla* LENGTH: 12cm

Rare vagrant to Europe from North America. Similar to Little Stint but with yellow legs. Breeding adult is grey-brown above with chestnut on cap, ear coverts, back and mantle. Winter adult lacks chestnut. Juvenile is buffish-brown above with reddish-brown on back, crown and ear coverts.

LEAST SANDPIPER

AMERICAN GOLDEN PLOVER
Pluvialis dominica LENGTH: 24cm

Rare vagrant to western Europe from North America. Similar to European Golden Plover but with longer legs and dark grey on underwing. Breeding adult is dark below and golden spangled above. Other plumages are grey-brown and golden spangled.

AMERICAN GOLDEN PLOVER

TEREK SANDPIPER
Xenus cinereus LENGTH: 22–25cm

Rare Asian vagrant to Europe. Plumage and bobbing gait recall Common Sandpiper but has diagnostic long, slightly upcurved bill. Has grey-brown upperparts, black 'V' marking on back, and pale underparts. Juvenile is similar to adult.

TEREK SANDPIPER

RED-NECKED STINT *Calidris ruficollis* LENGTH: 13–15cm

Very rare Asian vagrant to Europe. Similar to Little Stint with shorter bill and legs but longer wings and tail. Adult is grey above and white below; head is rufous in breeding season. Juvenile similar to winter adult but has reddish-brown on crown and mantle.

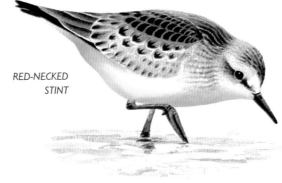

RED-NECKED STINT

SEMIPALMATED SANDPIPER *Calidris pusilla* LENGTH: 14cm

Rare vagrant to Europe from North America. Similar to Little Stint but with broad-based, blob-tipped bill. Juvenile and first autumn (plumages most likely to be seen in Europe) are overall grey-brown above, with reddish-brown feathering on mantle and back, and whitish below.

SEMIPALMATED SANDPIPER

PECTORAL SANDPIPER *Calidris melanotos* LENGTH: 21cm

Regular vagrant from North America. Recalls Dunlin but with longer neck and smaller head. Juvenile (plumage most likely to be seen in Europe) has buffish-brown upperparts, neck and breast. Shows neat division between streaks on breast and white underparts.

WHITE-RUMPED SANDPIPER *Calidris fuscicollis* LENGTH: 16cm

Vagrant from North America. Recalls winter-plumage Dunlin with longer body; longer wings extend beyond tail at rest. Bill has dull orange at base to lower mandible; white rump seen in flight. All birds are overall grey above and white below. Juvenile's back feathers have pale margins.

PECTORAL SANDPIPER
juvenile

WHITE-RUMPED
SANDPIPER

BAIRD'S
SANDPIPER

BAIRD'S SANDPIPER
Calidris bairdii LENGTH: 15cm

Autumn vagrant from North America. Similar to Dunlin but with shorter bill and elongated rear end. Juvenile (plumage typically seen in Europe) has grey-brown upperparts with scaly looking back; neck and breast are grey-brown and underparts are white.

SPOTTED SANDPIPER *Actitis macularia* LENGTH: 19cm

Vagrant from North America. Very similar to Common Sandpiper but with shorter tail. Breeding adult has grey-brown upperparts and white underparts with dark spots. Winter adult and juvenile have well-marked wing coverts.

LEFT: SPOTTED
SANDPIPER

SOLITARY
SANDPIPER

BELOW: BUFF-BREASTED
SANDPIPER
juvenile

SOLITARY SANDPIPER
Tringa solitaria LENGTH: 20cm

Rare vagrant from North America. Similar to Green Sandpiper but smaller, with proportionately shorter legs and longer wings; in flight, reveals dark rump, not white. Upperparts dark olive-brown, speckled with white spots. Underparts are mainly white.

LESSER YELLOWLEGS
Tringa flavipes LENGTH: 24cm

Annual vagrant from North America. Recalls Wood Sandpiper but with long, bright yellow legs. Winter adult and juvenile (plumages typically seen in Europe) have grey-brown head, neck and upperparts, spangled on back; underparts are greyish-white.

BUFF-BREASTED SANDPIPER *Tryngites subruficollis* LENGTH: 19cm

Annual vagrant from North America. Recalls small juvenile Ruff but distinguished by uniformly buff throat and underparts (white in Ruff), shorter, straighter bill and scaly appearance (especially in juvenile) to mantle and back. Legs are yellow in all birds.

WILSON'S PHALAROPE
Phalaropus tricolor LENGTH: 23cm

Vagrant from North America. Larger than other phalaropes, with longer bill and legs. Breeding adult has white underparts and throat with orange, red, black and grey on upperparts. Other plumages are pale grey above, white below; juvenile has dark feathers on back.

WILSON'S PHALAROPE juvenile

LESSER YELLOWLEGS juvenile

GREATER YELLOWLEGS

GREATER YELLOWLEGS

Tringa melanoleuca
LENGTH: 30cm

Rare vagrant from North America. Recalls Greenshank but legs are yellow. Winter adult and juvenile (plumages typically seen in Europe) have grey back and mantle with pale margins to feathers; juvenile has extensive white spotting on upperparts.

LONG-BILLED DOWITCHER

Limnodromus scolopaceus LENGTH: 28–30cm

Rare vagrant from North America. Recalls outsized Snipe. Breeding adult plumage essentially reddish-brown with dark markings. Winter adult has grey-brown upperparts and whitish underparts; juvenile similar but shows chestnut margins to mantle and back feathers.

IVORY GULL

Pagophila eburnea LENGTH: 40–42cm

Rare Arctic vagrant to northern Europe coasts. Adult has pure white plumage. Bill bluish but grading to yellow towards tip, which is red. Legs and feet black. Juvenile and first-winter birds are white with variable amounts of black spotting and grey feathering on face.

STILT SANDPIPER

Calidris himantopus LENGTH: 20cm

Rare vagrant from North America. Recalls a *Tringa* wader with longer legs; long bill has downcurved tip. Breeding adult has dark-streaked head and neck, black barring on underparts, and chestnut on crown and ear coverts. Other plumages are greyish above, whitish below.

LONG-BILLED DOWITCHER

STILT SANDPIPER

UPLAND SANDPIPER

Bartramia longicauda LENGTH: 27cm

Rare vagrant from North America. Recalls tiny, short-billed Curlew with yellowish legs and long wings and tail. Adult upperparts mottled brown; head, neck and breast buffish with dark streaks. Juvenile is similar but back feathers have pale margins.

UPLAND SANDPIPER

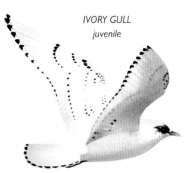
IVORY GULL
juvenile

ROSS'S GULL
juvenile

PALLAS'S GULL *Larus ichthyaetus* LENGTH: 59cm

Scarce winter visitor to eastern Mediterranean; rare vagrant elsewhere. Large gull with massive bill. Breeding bird has black hood; reduced to dark smudge around eye in winter. Juvenile has more extensive dark markings on wings and dark-tipped pink bill.

ROSS'S GULL winter adult

ABOVE: PALLAS'S GULL summer adult

BELOW: BONAPARTE'S GULL

BONAPARTE'S GULL

Larus philadelphia LENGTH: 29cm

Rare vagrant from North America. Similar to Little Gull but adult has black (not white) wingtips. Summer adult has black hood; winter adult has white head with dark smudges. First winter has dark diagonal band on inner upperwing and black trailing edge along entire wing.

1st winter

ROSS'S GULL *Rhodostethia rosea* LENGTH: 30–32cm

Rare Arctic vagrant to coasts. Small, long-winged gull with wedge-shaped tail and small bill. Winter adult (typical plumage seen in Europe) is pale grey and white on head and underparts. Subtle pink suffusion sometimes seen. Juvenile has dark zigzag on upperwings.

FRANKLIN'S GULL *Larus pipixcan* LENGTH: 34cm

Rare vagrant from North America. Adult is grey above, white below, with red bill and legs. In flight, upperwing has white trailing edge. Has black hood in summer, but just black band on nape in winter. First winter recalls adult but back is darker and tail is black-tipped.

FRANKLIN'S GULL
winter adult

RING-BILLED GULL

Larus delawarensis LENGTH: 45cm

Vagrant from North America. Similar to Common Gull but larger; its larger bill has a black band and its eye has yellow iris. Winter adult has brownish streaking on head and nape. First-winter bird has variably grey-brown upperparts with pale mantle and spotted head and neck.

LAUGHING GULL *Larus atricilla* LENGTH: 38cm

Rare vagrant from North America. Breeding adult has dark-grey mantle and upperwings; hood and wingtips black, bill and legs deep red. Winter adult similar but white head has dark smudges. First winter has grey back, grey-brown wing coverts and smudges around eye.

LAUGHING GULL
winter adult

RING-BILLED GULL
winter adult

LAUGHING GULL
1st winter

LESSER CRESTED TERN

Sterna bengalensis LENGTH: 34–36cm

Scarce in eastern Mediterranean; occasional elsewhere in tern colonies. Similar to Sandwich Tern but with more robust, orange-yellow bill. Breeding plumage adult has black cap; black on head confined to patch from eye to nape in non-breeding plumage.

LESSER CRESTED TERN

FORSTER'S TERN

Sterna forsteri LENGTH: 34–35cm

Rare vagrant from North America. Breeding adult recalls Common Tern but is larger, with longer legs. Non-breeding adult is extremely pale except for dark patch through eye. Bill and legs dark. First winter is similar to non-breeding adult but upperwings are less uniform.

FORSTER'S TERN

YELLOW-BILLED CUCKOO

Coccyzus americanus LENGTH: 28–30cm

Rare vagrant from North America. Juvenile (plumage likely to be seen here) has grey-brown upperparts with chestnut on flight feathers. Underparts whitish. Has narrow yellow eyering. Underside of tail is grey with white tips. Bill dark but base of lower mandible yellowish.

YELLOW-BILLED CUCKOO

COMMON NIGHTHAWK

Chordeiles minor LENGTH: 24–25cm

Rare vagrant from North America. Recalls European Nightjar but has shorter, forked (not rounded) tail and longer wings. Finely marked grey-brown plumage gives excellent camouflage against fallen leaves. White wing patch striking in flight. Adult male has white throat.

COMMON NIGHTHAWK

OLIVE-BACKED PIPIT

Anthus hodgsoni LENGTH: 14–15cm

Rare vagrant from Asia. Recalls Tree Pipit. Olive-green upperparts have little streaking. Underparts have dark spots on breast and flanks; belly and undertail white. Supercilium is buff in front of eye, white behind eye. Has black and white marks on ear coverts.

OLIVE-BACKED PIPIT

CITRINE WAGTAIL

Motacilla citreola LENGTH: 17–18cm

Scarce passage migrant (E) and vagrant (W). Breeding male has lemon-yellow head and underparts and black collar. Back grey and wings dark with two white wingbars. Yellow is less intense in other adults. First-winter birds pale grey above, white below; white wingbars.

CITRINE WAGTAIL adult male

RICHARD'S PIPIT

Anthus richardi LENGTH: 18cm

Vagrant from Asia. Large pipit with long tail, legs and hind-claw. Has streaked brown upperparts. Underparts pale buff with warm wash and dark streaks on breast. Head has streaked crown, buff lores and broad supercilium, palest behind eye. Bill long and stout.

RICHARD'S PIPIT

RICHARD'S PIPIT

BLACK LARK adult male

BLACK LARK *Melanocorypha yeltoniensis* LENGTH: 18–20cm

Rare vagrant from Asia. Plump-bodied lark with a stout bill. Breeding male is mostly black except for silvery edges to feathers on back. Female and immature have similar proportions to male but mostly scaly-looking plumage except for dark wings.

WHITE-THROATED ROBIN *Irania gutturalis* LENGTH: 17–18cm

Scarce breeding species in southeast Europe. Plump-bodied, thrush-like bird. Male has grey upperparts, black face with white throat, white supercilium and orange-red underparts. Female and immature lack male's black on head; orange is restricted to flush on flanks.

SIBERIAN RUBYTHROAT *Luscinia calliope* LENGTH: 14cm

Rare vagrant from Asia. Adult male is mostly grey-brown, palest on underparts, with pale supercilium, white submoustachial stripe and ruby-red throat. Adult female lacks male's red throat. First-autumn bird is similar to respective sex adult with pale tips to wing coverts.

WHITE-THROATED ROBIN male

RED-FLANKED BLUETAIL

SIBERIAN RUBYTHROAT

RED-FLANKED BLUETAIL

Tarsiger cyanurus LENGTH: 13–14cm

Occasional breeder in Finland, rare vagrant elsewhere. Adult male has blue upperparts and tail. Has white throat; underparts otherwise pale, flushed orange-red on flanks. Female and first-autumn birds have blue tail but other blue elements of male's plumage buffish-brown.

SIBERIAN STONECHAT

SIBERIAN STONECHAT

Saxicola maura LENGTH: 12.5cm

Rare vagrant from Asia. Similar to Stonechat. Male is more strikingly black and white with orange-red flush to breast. Note pure white, unstreaked rump and white wing panel. Adult female and immatures are buffish-brown above, paler below, with very pale rump.

DESERT WHEATEAR *Oenanthe deserti* LENGTH: 14–15cm

Rare vagrant from Middle East and Asia. All-black tail is diagnostic in all birds. Male recalls black-throated form of Black-eared Wheatear but black on face and throat links with black wings. Other elements of plumage pale sandy brown except for white rump.

DESERT
WHEATEAR

DESERT WHEATEAR
1st winter

SWAINSON'S THRUSH *Catharus ustulatus* LENGTH: 18cm

Rare vagrant from North America. All birds have conspicuous buffish-yellow eyering. Juvenile (plumage seen in Europe) has warm olive-brown upperparts, sometimes showing pale spots. Underparts greyish-white with black spots on neck. Legs pink in all birds.

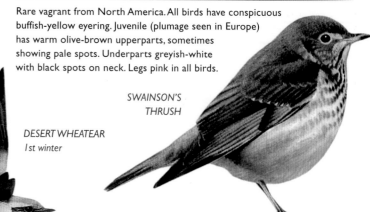

SWAINSON'S
THRUSH

VEERY *Catharus fuscescens* LENGTH: 17cm

Rare vagrant from North America. Recalls Nightingale with warm-brown upperparts and tail; underparts mostly greyish-white. Throat, sides of neck and upper breast have pale buffish wash and faint grey-brown spotting; note the faint, pale wingbar.

VEERY

GREY-CHEEKED THRUSH
Catharus minimus LENGTH: 18cm

Rare vagrant from North America. Similar to Swainson's but lacks that species' buffish eyering. Juvenile (plumage seen in Europe) is grey-brown above, greyish-white below, with dark spots on breast. Has buffish margins to wing coverts and tertials. Legs are pink.

GREY-CHEEKED
THRUSH

HERMIT THRUSH *Catharus guttatus* LENGTH: 17cm

Rare vagrant from North America. Recalls Thrush Nightingale with olive-brown head and back, reddish-brown lower rump and tail, and greyish-white underparts; shows dark spots on throat and upper breast; margins of primaries reddish-brown. Legs are pinkish.

HERMIT
THRUSH

AMERICAN ROBIN *Turdus migratorius* LENGTH: 25cm

Rare vagrant from North America. Adult male has grey upperparts, white 'eyelids' and dark streaking on throat; breast and belly are red. Adult female is similar but red is much less intense. Juvenile similar to female but even duller, appearing browner on upperparts.

AMERICAN
ROBIN

DARK-THROATED THRUSH *Turdus ruficollis* LENGTH: 25cm

Rare vagrant from Asia. Occurs as two races. Adult male always pale grey-brown above and white below; race *atrogularis* (most regular in Europe) has black breast; race *ruficollis* (Red-throated Thrush) has red breast. Females and juveniles duller than respective race males.

DARK-THROATED
THRUSH

EYEBROWED THRUSH
Turdus obscurus LENGTH: 23cm

Rare vagrant from Asia. Adult male has dark grey head with white supercilium, and white below eye and on throat. Has brown back and wings, and orange-red breast and flanks. Female and juvenile male are similar but colours are less intense.

EYEBROWED THRUSH

WHITE'S THRUSH *Zoothera dauma* LENGTH: 27cm

Rare vagrant from Asia. Recalls immature Mistle Thrush but overall appearance is more scaly. Adult's body feathers have numerous black crescent markings; wings buff-brown with pale feather margins. Juvenile's dark markings more rounded than crescent-shaped.

WHITE'S
THRUSH

SIBERIAN THRUSH
Zoothera sibirica LENGTH: 22cm

Rare vagrant from Asia. Adult male is blue-black with white supercilium; paler flanks show dark crescent-shaped markings; belly white. Juvenile male similar but overall paler. Female similar to juvenile male but dark elements of plumage are warm brown.

SIBERIAN
THRUSH

BLYTH'S REED WARBLER
Acrocephalus dumetorum LENGTH: 13cm

Breeds from Finland eastwards; rare vagrant elsewhere. Medium-sized, slim warbler; similar to Reed and Marsh Warblers. Adult is grey-brown above, pale below; note short primaries and dark-tipped lower mandible of bill. Juvenile similar but upperparts warmer brown.

BLYTH'S
REED
WARBLER

YELLOW-BROWED WARBLER
Phylloscopus inornatus
LENGTH: 10cm

Regular autumn migrant from Asia. Tiny, active warbler, between Goldcrest and Chiffchaff in size. Has greyish-green upperparts and greyish-white underparts. Note long, pale-yellow supercilium and double pale-yellow wingbar.

YELLOW-BROWED
WARBLER

PALLAS'S WARBLER
Phylloscopus proregulus
LENGTH: 9cm

Autumn vagrant from Asia. Tiny, active warbler; recalls Yellow-browed but smaller and more striking. Has greenish-yellow upperparts and greyish-white underparts. Note dark eyestripe, yellowish supercilium and crown stripe, two pale wingbars and yellow rump.

PALLAS'S
WARBLER

PADDYFIELD WARBLER
Acrocephalus agricola LENGTH: 13cm

Breeds from eastern Romania eastwards; vagrant elsewhere. Recalls Reed Warbler but plumage shows more contrast. Pale brown above with reddish rump. Note dark eyestripe and white supercilium. Underparts pale. Juvenile's plumage shows less contrast than adult.

PADDYFIELD
WARBLER

DUSKY WARBLER *Phylloscopus fuscatus* LENGTH: 11cm

Rare vagrant from Asia. Small, active warbler; similar to Chiffchaff but legs pink, not blackish, and plumage darker. Has mostly brownish upperparts and yellowish underparts. Note the bold, dull yellowish supercilium, often brightest in front of eye.

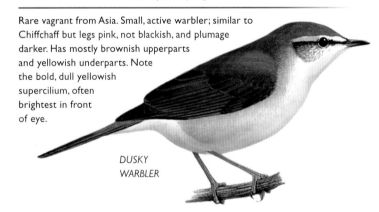

DUSKY
WARBLER

RADDE'S WARBLER *Phylloscopus schwarzi* LENGTH: 12cm

Rare autumn vagrant from Asia. Large, plump warbler with short, thick bill and proportionately large head; movements slower than similar warblers. Has brown upperparts and yellowish-buff underparts. Note broad, pale supercilium, palest behind eye. Legs are pale.

RADDE'S
WARBLER

BOOTED WARBLER *Hippolais caligata* LENGTH: 12cm

Rare autumn vagrant from Asia. Small and pale, similar to *Phylloscopus* warblers, but more stocky with more robust bill and pale lores. Adult has grey-buff upperparts and pale underparts, washed buff on flanks. Juvenile has darker upperparts and flanks than adult.

BOOTED WARBLER

DESERT WARBLER

SYKES' WARBLER *Hippolais rama* LENGTH: 11–12cm

Rare autumn vagrant from Asia. Similar to Booted Warbler with which it was formerly considered conspecific. Differs in paler grey-buff upperparts, paler, less buff-washed underparts, longer primary projection and marginally longer bill. Juveniles resemble adults.

SYKES' WARBLER

AZURE TIT

Parus cyanus LENGTH: 13cm

Occasional in Finland; rare vagrant elsewhere. All birds have largely white plumage. Head has narrow black stripe from eye to join black nape band. Back pale blue-grey and wings blue with white wingbar and white tips to secondary feathers. Tail blue with white tips.

TRUMPETER FINCH

AZURE TIT

DESERT WARBLER

Sylvia nana LENGTH: 12cm

Rare vagrant from Middle East and Africa. Small, extremely pale warbler. Generally skulking but sometimes perches on top of bush like Dartford Warbler. Has pale sandy buff upperparts (greyest on Middle Eastern race) and white underparts. Legs, bill and eye are yellow.

TRUMPETER FINCH

Bucanetes githagineus LENGTH: 12.5cm

Rare vagrant from Middle East and Africa. Small, compact finch with large, stubby bill; red in summer male but pinkish-buff in winter male and in female. Plumage is uniform buffish but male has pinkish flush to underparts and wings. Legs pinkish in both sexes.

RED-EYED VIREO

Vireo olivaceus LENGTH: 12cm

Rare autumn vagrant from North America. Has red eye, stout bill, greenish-brown upperparts and striking head pattern: broad white supercilium and patch under eye, dark line through eye and dark margin to grey crown. Underparts are whitish. Legs are bluish.

RED-EYED VIREO

AMERICAN REDSTART

COMMON YELLOWTHROAT *Geothlypis trichas* LENGTH: 12cm

Rare autumn vagrant from North America. Adult male has striking black mask, olive-brown upperparts and bright yellow throat and upper breast. Female and juvenile (latter is most likely plumage to be seen in Europe) lack black mask, having greyish lores and ear coverts.

COMMON YELLOWTHROAT

AMERICAN REDSTART *Setophaga ruticilla* LENGTH: 14cm

Rare autumn vagrant from North America. Has slaty black upperparts with red patches on sides of breast. Juvenile (most likely plumage seen in Europe) has grey-brown upperparts with orange-yellow on flanks and patches of yellow on wings and tail.

NORTHERN PARULA

Parula americana LENGTH: 11cm

Rare autumn vagrant from North America.
Adult male has blue-grey upperparts, yellow
throat and flush of orange on breast. Female
and first winters (latter is most likely
plumage seen in Europe) are similar
but breast markings are less striking
and flight feathers are fringed green.

BLACKPOLL WARBLER

Dendroica striata

LENGTH: 14cm

Rare autumn vagrant from North America.
All plumages show two striking white wingbars,
and white spots on outertail feathers. Female and first-autumn
birds (latter plumage is most likely in Europe) are heavily
streaked and washed buffish-yellow. All birds have dark legs.

NORTHERN
PARULA

BLACKPOLL
WARBLER

NORTHERN WATERTHRUSH

Seiurus noveboracensis

LENGTH: 14cm

Rare autumn vagrant from North America.
Superficially thrush-like warbler that bobs
up and down like a Dipper when feeding.
Sexes are similar and juvenile resembles
adult; upperparts are olive-brown and
underparts are off-white marked
with black spots.

NORTHERN
WATERTHRUSH

ROSE-BREASTED GROSBEAK

Pheucticus ludovicianus LENGTH: 20cm

Rare autumn vagrant from North America.
Adult male is mainly black above and white
below with red flush on breast. Other
plumages have similar overall pattern
but back is streaked brown, with white
wingbars, supercilium and moustachial
stripe; first-winter male has faint
pink flush to breast.

ROSE-BREASTED
GROSBEAK

YELLOW-RUMPED WARBLER *Dendroica coronata* LENGTH: 14cm

Rare autumn vagrant from North America. All birds have yellow rump. Breeding
male is streaked blue-grey with two white wingbars. Female and first-winter birds
(latter is most likely plumage seen in Europe)
much duller with streaked warm-brown
upperparts and two white
wingbars.

YELLOW-RUMPED
WARBLER

BLACK-AND-WHITE WARBLER *Mniotilta varia*

LENGTH: 12cm

Rare autumn vagrant from North America.
Plumage entirely black and white with prominent
streaking. All plumages are similar except that
first-autumn males have buffish wash to
sides of neck and flanks and have
greyish, not black, ear coverts.

BLACK-AND-WHITE
WARBLER

SCARLET TANAGER *Piranga olivacea* LENGTH: 16cm

Rare vagrant from North America. Breeding male is bright red with black wings
and tail. Winter male is olive-brown; female and first-winter male (latter is most
likely plumage to be seen in Europe) are olive-yellow.

SCARLET TANAGER

BALTIMORE ORIOLE *Icterus galbula* LENGTH: 18cm

Rare autumn vagrant from North America. Adult male has black head, breast and
upperparts, and orange rump and underparts. Female and juvenile (latter is mostly
likely plumage in Europe) are brown instead of black and dull orange-buff rather
than orange.

BALTIMORE
ORIOLE

GLOSSARY

Abrasion Wear and tear on feathers, which can change a bird's appearance dramatically. Pale parts wear more easily than dark; for example, white spots on gulls' wingtips wear off to leave a uniform dark colour.

Barring Narrow bands or stripes on a bird's plumage.

Basal knob Swelling seen at the base of the bill in some species of wildfowl.

Boreal Referring to northerly latitudes – those immediately south of the Arctic.

Calls Sounds uttered by birds other than song. In some non-passerines these may fulfill the same role as song, but they usually serve contact and alarm functions.

Carpal Area of feathers at wrist joint of wings, contrastingly marked in some birds of prey.

Carr Type of woodland; occurs in damp situations and normally comprises alder.

Cere Naked wax-like membrane at base of bill.

Courtship In order to mate and rear young successfully, pairs of most species must first break down their natural instinct to keep their distance, must reduce aggression and maintain a firm relationship, or pair bond; this is created and reinforced by courtship behaviour.

Coverts The name given to a group of feathers covering a particular part of a bird's body. Thus ear coverts cover the ear, undertail coverts are found on the undertail area and underwing coverts are found lining the inner part of the underwing. Those feathers on the upperwing not concerned with flight are also referred to as coverts; they are arranged in zones which are, from the leading edge backwards, referred to as greater, median and lesser coverts; those covering the bases of the primary feathers are called primary coverts.

Culmen Upper ridge of the bill.

Display Behaviour designed to demonstrate a bird's presence.

Diurnal Active during the day.

Eclipse A dull plumage, notable of male duck, acquired after breeding to reduce conspicuousness (ducks moult all their flight feathers and lose the power of flight for a short period while 'in eclipse').

Extralimital Outside the normal range.

Feral Precise definition means 'wild', but is used to describe a species or individuals once domesticated or captive but since released or escaped and living wild.

Flank Side of breast and belly.

Gape The opening or the corners of the mouth; 'to gape' is to hold the bill wide open.

Garrigue Sparsely vegetated habitat characteristic of arid, stony terrain in the Mediterranean region.

Gliding Effortless and usually level flight where wingbeats are not involved.

Hirundines Swallows and martins, members of the family Hirundinidae.

Immature Strictly speaking, it means not old enough to breed. But with birds this usually refers to a plumage state that precedes full adult plumage. Confusingly, some birds, such as eagles, are able to breed in immature plumage. Others, like the Fulmar, may not breed for several years even though visually indistinguishable from an adult.

Irruption The sudden large-scale movement of birds out of one area and their arrival into another; generally occurs in response to food shortage.

Jizz Field characteristics that are unique to a species.

Juvenile A bird in its first set of feathers, or juvenile plumage.

Lek Communal display ground.

Lores Region of feathers between the eye and the bill.

Malar stripe A marking originating at the base of the lower mandible of the bill.

Mandible One half of the bill.

Maquis Shrub-dominated vegetation typical of many parts of the Mediterranean region.

Migration Regular, seasonal movements of a species from breeding grounds to winter quarters; it is more or less predictable. Irregular movements caused by, for example, hard weather or food shortage also occur (*see* Fieldfare). Young birds invariably spread away from breeding areas in autumn – this type of movement is termed dispersal.

Mimicry Vocal mimicry is copying other sounds, natural or man-made; the precise reason for it is unknown.

Mobbing Small birds that discover a roosting owl or bird of prey, or sometimes a mammalian predator or snake, will flutter around or dive at it with loud calls, attracting mixed species to join in. The purpose is uncertain.

Moult Shedding and replacement of feathers or plumage in a regular sequence, which may or may not affect the appearance of the bird. Many species have feathers with dull tips that crumble away in spring to reveal brighter colours beneath. This is sometimes referred to as moulting by abrasion.

Nest Usually thought of as a structure to hold eggs. Some birds, however, dispense with nests and lay their eggs on the ground or on a ledge.

Nocturnal Active at night.

Partial migrant A species where only some individuals migrate.

Passage Refers to migrants and migration - a bird 'on passage' is *en route* to its winter or summer grounds. A 'passage migrant' is a species that appears in the spring and/or autumn but does not breed or spend the winter.

Passerine One of a large order of birds called the Passiformes, all members of which can perch (although many other birds can perch as well).

Pelagic Found in the open sea.

Plumage The whole set of feathers covering a bird. Also used to describe different combinations of colour and pattern according to sex, season or age (for example, summer plumage, adult plumage, etc.).

Predator An animal that eats other animals. Among birdwatchers the term is often used to describe an avian predator of other birds.

Primaries Outer flight feathers.

Preening Using the bill to clean and adjust the feathers.

Puszta East European grassy plain.

Raptor Bird of prey.

Resident A species that remains in a given area all year round.

Roost Rest or 'sleep', or the place where a bird or birds do this.

Scapulars Region of feathers between the mantle and the wing coverts.

Scrape Nest site of some wader species, where a small depression is made in the soil or gravelly substrate.

Secondaries Flight feathers in the middle of the wing.

Sedentary A non-migratory, non-dispersive species.

Soaring Effortless flight by broad-winged birds rising on heat thermals and updraughts.

Song Voice of a bird in a recognisable pattern for its species, be it an irregular flow or a repetitive phrase; intended to identify the individual and its species, to proclaim ownership of territory and/or attract a mate. Other vocal sounds are usually termed 'calls'.

Species A 'kind' of organism, basically isolated from others by its inability to cross-breed and produce fertile young. A subspecies is a recognisably different group (because of size or colour) within a species in a defined area. Apart from subspecies the remarkable feature of each bird species is the lack of variation within it, in terms of size, colour, pattern, voice, behaviour, food and nest; many other factors remain remarkably constant.

Speculum Coloured patch on a duck's wing, often used in display.

Steppe Treeless, grassy habitat associated mainly with Russia and eastern Europe.

Supercilium Stripe above the eye.

Taiga Forest type found at northerly latitudes, just before the tree-line is reached; often comprises spruce and birch.

Territory An area (or 'home range') occupied by a bird (or a pair), and which is defended against other individuals of the same species.

Tertials Inner flight feathers.

Thermalling Method of flight employed by broad-winged birds, including raptors and storks, where lift is provided by uprising currents of warm or hot air.

Tundra Northern, treeless habitat; normally characterised by the presence of permafrost.

Vagrant Usually a migrant that appears outside its normal range. During spring migration, southerly winds often induce migrants to overshoot. On autumn migration inexperienced juveniles are sometimes blown off course by strong winds or engage in 'reverse migration' (flying in the wrong direction).

Vermiculation Feather pattern where numerous worm-like lines create a close-packed pattern.

PICTURE CREDITS

All photographs used in this book were taken by Paul Sterry with the exception of those listed below; these can be identified using a combination of page number and subject.

From the files of Nature Photographers Ltd:

Frank Blackburn: 192 Green Woodpecker (top right); 196 Lesser Spotted Woodpecker at nest; 238 Marsh Warbler; 258 Willow Tit at nest. Mark Bolton: 162 Roseate Tern (all images); 163 Little Tern (bottom); 220 Alpine Accentor; 231 Ring Ouzel male; 234; Fan-tailed Warbler; 293 Two-barred Crossbill. T.D. Bonsall: 208 Tree Pipit nesting. Laurie Campbell: 52 Black-throated Diver summer; 74 Golden Eagle adult. Kevin Carlson: 114 Little Bustard male; 230 Rock Thrush male; 300 Rock Bunting. Colin Carver: 170 Stock Dove (top); 194 Great Spotted Woodpecker male. Hugh Clark: 196 Lesser Spotted Woodpecker flying; 214 Grey Wagtail flying; 262 Treecreeper flying; 292 Common Crossbill top. Andrew Cleave: 55 Black-necked Grebe winter; 109 Little Crake male; 154 Glaucous Gull (bottom right); 168 Little Auk colony. Peter Craig-Cooper: 72 Lammergeier adult; 111 Crested Coot. Ron Croucher: 21 Blue Tits; 179 Little Owl (centre). Michael Gore: 306 Cream-coloured Courser. Barry Hughes: 106 Chukar; 230 Blue Rock Thrush male; 243 Sardinian Warbler male; 301 Ortolan Bunting. Ernie Janes: 14 Snow Bunting flock; 15 Knot flock; 81 Long-legged Buzzard; 85 Marsh Harrier pair; 88 Goshawk; 89 Sparrowhawk male; 100 Red Grouse female; 111 Coot feeding young; 126 Knot winter flock; 126 Sanderling flying; 133 Curlew feeding; 133 Turnstone flying; 135 Bar-tailed Godwit winter; 173 Barn Owl with vole; 176 Long-eared Owl top right; 177 Short-eared Owl (bottom centre); 288 Lesser Redpoll. Keith Lugg: 90 Merlin juvenile. Hugh Miles: 103 Capercaillie female. Owen Newman: 93 Kestrel male perched. Philip Newman: 12 Song Thrush; 28 Barnacle Goose flying; 84 Hen Harrier female (both images); 84 Hen Harrier male; 100 Red Grouse male; 102 Black Grouse male and female; 292 Common Crossbill (bottom). David Osborn: 20 Merlin; 22 Whooper Swan flock; 61 Gannet; 68 Cattle Egret breeding plumage; 71 Black Stork head; 83 Osprey (both images); 90 Merlin male; 119 Grey Plover (bottom left); 126 Sanderling breeding plumage; 132 Turnstone breeding plumage; 151 Yellow-legged Gull standing; 159 Caspian Tern; 305 Black-browed Albatross. W.S. Paton: 178 Snowy Owl male; House Martin at nest; 107 Grey Partridge; 127 Greenshank nesting. Richard Revels: 48 Goosander female; 54 Great Crested Grebe with young; 75 White-tailed Eagle adult flying; 152 Lesser Black-backed Gull (top right); 153 Great Black-backed Gull (top left); 158 Sandwich Tern (bottom); 158 Sandwich Tern (top right); 160 Common Tern (bottom right); 160 Common Tern (top); 161 Arctic Tern (top); 163 Little Tern (top left); 164 Puffin flying; 165 Razorbill adult with chick; 165 Razorbill flying (both images); 166 Guillemot flying; 166 Guillemot (centre right); 171 Turtle Dove drinking. Peter Roberts: 142 Pomarine Skua adult flying. Don Smith: 173 Barn Owl flying; Tawny Owl flying. James Sutherland: 138 Jack Snipe (top). E.K. Thompson: 22 Whooper Swan adult head; 174 Tawny Owl adult perched. Roger Tidman: 17 Great Grey Owl; 18 Great Bustard; 19 Hoopoe and Bee-eater; 29 Egyptian Geese fighting; 47 Goldeneye flying; 49 Smew male flying; 53 Little Grebe wing flapping; 64 Bittern; 68 Great White Egret flying; 71 Black Stork flying; 72 Lammergeier juvenile; 74 Golden Eagle immature; 75 White-tailed Eagle adult; 75 White-tailed Eagle immature; 77 Spanish Imperial Eagle immature; 78 Short-toed Eagle perched; 79 Bonelli's Eagle (both images); 79 Booted Eagle (both images); 80 Rough-legged Buzzard; 84 Montagu's Harrier (female flying, male perched and male flying); 85 Marsh Harrier male (both images); 93 Kestrel (male flying and male hovering); 94 Lanner; 95 Gyr Falcon; 96 Red-footed Falcon female flying; 106 Red-legged Partridge; 111 Coot flying; 114 Great Bustard male and female; 114 Little Bustard female; 115 Oystercatcher winter plumage; 116 Avocet feeding and flying (bottom); 123 Temminck's Stint flying; 132 Whimbrel (bottom); 135 Bar-tailed Godwit summer plumage; 136 Ruff in flight; 137 Woodcock; 141 Arctic Skua dark phase flying; 147 Slender-billed Gull adult flying; 156 Black Tern 1st autumn; 157 White-winged Black Tern (bottom right); 158 Sandwich Tern (centre right); 159 Gull-billed Tern flying; 159 Gull-billed Tern standing; 175 Great Grey Owl; 178 Snowy Owl female; 181 Tengmalm's Owl; 184 Swift drinking; 185 Little Swift; 185 Pallid Swift; 188 Hoopoe; 198 Shorelark (bottom); 199 Woodlark juvenile; 202 Lesser Short-toed Lark; 204 Swallow flying; 206 Sand Martin flying; 213 Pied Wagtail male; 222 Bluethroat flying; 240 Melodious Warbler (both images); 244 Subalpine Warbler female; 245 Orphean Warbler 1st autumn; 249 Garden Warbler; 260 Bearded Tit; 281 Rock Sparrow; 283 Goldfinch juvenile; 289 Linnet; 290 Serin; 291 Hawfinch (bottom left and right); 294 Pine Grosbeak; 297 Cirl Bunting male (lower); 303 Lapland Bunting (top); 314 Trumpeter Finch. Derek Washington: 160 Common Tern (middle). Patrick Whalley: 255 Crested Tit.

From the files of the BTO Photolibrary:

Alan Drewitt: 104 Hazel Grouse.

Artists whose work appears in this book are as follows: Richard Allen, Norman Arlott, Trevor Boyser, Hilary Burn, John Cox, Dave Daly, John Gale, Robert Gillmor, Peter Hayman, Ian Lewington, David Quinn, Darren Rees, Chris Rose, Christopher Schmidt.